ORACLE®   *Oracle Press*™

P9-DMO-472

Oracle Mobile Application Framework Developer Guide

Build Multiplatform Enterprise Mobile Apps

Luc Bors

Mc
Graw
Hill
Education

New York   Chicago   San Francisco
Athens   London   Madrid   Mexico City
Milan   New Delhi   Singapore   Sydney   Toronto

Cataloging-in-Publication Data is on file with the Library of Congress

McGraw-Hill Education books are available at special quantity discounts to use as premiums and sales promotions, or for use in corporate training programs. To contact a representative, please visit the Contact Us pages at www.mhprofessional.com.

Oracle Mobile Application Framework Developer Guide: Build Multiplatform Enterprise Mobile Apps

1234567890 QFR/QFR 10987654

ISBN   978-0-07-183085-0
MHID   0-07-183085-5

Sponsoring Editor Paul Carlstroem	**Technical Editor** Joe Huang	**Production Supervisor** George Anderson
Editorial Supervisor Patty Mon	**Copy Editor** Margaret Berson	**Composition** Cenveo Publisher Services
Project Manager Vastavikta Sharma, Cenveo® Publisher Services	**Proofreader** Lisa McCoy	**Illustration** Cenveo Publisher Services
	Indexer Ted Laux	**Art Director, Cover** Jeff Weeks
Acquisitions Coordinator Amanda Russell		

We choose to go to the moon in this decade and do the other things, not because they are easy, but because they are hard, because that goal will serve to organize and measure the best of our energies and skills, because that challenge is one that we are willing to accept, one we are unwilling to postpone, and one which we intend to win, and the others, too.

—*John F. Kennedy*

About the Author

Luc Bors is an Oracle ACE and ADF Expertise lead at AMIS. He has many years of experience as a principal consultant and architect. He regularly writes articles for international magazines, web sites, and the AMIS technology blog. Luc is a frequent presenter at international conferences such as ODTUG KScope, Oracle OpenWorld, and UKOUG. In 2011, he was the best speaker at ODTUG KScope in Fusion Middleware Track. In 2012 and 2014, Luc participated in the Mobile Beta testing program and presented about Oracle Mobile Application Framework at several conferences.

About the Technical Editor

Joe Huang is part of Oracle's Mobile Platform product management team, focusing on evangelizing Oracle's mobile application development platform to developers and Oracle Partners alike. He has more than 20 years of experience in software development, and spent the last 10 years focusing on enterprise mobility. Joe joined Oracle through the Siebel acquisition in 2006, where he was part of Siebel's platform product management team. Prior to Siebel, Joe was with Computer Sciences Corporation (CSC), leading various development teams in creating innovative solutions for leading companies of the world. Joe received MS and BS degrees in Industrial Engineering from the University of California, Berkeley in the early 1990s and currently resides in the San Francisco Bay Area.

About the Reviewers

Chris Muir is a Senior Principal Product Manager for Oracle Corporation's Development Tools, including Oracle JDeveloper, ADF, and MAF. In a past life as a consultant, he spent time fooling, ah, convincing others he was an Oracle Fusion Middleware specialist, which paid off as he was awarded *Oracle Magazine's* 2009 Oracle ACE Director of the year award for his developer and user group efforts. He is also the founder of the ADF EMG, but we try not to hold this against him.

Frank Nimphius is a Senior Principal Product Manager in the Oracle Mobility and Application Tools Product Management team. Being with Oracle for more than 15 years, Frank currently focuses on customer enablement activities for the Oracle Application Development Framework (ADF) and Mobile Application Framework (MAF) products, providing technical help, training, and documentation for internal and external customers. He frequently writes about Oracle ADF and Oracle MAF in the *Oracle Magazine* and is the author of various articles and whitepapers published by Oracle or Oracle-related groups. Frank is the co-author of *Oracle Fusion Developer Guide* (McGraw-Hill Education, 2010). As a day-to-day contributor to the Oracle ADF and Oracle MAF community, Frank runs the ADF Code Corner web site, the MAF code corner web site, and the "OTN Forum Harvest" blog. Frank also co-authors the ADF Architecture Square web site and presents in various Oracle ADF Architecture and Mobile Application Framework YouTube training videos, as well as the Oracle Open World conference and other user group events. More than looking back at these footprints of the past, Frank enjoys looking forward to what is coming in Oracle ADF and MAF for him to be involved as a part of the Oracle community.

Contents

PART I
Understanding the Oracle Mobile Application Framework

PART II
Developing the Sample Application

Acknowledgments

A lot of time, blood, sweat, and tears went into this book, but without the help of others, this task would have been even harder. It has been two years since we first came up with the idea to write a book on Oracle Mobile Application Framework. I will never forget the moment when Chris Muir asked me if I was willing to write a book on Oracle's Mobile Framework. It took me a couple of days before I decided to take on the adventure. A lot has happened since. Given the fact that the first chapter was submitted for review over one year ago, you can imagine the amount of work that was put into this book.

I need to thank the team at McGraw-Hill Professional, Paul Carlstroem and Amanda Russell, my editorial coordinator, who had to cope with my planning skills and many times had to rewrite the planning.

Of course I'd like to thank Joe Huang, my technical reviewer, who did a great job in helping me with any kind of issue regarding the Oracle Mobile Application Framework.

This book would have never been possible without the help and dedication of Frank Nimphius and Chris Muir, who volunteered to review all chapters in the book. Due to the many changes in the product over the course of the last year, they even had to go over much of the content twice. Thanks, guys, for this effort; it is really highly appreciated.

A big thank you also to everybody at my employer, AMIS, who helped in any possible way by thinking with me, reviewing sections, and supporting me with infrastructure and hardware. A special thank you goes to Lucas Jellema who on several occasions was available for sparring about all things involved in "writing" a book. Lucas, you are an inspiration to me and you are always able to motivate me.

When I started writing this book, I realized that it would be a time-consuming undertaking. This had an impact on my family as well. First, I want to thank my parents, who never stopped inquiring about the status of the book and are always available when I need them. Thanks for supporting me and understanding that I didn't show up on several occasions due to my busy schedule.

Finally, a big hug and thank you goes to my wife Judith, who never stopped supporting me even when I was writing during our precious holidays. Without your support and sometimes necessary pressure to "get this over with," this book wouldn't have been possible. Also a big hug to my kids Olivier and Lisanne, who got to watch a bit more television every Saturday and Sunday when I was writing instead of playing. "Not sure if you will like it, but television time will be reduced now."

Foreword

I n the history of enterprise computing, there have been several transformations that have
fundamentally changed the way we work. In the 1980s, it was the emergence of the
PC and the advent of local IP-based networks enabling client-server computing. In
the 1990s, the interconnection of these networks formed the commercial Internet and the
birth of the Web. The turn of the twenty-first century saw the widespread adoption of
service-oriented architectures to simplify the interconnection of complex systems.

We are now in the midst of another such transformation. While smartphones and tablets
have been around for several years, they are just beginning to change the way we work. We
are at the beginning of the era of truly mobile computing.

Early devices such as the Apple Newton (1993) and the Palm Pilots (1996) were
personal digital assistants without any powerful communication capabilities and limited
user interface capabilities. BlackBerry brought the smartphone to the broader market with
networking in 1999. However, it wasn't until 2007 with the first Apple iPhone that the
multitouch interface took these devices to the modern era, beyond the limited functionality
of e-mail, calendars, and contacts. Apple again created a new category of computing in
2010 with the introduction of the iPad. Thousands of other devices followed the iPhone and
iPad in the modern smartphone and tablet categories.

When these multitouch devices first appeared, they were able to take advantage of the
web interface that most enterprise applications relied upon. However, that only scratches
the surface of the capabilities of these devices. Smartphones and tablets have significant
built-in capabilities beyond the browser, including location awareness, inertial sensors,
imaging capabilities, audio, and other biometrics that can be integrated into applications to
change the way we work. Add to that the unbounded possibilities of connected peripherals
and the potential begins to emerge for the creative thinker.

The limited screen layout of mobile phones requires specialized interface design. The ability for devices to continue to function when disconnected from networking requires on-device applications. On-device applications can better leverage device and peripheral capabilities than web applications will ever be able to. A new type of application has emerged.

We are just now entering the era of applications designed to take advantage of the capabilities of these devices. As a leader in enterprise software, Oracle is committed to helping our customers to fully leverage these possibilities. Mobile computing is one of the most transformational strategic initiatives we have embarked upon. It is truly the future of computing, and we realize that we are in the early days of opening the possibilities it holds.

Enterprises who wish to take advantage of these possibilities face many challenges. The proliferation of devices, operating systems, form-factors, and peripherals makes it difficult for any company to deliver and maintain solutions for these devices. As we've seen many times in our industry, tools have emerged to simplify the task and abstract away the differences. Hybrid development frameworks are doing that for mobile devices today, and the Oracle Mobile Application Framework is, without a doubt, the most advanced solution available.

Luc Bors is uniquely positioned to open the potential of Oracle Mobile Application Framework to developers. He has been a software architect for AMIS since 2008. As an Oracle ACE and a frequent speaker at technical conferences around the world, he has been educating developers on how to best leverage the latest technologies for years. He has won awards for his speaking at developers' conferences and is an active advocate of best practices in technology adoption.

Inside this book, you will find practical knowledge allowing the reader to quickly grasp the concepts behind Oracle Mobile Application Framework. He will take you from the basics to advanced design concepts and techniques to building truly usable multiplatform enterprise applications.

The potential of mobile computing is unbounded. Turn the page and create the future.

Bill Pataky
Vice President, Mobile Platform
Oracle

Introduction

Mobile Development is one of the hottest topics in many companies. With Oracle Mobile Application Framework, you are now able to create multiplatform applications based on a single code base. In this book, you will learn how to use the Oracle Mobile Application Framework (MAF) and find many useful examples.

In this book, you will find 18 chapters that will guide you through the MAF development principles and teach you how to create mobile applications for both iOS and Android.

Chapter 1: Introduction to Mobile Application Development

This chapter gives you an overview of the mobile landscape, including design, device, platform, and technology, before introducing Oracle's Mobile Application Framework (MAF).

Chapter 2: Setting Up Oracle JDeveloper and Your Development Platform

In this chapter you will learn how to set up your environments to build the platform-specific apps. The chapter does not go into details on how to prepare actual devices, but rather focuses on the configuration of JDeveloper to work with the appropriate SDKs.

Chapter 3: Oracle JDeveloper for Oracle Mobile Application Framework Development

Before you start developing, you get a quick guided tour in JDeveloper in order to become familiar with the most important windows, menus, and features of the Integrated Development Environment (IDE). This enables you to be even more productive in building and organizing your MAF applications. In this chapter you will be introduced to JDeveloper and learn how to find your way around in this development environment.

Chapter 4: Building AMX Pages

In this chapter you will learn how to use the Mobile Application Framework to create AMX pages and flows for your mobile application. More specifically, you will learn about the component libraries that are part of the framework and that help you develop the user interface in a component-driven way. Furthermore, you will see how you can create task flows to implement the flow in your application.

Chapter 5: Bindings and Data Controls

The binding layer is one of the most important layers in an Oracle MAF application. It abstracts business service implementation from the user interface and enables developers to work with business services in a declarative way. In this chapter you learn all about the concepts of the binding layer.

Chapter 6: Application Features

MAF applications can consist of multiple functional parts called features. In this chapter you will learn how to create application features and how to configure access to those features in the springboard and navigation bar.

Chapter 7: Using Web Services and the Local Database

The Mobile Application Framework offers several ways of retrieving and working with data. In this chapter you will learn how to get data into your application by calling web services, and how to work with an on-device database to store the data to survive application restarts. You will also be introduced to the concept of property change events and provider change events that can be used to make the application's UI respond to data change events.

Chapter 8: Device Interaction

Using device interaction enables you to really make the app stand out from what you would have done with a regular desktop application. With MAF you are able to reach out to the device and use the services available to allow the user to get contextual information on where they are, take pictures, share and access contacts, send e-mails and SMS, and more. In this chapter you will learn all about device interaction.

Chapter 9: Debugging and Testing Oracle Mobile Application Framework Applications

Testing and debugging of an MAF application is probably one the most important keys to success. A thoroughly tested application will result in happy users. The process of testing and debugging involves several phases that you will learn in this chapter.

Chapter 10: Security and Deployment

Security always is a big issue when building applications, and in a mobile context, this issue even becomes bigger. The Oracle Mobile Application Framework offers great support for building secure mobile applications. You will learn how to do this in this chapter.

Deployment to the supported platforms also is a more or less declarative process. You will learn how to configure the specific requirements for the supported platforms.

Chapter 11: Explaining the TAMCAPP Sample Application

This chapter describes the sample application TAMCAPP, which consists of several features that all together cover the possibilities that you have with the Oracle MAF Framework. This chapter gives you a glimpse of the functionality contained in TAMCAPP.

Chapter 12: Developing the Springboard

In this chapter you will learn how to set up the TAMCAPP application and how to build the custom springboard that is used in this app.

Chapter 13: Building the Conference Session Feature

In this chapter you learn how to work with the SQLite database and how to synchronize with the enterprise. Besides this, the MAF Data Visualization Tools will be used, and you will learn how to download and view documents.

Chapter 14: Building the Attendees Feature

In this chapter you learn some smart techniques for implementing user-friendly UX patterns for searching and navigating in an Oracle MAF application. Besides that, you also learn how to navigate programmatically and work with the binding layer programmatically. Finally, you will also be introduced to invoking the phone function and Skype, and you will learn how to upload an image to the server database.

Chapter 15: Developing the Maps and Social Network

Maps tell you where you are. In this chapter you will learn how to use both thematic maps and geographical maps to show information in a more visible way. You will also learn techniques to use Google APIs and Twitter APIs to embed Twitter feeds in your MAF application.

Chapter 16: Configuring Security and Preferences

Security is very important in mobile apps. The Oracle Mobile Application Framework provides you with functionality that enables you to secure applications and features. Besides that, you can use Oracle MAF security to conditionally show and hide page content and to protect feature content from unauthorized access. Oracle MAF also enables you to define user preferences so that they can customize the appearance and behavior of the app.

In this chapter you will learn how to secure TAMCAPP and how to make TAMCAPP configurable by using preferences.

Chapter 17: Implementing Push Notifications

Push notifications are a great mechanism to push information to the users of an Oracle MAF application. The TAMCAPP application can respond to a notification and invoke functionality required for the user to take action based on the payload of the notification. In this chapter you learn how to set up both Apple Push Notification Service and Google Cloud Messaging Service.

Chapter 18: Enhancing TAMCAPP

This last chapter tops off the book with some additional tips and tricks. The importance of applications interacting with each other and how this can be achieved by using URL schemes will be explained. The fact that devices come in virtually any size makes it important for your application to respond to the size of the device. Oracle MAF enables you to do so and also provides you with several layout components, specifically targeting tablet layouts. The implementation of threads that run in the background also adds extra power to your application. Finally, you will learn about custom components and Cordova plugins.

Intended Audience

This book is suitable for the following readers:

- Developers who need to build Oracle MAF applications
- Technical managers or consultants who need an introduction to Oracle MAF

No prior knowledge of mobile development is assumed. Everything you need to know to become a master is contained in this book.

I hope you enjoy this book!

PART

I

Understanding the Oracle Mobile Application Framework

CHAPTER
1

Introduction to Mobile
Application Development

The obvious reason for you to buy this book is that you want to start building mobile applications with Oracle tooling. Before you get started, you must understand some of the history, principles, and technologies used in modern-day mobile development. This chapter will give you an overview of the mobile landscape, including design, device, platform, and technology, before introducing Oracle's Mobile Application Framework (MAF). But before this, let's start with looking back to when there was no mobility at all.

A Short History

On April 3, 1973, Motorola employee Martin Cooper stood in midtown Manhattan and placed a call to New Jersey. Using a prototype of what would become the Motorola DynaTAC 8000x, the world's first commercial cell phone, Cooper stood near a 900-MHz base station on Sixth Avenue in New York City and placed a call to the headquarters of Bell Labs in New Jersey. Back then, no one was yet thinking of watching movies on their telephones, or playing games on them, or writing letters on them that would fly through space and end up on someone else's phone. But Cooper already understood that the big trick would lie in making the phones smaller and lighter. And this is exactly what happened (Figure 1-1).

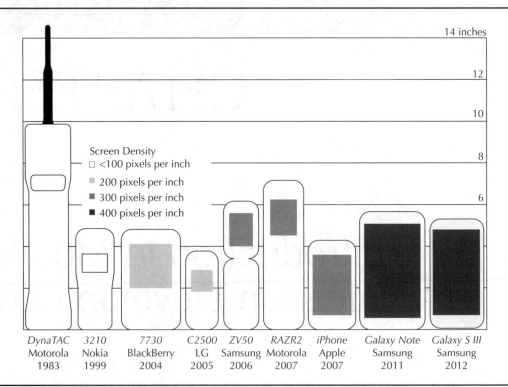

FIGURE 1-1.   *Size of smartphones from 1983 to 2012 (Source: http://qz.com/42150/a-history-of-mobile-devices-told-through-screen-sizes/)*

When I started working in IT in the mid-nineties, there was nothing mobile except for the end users themselves. A lot has changed since then. Over the last two decades, there has been a massive shift where the work we traditionally did on desktop PCs moved to laptops, and later our mobile phones became "smart," fully featured computers in their own right as they moved way beyond just a simple phone to a fully working, mobile office.

In the beginning, the very first mobile devices didn't support any kind of apps. My first encounter with mobile development was in 2004 when I created an HTML UI for a hand-held barcode scanner, calling out to a web service to retrieve product and stock information. The first real apps I created were apps for BlackBerry and Windows mobile devices. These apps were built with the Oracle Mobile Client Framework, which was retired in 2010. That's when Oracle started to work on the ADF Mobile framework, which was released in 2012. Based on what was learned from ADF Mobile, in mid-2014 Oracle launched a completely new framework. This framework is known as the Oracle Mobile Application Framework, in short, Oracle MAF.

NOTE
"MAF" is the abbreviation of Mobile Application Framework and is pronounced M-A-F.

Mobile Design Principles

When you design for mobile, you need to understand that designing for mobile is significantly different from designing desktop applications. There is a great set of design principles available, and in this section you will learn about these design principles. At the core of these principles is the fact that it is all about the end user. Mobile workers have different needs and priorities than their colleagues who remain in one location throughout the day.

Some characteristics of the activities of mobile users include completing tasks in short spurts, moving from place to place, and being frequently distracted by changes in their physical environment.

For example, let's take a look at a person completing an online form for a rental car reservation while waiting to get on an airplane. When the gate opens, this person must get in line. Then he gets a call from his office to confirm the hotel reservation that he submitted earlier. By the time he enters the plane and finds his seat, he has probably forgotten the place in the rental car form completion process. Therefore, tasks need to be simple, easily recoverable, and fast; anything more than a few minutes to complete a task will not be workable in a mobile application.

Kids use mobile devices to play games, but in the business world, at their core mobile devices are about connecting people and the systems people use to do their job. Collaboration and communication are central to the mobile experience. Integrating Short Message Service (SMS), Multimedia Message Service (MMS), instant messaging (IM), e-mail, and phone calls into the application can make task completion more efficient. For example, when regional sales managers are reviewing results by store location, they may scroll to a specific store and call the store manager by tapping the phone number on the screen. Mobile application design provides unique opportunities to leverage built-in communication functionality.

When transitioning to mobile design, an application designer's first thoughts often focus on constraints, such as the small screen size. However, mobile applications are not just limited versions of desktop applications; they are compact apps that support constant updates, decision making, and data entry. With lower costs, portability, and better computing power, mobile devices have become a platform for providing analytics and unique functionality. Sales professionals know where to go next by viewing mapped routes of upcoming sales appointments, managers stay updated with real-time performance metrics, and retail merchandisers stay current by taking pictures of competitor product marketing materials.

If mobile applications are not well designed, users will not use them. The following design principles are fundamental to maximizing the adoption of mobile applications.

During the design stage, consider the tasks a mobile user will be performing, keeping in mind that hand-held usage is different from that of a laptop or desktop computer. How will your Mobile application help users get their jobs done? How will the users interact with the device? The more streamlined the application, the more they will use it. The next steps are to determine whether the application is required to work in a connected or disconnected mode; understand the device services integration requirements; determine the server-side data source and protocol. When designing server-side services, it is critical to provide optimizations for mobile access: if server-side web services are complex, requiring many round trips, for example, it would be difficult for the mobile application to consume them. This is not only due to the amount of data that needs to be passed, but also the amount of client-side logic that must be written to process the results. It is preferable to expose a set of server-side interfaces provided specifically for mobile that provide quick, efficient results.

The secret of writing good mobile applications lies in the understanding of functional and data partitioning, and how to make it easy for users to complete the task at hand. Wireframes offer a great help for designing mobile user interfaces that are easy to use and understand.

You also need to understand the business services that must be developed on the device, such as all Java modules and controls that need to be created. In addition, you should create wireframes for the views and flow in the application, which can help you to visualize the application functionality and assist in the development process. As a final design step, you should consider how to partition the application functionality into separate application features that represent a group of functionality and associated views. Then you can start designing the client user interface and task flows by creating wireframes.

As mentioned before, mobile development and design are different from desktop design and development. If you want to create a best-practice mobile app that satisfies your users, you should obey the most important mobile design principles. When you stick to these principles, you are likely to create a successful mobile app. These principles are explained next.

First, you must know your end users. Before designing, spend time getting to know the role of your end users and the specific needs that they will have while mobile. Understanding key characteristics of your users, their work environments, and the tasks that they perform will help ensure that your product has the right features and optimal user experience.

TIP
You can use Personas during the design phase of your mobile app. Personas are fictional characters created to represent the different user types. By thinking about the needs of a fictional Persona, designers may be better able to infer what a real person might need.

Next, you must define the essential mobile tasks. When assessing how to convert an existing desktop application into a mobile design, be aware that the key task for the desktop may be quite different from that of the mobile. It is best to think through the mobile use case rather than relying on the desktop workflows. Do not hesitate to eliminate tasks that are not essential to the mobile requirements. Successful mobile applications are frequently simplified to primary tasks, such as searching for coworkers or managing task lists.

Also, application design must be contextual. Mobile applications are used in trains, warehouses, taxis, oil platforms, and more where there may be poor connectivity, loud distracting noises, limited access to the touch screen though gloves, and other constraining factors. Designs must work in the target work environment and maximize context awareness of the mobile device. A GPS-enabled device that maps sales representatives' locations helps them arrive at their next appointments on time.

It is important to create a flattened navigation model. With limited time and concentration, users do not want to, and in many cases are incapable of, traversing deep data structures to complete a task. A flattened navigation model gives users quick access to the most important tasks without having to fully concentrate on the task at hand. Once users begin their work, in terms of navigation through the application, you should provide a clear understanding of where they are and how they can return to their starting point if they mess things up. Instead of having a user log in, access a section, find an object, and then perform a task, a flattened navigation model provides quick access to the mobile task immediately after login.

Next, think and design for "two-minute" tasks. Typically, mobile devices are used for short tasks, while laptop and desktop computers are used for more extended work. Mobile users will not tolerate designs that require a lot of data entry or multistep flows because this takes too much time and concentration. Mobile users need to get to work fast and complete their tasks quickly. Tasks should be simple and quick to complete. If you can prefill data for them or hide nonessential fields for the most part, this will speed up the data entry exercise.

Also, it can be useful to integrate analytics. Analytics and business intelligence are not limited to the desktop. Mobile users need analytics that work for small screens. A color-coded graph of sales data draws immediate attention to good, moderate, and bad situations. Compare this to a large table of text data that takes minutes to read. The first step in determining which analytics will be useful is to understand the mobile use case and how to integrate analytics that help decision making. A needless insertion of analytics takes up valuable real estate and makes it harder for mobile workers to do their jobs.

It is essential that you simplify the search process. Search is a very important part of mobile applications and must be quickly accessible. Because mobile data entry is more difficult, simplify search entry requirements to a single field when possible and place the field above related data. If a user is on an inventory screen within a hand-held application and initiates a search for an item, all results should relate to inventory attributes. Do not require the user to enter text in multiple fields.

Make use of the power of the device and embed collaboration. You can embed collaboration into workflows, and include triggers to call a person, connect to a social network, and text using SMS and IM. Social networking is used heavily within the work environment and demonstrates the importance of keeping in touch with colleagues and affiliated professionals.

Do not show all information at once. Because screen real estate is small, you must consider the type and quantity of data that you display when designing the application. Information must be summarized with basic overviews and limited actions. Details and additional actions should be available in drill-down pages.

Reduce free-text input and instead use select lists, single or multiple-choice components like check boxes and radio buttons, and similar. Even with all the beauty in mobile, the virtual keyboard hasn't yet found its way into everyone's hearts.

Finally, it is important to leverage the mobile platform. Mobile applications can be built to run in the browser or as native applications installed on the device. Enterprise applications should leverage mobile capabilities that enable a user to tap a phone number to call or text, touch an address to map its location, and rotate the device for an alternative view. Native enterprise applications enable more integration than those applications run in the browser and provide the ability to transfer enterprise data to local built-in applications, such as calendars and contacts, so that users can view important business information without signing in. Understanding each platform and maximizing the appropriate mobile actions will ensure a productive and natural mobile experience.

Mobile Platforms

Mobile application development is targeted for one or multiple mobile platforms. These platforms are the operating system that runs on the mobile device. There are many mobile platforms. Some of them are relatively new and/or unknown such as Bada and Tizen, while others are already gradually disappearing, such as BlackBerry and Symbian (Figure 1-2).

From the perspective of this book, there are two platforms that you need to know, Apple's iOS and Google's Android.

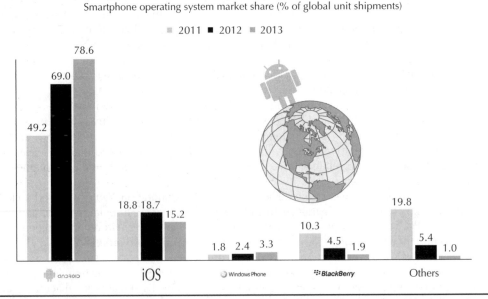

FIGURE 1-2. *Global smartphone operating system market share (Source: http://www.statista .com/chart/1899/smartphone-market-share/)*

What Is iOS?

The iOS operating system is owned, developed, and distributed by Apple. iOS was released in 2007 originally for the iPhone and iPod Touch, and has been extended to support other Apple devices such as the iPad and Apple TV. iOS can only be used on Apple-produced hardware and is not licensed for installation on other hardware. iOS is derived from OS X and is also seen as Apple's mobile version of the OS X operating system used on Apple computers.

The user interface of iOS is based on the concept of direct manipulation, using touch gestures rather than a mouse. Interface control elements consist of sliders, switches, and buttons. Interaction with the OS includes gestures such as swipe, tap, pinch, and reverse pinch, all of which have specific definitions within the context of the iOS operating system and its multitouch interface. Internal accelerometers are used by some applications to respond to shaking the device (one common result is the undo command) or rotating it in three dimensions (one common result is switching from portrait to landscape mode).

What Is Android?

Android is a Linux-based operating system designed primarily for touchscreen mobile devices such as smartphones and tablet computers. Initially, the operating system was developed by Android, Inc., which Google later bought in 2005. The first Android-powered phone was sold in October 2008.

The opposite of iOS Android is open source, and Google releases the code under the Apache License. This open source code and permissive licensing allows the software to be freely modified and distributed by device manufacturers, wireless carriers, and enthusiast developers. Additionally, Android has a large community of developers writing applications ("apps") that extend the functionality of devices, written primarily in a customized version of the Java programming language.

These factors have allowed Android to become the world's most widely used smartphone platform. Android's open nature has further encouraged a large community of developers and enthusiasts to use the open source code as a foundation for community-driven projects.

What About Windows?

There's a broad set of Windows mobile solutions, including Windows 8 Pro Tablet, Windows RT, and Windows Phone. Windows Phone is a series of proprietary mobile operating systems developed by Microsoft, and is the successor to its Windows Mobile platform. With Windows Phone, Microsoft created a new user interface.

Additionally, the software is integrated with third-party services and Microsoft services, and sets minimum requirements for the hardware on which it runs. Because of the multiple Windows-related mobile platforms and fragmented market share, Oracle hasn't yet supported any Windows platforms. It looks as if Oracle is waiting to see which Windows platform (if any) gets market share before implementing a solution. This is probably the main reason why Windows Phone is currently not supported by Oracle MAF.

What Technologies Do I Need to Know?

When you start developing mobile applications with the Oracle Mobile Application Framework, you might encounter a number of techniques that you have never used or even have never heard of. What technologies are important and which ones do you really need to know? The most important ones are discussed in the next sections.

HTML5

"HTML" stands for Hyper Text Markup Language, which is most of the code that makes up the web pages we view each day. "HTML5" refers to the fifth generation of the original language. Many features of HTML5 have been built with the consideration of being able to run on low-powered devices such as smartphones and tablets. It was specially designed to deliver rich content without the need for additional plugins.

The current version delivers everything from animation to graphics, music to movies, and can also be used to build sophisticated web applications. HTML5 is also cross-platform. It is designed to work whether you are using a PC, or a tablet, a smartphone, or a Smart TV.

CSS3

"CSS" is an acronym for Cascading Style Sheets, a web-based markup language used to describe the look and formatting of a web site to the browser, most commonly used in HTML or XHTML web pages. "CSS3" simply refers to the latest version of CSS, with additional capabilities compared to the first two generations. Because of its modular structure, CSS3 allows developers to build content-rich web pages with relatively lightweight code requirements. That means fancier visual effects, better user interfaces, and most importantly, cleaner pages that load faster than ever before.

JSON

JSON (JavaScript Object Notification) is a text-based open-standard data interchange format. JSON is easy for humans to read and write, and for software, it is easy to parse and generate. It is based on the JavaScript scripting language. Despite its relationship to JavaScript, it is language independent. There are many JSON parsers available in several programming languages, which makes JSON an ideal language for data exchange.

Apache Cordova and PhoneGap

PhoneGap is a mobile development framework that enables software programmers to build applications for mobile devices using JavaScript, HTML5, and CSS3, instead of device-specific languages such as Objective-C for the Apple iOS platform. The resulting applications are hybrid, meaning that they are neither truly native (because all layout rendering is done via web views instead of the platform's native UI framework) nor purely web-based (because they are not just web apps, but are packaged as apps for distribution and have access to native device APIs). The software underlying PhoneGap is Apache Cordova. The software was previously called just "PhoneGap." Apache Cordova is open source software.

NOTE
Throughout this book you may find that the terms Cordova and PhoneGap are used interchangeably. Both refer to exactly the same open source platform and library to enable you to create mobile applications built using HTML, JavaScript, and CSS. In 2011, the PhoneGap codebase moved to an open source Apache Software Foundation project under the name Cordova. Adobe still distributes the library under the PhoneGap name. Essentially, both the PhoneGap and Cordova projects are the same, and refer to the same free, open source library.

A Challenge in Mobile Development

Essentially, developers can choose from three different application approaches, each with its own set of pros and cons. First, there are native applications. These refer to apps built for and installed on a specific platform, such as iOS or Android, using a platform-specific software development kit (SDK). For example, apps for Apple's iPhone and iPad are designed to run specifically on iOS and are written in Xcode/Objective-C. Android has its own variation of Java, Windows uses C#, and so on. Native apps written for one platform cannot be deployed on another. Native apps offer fast performance and access to native-device services, but require additional resources to develop and maintain each platform, which can be expensive and time consuming.

Next there are mobile web applications. Unlike native apps, mobile web apps are not installed on the device; rather, they are accessed via a web browser. These are server-side applications that render HTML, typically adjusting the design depending on the type of device making the request. There are no program coding constraints for writing server-side apps—they can be written in any programming language. These apps work across platforms, but are limited to what you can do through a browser and require Internet connectivity. Oracle supports mobile web applications via MAF Faces (for tablets) and MAF Mobile browser (Trinidad) for smartphone and feature phones.

Finally, there are hybrid mobile applications. Hybrid apps combine technologies from native and mobile web apps to gain the benefits of each. These apps are installed on a device, like a pure native app, while the user interface (UI) is based on HTML5. This UI runs locally within the native container, which usually leverages the device's browser engine. The advantage of using HTML5 is a consistent, cross-platform UI that works well on most devices. Combining this with the native container, which is installed on-device, provides mobile users with access to local device services, such as camera, GPS, and local device storage. Native apps may offer greater flexibility in integrating with device native services. However, since hybrid applications already provide device integrations that typical enterprise applications need, this is typically less of an issue. Oracle Mobile Application Framework is an HTML5 and Java hybrid framework that targets mobile app development to iOS and Android from one code base.

So what is the best approach?

While coding native applications, you will have to write the code in different languages, based on the platform. You will then have to compile the code for each platform and build binary packages that can run on the device. Upgrading the application to support the next version means you have to go back and redo the whole exercise of checking/fixing your code, rebuilding, and repackaging. Of course, there are advantages to using native applications. The performance of your application could be a very crucial factor. There are certain applications where you have to go native, especially when you expect real-time responses, as in games or command-and-control systems like drone remote controls. Also, with native apps, you can access core OS and device features, such as camera, accelerometer, contacts, and calendar. This is not easily done today with HTML5.

Access to enterprise applications with mobile devices is the standard nowadays rather than the exception. Such mobile applications increase efficiency because, unlike desktops, they can be used at any place at any time; but this also has a drawback. The speed with which mobile platforms are evolving creates big challenges for enterprises. Smartphones such as iPhone and tablets (iPad) are powerful platforms. However, when you need to develop for different mobile platforms, you usually need different tools and languages for developers. Developing mobile applications for each platform from the ground up typically means maintaining multiple code paths. Besides that, where do you find developers who are expert in all mobile platforms and their associated programming languages? And what if you find one? Can you afford to hire that developer? The Oracle Mobile Application Framework addresses these and more challenges.

Introducing Oracle Mobile Application Framework

Oracle Mobile Application Framework (MAF) enables rapid and declarative development of rich, on-device mobile applications. Oracle MAF-based applications are built using the Oracle MAF extension in Oracle JDeveloper or by using Eclipse and the Oracle Enterprise Pack for Eclipse (OEPE). Developers only need to write an application once, and then they can deploy the same application across multiple leading mobile platforms such as Android and Apple iOS. This means that MAF enables developers to build applications that are portable across devices and operating systems while still leveraging the device-specific capabilities and delivering an excellent user experience. Applications developed with Oracle MAF can be designed for phone and/or tablet form factors and can be packaged for either Apple iOS or Google Android. The applications will adapt to the form factor.

The Mobile Application Framework Runtime Architecture

In order to start mobile application development with Oracle MAF, you need to have some basic understanding of the MAF Runtime Architecture (Figure 1-3). Note that this section does not intend to go into detail about the various components. Its main purpose is to give you an

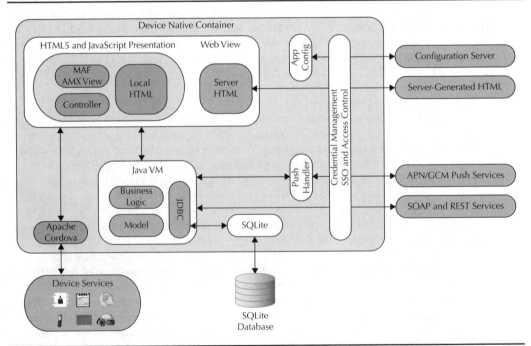

FIGURE 1-3. *The Oracle Mobile Application Framework Runtime Architecture*

overview of all components involved in the MAF Runtime Architecture. Further details will be covered throughout the book. Oracle MAF applications run in an application container that is compiled as a device-native application binary. It provides the runtime environment for a MAF application to run as an on-device native application right in the mobile device's operating system (such as iOS or Android) The container not only hosts the client-side components of the MAF application, but it also provides navigation utilities such as a springboard and a navigation bar, both enabling access to the specific application features.

Inside the device-native container you find several components of the MAF Runtime Architecture.

First, there is the web view. The web view uses the web engine of the mobile device to display web-based content. The web view is the primary mechanism to render and display the user interface of the Oracle MAF application. The user interface can be made up of several different technologies: Server HTML, Local HTML, and MAF AMX views.

Server HTML, for example, an ADF Faces or Java Server Faces application, represents a remote server–generated HTML-based web interface. It is delivered to the MAF application as a web page just as a regular HTML page is rendered in a browser. All of the HTML, business logic, and page flow are generated on a remote server. By using the Cordova JavaScript APIs, these server HTML pages can access device services such as the camera. In order to access these device features, the server HTML needs to be rendered inside the MAF application.

Local HTML, such as pages created using JQuery Mobile, refers to web pages that are directly embedded within and deployed as part of the MAF application. Local HTML files can access device-native features through the JavaScript APIs supported by Cordova.

MAF AMX views are based on the MAF AMX technology that delivers a JSF-like development experience to working with an HTML5-based user interface. MAF AMX views are defined using UI and code editors provided by JDeveloper and Oracle Enterprise Plugins for Eclipse (OEPE). These views are embedded into a MAF application and deployed to a mobile device. At run time, the JavaScript engine in the web view renders MAF AMX view definitions as HTML5 components. Of the implementation approaches provided by MAF, application features developed using the MAF AMX components provide the most authentic device-native user experience through their extensive support of animation and gestures.

The controller is represented by a mobile version of Oracle ADF Controller that supports a subset of Oracle ADF task flow components available to a server-based Oracle ADF application. Both bounded and unbounded Oracle ADF task flows are supported, as well as a subset of events and scopes that are supported by the server-based ADF.

Java provides a Java runtime environment for MAF application. This Java Virtual Machine (JVM) is implemented in device-native code, and is embedded (or compiled) into each instance of the MAF application as part of the native application binary. The JVM is currently based on the JavaME Connected Device Configuration (CDC) specification. This JVM will be upgraded to be based on JavaSE8 in the near future. Inside the JVM you find three other components of the MAF Runtime Architecture.

First, there are managed beans. These are Java classes that can be created to extend the capabilities of MAF, such as providing additional business logic for processing data returned from the server. Managed beans are executed by the embedded Java support, and therefore must conform to the JavaME CDC specifications at the time this book is published.

The next component is the model. The model contains the binding layer that provides an interface between the business logic components and the user interface, as well as the execution logic to invoke REST or SOAP-based web services.

Finally, JDBC is part of the JVM. This enables a MAF application to connect to an on-device database. This is a data store that resides on the device. In MAF, this is implemented as encrypted SQLite database, which in Figure 1-8 is represented by "SQLite Local Database." CRUD operations are supported to this local data store through the Java layer, using JDBC-based APIs.

The app config refers to services that allow application configurations to be downloaded and refreshed. For example, URL endpoints for a web service or remote URL connection. Application configuration services download the configuration information from a WebDav-based server-side service.

Credential management and access control refers to client-side services that provide security-related services for a MAF application, for example, a local credential store that securely caches user credentials to support an offline authentication, or access control services that display or hide application features based on user access privileges.

Apache Cordova is an open source code library that provides a common JavaScript API to access various mobile device services, such as the camera. Cordova provides a majority of the device services integration for a MAF application. Cordova JavaScript APIs are further abstracted as device data controls in the JDeveloper design time for MAF AMX-based views, allowing for integration of device services by simply dragging and dropping data controls to their MAF AMX views.

Server-Side Components of the Oracle Mobile Application Framework Runtime Architecture

On the server side, the configuration server refers to a WebDav-based server that hosts configuration files used by the application configuration services. The configuration server is delivered as a reference implementation. Any common WebDav services hosted on a common J2EE server can be used for this purpose.

Server-generated HTML refers to any framework for developing server-side applications that can be used for implementation of the remote URL MAF application feature. Also, a MAF application can use server-side SOAP and REST services to obtain data from server-side sources.

Finally, a MAF application can use APNS/GCM push services that allow for push notifications to the MAF application.

Developing with the Oracle Mobile Application Framework

When you start working with the Oracle Mobile Application Framework, you will typically go through several stages: design, develop, deploy. These stages are explained briefly in the next sections and in more detail throughout the rest of this book.

Design the Oracle Mobile Application Framework Application

During the design stage, consider the tasks a mobile user will be performing, keeping in mind that hand-held usage is different from that of a laptop or desktop computer. Work with the design principles explained previously in this chapter. How will your MAF application help users get their jobs done? How will the users interact with the device? The more streamlined the application, the more they will use it. The next steps are to determine whether the application is required to work in a connected or disconnected mode, understand the device services integration requirements, and determine the server-side data source and protocol. When designing server-side services, it is critical to provide for optimization for the mobile access: if server-side web services are very complex, it would be difficult for the mobile application to consume them. This is not only due to the amount of data that needs to be passed, but also the amount of client-side logic that must be written to process the results. It is preferable to expose a set of server-side interfaces provided specifically for mobile. You also need to understand the client business services that must be developed, such as all Java modules and data controls that need to be created. In addition, you should create wireframes for the views and task flow in the application, which can help you to visualize the application functionality and assist in the development process. As a final design step, you should consider how to partition the application functionality into separate application features that represent a group of functionality and associated views. Then you can start designing the client user interface and task flows by creating wireframes.

Develop the Oracle Mobile Application Framework Application

Before you can start developing, you must first set up your development environment. You need to download and install the MAF extension or the plugin, and then install the necessary components and complete the required setup for development and deployment. All of this will be discussed in Chapter 3.

When creating your MAF application using JDeveloper or OEPE, you use the MAF application creation wizard and dialog boxes rather than code from the outset. This is one of the key features of JDeveloper and Oracle's development tooling, that wizards and smart editors supplement many of the repetitive tasks, and you only need to code by exception.

NOTE
Oracle supports two IDEs with MAF: Oracle JDeveloper and Eclipse through Oracle Enterprise Pack for Eclipse (OEPE). OEPE, like JDeveloper, is available as a free download from the Oracle Technology Network (OTN) web site. There will be three Eclipse plugins for MAF: one for design time, one for runtime deployment, and one for sample applications. These plugins are all added to Oracle Enterprise Plugin for Eclipse.

The artifacts that result from creating the application include descriptor files for the MAF application and for the application features, default images for icons and tabs for all supported platforms, and a set of data controls used for accessing the services of a mobile device (such as camera, GPS, or e-mail).

When implementing the application features, you perform a thorough evaluation of the business need to determine which application features should be included within the MAF application. Using the overview editors provided by MAF, your tasks for implementing an application feature include identifying its type (HTML, remote URL, or MAF AMX, or native UI), its display properties (display name, navigation bar, and springboard icon), and its display behavior as dictated by both the mobile device capabilities and the user role.

Deploy the Oracle Mobile Application Framework Application

During the application deployment stage, you start with creating a deployment profile that will support devices and simulators for its respective platform. Creating a deployment profile may include selecting the display icon used for the MAF application itself in various orientations (such as landscape or portrait) and setting the application's signing options (such as debug or release). You then proceed to deploying your application to the mobile device or simulator.

NOTE
With MAF applications, it is required that you deploy to the device or simulator before attempting any testing and debugging; in other words, the application cannot be run until you deploy it. Once the application has been deployed, it can be tested, debugged, and optimized.

Other Tasks During Application Development

Enabling and configuring security for the application typically require configuring the login server, such as the Oracle Identity Connect server, or it can be any web page protected by the basic HTTP authentication mechanism. In addition, you may have to configure the access control server.

After ensuring that your application functions as expected at a basic level, you can implement the Java code to access the server-side data. For connected applications, these Java classes should invoke web services directly. If your application uses SOAP or REST XML-based data sources, you invoke web services through data controls, with the assistance of a set of helper classes that you can invoke from your code to invoke the data controls and return data. If your application uses JSON-based data sources, your code should directly invoke the JSON service and return data, after which you need to parse the JSON data from the server and populate the objects holding data collections accordingly. For disconnected applications, your code should populate the local SQLite database. Then, the code that backs the user interface can retrieve data from the SQLite database instead of directly invoking web services.

Ensure that after adding security to your application and enabling access to the server-side data, the application deployment runs as expected and the application is ready for the final testing and debugging.

Deploy the Oracle Mobile Application Framework Application to Production

Deploying the application to the production environment typically involves publishing to an enterprise server, the enterprise App Store, the Apple App Store, or an application marketplace, such as Google Play. After you publish the MAF application, end users can download it to their mobile devices and access it by clicking the designated icon. The application features bear the designated display icons and display as appropriate to the end user and the end user's device.

Summary

Mobile development has gone through many stages of evolution over the last couple of decades, starting with the first mobile call in 1973 all the way to modern smartphones. Modern mobile devices require modern development frameworks. Oracle's Mobile Application Framework enables you to build hybrid on-device applications for both the Android and iOS platform.

In this chapter you were introduced to

- Technologies involved in mobile development
- Mobile design principles
- The Oracle Mobile Application Framework
- Steps involved in developing a MAF application

CHAPTER
2

Setting Up Oracle JDeveloper and Your Development Platform

Developing for Android and iOS with JDeveloper requires you to install some additional tools. This is because during deployment, MAF applications are built using the platform-specific SDKs. In the case of Android, JDeveloper uses the Android SDK, which is available for both Microsoft Windows and Apple OS X. For iOS, JDeveloper uses Apple's XCode, which is only available on Apple's OS X. Therefore, you need to install the relevant SDKs that you want to use, of course being aware that iOS development will require a Mac, but Android deployments can be done on both a Mac and a PC.

In this chapter you will learn how to set up your environments to build the platform-specific apps. This chapter does not go into details on how to prepare the actual devices, but rather focuses on the configuration of JDeveloper to work with the appropriate SDKs.

NOTE
While Linux is also a supported platform for Android development via MAF, it won't be discussed in this book.

Preparing for Android Development

When you are developing a MAF application for Android, you need to download the Android SDK. JDeveloper uses this SDK to build the application for the Android platform. The Android SDK can be downloaded from http://developer.android.com/sdk/index.html. The site will prompt you to download the SDK for your OS. In addition to the download link, the web site (Figure 2-1) contains other information such as documentation and samples, where specifically the documentation can be useful for understanding what utilities are coupled with the Android SDK.

Downloading and Installing Android APIs

After downloading and unzipping the Android SDK, you will find that the SDK includes the most recent API version. As long as MAF supports this API version, you don't need to download additional API packages. If you need to download and install additional Android API versions that you need for development, you can invoke the SDK Manager.

NOTE
MAF doesn't necessarily support the latest version of the Android API. Always check http://otn.oracle.com for supported versions of the Android API.

These API versions correspond to different Android operating system versions; for example, API 15 maps to Android 4.0.3 Ice Cream Sandwich. Note that MAF is only certified against specific Android APIs. Consult Oracle's certification matrix for specific information on what versions are supported for your version of MAF.

TIP
On Windows, double-click the SDK Manager.exe file at the root of the Android SDK directory. On Mac or Linux, open a terminal and navigate to the tools/ directory in the Android SDK, then start the "android" executable.

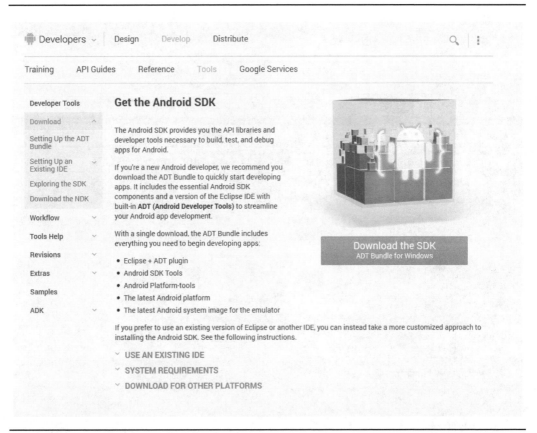

FIGURE 2-1. *Android SDK download web site*

In order to download and install the API versions, you have to check the boxes in front of the API version that you need, as well as agreeing to the license in the corresponding install dialog. After installation, the SDK Manager shows you exactly what was installed (Figure 2-2).

MAF also requires that you install the "Google Cloud Messaging for Android Library." MAF needs this library in order to be able to receive push notifications, a feature you can optionally build into your MAF applications. You can find this component in the "Extras" section of the Android SDK Manager (Figure 2-3).

The Android Emulator

With all the required Android SDKs and extras installed, you can now continue and test your Android setup. When building MAF applications, you probably want to test them first using the Android Emulator instead of running on a real device. In order to test on the Android Emulator, you need to create virtual devices.

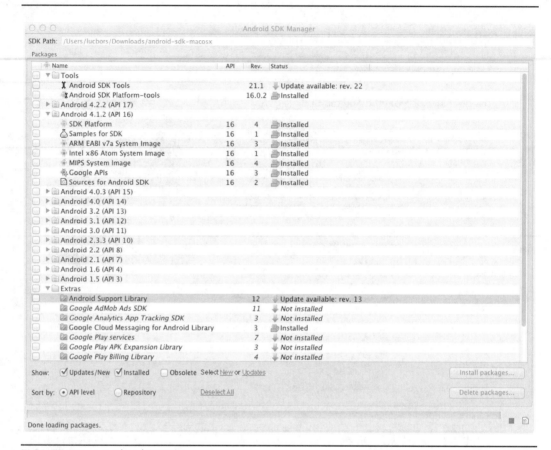

FIGURE 2-2. *Android SDK Manager*

Extras		
Android Support Library	12	⬇ Update available: rev. 13
Google AdMob Ads SDK	11	⬇ Not installed
Google Analytics App Tracking SDK	3	⬇ Not installed
Google Cloud Messaging for Android Library	3	Installed
Google Play services	7	⬇ Not installed
Google Play APK Expansion Library	3	⬇ Not installed
Google Play Billing Library	4	⬇ Not installed
Google Play Licensing Library	2	⬇ Not installed
Google USB Driver	7	✗ Not compatible with Mac C
Google Web Driver	2	⬇ Not installed
Intel x86 Emulator Accelerator (HAXM)	3	Not installed

FIGURE 2-3. *Extras section*

An Android Virtual Device (AVD) is a configuration set that lets you emulate an actual Android device on your PC or Mac by defining hardware and software. The easiest way to create an AVD is to use the graphical AVD Manager. The AVD Manager can be started from the command line by calling the android tool from the <sdk>/platform-tools/ directory, then selecting the Tools menu and the Manage AVDs submenu option. The AVD Manager has an easy-to-use user interface to manage your AVD configurations. After creating an AVD, you can see its details to check whether the configuration fits your needs (Figure 2-4).

In an AVD you can define the hardware features of the virtual device. For example, you can define whether the device has a camera, how much memory it has, and more. You also need to define what version of the Android platform will run on the virtual device. You can create as many AVDs as you need. To test your application, you should create an AVD for each general device configuration with which your application is compatible and test your application on each one.

NOTE
You need to be careful not to "overspecify" your AVDs. This will inevitably lead to a drop in performance of the emulator.

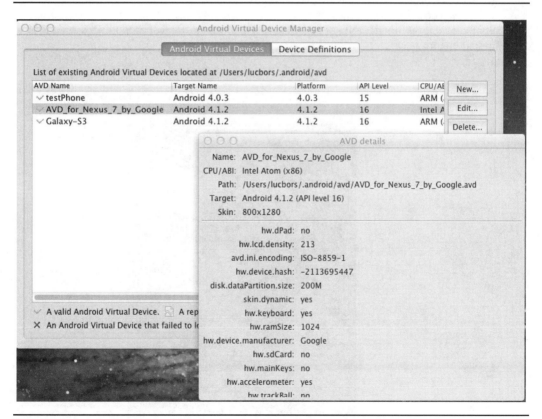

FIGURE 2-4.   *Android Virtual Device Manager*

Once you've configured the actual AVD, you can then use it to start the Android Emulator. The Emulator lets you prototype, develop, and test Android applications without using a physical device. The Emulator mimics the hardware and software features of the mobile device. Of course, you cannot make actual phone calls or send text messages. It also provides a screen in which your application is displayed, together with any other active Android applications (Figure 2-5).

There is one major drawback: As the Android Emulator attempts to emulate the complete device right down to the ARM CPU instruction set, the Android Emulator is very slow, and this is a frustration of many Android developers. Luckily, there is an alternative solution.

Android Emulator Intel HAXM Software

When working with the Android Emulator, you will very soon start asking yourself, "How do I make the Android Emulator faster?" Unfortunately, the default Emulator written by Google is notoriously slow even for Android developers.

Luckily, there is a solution in the form of Intel's x86 Hardware Accelerated Execution Manager (HAXM). For all intents and purposes, HAXM can be thought of as a set of drivers that plug the Android Emulator directly into your PC or Mac's accelerated hardware, with the goal of making the Android Emulator fast enough for real development, and saving you from tearing your hair out too!

Intel's HAXM software is available for Windows, Mac, and Linux machines. In order for it to work, your computer must have an Intel CPU with support for Intel VT-x, EM64T, and Execute Disabled (XD) Bit functionality at the BIOS level. Fortunately, most modern PCs and laptops meet these demands.

FIGURE 2-5. *The Android Emulator running Nexus 7*

You can download the Intel HAXM software via the Extras option in the Android SDK Manager (Figure 2-6).

However, this only downloads the software; it does not install the software. To install the software, search under your Android SDK installation directory for IntelHaxm.exe on Windows or IntelHAXM.dmg on OS X, and run the associated programs. For example, on Windows, if you haven't changed any of the default settings, you should find the executable located under C:\Program Files\Android\android-sdk\extras\Intel\Hardware_Accelerated_Execution_Manager\IntelHaxm.exe.

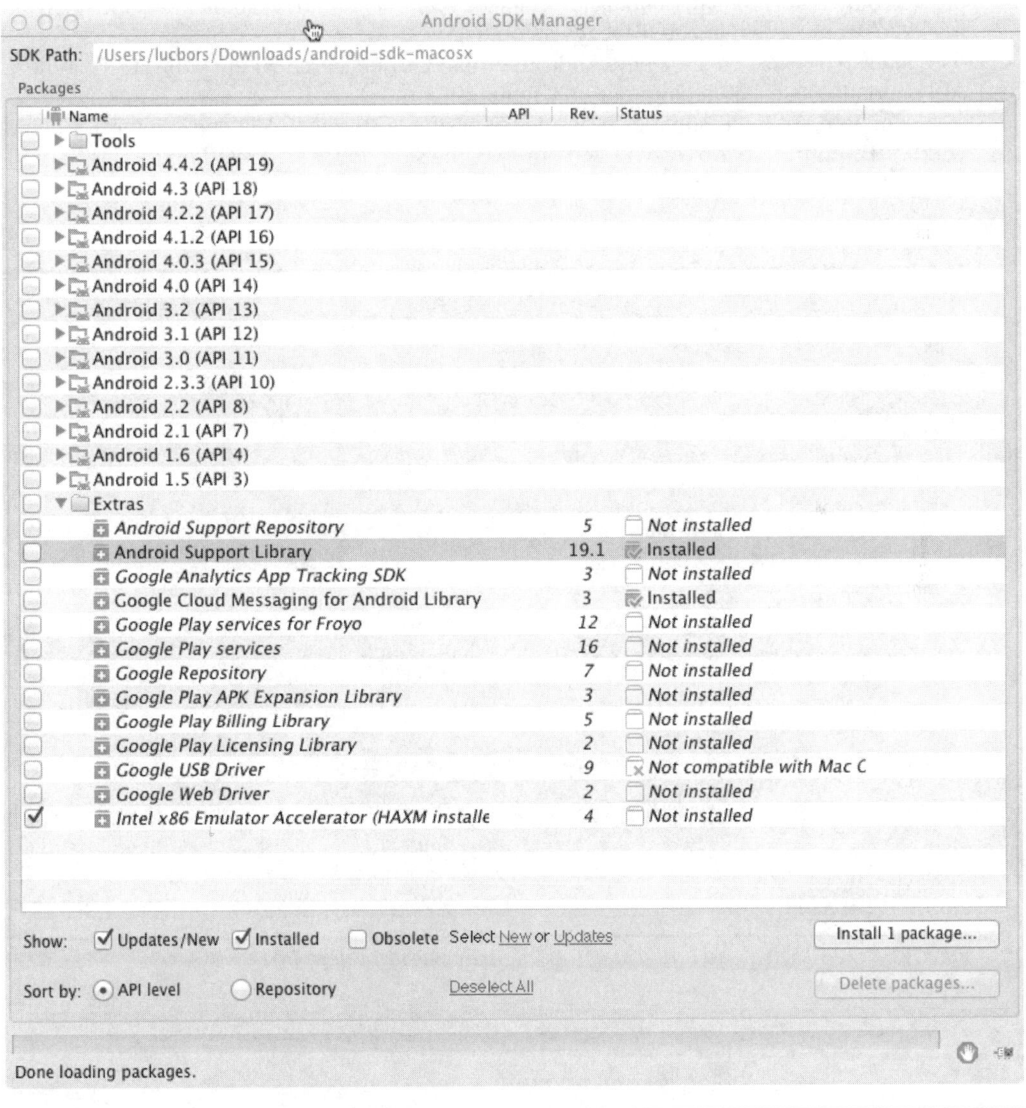

Name	API	Rev.	Status
▶ Tools			
▶ Android 4.4.2 (API 19)			
▶ Android 4.3 (API 18)			
▶ Android 4.2.2 (API 17)			
▶ Android 4.1.2 (API 16)			
▶ Android 4.0.3 (API 15)			
▶ Android 4.0 (API 14)			
▶ Android 3.2 (API 13)			
▶ Android 3.1 (API 12)			
▶ Android 3.0 (API 11)			
▶ Android 2.3.3 (API 10)			
▶ Android 2.2 (API 8)			
▶ Android 2.1 (API 7)			
▶ Android 1.6 (API 4)			
▶ Android 1.5 (API 3)			
▼ Extras			
Android Support Repository		5	Not installed
Android Support Library		19.1	Installed
Google Analytics App Tracking SDK		3	Not installed
Google Cloud Messaging for Android Library		3	Installed
Google Play services for Froyo		12	Not installed
Google Play services		16	Not installed
Google Repository		7	Not installed
Google Play APK Expansion Library		3	Not installed
Google Play Billing Library		5	Not installed
Google Play Licensing Library		2	Not installed
Google USB Driver		9	Not compatible with Mac C
Google Web Driver		2	Not installed
Intel x86 Emulator Accelerator (HAXM installe		4	Not installed

SDK Path: /Users/lucbors/Downloads/android-sdk-macosx

Packages

Show: ☑ Updates/New ☑ Installed ☐ Obsolete Select New or Updates   Install 1 package...

Sort by: ⦿ API level ◯ Repository   Deselect All   Delete packages...

Done loading packages.

FIGURE 2-6. *Installing the HAXM software*

NOTE
Once you've installed HAXM, note that on Windows 8.1+ or OS X 10.9+ at the time this book was published, a hotfix is required; otherwise, the software will hang your machine. This hotfix and how to install it can be found at:
http://software.intel.com/en-us/android/articles/intel-hardware-accelerated-execution-manager-end-user-license-agreement-macos-hotfix.

With the HAXM software successfully installed, next within your Android SDK Manager, for the Android version you are building for (Android 4.2.2 API 17, for example), you then download the Intel x86 Atom System Image for that version (Figure 2-7).

Finally, you must create a new Android Virtual Device (AVD) where you select for the CPU/ ABI option the Intel Atom (x86) option (Figure 2-8).

From here, as in the previous examples, you simply start the AVD and use this for deploying your MAF application too. As you will observe, the start time and overall performance of the Android Emulator is faster and much less painful for development.

Android SDK Manager

SDK Path: /Users/lucbors/Downloads/android-sdk-macosx

Packages

Name	API	Rev.	Status
▶ ☐ Tools			
▶ ☐ Android 4.4.2 (API 19)			
▶ ☐ Android 4.3 (API 18)			
▼ ☐ Android 4.2.2 (API 17)			
☐ Documentation for Android SDK	17	2	Installed
☐ SDK Platform	17	2	Installed
☐ Samples for SDK	17	1	Installed
☐ ARM EABI v7a System Image	17	2	Installed
☑ Intel x86 Atom System Image	17	1	Installed
☐ MIPS System Image	17	1	Installed
☐ Google APIs	17	3	Installed
☐ Sources for Android SDK	17	1	Installed
▶ ☐ Android 4.1.2 (API 16)			

Show: ☑ Updates/New ☑ Installed ☐ Obsolete Select New or Updates   Install 1 package...

Sort by: ⦿ API level ○ Repository   Deselect All   Delete 1 package...

Done loading packages.

FIGURE 2-7. *Download and install the Intel x86 Atom System Image.*

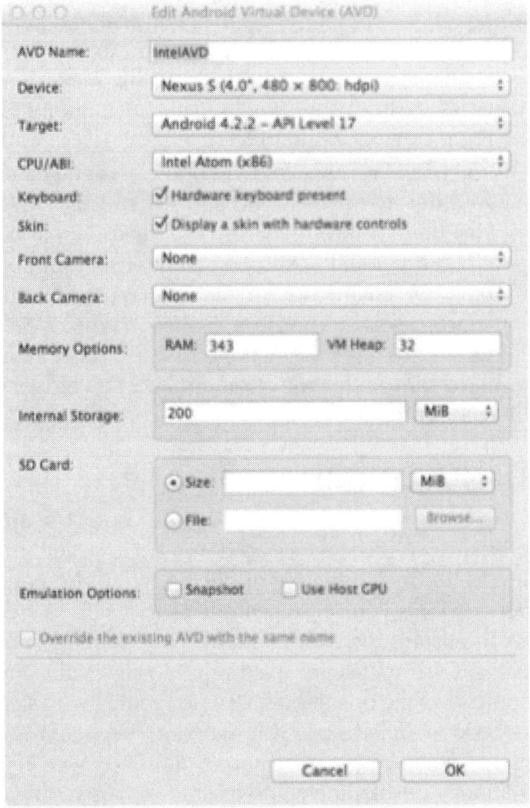

FIGURE 2-8. *Create a new Android Virtual Device.*

Preparing for iOS Development

In contrast to Google and Android development, Apple does not allow you to develop applications for iOS with Xcode and deploy to an actual device for free. You need to be a member of the iOS Developer Program. However, you can join the free version of the iOS Developer Program, which would allow you to download Xcode and develop/test the app. You just can't deploy it to an actual device.

The setup for deploying to an actual device is a little bit more complicated than with Android. All steps you need to take before starting iOS development are explained in the next sections.

The iOS Developer Program and the Apple ID

To register for any of the iOS Developer Programs, you will need an Apple ID. As a consumer who owns an iOS device, you probably already have an Apple ID, but preferably, you should create a separate Apple ID using an e-mail address that is shared within the enterprise where you work. The Apple ID can be created at the Apple web site at the following URL: https://appleid .apple.com/cgi-bin/WebObjects/MyAppleId.woa/.

The easiest way is to create your Apple ID in one go when you sign up for the iOS Developer Program. There are two different (three if you also count the iOS University Program) iOS Developer Programs. First there is the standard program known as the IOS Developer Program, which is designed to allow individual developers to publish your apps to the iTunes App Store. Second, there is the Apple iOS Enterprise Program. You must sign up for the Enterprise Program if you wish to distribute proprietary in-house iOS apps to employees within your organization. To sign up for the Enterprise Program, you can go to https://developer.apple.com/programs/ios/ enterprise/. If you want to sign up for the standard iOS Developer program, you can go to https://developer.apple.com/programs/ios/.

Application Distribution

For the purposes of this book, you'll likely only deploy your MAF applications to iOS using the iOS Simulator or your own iPhone or iPad devices. However, for a real development effort, at some stage you'll want to distribute your application to others, and you'll do this through the Apple iOS Developer accounts you've just enrolled in.

To do this, a few things are required. First of all, you need to create development and distribution certificates. Certificates are used to code-sign your app or installer package. Code-signing your app allows the operating system to identify who signed your app and to verify that your app has not been modified since you signed it. There are two kinds of certificates. The first one is the Development Certificate to run an app on an iOS device and use store technologies during development. During development and testing, you are required to sign all iOS apps that run on devices. The second one is a Distribution Certificate to distribute your app on designated devices for testing or to submit it to the store. Distribution certificates are used to submit your app to the App Store.

Certificates can be created in the Certificates, Identifiers & Profiles part of the Developer Member Center at https://developer.apple.com/account/ios/certificate/certificateList.action. The site has clear instructions on how to request these certificates. Make sure to get both a Developer and a Distribution certificate.

Next, you need to create an App ID. Every application needs an App ID that is used inside the Developer Program to uniquely identify your app from all others. You can create one in the Member Center at https://developer.apple.com/account/ios/identifiers/bundle/bundleList.action. iOS uses the App ID, for instance, to allow your application to connect to the Apple Push Notification service. An App ID is a two-part string used to identify one or more apps from a single development team. The string consists of a *Team ID* and a *bundle ID search string*, with a period (.) separating the two parts. The Team ID is supplied by Apple and is unique to a specific development team, while the bundle ID search string is supplied by you to match either the bundle ID of a single app or a set of bundle IDs for a group of your apps. The recommended practice is to use a reverse-domain name–style string for the bundle ID portion of the App ID. An example App ID would be ABCDE12345.com.yourcompany.yourapp.

Finally, you will need provisioning profiles. A provisioning profile is a combination of an App ID and a certificate and will allow you to distribute your app. You can have development profiles or distribution profiles. This allows devices to actually run the app. All iOS apps require that you use provisioning profiles during development. For iOS apps, you cannot run an app on a device (an iPhone or iPad) until you provision that device for development. Provisioning is the process of preparing and configuring an app to launch on devices. During development and testing, you designate the devices that can launch your app. When you submit your app to the store, you just provision your app (distribution profile).

Downloading Xcode

Once you have finished all the administration tasks, you still need to install the SDK for developing iOS apps. This SDK is Xcode. The latest version of Xcode is available from the Apple App Store. Older versions are available from the Xcode web site: https://developer.apple.com/xcode/. This web site (Figure 2-9) hosts all versions of Xcode, including documentation. Also, it has a link that guides you to the App Store, where you can download Xcode.

FIGURE 2-9. *The Apple Xcode web site*

NOTE
MAF doesn't necessarily support the latest version of Xcode. Before downloading Xcode, always check http://otn.oracle.com for supported versions.

You can also obtain Xcode directly from the Apple App Store (Figure 2-10). Simply search for Xcode and the application will show up for you to download and install.

Launching the iOS Simulator

Xcode ships with the latest iOS Simulator. To get the iOS Simulator into Launchpad or into the Dock, you can use the following steps: From the Finder, press COMMAND-SHIFT-G and paste in the following path:

```
/Applications/Xcode.app/Contents/Developer/Platforms/iPhoneSimulator.platform/
Developer/Applications/
```

Now you can drag the iOS Simulator into the Dock. When you start the iOS Simulator, it shows you the iPhone with default apps installed.

You can use it as if it were a real device (Figure 2-11). You can also switch from iPhone to iPad via the Hardware | Device menu.

Using Multiple Versions of iOS Simulator

As mentioned earlier, Xcode ships with the latest version of the iOS Simulator. If you need to develop for older iOS operating system versions, you can download and install these versions via Xcode. You open Xcode, go to the Xcode | Preferences menu, and from the preferences, select the

FIGURE 2-10. *Xcode in the App Store*

FIGURE 2-11.   *The iOS Simulator in action*

Downloads section (Figure 2-12). Simply click the "Check and Install Now" button for the versions you want to use.

If you are running the iOS Simulator, you can switch to and from all the installed versions as shown in Figure 2-13. Later when you are really building MAF applications with JDeveloper, you can tell JDeveloper what version of the Simulator the application must be deployed to. That enables you to test the app against different versions of iOS.

TIP
When you start deploying your MAF application to the Simulator and the application doesn't appear, it could be because you have the wrong version selected in the Simulator; try switching versions.

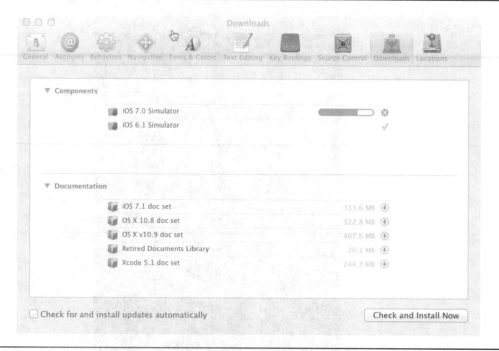

FIGURE 2-12. *Xcode Preferences to download iOS Simulators*

FIGURE 2-13. *Switching iOS versions*

Setting Up Oracle JDeveloper

Once you have the relevant Android SDK or XCode software installed, your final configuration steps are to tell JDeveloper where it can find them on your local machine. The first step is to download and install the JDeveloper extension for MAF. This extension can be installed via the "Check for Updates" menu in JDeveloper.

TIP
For MAF, if for some reason you cannot use the "Check for Updates" feature, you can go to the JDeveloper Extensions web site on OTN and download the extension from there.

This downloaded extension can then be installed via "Check for Updates" from the local file system.

After installing the MAF extension, you are almost ready to start developing your first MAF application. There are just a couple of properties that need to be set in the JDeveloper preferences. These settings enable JDeveloper to locate the platform-specific SDKs. You need to open JDeveloper and access the Preferences.

NOTE
The Preferences menu item has different locations depending on your operating system. On Windows, it can be found under Tools | Preferences. On Mac, it is under JDeveloper | Preferences.

In the Preferences window you find the option Mobile Application Framework, and when you expand that option, you'll see options for the Android Platform and iOS Platform. Each platform page contains the path and configuration parameters for the supported mobile platform you selected.

NOTE
At the time of writing, the supported platforms are Android and iOS. If in the future Oracle decides to support extra platforms, configuration of these platforms is most probably also here. Also note that MAF is supported in JDeveloper 12.1.3.

Setting Up Oracle JDeveloper for Android Development

To set up Android Development in JDeveloper (Figure 2-14), you need to select the Android Platform option and tell JDeveloper where the Android SDK is installed. JDeveloper will try to complete most of these settings for you, but you need to check them carefully to ensure they do point to a valid SDK installation.

Also you need to provide the signing credentials. These signing credentials are used when JDeveloper uses the Android SDK to build the application. If you use debug mode, you can use the default setting. If you want to use release mode, you need to use the Java key tools to generate a certificate. A typical command that you would issue for this on the command line would be:

```
keytool –genkey –v –keystore <Keystore Name>.keystore –alias <Alias Name>
-keyalg RSA –keysize 2048 –validity 10000
```

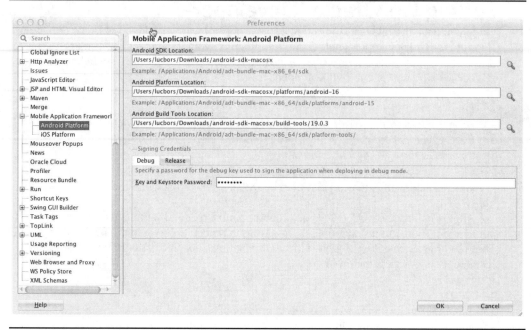

FIGURE 2-14. *JDeveloper Android preferences*

You then enter the name and password of the generated key in the JDeveloper Android preferences for Android release mode.

Setting Up Oracle JDeveloper for iOS Development

For configuring iOS development in JDeveloper (Figure 2-15), you select iOS from the list of supported platforms. Now you need to specify the iOS Simulator SDK location, the location of the Xcode build utility, and the location of iTunes. The iTunes location is used by JDeveloper to deploy the application to iTunes for synchronization to the device. As a reminder, because Xcode and the associated iPhone Simulator can only be installed on a Mac, it only makes sense to configure these settings if you're running JDeveloper on a Mac.

NOTE
You must have run iTunes and the iOS Simulator at least once before you configure their directory locations in the Mobile Application Framework iOS Platforms preferences page. If you miss these steps, often the deployments will fail from JDeveloper because the license conditions haven't been agreed to by the XCode/iTunes command-line utilities.

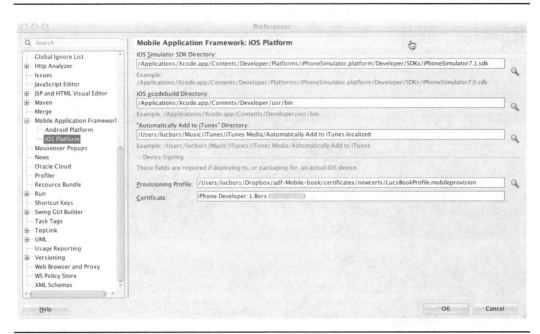

FIGURE 2-15. *JDeveloper iOS preferences*

Finally, you need to provide JDeveloper with signing information such as provisioning profile and a Developer Certificate. You can use the profile and certificate as discussed in the section "Preparing for iOS Development."

Summary

Developing with MAF requires you to configure and install extra tooling. In this chapter you learned how to set up these additional tools and how to configure JDeveloper for MAF development.

- Setting up the Android SDK
- Using the Android Emulator
- Obtaining an Apple ID and certificates
- Setting up Xcode
- Using the iOS Simulator

CHAPTER
3

Oracle JDeveloper for Oracle Mobile Application Framework Development

I n the previous chapters you learned about the Oracle Mobile Application Framework and how to set up your development environment in order to work with Oracle MAF.

Before you can actually start building your MAF applications, it is recommended that you take a quick guided tour of JDeveloper in order to become familiar with the most important windows, menus, and features of the Integrated Development Environment (IDE). This enables you to be even more productive in building and organizing your MAF applications. In this chapter you will be introduced to JDeveloper and learn how to find your way around in this development environment.

Quick Overview of Oracle JDeveloper

JDeveloper is a free tool that Oracle supplies to help developers build applications in the Oracle Fusion Middleware (FMW) stack. The tool is created to make developers as productive as possible and promotes both the declarative development model and the ability to write code.

Oracle JDeveloper integrates development features for Java, SOA, Web 2.0, database, XML, web services, and mobile development into a single tool. It covers the full development life cycle from initial design and analysis, through the coding and testing phases, all the way to deployment.

NOTE
You need the full Studio Edition of JDeveloper for MAF development.

JDeveloper is an IDE that focuses on increasing developers' productivity by offering a visual and declarative approach to application design that provides a simpler way to define the components that construct an application, thereby simplifying and eliminating tedious coding.

After you have installed JDeveloper and started (Figure 3-1) it for the first time, JDeveloper prompts you to select a "startup role" (Figure 3-2).

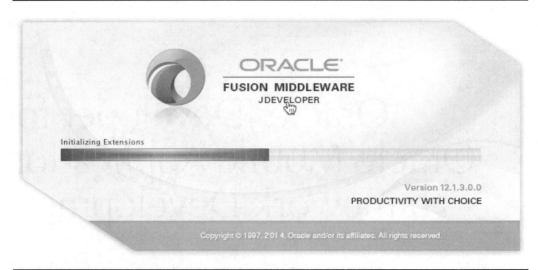

FIGURE 3-1. *The JDeveloper Startup window*

NOTE
JDeveloper ships with an installer that you must use to install the IDE. For platform-specific requirements and installation, you must refer to the "Installing Oracle JDeveloper" guide in the Oracle Fusion Middleware Documentation Library.

After you have installed JDeveloper and started it for the first time, JDeveloper prompts you to select a "startup role" (Figure 3-2).

This will configure JDeveloper with the features you need to perform the tasks of your choice. If you pick Studio Developer, you will get all the features available in JDeveloper.

NOTE
You must pick Studio Developer to be able to develop MAF applications.

Next uncheck the box "Always prompt for role selection on startup" so you aren't prompted each time you start JDeveloper.

NOTE
You can always change the role and also re-enable the "Prompt at startup" option from within JDeveloper by simply invoking the Tools menu and choosing the Switch Roles option in this menu (Figure 3-3).

FIGURE 3-2. *Choose your role to preconfigure JDeveloper.*

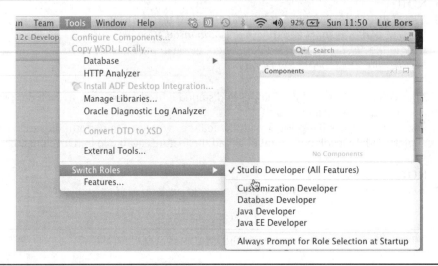

FIGURE 3-3. *Changing the JDeveloper role*

When JDeveloper starts, after dismissing the "tip of the day" and "Oracle usage Reporting" messages, you will see a more or less empty IDE. Now you can start the guided JDeveloper tour.

Exploring and Customizing the Oracle JDeveloper IDE

JDeveloper is an out-of-the-box Integrated Development Environment (IDE). It ships with its default settings and default styles. There are many preferences that can be changed by individual developers, and it is beyond the scope of this book to go into detail on all of them. There are, however, several parts of the IDE that you will be using throughout the development of an Oracle MAF application. These parts need further investigation in order to get you started.

The Windows in Oracle JDeveloper

In order to get comfortable with JDeveloper, you must learn to recognize all the windows and panels in JDeveloper and you must be able to manage them. JDeveloper uses several windows and panes to show different kinds of content. Most of these windows can be moved around and positioned independently of the other windows.

When you start JDeveloper, you get a predefined IDE layout that looks a lot like what you see in Figure 3-4.

Usually, the default setup, as suggested by JDeveloper, works fine. After working with JDeveloper for a while, you might find the default positions of the windows and panes are not quite what you want. You can rearrange the IDE windows, allowing you to organize them in a manner to your liking. If this gets too confusing, you can revert to the factory settings by invoking the Windows menu and selecting "Reset Windows To Factory Settings."

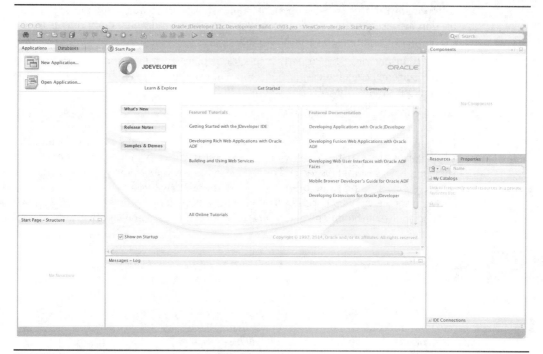

FIGURE 3-4. *JDeveloper initial and default IDE*

The windows (Figure 3-5) that you will probably use the most are the following:

- **Application Navigator** This is the main container for an application in JDeveloper. It holds panels to manage application content. These panels include:
    - **Projects Panel** This is the panel that you will use to navigate the artifacts of your application, mainly source code. You can invoke the right mouse button menu on an artifact to create, view, and edit artifacts. You can also double-click an artifact to open it in the appropriate editor.
    - **Data Control Panel** This panel shows the "data model" for the current application. You will use the Data Control panel when building the application's user interface. The Data Control panel enables you to drag and drop parts of the data model to create user interface items.
- **Application Resources** This contains all application-wide resources and configuration files. Whatever happens here applies to the whole application. You will find connections used in the application and also application images for iOS and Android such as splash screen images.
- **Structure Window** This window displays a hierarchical view of the currently selected object. When it displays the structure of a Java file, you will see methods and member variables of the class. You can click a node in the structure window, let's say a method of a Java class, and that same method is automatically highlighted in the corresponding source editor. This makes the Structure window a valuable asset when working with large classes or complex structures.

- **Component Palette** The Component Palette shows you available elements that can be used in the visual editor. For instance, you can drag and drop UI components from the Component Palette on an MAF AMX page.

- **Property Inspector** The Property Inspector displays a list of properties and their values for the currently selected component. You will use the Property Inspector mainly to view and edit properties of MAF components.

- **Editor Window** This is the part of the IDE where you do all the work. It usually appears in the center of JDeveloper and is the window where you do the editing of all artifacts. No matter what kind of file, a Java class, an XML file, configuration files, or diagrams, the editing takes place in the editor window. The editor will, depending on the file type that it is showing, have several tabs located on the bottom. These tabs allow you to switch between different views of the same file. For an MAF mobile page you can, for instance, switch between source view and preview. For a configuration file, you can switch between overview (for declarative development) and source view for doing the same task by hand-coding.

NOTE
JDeveloper synchronizes the content of the different tabs of the editor window so that changes in the visual editors are immediately reflected in the code or source editors and vice versa. Also, JDeveloper synchronizes the editor window and the Structure window as well as the Property Inspector and the editor window. This means that you have several options to do the same task, but the result will be the same.

All of the panel and windows mentioned earlier are highlighted in Figure 3-5.

There is also a History tab. Switching to this tab enables you to compare several versions of a file. You will see what changed in the current version compared to an older version (Figure 3-6).

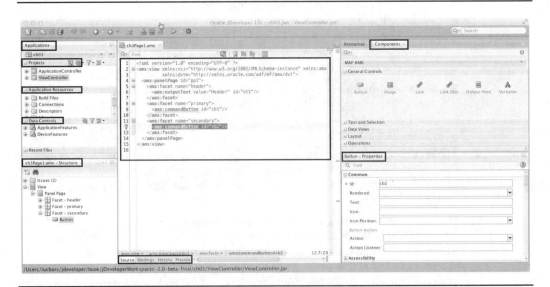

FIGURE 3-5. *JDeveloper windows and panels*

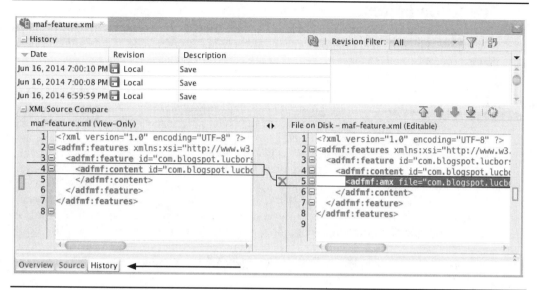

FIGURE 3-6.   *JDeveloper File History feature*

Oracle JDevelopers' Local History

JDeveloper will keep a local history of each file as long as you configure JDeveloper to do so. You can change this setting in the JDeveloper Preferences. Depending on your settings, JDeveloper will keep the history for a couple of days (Figure 3-7).

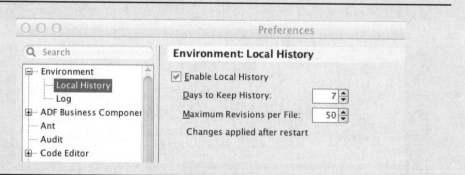

FIGURE 3-7.   *JDeveloper Local History preferences*

If you take a vacation, on returning, you might get an unpleasant surprise when invoking the history feature to find that all history is gone because, by default, it is only saved for seven days. Be careful not to fully rely on this for version control. You will learn about version control options later in this chapter. The History tab, whether associated with a version control system or not, can be a life saver if you messed with a previously working state of your code.

The Code Editor

The editor window can contain all kinds of content. The way this content is initially displayed can be configured in the JDeveloper preferences. If you want to open a file in a different kind of editor, you can simply change this setting in the File Types preferences (Figure 3-8).

TIP
When you open JDeveloper, it loads all files that were open when JDeveloper was last closed. When the default editor is "Preview" or "Design," the windows can take a little time to render as JDeveloper initializes. The "Source" editor is slightly faster, and when you tend to leave files open when closing JDeveloper, "Source" is definitely the preferred default.

In the code editor, you can (obviously) edit code. This can be Java files, XML files, and also property files, text files, JavaScript files, and Cascading Style Sheets (CSS). The way this code is displayed, colors, fonts, layout, can all be configured in JDeveloper. This can be achieved in the JDeveloper preferences under the Code Editor node. Many settings can be changed at the different

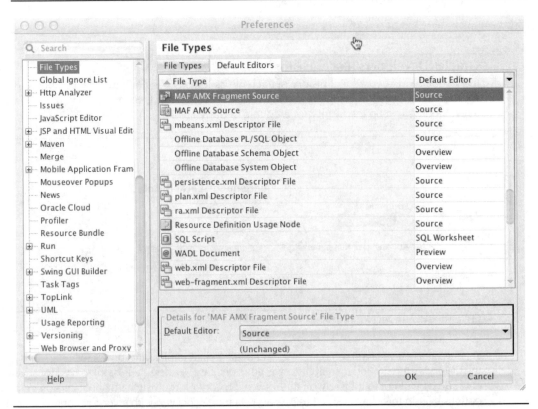

FIGURE 3-8. *Changing a file's default editor*

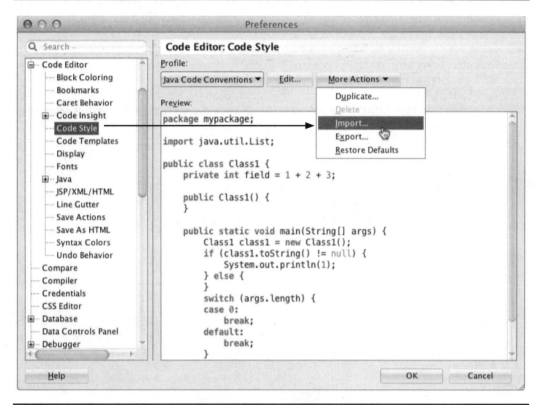

FIGURE 3-9. *JDeveloper code editor preferences*

nodes, and you can even add your own "code style" by importing a code style template (Figure 3-9). This makes sure that all developers use the same code style.

Creating an Oracle Mobile Application Framework Application

Now that you know your way around in JDeveloper and with all IDE preferences in place, it is now time to create your first MAF application. You can create a new MAF application in several ways. You can either use the New icon in the toolbar, the New Application in the Application Navigator or simply use the File | Application| New menu. If you choose to create a new application, JDeveloper will give you a choice of what kind of application you want to create.

TIP
Instead of the options mentioned earlier to display the New Gallery, you can also press CTRL-N.

Because JDeveloper is an IDE for many Oracle Fusion Middleware solutions, it enables you to create many different kinds of application types based on what you are building. For this book, you want to create a new Mobile Application Framework Application (Figure 3-10).

When you click OK, JDeveloper guides you through a wizard that you can use to configure the parent-level MAF application. In the first step (Figure 3-11), define the application name and the directory on the file system where the application files are stored. You can also enter the Application Package Prefix. This will act as a root Java package structure for all files that are created in your application. This helps you to structure the content of your application. Make sure to think about a package-naming convention to ensure that what you build is located in unique paths to avoid naming conflicts.

NOTE
Application Package Prefix and Directory are not the same. A "Directory" is specific to your development computer, whereas the "Application Package Prefix" is abstracted from the file system of any computer.

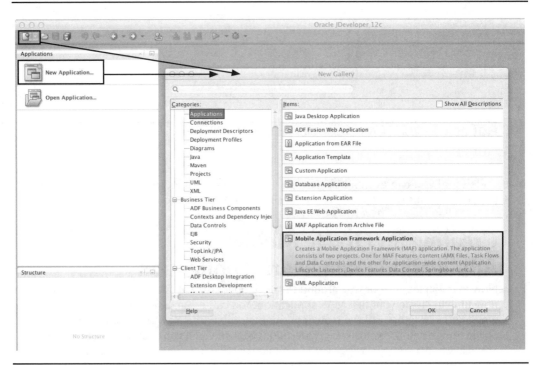

FIGURE 3-10. *Choose Mobile Application Framework Application in the New Gallery.*

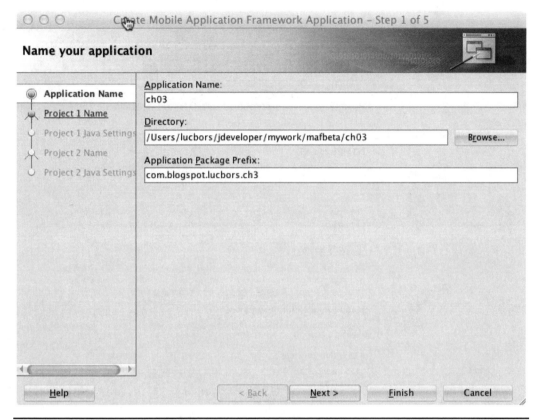

FIGURE 3-11. *Creating a new MAF application – step one*

Step two (Figure 3-12) is the creation of the projects within the MAF application. An MAF application typically consists of two projects. The first project is the ApplicationController. This project is used to store all application-level artifacts in your MAF application. The name "ApplicationController" is entered by default. Also, the directory where the project files are stored must be set in this step of the wizard. The directory is derived from the application directory that was set in step one. Also note the project features. JDeveloper adds the project features to the project. Information about exactly what features are needed is derived from an application template.

TIP
JDeveloper uses application templates to set up and configure newly created applications. You can find the application and project templates by using the Application menu; select Manage Template.

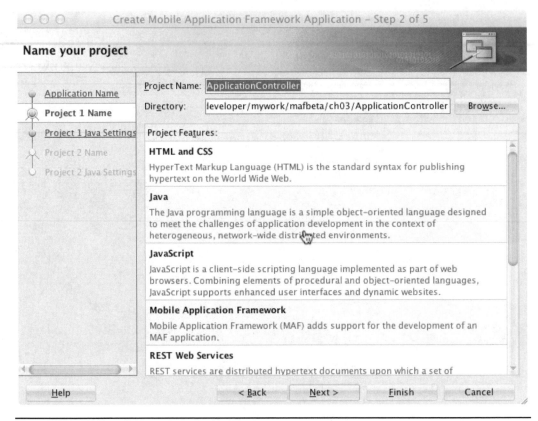

FIGURE 3-12. *Creating a new MAF application – step two*

In step three (Figure 3-13) of the wizard, you configure the Java settings. This means that you define a default package for the project. This defaults to the default package that is set at application level, suffixed with "application." You must also configure the Java Source Path and the Output Directory. The first determines where your Java Source files are stored. Note that this is the root path. The actual files will be stored after the default package is added to this root path. The same applies to the Output Directory where your class files (compiled Java classes) are stored.

The final two steps of the wizard are the same as steps 2 and 3, with the difference that the final steps apply to the ViewController project instead of the ApplicationController project. Just enter the settings (or accept the defaults) and finish the New MAF Application wizard.

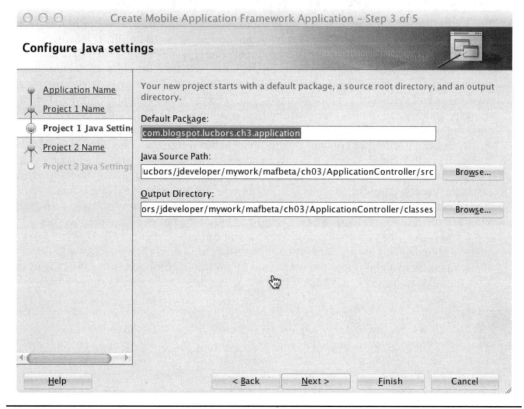

FIGURE 3-13. *Creating a new MAF application – step three*

Oracle Mobile Application Framework Development in Eclipse

In this book, the JDeveloper IDE is used to explain Oracle MAF and the development process. If the IDE of your choice is Eclipse, you can also develop MAF applications. In order to enable MAF development in Eclipse, you must first install Oracle Enterprise Pack for Eclipse (OEPE). OEPE provides a set of plugins for the Eclipse IDE designed to create, configure, and deploy Oracle MAF applications. If Eclipse is your preferred IDE, you most probably know your way around in Eclipse. Configuration of the Eclipse IDE is beyond the scope of this book.

After installing OEPE in Eclipse, you must open the perspective dialog in Eclipse and select Oracle MAF. When you click OK, the Eclipse IDE updates to a new set of views and editors that are best suited to developing Oracle MAF applications.

To start working, from the main menu, select File | New | Other. Then in the New wizard, expand Oracle, then Mobile Application Framework, and from the list of available Oracle templates, select MAF Application.

Now the new MAF application is created and you can start developing this new MAF application using the explanations and sample used in this book. There might be small differences, but in essence the application development is the same.

Version Control in Oracle JDeveloper

Previously, the local history feature of JDeveloper was mentioned. This works to some extent as long as you are working as the one and only developer on the project. However, during application development, there are most probably more developers involved than just one. This means that you will be working together on the same code base. In order to identify changes and to ensure that developers work with the latest version of the program, you can (must) use a version control system. JDeveloper enables you to connect to a version control system and to manage your source control from within the JDeveloper IDE. JDeveloper supports several different version control systems.

By default, JDeveloper contains plugins that enable you to use either Subversion (subversion .tigris.org) or GIT (git-scm.com). It is easy to configure JDeveloper to use Subversion or GIT. You can version an application via the Team | Version Application menu. JDeveloper allows you to select the Version repository (Figure 3-14). After selecting the repository of your choice, JDeveloper starts an import wizard where you must enter the repository-specific settings. Refer to the JDeveloper online help for specific setup and requirements for GIT and Subversion.

If you prefer other version control systems, you can use "Check for Updates" and see if there is an extension for the version control system of your choice that is available for JDeveloper. There will probably be extensions for version control systems such as ClearCase, ConcurrentVersionsSystem (CVS), and Perforce.

TIP
The JDeveloper online help contains information on how to set up and use your own version control system.

FIGURE 3-14. *Version application in JDeveloper*

Summary

Before starting with MAF development, it is very useful to know your development tool of choice. You will be working with it a lot, and you will get used to how JDeveloper supports mobile application development. Once you are familiar with JDeveloper, the IDE offers you many ways to customize the environment so it will meet your needs. In this chapter you learned

- How to configure JDeveloper startup roles
- How to find your way around in JDeveloper
- How local history works and how to use version control systems
- How to create an Oracle MAF application

CHAPTER
4

Building AMX Pages

A good user interface and user experience are the keys to success for mobile applications. The users of your mobile application want to accomplish tasks. Every function of your mobile application should be targeted toward helping them to complete their task, and everything else should be discarded. Vendors such as Apple and Google are well known for their mobile applications that ooze user experience through well-orchestrated user interfaces. They did extended research to ensure that users know exactly what to expect when they press a button, swipe the screen, or touch an icon. When you develop a custom interface that does not work in this way, users will get confused, and this can potentially put them off using your mobile product permanently.

In this chapter you will learn how to use the Mobile Application Framework to create AMX pages and flows for your mobile application. More specifically, you will learn about the component libraries that are part of the framework and that help you develop the user interface in a component-driven way. Furthermore, you will see how you can create task flows to implement the flow in your application.

First, let's take a look at the framework, and more specifically, the role of the AMX pages and the controller in the framework's architecture (Figure 4-1).

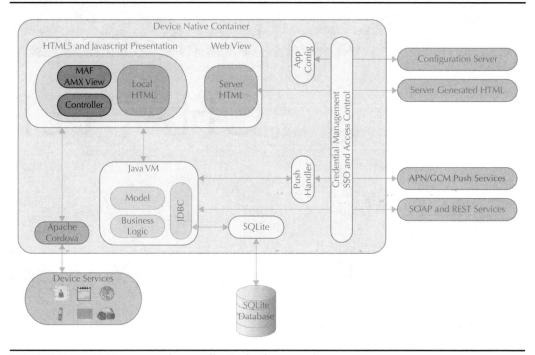

FIGURE 4-1. *AMX pages and controller in the framework*

The AMX views and the controller are responsible for rendering the user interface and controlling navigation at run time in the device's web view. These parts of the framework are not involved directly in connecting to data sources such as web services, nor are they involved in device interaction. They are only involved in rendering the HTML5 views and navigation.

The examples that are used throughout the chapter retrieve data from plain old Java objects (POJOs). In order to show this data in the application, the binding layer will be used. The binding layer part of the framework will be discussed in Chapter 5. There is no need yet to try to understand these parts, as we will focus on building the user interface with the available UI components and how to implement task flows and navigation.

Introducing Component-Based Development

Component-based development is like building with LEGOs. You have a set of bricks and you can use them to build a car or house or whatever you like. Each brick has its own specific properties and they can be combined in any way you like.

The components in a component library are pretty much like LEGOs. They are predefined; they have their own properties and behavior. There is no need to have a deep understanding of how this is implemented. You can look at them as black boxes that can be combined into a fully functional user interface. They can be combined in any way you like to create many different kinds of user interfaces.

The same is true for the Mobile Application Frameworks component library. You can develop AMX pages by using components from the framework's component library. This component library consists of many predefined components that have properties to configure them.

Let's take a closer look at the components that are available.

Available Components in the Oracle Mobile Application Framework

The MAF component library holds all components that you need to build a mobile application with MAF. The MAF component library consists of two broad categories. The first contains common components that can be used to create the user interface. The second contains components that are specifically created for data visualization, such as graphs, gauges, maps, and so on. You will learn about both categories in the following sections.

As you can see from Figure 4-2, the common components are grouped into further subcategories. This makes it easier for developers to find the components.

TIP
If you do not exactly know where to find a component, you can use the search functionality of the Component Palette (Figure 4-3). This enables you to quickly locate a component.

Let's take a look at a basic example of how you can use the Component Palette. The Oracle MAF component library contains a component named Input Text. You can find that component in the Component Palette in JDeveloper under the "Text and Selection" category. The Component Palette can be used to drag and drop a component into an AMX page as you can see in Figure 4-4.

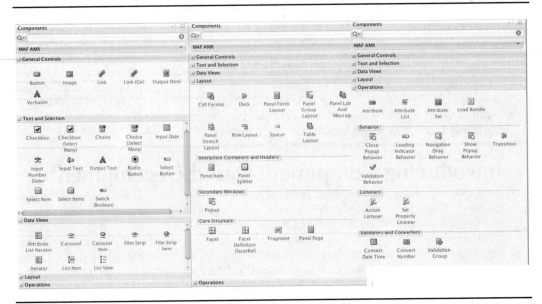

FIGURE 4-2. *Components available in the MAF component library*

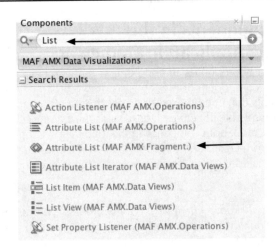

FIGURE 4-3. *Searching in the Component Palette*

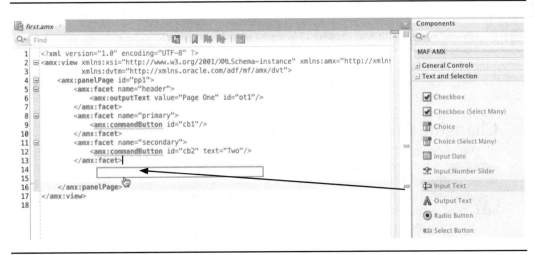

FIGURE 4-4.   *Drag and drop from the Component Palette.*

When you drag the Input Text component from the palette onto an Oracle MAF AMX page, JDeveloper creates an input text field for you:

```xml
<?xml version="1.0" encoding="UTF-8" ?>
<amx:view xmlns:xsi=http://www.w3.org/2001/XMLSchema-instance
          xmlns:amx=http://xmlns.oracle.com/adf/mf/amx
          xmlns:dvtm="http://xmlns.oracle.com/adf/mf/amx/dvt">
   <amx:panelPage id="pp1">
      <amx:facet name="header">
         <amx:outputText value="Header" id="ot1"/>
      </amx:facet>
      <amx:facet name="primary">
         <amx:commandButton id="cb1"/>
      </amx:facet>
      <amx:facet name="secondary">
         <amx:commandButton id="cb2"/>
      </amx:facet>
      <amx:inputText label="label1" id="it1"/>
   </amx:panelPage>
</amx:view>
```

TIP
If you feel confident, you can omit using the Component Palette. Instead of dragging and dropping, it is also possible to directly type the component into the AMX source. The result will be the same.

The properties of this Input Text component are available through the Property Inspector and can be changed. You will learn about this in the next section.

Changing Component Properties

All components of MAF have a set of properties. These properties determine the runtime appearance, behavior, and style of the components. The properties can be changed in the Property Inspector. The Property Inspector can be displayed in both vertical and horizontal layout. The horizontal layout uses tabs to group the properties, whereas the vertical layout uses an accordion to group the properties.

Both orientations (Figure 4-5) display the same properties. In the Structure window, the Property Inspector can be invoked from the context menu on the component as displayed in Figure 4-6.

TIP
If you are new to JDeveloper and the Mobile Application Framework, the Property Inspector offers a very convenient way of changing the properties of a component. Changing properties is immediately reflected in the XML that defines the Mobile AMX page. When you gain confidence and experience, you will probably find that working directly inside the XML code is easier as you know what code to type. The result is the same, but the speed of development usually is faster. The code editor offers autosuggest lists for both components and properties (Figure 4-7).

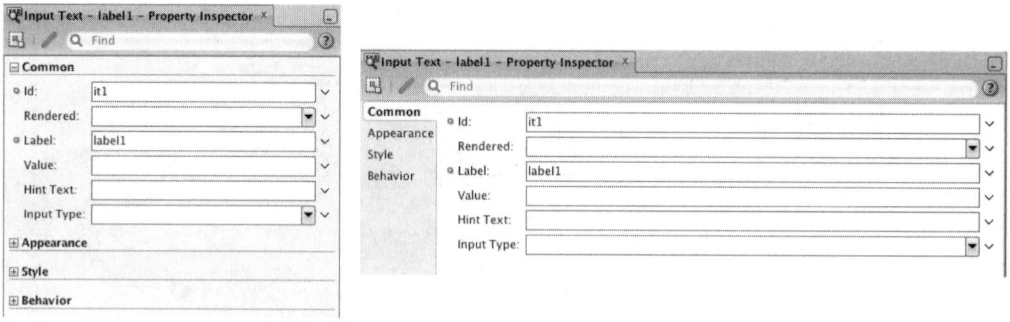

FIGURE 4-5. *Property Inspector in vertical (left) and horizontal (right) layout*

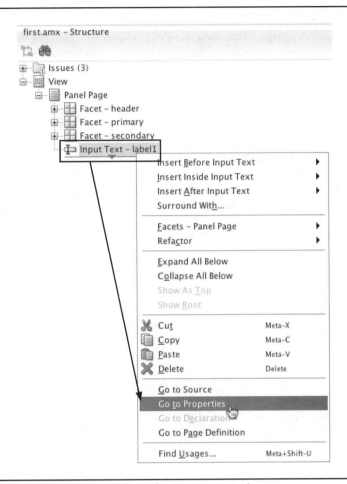

FIGURE 4-6. *Invoking the properties from the Structure window*

FIGURE 4-7. *Autosuggested properties in the source editor*

Layout Components

Mobile applications usually follow best practices in terms of laying out the page. These layouts for different platforms such as iOS and Android are described in standards and guidelines provided by Apple and Google. Many of these layouts can be created with the Oracle Mobile Application Framework's mobile layout components.

There are several layout components, such as tableLayout, rowLayout, cellFormat, and panelSplitter, all of which will be explained throughout this chapter. When you build an AMX page, you will first have to create a "skeleton," or core structure, for your AMX page. This structure will have one single "view" component as the outer layout component. An example of such a "skeleton" structure is displayed in the next code sample. This "view" component cannot be configured, as it has no attributes. The framework, however, needs this component to be the outer container for all components on an AMX mobile page. Usually, the next component in the page's component tree is the panelPage component, which will be discussed next.

```xml
<?xml version="1.0" encoding="UTF-8" ?>
    <amx:view xmlns:xsi=http://www.w3.org/2001/XMLSchema-instance
            xmlns:amx=http://xmlns.oracle.com/adf/mf/amx
            xmlns:dvtm="http://xmlns.oracle.com/adf/mf/amx/dvt">
    <amx:panelPage id="pp1">
        <amx:facet name="header"/>
        <amx:facet name="primary"/>
        <amx:facet name="secondary"/>
    </amx:panelPage>
</amx:view>
```

You do not have to use the panelPage if you don't want to, but it is a very powerful component that helps you build your mobile AMX pages. The panelPage component has four facets defined. Facets are placeholder components that make sure that whenever a page is rendered, the facets' content is always displayed on a predefined position. The facets for a panel page are the following:

- **Header** This facet usually contains the title for the mobile page and is rendered at the top of the mobile page.
- **Footer** The footer is rendered at the bottom of the mobile page.
- **Primary** Usually contains a button, most often to navigate back to the previously displayed view.
- **Secondary** Also used to display a button; for instance, to navigate to a next view.

If you create a new AMX page, JDeveloper asks you what facets you want to use, as displayed in Figure 4-8.

NOTE
You do not have to pick any of the facets at this time. They can always be added later by invoking the context menu on the panel page and selecting the available facets or by simply typing the code for the facet components in the code editor.

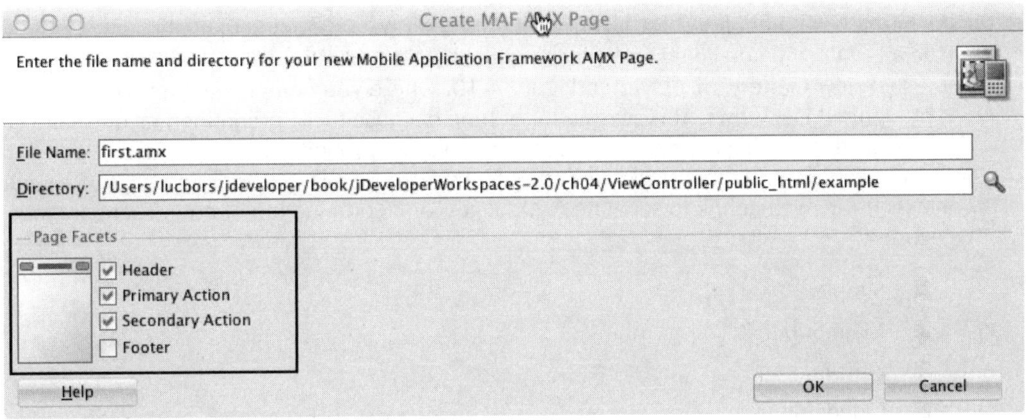

○ ○ ○   Create MAF AMX Page

Enter the file name and directory for your new Mobile Application Framework AMX Page.

File Name: | first.amx

Directory: | /Users/lucbors/jdeveloper/book/jDeveloperWorkspaces-2.0/ch04/ViewController/public_html/example

Page Facets

☑ Header
☑ Primary Action
☑ Secondary Action
☐ Footer

Help   OK   Cancel

FIGURE 4-8. *Pick the page facets for the new AMX mobile page.*

The panelPage component will render content that can scroll in between the header and footer facets of the AMX page as you can see in Figure 4-9. This figure displays a screenshot of the MAF application that will be used throughout this section to explain the use of several layout components.

FIGURE 4-9. *Sample panel page with header and footer*

The List View

MAF has several predefined list layouts, all with their own specific characteristics. When you create a List View by dragging and dropping a collection from the data control, JDeveloper shows you a ListView Gallery, displayed in Figure 4-10, where you can pick any of over 50 (currently 64) predefined List Views. This saves a lot of time because these predefined layouts take care of the hard work of setting the right combination of display properties.

You can pick any of the predefined layouts. This can be a layout with an image, a layout that contains list items that link to separate AMX pages, or a combination of both. There are four main categories:

- Simple
- Main-Sub text
- Start-End
- Quadrant

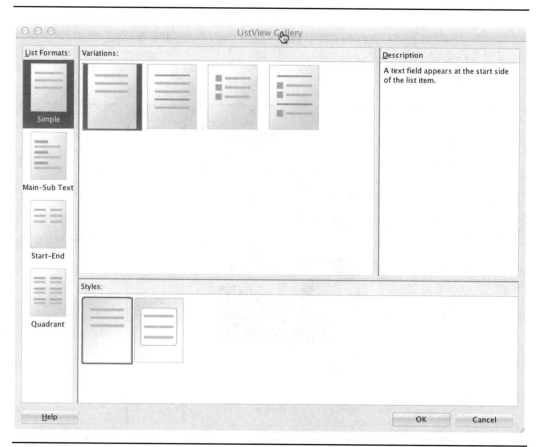

FIGURE 4-10. *Create a new List View from the ListView Gallery.*

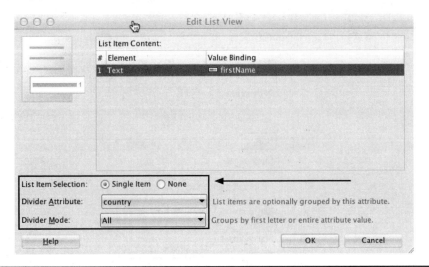

FIGURE 4-11. *Edit List View editor*

When you create a list, you have several settings to consider. These settings must be configured in the Edit List View editor that shows up once you select one of the predefined layouts. Figure 4-11 shows the Edit List View editor after picking a Simple List from the predefined layouts.

List Item Selection

When you create a list, you can configure the list to support list item selection. When you use Single Item, the list will be configured in such a way that the selected list item is made the current item in the collection that the list is based on. A SelectionListener attribute and a selectedRowKeys attribute are added to the List View to accommodate list item selection. If you select None, selection is not possible.

Using a Divider

When you create a list, you can also configure a divider attribute for the list. The divider attribute is used to group list items together. Divider mode can be set to two different values. In both options, you can use the showDividerCount attribute, which will display the number of entries for that specific group. The first option is to use the complete value of the divider attribute, for instance, to group list items by day of the week or by country. An example of this is displayed in Figure 4-12.

```
<amx:listView var="row"
              value="#{bindings.attendees.collectionModel}"
              fetchSize="#{bindings.attendees.rangeSize}"
              selectedRowKeys="#{bindings.attendees.collectionModel.selectedRow}"
              selectionListener="#{bindings.attendees.collectionModel.makeCurrent}"
              dividerAttribute="country"
              dividerMode="all"
              showMoreStrategy="autoScroll"
              bufferStrategy="viewport" id="lv1">
```

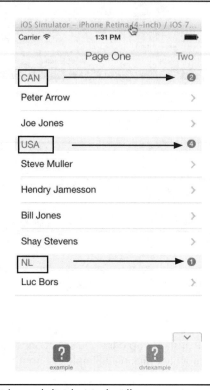

FIGURE 4-12. *List with divider and dividerMode All*

The other option is to use the first letter of the dividerAttribute. This would typically be used when ordering a list, for instance, by Last Name, as you can see in Figure 4-13. When you use the firstLetter dividerMode, MAF will also create an alphabet indexer with those letters that have entries in the list highlighted.

```
<amx:listView var="row"
             value="#{bindings.attendees.collectionModel}"
             fetchSize="#{bindings.attendees.rangeSize}"
             selectedRowKeys="#{bindings.attendees.collectionModel.selectedRow}"
             selectionListener="#{bindings.attendees.collectionModel.makeCurrent}"
             dividerAttribute="lastName"
             dividerMode="firstLetter"
             showMoreStrategy="autoScroll"
             bufferStrategy="viewport" id="lv1">
```

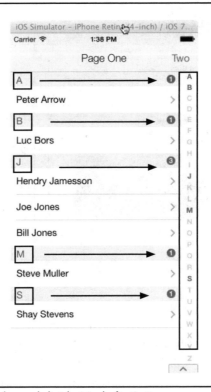

FIGURE 4-13.   *List with divider and dividerMode firstLetter*

NOTE
The divider itself does not sort the data. In order to have the data in the list displayed properly, it needs to be sorted. This is something you would typically do in a Java method.

Creating Your Own List View Layout

Although there are plenty of options to pick from, there are definitely circumstances where the predefined layouts do not meet your requirements. If that happens to be the case, you need to know how to create your own layout. Let's take a look at the following example, which is based on a Twitter client. Looking at the layout in Figure 4-14, you can see the several layout areas.

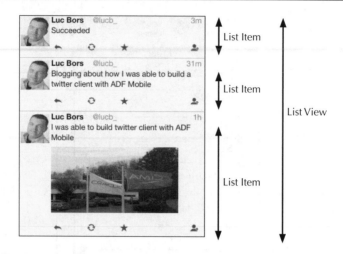

FIGURE 4-14. *A List View in action*

The components are easily recognizable. First, you can see a listView component with nested listItems components. This implementation is straightforward.

```
<amx:listView var="row" value="#{bindings.timeline1.collectionModel}"
    selectedRowKeys="#{bindings.timeline1.collectionModel.selectedRow}"
    selectionListener="#{bindings.timeline1.collectionModel.makeCurrent}"
    showMoreStrategy="autoScroll" bufferStrategy="viewport"
    fetchSize="#{bindings.timeline1.rangeSize}" id="lv1">
  <amx:listItem showLinkIcon="false" id="li1">

  <!—content of list view goes inhere -->

  </amx:listItem>
</amx:listView>
```

The next step is to analyze the layout more precisely and determine what layout component you need to use in order to achieve this layout.

The content of the List Items consists of several layout areas. Looking from the top down in Figure 4-15, there are four rows that can be recognized. The first row contains the header, the second row contains the text of the tweet, and the third row is optional and contains an image if one is tweeted. Finally, the fourth row contains icons to retweet, favor, or reply to a tweet and the possibility to follow the Twitter handle.

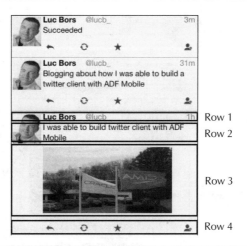

FIGURE 4-15. *The Table Layout component in action*

A layout with multiple rows can best be implemented by using a table layout component with multiple row layout components. In this case, four row layout components must be used. This table layout component is a child of the List Item component. By setting the width property to 100 percent, you make sure that the component takes up all available horizontal space.

```
<amx:tableLayout width="100%" id="tl2">
    <amx:rowLayout id="rl2">
        <!—header goes here -->
    </amx:rowLayout>
    <amx:rowLayout id="rl3">
        <!—tweet goes here -->
    </amx:rowLayout>
    <amx:rowLayout id="rl6" rendered="#{row.photo!=''}">
        <!—image goes here -->
    <amx:rowLayout id="rl4">
        <!—footer goes here -->
    </amx:rowLayout>
</amx:tableLayout>
```

So far, this is still a pretty simple layout to create. All content in the rows is embedded in cell components. These are responsible for the specific layout within the rows and table.

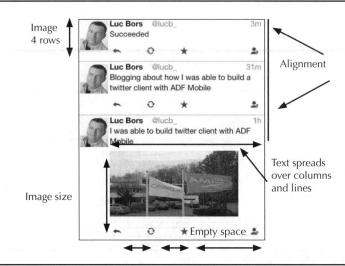

FIGURE 4-16. *Specific layout features*

When you look at the individual rows, you can see several components and some specific alignments, which are highlighted in Figure 4-16. Let's look at this on a row-by-row basis and explain the possibilities. In the first row, there is the image of the Twitter account itself, followed by name, handle, and the time of the tweet.

You can clearly recognize these four parts, and they reside in their own cellFormat component. CellFormat components are the actual content containers. By using the width property and the halign property, the row is rendered as a one-row component, where the first cell spans four rows and has a fixed width, and the second and third cell use 20 percent of the available width each. The fourth cell aligns its content to the end in order to have the tweet time at the end of the line. This is part of the first row; however, it stretches below that first row. This can be achieved by using the rowspan attribute of the cell that contains the image.

```
<amx:rowLayout id="rl2">
    <amx:cellFormat width="54px" halign="center" valign="top"
                    rowSpan="4" id="cf5">
        <amx:image id="i7" source="/images/#{row.image}.png"
                   inlineStyle="height:48px;width:48px;margin-top:4px" />
    </amx:cellFormat>
    <amx:cellFormat width="20%" height="12px" id="cf4">
        <amx:outputText value="#{row.name}" id="ot1"
                        inlineStyle="font-size:small; font-weight:bold;"/>
    </amx:cellFormat>
    <amx:cellFormat width="20%" height="12px" id="cf4a" halign="end">
```

```
        <amx:outputText value="@#{row.handle}" id="ot1a"
                        inlineStyle="font-size:small; color:Gray;"/>
    </amx:cellFormat>
    <amx:cellFormat width="50%" height="12px" id="cf14" halign="end"
                    columnSpan="2">
        <amx:outputText value="#{row.when}" id="ot3"
                        inlineStyle="font-size:small;color:Gray;"/>
    </amx:cellFormat>
</amx:rowLayout>
```

In the second row, the text of the tweet is displayed. For the displayed text to take the horizontal space available, you must understand how the layout mechanism works. When building layouts with the table, row, and cell components, the following strategy is used by the framework: The second and consecutive rows' layout is determined based on the first row's layout. In order for the tweet text to take more space than just one cell, the columnSpan property must be used. In this case, columnSpan 4 is used to make the tweet text stretch over all columns of the first row. For wrapping the text, an inline style property is used. This could also be implemented as a style class that resides in a CSS file.

```
<amx:rowLayout id="rl3">
    <amx:cellFormat width="100%" height="12px" id="cf6"
                    halign="start" columnSpan="4">
        <amx:outputText value="#{row.text}" id="ot2"
        inlineStyle="font-size:small;text-wrap:normal;white-space:pre-wrap;"/>
    </amx:cellFormat>
</amx:rowLayout>
```

Next is the image that is conditionally displayed. For this image, a fixed size can be used so no matter what the size of this image is, it always takes the same amount of space.

```
<amx:rowLayout id="rl6" rendered="#{row.photo!=''}">
    <amx:cellFormat id="cf9">
        <amx:image id="i15" source="/images/#{row.photo}.png"
                   inlineStyle="height:108px; width:216px;"/>
    </amx:cellFormat>
</amx:rowLayout>
```

Third are the four icons in the bottom row. These icons are all displayed in their own cells, and you can use the width property to size the cells and the halign property to tell the cell components where their content must be rendered relative to the cell boundaries.

```
<amx:rowLayout id="rl4">
    <amx:cellFormat id="cf7" height="12px" width="20%" halign="start">
        <amx:commandLink id="cl8">
            <amx:image id="i8" source="/images/tlal-Reply.png"
                       inlineStyle="height:24px; width:24px;"/>
        </amx:commandLink>
    </amx:cellFormat>
    <amx:cellFormat id="cf11" height="12px" width="20%" halign="start">
```

```
        <amx:commandLink id="cl9">
           <amx:image id="i9" source="/images/tlal-Retweet.png"
                      inlineStyle="height:24px; width:24px;"/>
        </amx:commandLink>
     </amx:cellFormat>
     <amx:cellFormat id="cf13" height="12px" width="20%" halign="start">
        <amx:commandLink id="cl10">
           <amx:image id="i10" source="/images/tlal-Favorites.png"
                      inlineStyle="height:24px; width:24px;"/>
        </amx:commandLink>
     </amx:cellFormat>
     <amx:cellFormat id="cf12" height="12px" width="20%" halign="end" >
        <amx:commandLink id="cl11">
           <amx:image id="i11" source="/images/tlal-User-Add.png"
                      inlineStyle="height:24px; width:24px;"/>
        </amx:commandLink>
     </amx:cellFormat>
  </amx:rowLayout>
```

The PanelSplitter Component

The panelSplitter layout component is a component that can be used to conditionally render different parts of a UI without having to navigate to a different AMX view. This can also be explained based on the Twitter client sample. Figure 4-17 shows the same mobile application, but now with some links displayed just below the header.

The panelSplitter component has a selectedItem property. This property determines which one of the panelItem children of the panelSplitter component is visible for the end user at a given moment. The sample contains three panelItems, each of which renders its own specific content. A panelItem's content is visible to the user whenever the id of the panelItem matches the value of the selectedItem property of the panelSplitter component. This is dynamic and can be set at run

FIGURE 4-17. *Using links to control a panelSplitter component*

time. To switch between the panelItems, the Home, Discover, and Activity (Figure 4-16) links can be used. Invoking these links will set the value of the activePanel property.

```
<amx:panelSplitter selectedItem="#{pageFlowScope.UiBean.activePanel}"
                   animation="slideLeft">
    <amx:panelItem id="home">
       <!—List view from previous section goes here -->
    </amx:panelItem>
    <amx:panelItem id="discover">
       <!—List view from previous section goes here -->
    </amx:panelItem>
    <amx:panelItem id="activity">
       <!—List view from previous section goes here -->
    </amx:panelItem>
</amx:panelSplitter>
```

The panelSplitter component is also typically a component that you would use to create tablet layouts where you have a list on the left side and detail content on the right side. You will learn more about how to use the panelSplitter component in Chapter 18, where the panelSplitter component is used to create the tablet layout for the sample app.

Switching between displayed components can also be achieved by the deck component. The deck component uses commandLinks to render the content instead of the panelItems in the previous example. You can use a setPropertyListener to set the value of the child to be displayed, and the deck component supports animated transitions.

```
<amx:deck displayedChild="#{pageFlowScope.UiBean.activePanel}">
    <amx:commandLink id="home">
       <!—List view from previous section goes here -->
       <amx:setPropertyListener from="discover"
              to="#{pageFlowScope.UiBean.activePanel}" type="swipeStart"/>
    </amx:commandLink>
    <amx:commandLink id="discover">
       <!—List view from previous section goes here -->
       <amx:setPropertyListener from="activity"
              to="#{pageFlowScope.UiBean.activePanel}" type="swipeStart"/>
       <amx:setPropertyListener from="home"
              to="#{pageFlowScope.UiBean.activePanel}" type="swipeEnd"/>
    </amx:commandLink>
    <amx:commandLink id="activity">
        <!—List view from previous section goes here -->
       <amx:setPropertyListener from="discover"
              to="#{pageFlowScope.UiBean.activePanel}" type="swipeEnd"/>
    </amx:commandLink>
    <amx:transition transition="slideRight" triggerType="backNavigate"
                 id="t1"/>
    <amx:transition transition="slideLeft" triggerType="forwardNavigate"
                 id="t2"/>
</amx:deck>
```

Working with Gestures

Since the creation of touchscreens, there is an extra dimension to application interaction. Mobile devices with touchscreens support finger gestures and thus enable you to use your fingers to control the application.

You can use one-finger gestures such as swipe up and down, and from left to right and also use the so-called taphold gesture. There are also two-finger gestures such as spread to zoom in and pinch to zoom out.

MAF supports many of these gestures and enables you to have the users control the MAF application in a way that they are used to. Oracle MAF supports the following gestures: SwipeLeft, SwipeRight, SwipeUp, SwipeDown, SwipeStart, SwipeEnd, and TapHold.

How to Use Gestures

There are several components that you can use to implement gesture support. They are not responsible for rendering any UI components, but they are operations or Listeners. These components are setPropertyListener, setActionListener, showPopupBehavior, and closePopupBehavior and can be added as child components of other components. Components that support these Listeners include, among others, the commandButton and listItems components. Also, some of the Data Visualization components that will be discussed later use this to trigger popups.

To implement the actual gesture support, you can use the "type" attribute of these components. This attribute holds the value of the gesture that it responds to.

For instance: If you want to open a popup when the user tapholds a listItem, you would typically use type="tapHold" as shown in the code sample:

```
<amx:listView id="lv"  value="#{bindings.data.collectionModel}" var="row">
    <amx:listItem action="gosomewhere">
        <amx:outputText id="ot1" value="#{row.description}"/>
        <amx:showPopupBehavior type="tapHold" alignid="pp1"
                               popupid="pop1" align="startAfter"/>
    </amx:listItem>
</amx:listView>
```

You can see all available gestures for a component in the Property Inspector or in the source editor (Figure 4-18).

Common patterns, such as "Swipe left to delete" and "Taphold to open a popup window," will be discussed in later chapters.

One other pattern is "Pull down to refresh." This pattern is used by many applications to refresh List Views. In the Mobile Application Framework, this can be implemented by using the setActionListener with the type "swipeDown":

```
<amx:listView var="row"
    value="#{bindings.allLocations.collectionModel}"
    fetchSize="#{bindings.allLocations.rangeSize}" id="lv1">
    <amx:listItem id="li1">
        <amx:actionListener type="swipeDown"
            binding=
                "#{pageFlowScope.locationsBackingBean.checkForUpdates}">
```

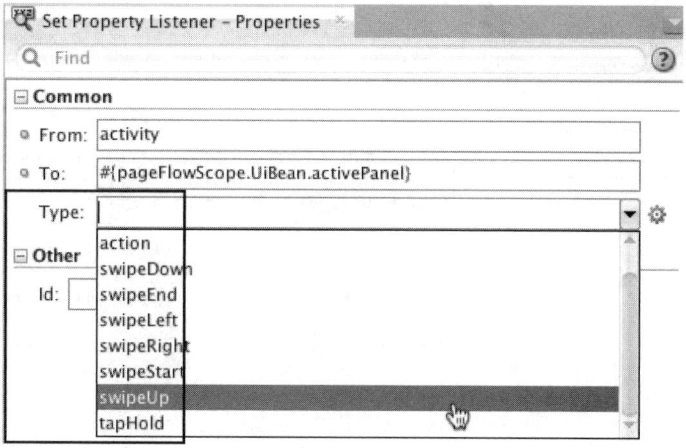

FIGURE 4-18. *Allowed values for the Type attribute*

When implementing this, the actionListener component on the list item fires the checkForUpdates method whenever the user swipes down.

NOTE
The checkForUpdates method is a custom method that is implemented in a backing bean. You will learn later how to implement backing beans.

Reordering Items in a List

There is a special gesture that can be implemented without coding. It is provided by the framework to rearrange items in a list. You can simply drag items to a new position in that list.

Here is how this "drag to reorder" can be implemented. Let's take another look at the listView that was created previously. This listView is a rather static view, but we can add some behavior to it. You can achieve this by using the editMode property of the listView. When this is set to true, listItems can be moved by the user. An example of this is displayed in Figure 4-19.

```
<amx:listView var="row" id="lv1"
    value="#{bindings.attendees.collectionModel}"
    fetchSize="#{bindings.attendees.rangeSize}"
    editMode="true">
    <amx:listItem id="li1">
        <amx:outputText value="#{row.firstName} #{row.lastName}" id="ot2"/>
    </amx:listItem>
</amx:listView>
```

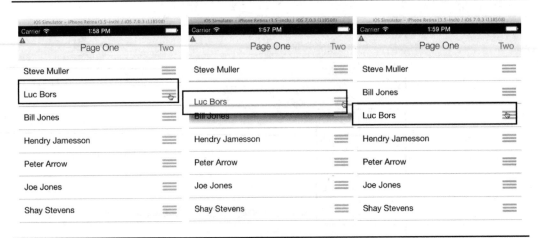

FIGURE 4-19. *Reordering items in a list*

Skinning Oracle Mobile Application Framework Applications

Skinning is a mechanism that is used to give the Oracle MAF application its specific look and feel in terms of colors and fonts. It is configured in an application by three different files. The default skin family that is used by an Oracle MAF application is defined in the maf-config.xml file.

```
<?xml version="1.0" encoding="UTF-8" ?>
    <adfmf-config xmlns="http://xmlns.oracle.com/adf/mf/config">
        <skin-family>mobileAlta</skin-family>
</adfmf-config>
```

The next file that is needed to configure skinning, if you use a custom skin or a skin extension, is the maf-skins.xml. If you do not want to change the default skin, this file will remain empty. If you do want to change the existing skin, or create a new one, you will make modifications to this file.

Let's take a look at the possible modifications:

■ You can customize the default skin by first creating a new CSS file.

■ You can create an addition to an existing skin by defining the "skin-addition" attribute in the maf-skins.xml.

■ You can create a whole new skin for your Oracle MAF application. This can be done by adding a new <skin> element to the maf-skins.xml without using the <extends> element.

The actual definition of the skin is done in the maf-skins.xml file as displayed in Figure 4-20.

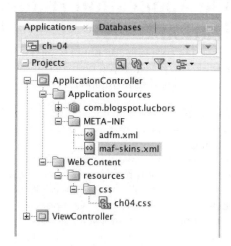

FIGURE 4-20. *maf-skins.xml*

This file needs to have a reference to the CSS file that contains the adjusted styles.

A new CSS file can be created in the ApplicationController project of our mobile application. You can do this by invoking the New Gallery, and under the Web Tier option, select HTML | CSS File. Once the CSS file is created, remove the default content that JDeveloper adds to the new CSS file, as we will add our own.

Now you have an empty CSS file. Before you add new styles to the CSS file, it is better to first define a skin addition to ensure that this CSS file will be picked up at run time. To do this, open the maf-skins.xml file, located in the META-INF directory of your ApplicationController project. Then drag and drop skin-addition from the Component Palette onto this file. Specify mobileAlta as the skin id, and select the CSS file you just created to set the style sheet property.

TIP

If you want to take a look at the default styles used by MAF, you can find these in the amx.css file. This file resides in the www\css directory. To access this directory, you must first deploy a MAF application to a simulator or device and then traverse to the deploy directory (for example, C:\JDeveloper\mywork\application name\deploy). The www\css directory resides within the platform-specific artifacts generated by the deployment. For iOS, this is the temporary_xcode_ project directory, and for Android, this is the assets directory.

```xml
<?xml version="1.0" encoding="UTF-8" ?>
    <adfmf-skins xmlns="http://xmlns.oracle.com/adf/mf/skin">
        <skin-addition id="s1">
            <skin-id>mobileAlta</skin-id>
            <style-sheet-name>css/tamcapp.css</style-sheet-name>
        </skin-addition>
</adfmf-skins>
```

Oracle Mobile Application Framework's Data Visualization Tools

So far, we have been discussing common components such as input components and layout components. The framework also provides you with an extensive set of Data Visualization Tools (DVTs). These DVTs can be used to display information in a graphical format to help better understand the underlying data.

Let's take a look again at the example that was used to explain the divider attribute earlier in this chapter. When this data is displayed in a list, the user of the application can only see the data that is currently visible in the viewable area of the application. If they wanted to know how many attendees live in certain countries, they would have to count and group these by hand. If this information is displayed in a graph, it is much easier to see how this distribution is. As with the other components from the Mobile Application Framework component library, the Data Visualization components are available from the Component Palette (Figure 4-21).

In the next section, one component from each category will be explained. Not all components are the same, but we will explain one of them per category, so that you will get an idea of how they work. First, you will learn how to implement a bar chart; next, you will work with a gauge component; and finally, you will see how to work with a map component.

Creating a Bar Chart

A bar chart is a chart that uses either horizontal or vertical bars to show comparisons among categories. One axis of the chart shows the specific categories being compared, and the other axis represents the value. In this example, you will learn how to create a bar chart that shows the number of attendees per country.

When you drag and drop the collection from the data control onto your page (Figure 4-22), JDeveloper shows you several options to create a chart. There are nine main categories and within

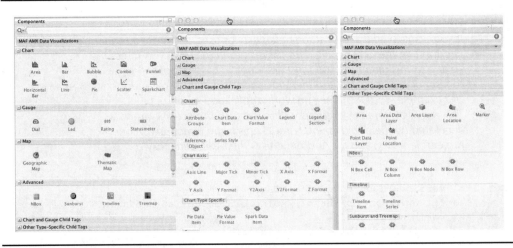

FIGURE 4-21. *MAF AMX Data Visualization Components*

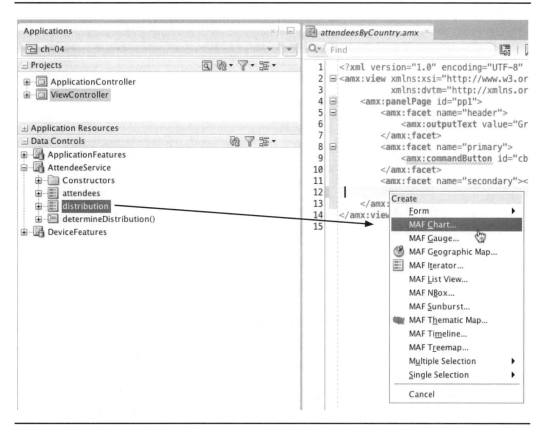

FIGURE 4-22. *Drag and drop as a mobile chart*

each category there can be multiple types of charts. Each of the types again can have multiple Quick Start layouts. All of this is to help you as a developer create charts very quickly with as little coding as necessary. In the case of this sample, just pick a bar chart without a legend as displayed in Figure 4-23.

When this option is selected, all you need to do is tell JDeveloper what attributes you want to use for the bars and for the x-axis. For this example, we want a bar for each country, and the height of the bar should display the number of attendees in that country. This configuration is displayed in Figure 4-24.

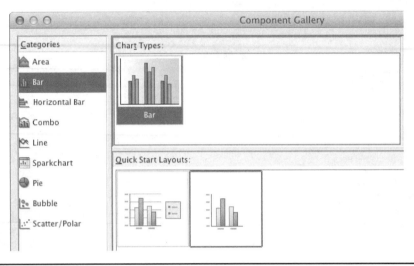

FIGURE 4-23. *Chart Component Gallery*

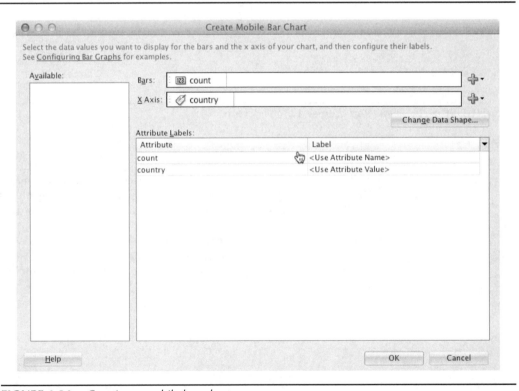

FIGURE 4-24. *Creating a mobile bar chart*

Closing the Create dialog results in the following code:

```
<dvtm:barChart var="row" value="#{bindings.distribution.collectionModel}"
                animationOnDisplay="auto" id="bc1">
    <amx:facet name="dataStamp">
       <dvtm:chartDataItem group="#{row.country}" value="#{row.count}"
                        series="#{bindings.distribution.hints.count.label}"
                        id="cdi1"/>
    </amx:facet>
    <dvtm:yAxis majorIncrement="1" minorIncrement="1"/>
    <dvtm:legend rendered="false" id="l1"/>
</dvtm:barChart>
```

At run time, the result is a bar chart, displayed in Figure 4-25, just as expected.

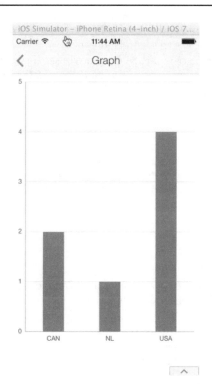

FIGURE 4-25. *A bar chart at run time*

Using Gauge Components

Gauge components are typically used to display a single data value relative to a given threshold. There are four different types of gauge components:

- **LED Gauges**   Show value by means of a single colored image
- **Status Meter Gauges**   Pressure or critical volume
- **Dial Gauges**   For instance, to show speed or temperature
- **Rating Gauges**   Show ratings, for instance, 3 on a scale of 5

You will learn about the dial and rating gauges in a later chapter.

Using the Map Component

The final component example in this chapter will explain how to use map components. When you look at address information, this usually doesn't make sense unless you are familiar with the city or neighborhood that the specific address is in. The Data Visualization Tools enable you to plot a specific address on a map. Here is how this works.

Again, you can use "drag and drop as". In this case, you need to pick MAF Geographic Map from the popup menu as you can see in Figure 4-26.

When you pick MAF Geographic Map, you will see a popup (Figure 4-27) where you can configure the Mobile Geographic Map. You can create data points based on coordinates, but for this sample, the address will be used.

After dismissing the Create Mobile Geographic Map popup, you will see the XML code that is created for you:

```
<dvtm:geographicMap id="map1">
    <dvtm:pointDataLayer value="#{bindings.attendees.collectionModel}"
                         id="pdl1" var="row">
        <dvtm:pointLocation address="#{row.streetAddress}" id="ptl1"
                            type="address">
            <dvtm:marker id="mrk1"/>
        </dvtm:pointLocation>
    </dvtm:pointDataLayer>
</dvtm:geographicMap>
```

At run time, the map will show a point for all "attendees" in the collection, and each of those points will be plotted at the address for that particular attendee.

Configuring the Map Component

The Geographic Map Component can use either Google Maps as a map provider or Oracle's Map Viewer. By default, MAF uses Google. Figure 4-28 shows the Map Component using the Google Maps provider.

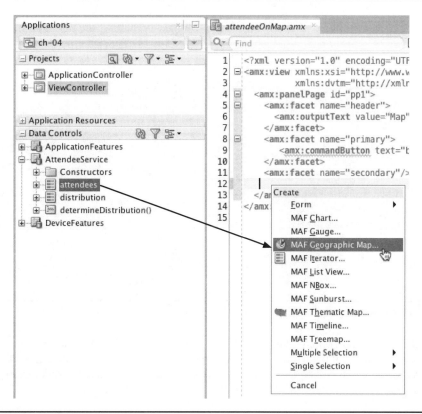

FIGURE 4-26. *Drag and drop as geographic map.*

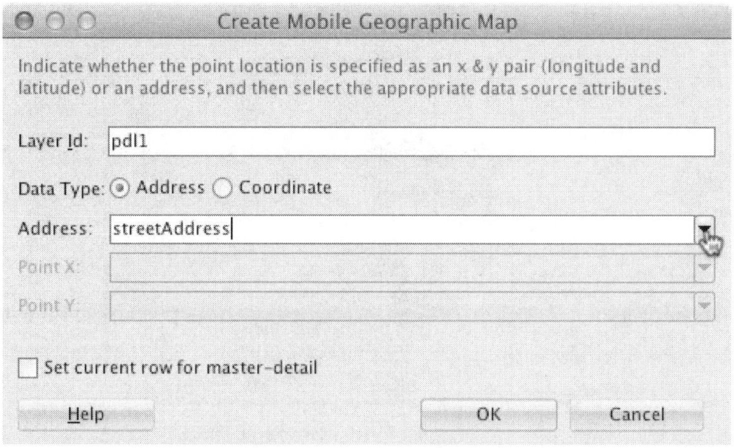

FIGURE 4-27. *Map configuration for geographic map points*

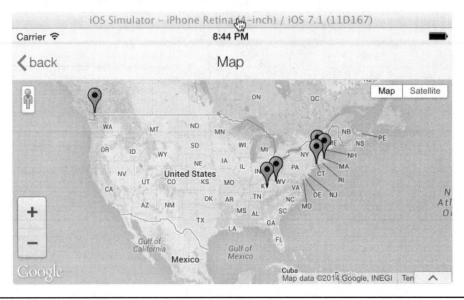

FIGURE 4-28. *A geographic map based on Google Maps viewer*

The definition of which map provider should be used by the MAF application is configured in the adf-config.xml file (Figure 4-29), which can be found as an application-level resource. The file is created when you create a new mobile application and is used to define application-level properties.

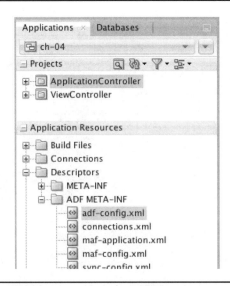

FIGURE 4-29. *The adf-config file*

The following code fragment shows configurations for both googleMaps and oraclemaps as the map provider. You will have to "uncomment" one of them in order to use the corresponding map viewer.

```
<adf:adf-properties-child
             xmlns="http://xmlns.oracle.com/adf/config/properties">
    <adf-property name="adfAppUID"
             value="ChapterFive.com.blogspot.lucbors.ch5"/>

<!-- google maps -->
    <adf-property name="mapProvider" value="googleMaps"/>
    <adf-property name="geoMapKey" value=""/>
<!-- -->

<!-- oracle maps -->
    <adf-property name="mapProvider" value="oraclemaps"/>
    <adf-property name="mapViewerUrl"
             value="http://elocation.oracle.com/mapviewer"/>
    <adf-property name="baseMap" value="ELOCATION_MERCATOR.WORLD_MAP"/>
<!-- -->
</adf:adf-properties-child>
```

The Oracle Map viewer is a little bit more critical on the data that you supply for the points. In Figure 4-30, you see an Oracle Map based on the same data points as the previously displayed Google Map. Note that the points are less accurate.

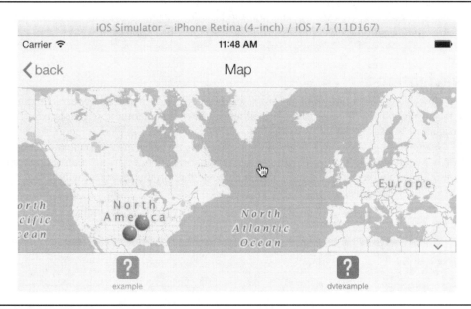

FIGURE 4-30. *A geographic map based on Oracle Map Viewer*

Oracle Mobile Application Framework Task Flows Explained

The Mobile Application Framework enables you to create AMX application features that have both bounded and unbounded task flows. A bounded task flow is also known as a task flow definition and represents the reusable portion of an application. These bounded task flows have a single entry point and no exit points. They have their own collections of activities and control flow rules, as well as their own memory scope and managed-bean life span. Unbounded task flows are not reusable and can have multiple entry points. It is a best practice to implement your task flows as bounded task flows, as this enables you to reuse the functionality and to work in a modular way.

Task flows help you to visually create the flow between pages and other activities within an application feature. Task flows can be visualized in a task flow diagram. When we look at the development of task flows, it is best to start from the task flow diagram. The task flow diagram can be used to construct a task flow in a visual way. You can add elements to this diagram and draw navigation paths known as control flow rules between them. This also helps you to implement routing decisions, method calls, and wildcard navigation. You will learn how to implement the task flow shown in Figure 4-31 when you develop the sample application.

For now, we will just focus on the basic features of task flows. The components available for constructing Oracle MAF task flows can be found in the Component Palette in the context of the task flow diagram.

TIP
You can create task flows in two different ways. The first is to use nonexisting pages and define the flow between them. Afterward, the pages can be created by double-clicking them on the task flow diagram. A second way is to construct your task flow from existing pages. You can drop existing pages on the task flow diagram and then define navigation between them. You can also mix both approaches.

Navigation

Many mobile applications will have some kind of navigation defined between the different parts of the application. In this section, you will learn how MAF enables you to define and invoke navigation. To explain how this works, the sample task flow displayed in Figure 4-32 will be used.

Navigation between AMX pages is defined in the AMX task flow. You can add a navigation case between two AMX view activities. This navigation is defined by a "control flow rule." This control flow rule has a source and a destination, defined in the "From Activity ID" and the "To Activity ID," respectively.

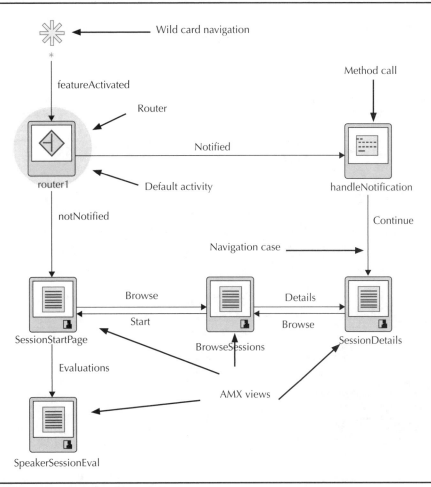

FIGURE 4-31. *A more complex task flow*

Besides navigating between activities, a control flow rule can be configured to implement animated page transitions. Sliding, flipping, and fading are supported.

To actually navigate between two AMX views, you need an action component such as a command button, command links, or list items. These components have an "action" attribute that can be used. The possible values for the action attribute are derived from the defined navigation rules in the corresponding task flow. Figure 4-33 shows available actions "goToSecond" and "goToThird," which are navigation rules.

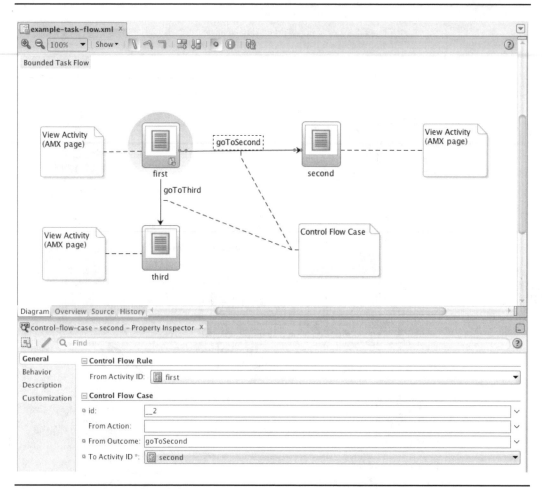

FIGURE 4-32. *A sample task flow with two navigation cases*

FIGURE 4-33. *Available values for action*

NOTE
A back action (__back) is automatically available to enable navigation to the previously visited page.

```xml
<?xml version="1.0" encoding="UTF-8" ?>
<amx:view xmlns:xsi=http://www.w3.org/2001/XMLSchema-instance
          xmlns:amx=http://xmlns.oracle.com/adf/mf/amx
          xmlns:dvtm="http://xmlns.oracle.com/adf/mf/amx/dvt">
    <amx:panelPage id="pp1">
        <amx:facet name="header">
            <amx:outputText value="Header" id="ot1"/>
        </amx:facet>
        <amx:facet name="primary">
        </amx:facet>
        <amx:facet name="secondary">
            <amx:commandButton id="cb2" action="goToSecond" text="Two" />
        </amx:facet>
        <amx:listView var="row" value="#{bindings.attendees.collectionModel}"
                    fetchSize="#{bindings.attendees.rangeSize}" id="lv1">
            <amx:listItem id="li1" action="goToThird">
                <amx:outputText value="#{row.firstName} #{row.lastName}"
                            id="ot2"/>
            </amx:listItem>
        </amx:listView>
    </amx:panelPage>
</amx:view>
```

Global Navigation

MAF also knows the concept of global navigation. This is navigation that is defined in such a way that it can be invoked from all view activities in the task flow, without individual control flow rules having to be defined for every possible path. To implement global navigation, a "wildcard control flow rule" can be used.

To create a wildcard flow, drag the Wildcard Control Flow Rule element from the Component Palette onto the task flow diagram of the called flow. Create a control flow case from the wildcard element to the task flow activity to call and define a name for the navigation case.

The wildcard is defined by an asterisk symbol (*) as the value of the from-activity-id element (Figure 4-34).

```xml
<control-flow-rule>
    <from-activity-id>*</from-activity-id>
        <control-flow-case>
            <from-outcome>goToFourth</from-outcome>
            <to-activity-id>fourth</to-activity-id>
        </control-flow-case>
</control-flow-rule>
```

This implementation results in "goToFourth" navigation being available on all view activities.

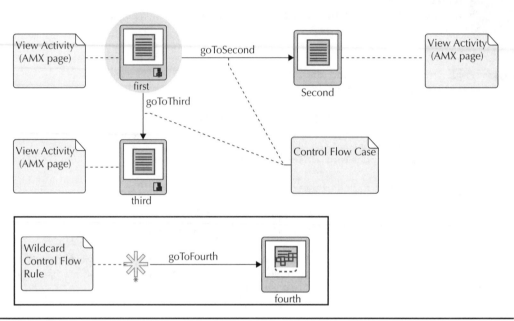

FIGURE 4-34. *Wildcard control flow rule*

Summary

The Oracle Mobile Application Framework offers an extensive set of user interface components that can be used to build mobile AMX pages. In addition, there is a set of Data Visualization Tools that can be used to build interactive dashboards. This chapter does not explain all of the available components, nor are all properties discussed. However, after reading this chapter, you should have a general understanding of how component-based development works. A lot of the Oracle Mobile Application Framework components will be discussed later on in this book in the context of the sample application.

In this chapter you learned

- What component-based development is
- What components are available in the Oracle MAF component library
- What are common characteristics of these components
- How to work with layout components
- How to work with Data Visualization Tools
- How to build mobile task flows

CHAPTER
5

Bindings and
Data Controls

One of the great advantages of Oracle MAF over other mobile frameworks is the fact that it has declarative support for building the user interface. This declarative support, as was explained in Chapter 4, enables a developer to create parts of the application without having to write code. On the other hand, Oracle MAF enables you to separately retrieve data from web services and POJOs and also from a SQLite database. For any application where the implementation of the user interface is separated from the implementation of the business services, these two tiers need to be bound together. To enable this, the framework uses a specific layer called data binding or the MAF Model. This Model layer is an architectural layer that binds the UI of your application to the back-end business services such as web services, and as such is the framework's implementation of decoupling the user interface from business services. Using the MAF Model comes with many advantages that enable developers to be very productive. The main advantages of the MAF Model are

- Drag-and-drop creation of databound components
- No need to understand the implementation of the underlying business services
- No need to write Java code to handle standard interactions between the business services and the view layer.
- The ability to declaratively add validation rules, UI hints, default attribute values, and other business logic to your business services as metadata without changing the code in the business services themselves. These declarative enhancements to the data model are propagated to any components that are created from the data control.
- The ability to work with multiple types of business services in the same way.

It is important to understand the basics of the MAF Model architecture in order to use the MAF Model.

The MAF Model consists of two parts. The first part is the data control and the second part is the declarative bindings. Data controls abstract the implementation technology of a business service by using a metadata interface to describe the service's operations and data collections, including information about the properties, methods, and types involved. There is no difference between a data control created from a web service and a data control created from a POJO. This saves developers having to learn the APIs over every single business service type; the data control allows the developer to treat them all generically through the data control API.

The second part, the declarative bindings, are used to bind services that are exposed by data controls to UI components and abstract the details of invoking methods or accessing data from data collections in a data control.

At run time, the two parts are combined as the MAF Model layer reads the information describing the data controls and bindings from the appropriate XML files and then implements the two-way connection between the user interface and the business service. Specific details of this mechanism are explained later in this chapter.

When you take a look at the MAF Mobile architecture (Figure 5-1), you will notice a part called Model. The Model layer is responsible for exposing data services and using these on Mobile AMX pages or inside Java code (Figure 5-2). There is definitely a lot of framework magic

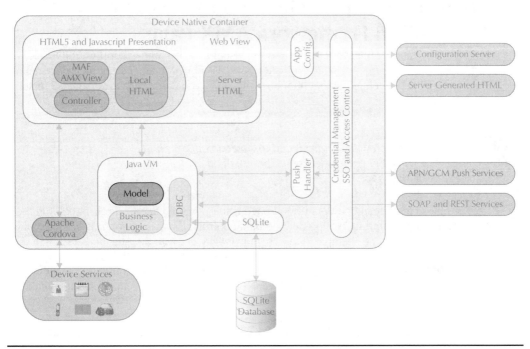

FIGURE 5-1. *The Model layer in the context of the framework*

involved behind the scenes to save the developer much repetitive coding, but for using the Model layer, there is no need to get into the details of all of this magic. However, it is very important to understand the principles and mechanisms that are involved in the Model layer.

This chapter will explain the Model layer and also how to work with the layer both in a declarative and programmatic way.

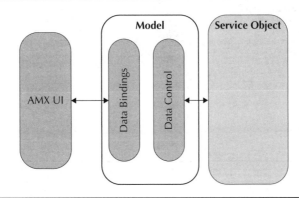

FIGURE 5-2. *MAF Model standing between data services and the UI*

Creating a Simple Data-Bound Mobile Application Framework AMX Page

To start understanding the Model layer and the visual and declarative support in JDeveloper, it is best to just start with creating a simple data-bound MAF AMX page. By taking it one step at a time, you will get a feeling of what happens when such a data-bound AMX page is created and what files are involved.

NOTE
In this section, you will be introduced to several concepts and artifacts involved in the Model layer. These will be explained in later sections of this chapter.

The first step in creating a data-bound page is to open the Data Controls panel. On the Data Controls panel, you find several predefined data controls. These data controls are created for you by the framework. For the example in this chapter, we'll work with the AttendeesService data control, which you will create. This data control exposes the Attendees collection so it can be used on an AMX page. Once the AttendeesService data control is created, the Attendees collection can be dropped (Figure 5-3) from the data control onto an existing AMX page and wired up with numerous

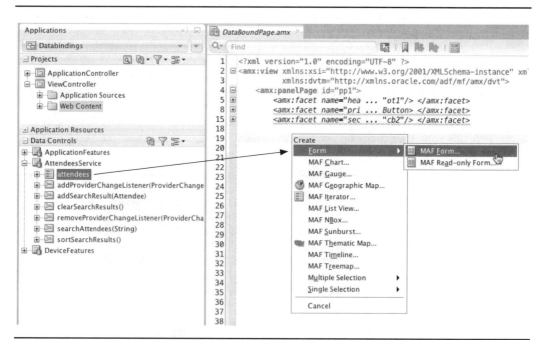

FIGURE 5-3. *Dragging and dropping from the data control*

UI components automatically by JDeveloper, saving the developer much tedious work in creating the bulk of the app's pages.

JDeveloper shows the User Interface controls that are available for the Attendees collection. Of all available options, for this example, a simple MAF Form is used.

JDeveloper shows an Edit Form Fields dialog, and after you accept the defaults, the data-bound AMX page is created for you, and it contains inputText components for all the attributes in the Attendees collection.

```
<amx:panelFormLayout id="pfl1">
    <amx:inputText value="#{bindings.id.inputValue}"
                   label="#{bindings.id.hints.label}" id="it5"/>
    <amx:inputText value="#{bindings.firstName.inputValue}"
                    label="#{bindings.firstName.hints.label}" id="it3"/>
    <amx:inputText value="#{bindings.lastName.inputValue}"
                   label="#{bindings.lastName.hints.label}" id="it2"/>
    <amx:inputText value="#{bindings.country.inputValue}"
                   label="#{bindings.country.hints.label}" id="it7"/>
    <amx:inputText value="#{bindings.email.inputValue}"
                   label="#{bindings.email.hints.label}" id="it1"/>
    <amx:inputText value="#{bindings.phone.inputValue}"
                   label="#{bindings.phone.hints.label}" id="it6"/>
    <amx:inputText value="#{bindings.photo.inputValue}"
                   label="#{bindings.photo.hints.label}" id="it4"/>
</amx:panelFormLayout>
```

You see that the code contains several entries of the form "#{bindings.<attributeName>.<property>}". These expressions are called EL expressions and refer to the binding container, also known as PageDefinition. All of these terms, EL expressions, the bindings keyword, and the PageDefinition, are explained later.

The AMX page is not the only file affected by the drag and drop. A lot more just happened. Several other files were created or changed. In the project navigator, these files are displayed in italics (Figure 5-4).

The DataBindings.cpx file is created and so is the <PageName>PageDef.xml. Both files are core elements of the MAF Model layer, and in the following sections, you will learn their responsibilities.

NOTE
The page definition file's name defaults to <PageName>PageDef.xml, where <PageName> refers to the name to which the PageDefinition file belongs.

Also, the adfm.xml file was created in the META-INF directory under adfmsrc.

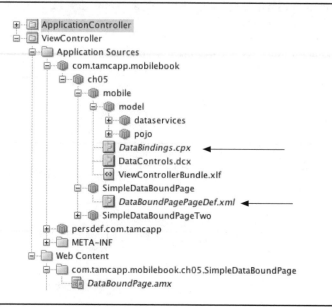

FIGURE 5-4. *What happens when the first page definition is created?*

Responsibilities of the Files Involved in the Model Layer

When the Attendees collection was dropped on the page, several XML files were created. All these files have their own responsibilities in a mobile application. All files are related in one way or another. In the next sections, you will learn what the files do and how they are related (Figure 5-5).

At run time, these XML files are translated into instances of lightweight Java classes (binding objects). The framework works with these classes to provide interaction between business services and their data, and the user interface.

adfm.xml

The adfm.xml file acts as a registry of registries and maintains the path to other configuration files such as the DataBindings.cpx and DataControls.dcx. The framework uses this file both at design time and run time. At run time, the framework reads the file and loads the configuration files as needed.

DataControls.dcx

The DataControls.dcx file is a file that contains the definition and configuration of all data controls in the project. You will learn about data controls in more detail later in this chapter.

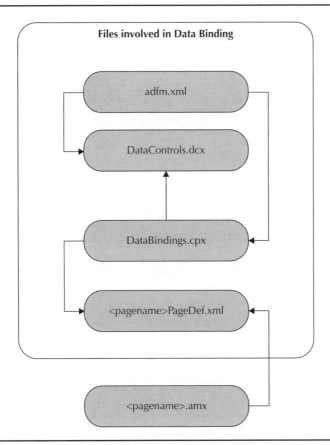

FIGURE 5-5. *Files involved in data binding*

DataBindings.cpx

The DataBindings.cpx file acts as a registry for mapping mobile pages and their corresponding PageDefinition files, and it defines the runtime-binding context for the MAF application. When a page contains MAF bindings, at run time, the interaction with the business services is managed by the application through a single object known as the binding context. The binding context is a runtime map (named data and accessible through the EL expression #{data}) of all data controls and page definitions within the application.

The relation between page and pageDefinition is obvious when you take a look at the DataBindings.cpx file that was created when the Attendees collection was dropped on the AMX page. Figure 5-6 also shows an entry for Data Control Usages.

DataBindings.cpx ×
Data Binding Registry

This file defines the Oracle MAF binding context for your application. JDeveloper creates this file the first time you data bind a UI component.

□ **Page Mappings**

path	usageId
/com.tamcapp.mobilebook.ch05.SimpleDataBoundPage/DataBoundPage.am	com_tamcapp_mobilebook_ch05_mobile_DataBoundPagePageDef

□ **Page Definition Usages**

id	path
com_tamcapp_mobilebook_ch05_mobile_DataBoundPagePageDef	com.tamcapp.mobilebook.ch05.SimpleDataBoundPage.DataBoundPagePageDef

□ **Data Control Usages**

id
AttendeesService

FIGURE 5-6. *The DataBindings.cpx overview editor*

NOTE
The DataBindings.cpx file must have a unique fully qualified name in a MAF application. This means that when you have features from independently developed MAF applications combined in one MAF application, all the DataBindings.cpx files must be on a different path. You will learn later how to do this. The naming convention for the path of a DataBindings.cpx file would typically involve an application-specific part, for instance:
    *com.tamcapp.mobilebook.**appone**.mobile.databindings.cpx*
    *com.tamcapp.mobilebook.**apptwo**.mobile.databindings.cpx*
The location of the DataBindings.cpx file is derived from the View Controller package naming, which derives its package name from the default package name you define when creating the mobile application.

The DataBindings.cpx file is created when the first PageDefinition file in an Oracle MAF application is created, which itself is typically created when you drag and drop data control components onto a page as shown in the earlier Figure 5-3. Once the DataBindings.cpx file is available, on every subsequent creation of a PageDefinition file, the DataBindings.cpx file is changed. The changes involve the creation of a new Page Mappings entry and a new Page Definition Usage.

NOTE
There is an option to use one single PageDefinition file for all pages in a task flow. In order to achieve this, you need to go into the DataBindings .cpx file and manually edit this file for all mobile pages to be associated with the same PageDef.xml file. The advantages are obvious. You need to define the iterator binding only in one PageDefinition file instead of two, and the overall size of the application is less. The disadvantage, however, is that pages are seldom showing the same level of information, and thus you pollute the PageDefinition file with information not used by a page. Thus, the recommendation is to go with an individual PageDefinition file for each mobile page.

The PageDefinition File

As seen in one of the previous sections, the PageDefinition file is created when a data collection, an attribute, or an operation is dragged from the data control and dropped in the page. It contains the bindings that support the user interface components on a page. At run time, this file is used by the Model layer to instantiate the bindings of the page. The bindings of the page are available by using the EL expression #{bindings}. This expression always evaluates to the binding container for the current page.

NOTE
The PageDefinition file can also be created by invoking the context menu (Figure 5-7) on an MAF AMX page and selecting Go to Page Definition. If there is no PageDefinition available for the AMX Page, JDeveloper will ask you to confirm the creation of a new PageDefinition.

A PageDefinition generally contains three main sections:

■ Parameters
■ Executables
■ Bindings

All of these will be explained. The code sample shows the XML representation of a PageDefinition file with the three main sections highlighted.

```xml
<?xml version="1.0" encoding="UTF-8" ?>
<pageDefinition xmlns=http://xmlns.oracle.com/adfm/uimodel
version=" 12.1.3.11.19" id="DataBoundPagePageDef"
Package="com.tamcapp.mobilebook.ch05.SimpleDataBoundPage">
  <parameters/>
  <executables>
     <variableIterator id="variables"/>
      <iterator Binds="root" RangeSize="25" DataControl="AttendeesService"
             id="AttendeesServiceIterator"/>
      <accessorIterator MasterBinding="AttendeesServiceIterator" Binds="attendees"
             RangeSize="25" DataControl="AttendeesService"
```

```
                    BeanClass="com.tamcapp.mobilebook.ch05.mobile.model.pojo.Attendee"
                 id="attendeesIterator"/>
    </executables>
    <bindings>
        <attributeValues IterBinding="attendeesIterator" id="id">
            <AttrNames>
                <Item Value="id"/>
            </AttrNames>
        </attributeValues>
     <!--
        ....... More attributeValues
     -- >
     <action IterBinding="attendeesIterator" id="Next"
             RequiresUpdateModel="true" Action="next"/>
     <action IterBinding="attendeesIterator" id="Previous"
             RequiresUpdateModel="true" Action="previous"/>
    </bindings>
</pageDefinition>
```

The PageDefinition can also be represented in an overview editor, showing exactly where each and every binding is derived from. In Figure 5-8, you can see the origin of the id attribute leading back to the Attendees collection in the data control. This figure also shows the Bindings and Executables section of the PageDefinition.

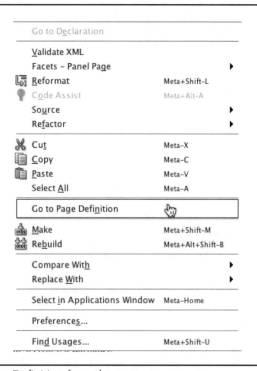

FIGURE 5-7.   *Go to Page Definition from the context menu*

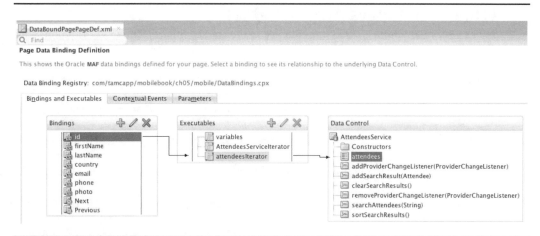

FIGURE 5-8. *PageDefinition overview*

In the sample page based on the Attendees collection, there are action bindings and attribute bindings. That is not all you can do. There are more binding types available.

What Binding Types Are Available?

In the PageDefinition file, you can define all kinds of bindings. There are three types of binding objects. The first are the value bindings. Value bindings are used to display data in UI components by referencing an iterator binding. Each UI component on a page that will display data from the data control is bound to a binding object.

There are a number of different binding objects:

- **Attribute bindings**   Binds text fields to a specific attribute in an object.
- **Tree bindings**   Binds an entire table or tree to a data collection to show all rows.
- **List bindings**   Binds list items to all values of an attribute in a data collection.
- **Graph bindings**   Binds a graph to the source data.

Next, there are the Method Action bindings. These bind command components, such as buttons or links, to custom methods on the data control that you want the user to be able to invoke. A Method Action binding object encapsulates the details about how to invoke a method and what parameters (if any) the method is expecting. This is the kind of binding that you would create to use device features.

Finally, there are the Action bindings. The Action bindings bind command components, such as buttons or links, to built-in collection-level operations, such as Create, Delete, Next, or Previous.

What Executables Are Available?

You can define multiple kinds of executables in the PageDefinition. The most common ones are the iterators. An iterator is populated by a collection and represents a row set with a current row pointer; the expression seen in the previous section #{bindings.firstName.inputValue} actually evaluates to "the firstName of the record that the Attendees iterator is pointing to in the Attendees collection."

The connection between the firstName attribute and the Attendees iterator is defined in the PageDefinition file.

Then there is the InvokeAction executable. An InvokeAction executable calls an existing action or method binding defined in the action bindings during any phase of the page life cycle. You can use the InvokeAction executable to invoke a method when an AMX view is initially loaded in MAF.

Finally, there is the Method Iterator. This binds to an iterator that iterates over the collections returned by custom methods in the data control. Such a Method Iterator is always related to a Method Action binding object. The Method Action binding encapsulates the details about how to invoke the method and what parameters (if any) the method is expecting. The Method Action binding is itself bound to the method iterator, which provides the data.

The Data Control

The data control abstracts the data service layer. It is an XML definition of the underlying data service and it describes this data service, including the exposed attributes and operations. Because of this abstraction, a developer can work with the data control in a similar way, regardless of the technical implementation of the underlying business service. In Oracle MAF, you can use Bean data controls and web service data controls. The data control enables you to declaratively bind user interface components to data services. Oracle MAF highly relies on the usage of data controls for getting its data from any kind of data source into the user interface.

The Creation of a Bean Data Control

A Bean data control can be created from a Java class in two different ways. The easiest way is to simply drag the class and drop it on the Data Controls panel. The other way is to invoke the context menu on the class and select Create Data Control (Figure 5-9).

After the Bean data control is created, it can be found in the Data Controls panel.

TIP
If you do not see the new data control immediately, you have to invoke the Refresh button in the Data Controls panel.

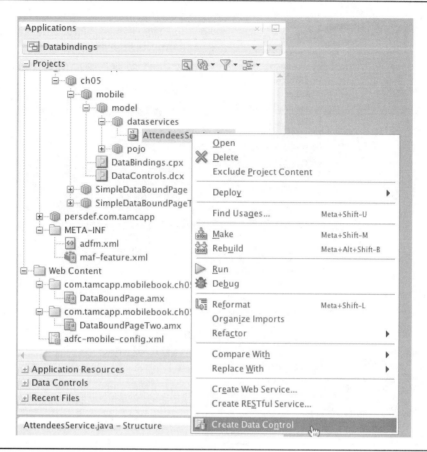

FIGURE 5-9. *Create Data Control menu option*

The data control based on the Attendees class contains a collection based on the Attendees array in the class, instance variables for all attributes in the Attendees object, built-in operations for the collection, and finally operations for all methods in the Attendees class (Figure 5-10).

The data control contains an Attendees collection that is derived from the Attendees collection in the corresponding Java class. The attributes are derived from the Attendees object. The operations all refer to methods in the Java class. Each method will result in an operation on the data control. So all of these explain themselves as they are based on the Attendees Java class that we created. But what about the built-in operations? Where did these come from and what do they do?

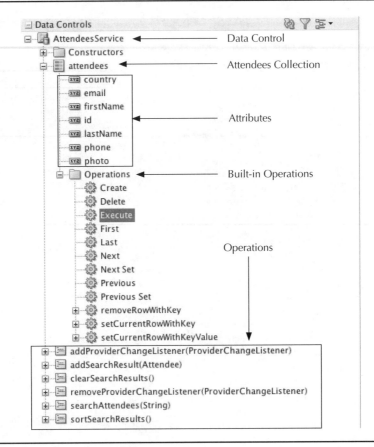

FIGURE 5-10. *Data Control overview*

Built-in Operations

The built-in operations are part of the framework's binding layer, and you get them for free. These operations enable you to navigate the collection, add or remove rows, and set the current row.

- **Create**   This operation is available to create a new row in the collection.
- **Delete**   This operation is used to delete the current row from the collection.
- **Execute**   This operation will execute and refresh the current collection.
- **First**   This operation sets the first row to be the current row.
- **Last**   This operation sets the last row to be the current row.
- **Next**   This operation sets the next row in the collection as the current row.
- **Next Set**   This operation moves to the next set in the collection.

- **Previous**   This operation sets the previous record as the current row.
- **Previous Set**   This operation moves to the previous set in the collection.
- **removeRowWithKey**   The key value is provided for this operation to remove the row matching the corresponding key.
- **setCurrentRowWithKey**   Sets the current row in the collection based on the key passed in.
- **setCurrentRowWithKeyValue**   Sets the current row in the collection based on the key value.

All of these operations can be used on a page by simply dragging and dropping them from the Data Controls panel onto the AMX page. The following example shows how to navigate to the next or previous row in the collection—all handled by the binding layer without writing any code.

The two buttons on the page refer to an action binding in the page's binding container. The ids of these action bindings are, respectively, "Previous" and "Next."

```
<amx:commandButton actionListener="#{bindings.Previous.execute}"
                   text="Previous"
                   disabled="#{!bindings.Previous.enabled}" id="cb4"/>
<amx:commandButton actionListener="#{bindings.Next.execute}"
                   text="Next"
                   disabled="#{!bindings.Next.enabled}" id="cb3"/>
```

The actionListener attribute in both buttons contains an EL expression that resolves to the action bindings for Next and Previous in PageDefinition. These action bindings will invoke the Previous and Next action on the attendeesIterator.

```
<action IterBinding="attendeesIterator" id="Next"
        RequiresUpdateModel="true" Action="next"/>
<action IterBinding="attendeesIterator" id="Previous"
        RequiresUpdateModel="true" Action="previous"/>
```

The setCurrentRowWithKey is an operation that you can use when navigating from a List to a Details of the selected list entry. You will learn more on this throughout the book.

The Data Controls Overview Editor

The overview editor for the DataControls.dcx file provides a view of the hierarchies of data control objects and exposed methods of your data model. You can open the data control and get a visual representation of all collections, attributes, and operations available on this data control, as you can see in Figure 5-11. You can change the settings for a data control object by selecting the object and clicking the Edit icon.

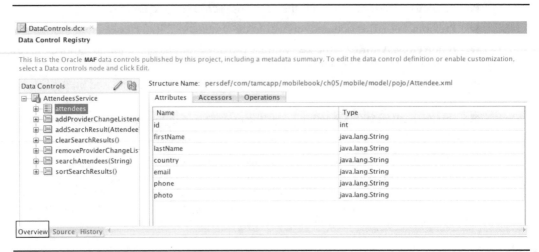

FIGURE 5-11. *DataControls.dcx visual representation*

How the Different Parts Connect

In the previous sections you learned the separate parts of the Model layer, and in this section you will learn how these parts work together to create interactive data-bound pages.

Figure 5-12 shows how data controls are used to disclose (data) services via Expression Language (EL) and bindings. The individual parts in this figure have different responsibilities. You will now learn those responsibilities.

- **EL**   Expression Language is a syntax that defines the linkage in an AMX page to another source. This is resolved during rendering of the page and ties data to the UI. EL expressions are typically "active" connections, and when the underlying data that the EL expression points to changes, the corresponding UI is updated.

- **Bindings**   Each AMX page has a backing page that holds its bindings called a Page Definition file. There is a file called the datacontrols.cpx file that tells the framework the names of each backing Page Definition for each AMX page.

- **Data Controls**   A data control is a wrapper that allows the framework to bind to data in an abstract way regardless of its source. The data can be a Java class, a web service, or any other source. The datacontrols.dcx file contains the listing of all data controls defined for the project. Data controls are visualized in the Data Controls panel, which allows the developer to drag and drop from there to the source/structurePane in order to create data-bound components.

- **Managed Beans**   A managed bean is simply a Java class defined on a task flow with an identifier and a scope. You can define managed beans in the top-level unbounded task flow (adfc-mobile-config.xml) or in individual bounded task flows. The scope of the managed beans consists of application (the entire application can access this instance), pageFlow (any other page in the same task flow can access this instance), or view (only the page that created it can access this instance).

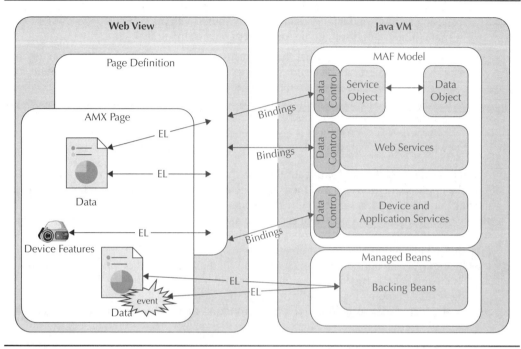

FIGURE 5-12. *How the MAF Model interacts with services and AMX pages*

Expression Language

A typical MAF data-binding EL expression uses the following syntax to reference any of the different types of binding objects in the binding container:

```
#{bindings.BindingObject.propertyName}
```

■ bindings is a variable that identifies that the binding object being referenced by the expression is located in the binding container of the current page. All MAF data-binding EL expressions must start with the bindings variable.

■ BindingObject is the ID, or, for attributes, the name, of the binding object as it is defined in the page definition file. The binding object ID or name is unique to that page definition file. An EL expression can reference any binding object in the page definition file, including parameters, executables, or value bindings.

■ propertyName is a variable that determines the default display characteristics of each data-bound UI component and sets properties for the binding object at run time. There are different binding properties for each type of binding object.

■ **Data Object** A Java class that is defined to be a data holder for the object. It represents a single "row" of data and defines the attributes with appropriate getters/setters for the data. It does not, itself, do the retrieval of data from another store.

■ **Service Object** A Java class that is used to define the CRUD operations on an object. It returns other data objects from a store based on functions provided by the developer. There is no specific interface for this object, and its definition is left for the developer, but we define its definition here. It is typical for a Service Object to use JDBC to access a local store or use web services to get its data and then fill arrays of Data Objects to be returned. A Service Object is also the class that a developer would create a data control wrapper on to expose its methods in the Data Controls panel.

At run time, the MAF Model layer reads the information describing the data controls and bindings from the appropriate XML files and then implements the two-way connection between the user interface and the business service. How this works (Figure 5-13) can be explained by using a simple example of an AMX page that shows the name of an employee that is retrieved from a service. The AMX page contains a component whose value property is set with an EL expression #{bindings.name.inputValue}. The framework evaluates this expression and knows what to do next. It will look up (1) the attribute binding for "name" in the PageDefinition file of the AMX page.

It is clear what this PageDefinition file is because it is registered in the databindings.cpx file.

The attribute binding for "name" also holds the reference to the iterator that is being used to retrieve the "name" data from (2). One of the properties of this iterator is from which data control

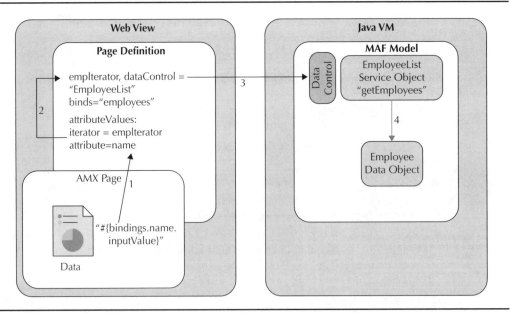

FIGURE 5-13. *How data binding works at run time*

the collection originates. This is looked up (3), and the collections getter method is called to retrieve (4) the data from the underlying Employees Data object and return this data all the way back to the user interface.

Implementing Validations

The binding layer can also be used for validation. You can define declarative validations on the attributes of the Java class. There are several types of validations that can be defined on the attributes. Each attribute can have multiple validations defined. If you want to add a validation rule to an attribute, you have to open the data control structure file for the corresponding Java class.

This file is not available until you create it by invoking the Edit Definition option on the collection in the data control (Figure 5-14).

Once it is created, you are able to open it in the editor (Figure 5-15) and edit the attributes. There are a lot of things to be edited, such as UI hints, indicating that an attribute is a key attribute and more. But for this section, we will look at validations.

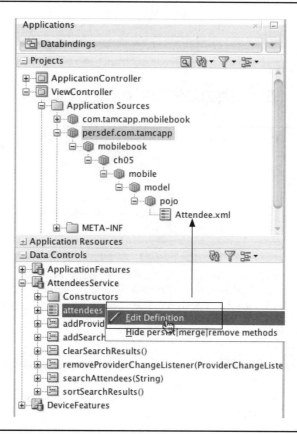

FIGURE 5-14. *Create the data control structure file.*

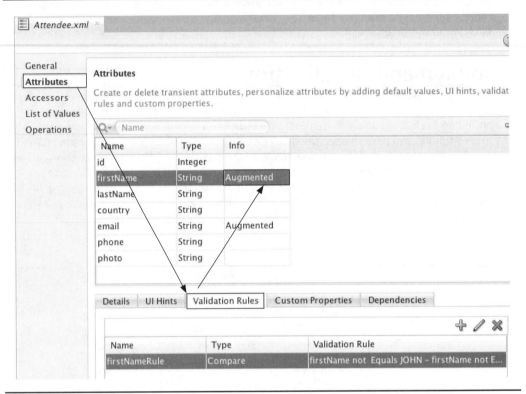

FIGURE 5-15. *Overview of the attributes of the Attendees POJO with validation rules*

As mentioned before, there are multiple validation types, and inside the types there are many different operators and compare types. You can, for instance, define a "compare" validation rule—that's where you check whether or not an attribute "equals" a literal value.

NOTE
Although the Add Validation Rule dialog implies that you can use "Regular Expression" and "Script Expression," these two options do not work (Figure 5-16). You can add them, but at run time, this will cause an error saying that the framework "cannot create the validator."

In the example used for this section, you will learn how to add a simple validation to prevent the user from entering the same value for First Name and Last Name. All of this can be done declaratively on the Rule Definition tab (Figure 5-17) when you add a validation to an attribute. So in this case, we need to pick a "Compare" validator with the operator "Equals."

The First Name needs to be compared with the Last Name. To instruct the framework to do this, you must pick "Expression" in the "Compare With" section. Finally, enter the "Expression" that will be used for the comparison, in this case "lastName."

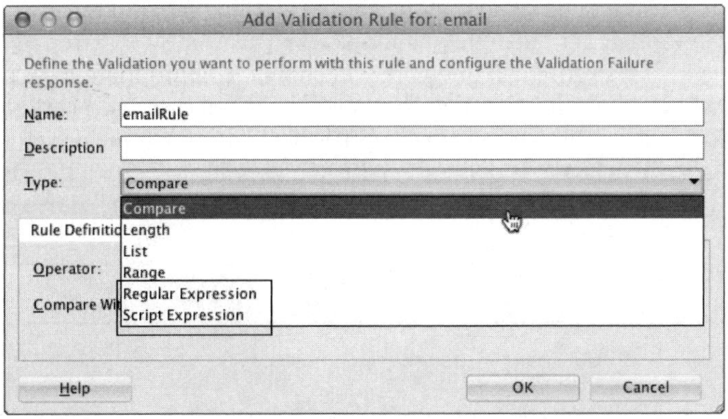

FIGURE 5-16. *The editor shows Regular Expression and Script Expression.*

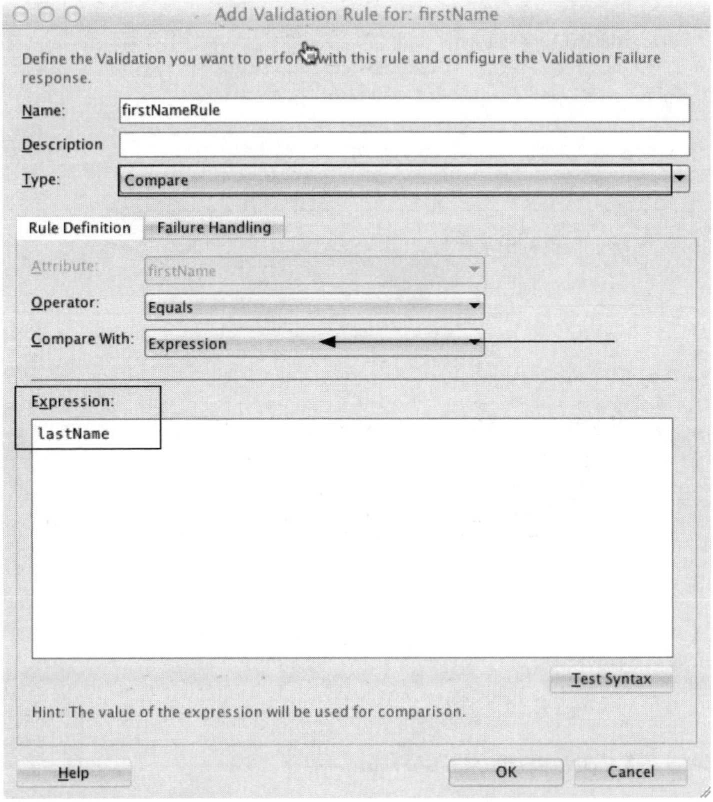

FIGURE 5-17. *Add a validation rule.*

After the validation rule is defined, you can also add properties on what to do if the validation rule is violated. This can be done on the Failure Handling tab. On this tab, you can configure the severity of the validation to be either "Informational Warning" or "Error" (Figure 5-18). Depending on what severity is picked, the framework will show the appropriate Error or Warning popup at run time whenever the validation fails. For our sample validation on Last Name and First Name, it doesn't really make sense to throw an error. This validation will be implemented as a warning.

The text for the message is defined on this tab as well. You either type a new message in the Message Text box, or pick an existing one from a resource bundle by invoking the search icon.

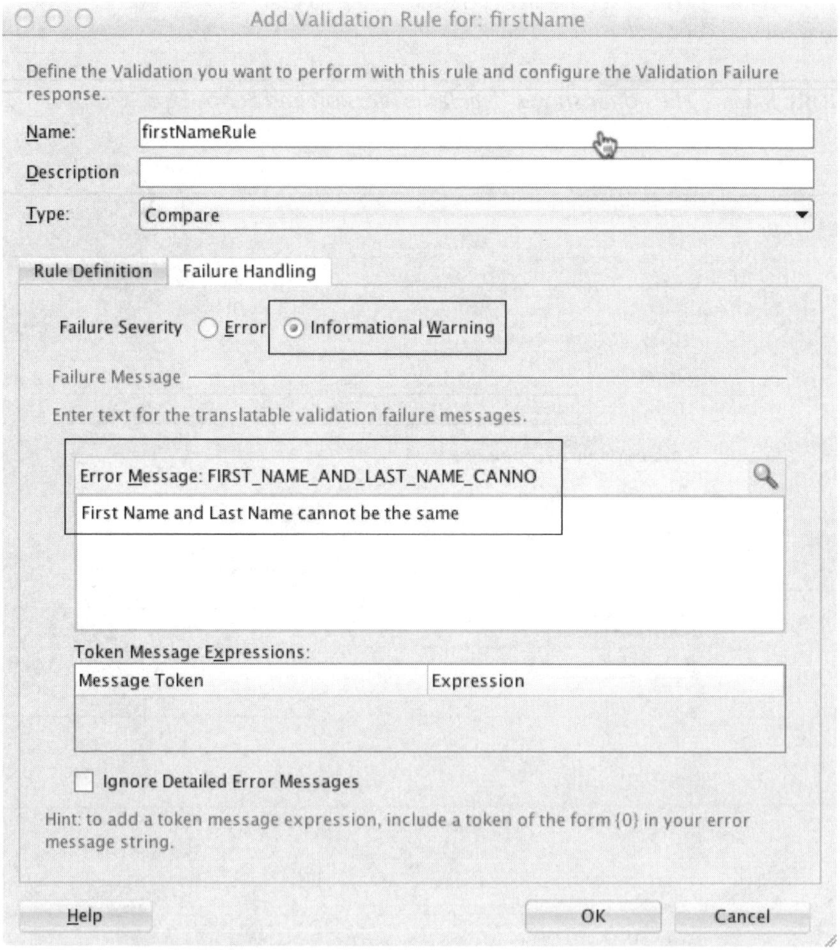

FIGURE 5-18. *Validation rule; failure handling*

Interacting with the User

Whenever user input is submitted, the validation is triggered. For the input text fields, this happens when the user leaves the field. The validation rule implemented in the previous section would lead to the warning displayed in Figure 5-19. This figure also shows the same validation message as an error. This can be achieved by changing the validation failure severity from Informational Warning to Error.

There is another scenario, and that is to trigger validation whenever a user taps a button. In order to actually execute the validation in such an event and to inform the user of any validation errors or warnings, the UI components involved in this validation must be surrounded by a validationGroup, and the button must define a validation behavior. This validation behavior should reference the id of the validation group.

For the example used in this section, you need to put the firstName input component inside a validation group whose id is set to "name."

```
<amx:validationGroup validateCondition="always" id="name">
    <amx:panelFormLayout id="pfl1">
        <amx:inputText value="#{bindings.firstName.inputValue}"
                       label="#{bindings.phone.firstName.label}" id="it2"/>
    </amx:panelFormLayout>
</amx:validationGroup>
```

To trigger the validation, the two navigation buttons must have a validation behavior defined, and the group attribute of this validationBehavior component must refer to the id of the validationGroup surrounding the firstName field.

```
<amx:commandButton actionListener="#{bindings.Previous.execute}"
                   text="Previous"
                   disabled="#{!bindings.Previous.enabled}" id="cb4">
    <amx:validationBehavior group="name"/>
</amx:commandButton>
<amx:commandButton actionListener="#{bindings.Next.execute}"
                   text="Next"
                   disabled="#{!bindings.Next.enabled}" id="cb3">
    <amx:validationBehavior group="name"/>
</amx:commandButton>
```

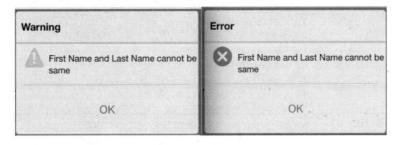

FIGURE 5-19. *Warning (left) or Error (right) displayed after validation failed*

Other Data Controls Used by Oracle Mobile Application Framework

In the previous section you learned how to create and use a POJO data control (aka Bean data control). This kind of data control can be used to link a specific class to a specific User Interface and have interaction between them. There are four other data controls that can be used by Oracle MAF.

The first two are the DeviceFeatures and ApplicationFeatures data controls. These are defined at the application level and disclose operations to interact with the device services and the applications features (what's in a name). Both data controls appear within the Data Controls panel of the application (Figure 5-20). There is nothing that you as a developer need to do to create these data controls. They are created for you each time you create a new mobile application.

You will learn how to work with these data controls in Chapter 6 (ApplicationFeatures) and Chapter 8 (DeviceFeatures), respectively.

Then there is the URL data control. This data control enables you to access and consume data from specified URLs. You can use a URL data control to enable access to RESTful web services.

Finally, there is the web service data control. This data control is the most common way of communicating with web services in MAF. A web service data control can be created based on the WSDL for an existing web service. You will learn how to do this throughout this book.

FIGURE 5-20. *The device and application features data controls*

Working with Bindings Programmatically

The binding layer of the framework provides you with a lot of declarative functionality. However, you will definitely run into situations where this declarative behavior is not enough. As an example, what if you need to retrieve the value from a binding and programmatically undertake some work based on that value? Luckily MAF has several APIs that you can use to work with the binding layer programmatically for either accessing bound data values or executing operations and methods. An example of this might be when you want to combine two or more data-bound method calls into a single button action. The methods involved in working with the binding layer can be found in the AdfmfJavaUtilities class.

Getting and Setting Bound Attribute Values

Getting and setting bound attribute values in Java can be very useful, for instance, if you need to transfer the value of a bound input component to the value of a bound search method. For this you can use the ValueExpression object and its getValue() and setValue() methods. The ValueExpression can be retrieved from the getValueExpression() method in the AdfmfJavaUtilities class.

```
ValueExpression veFirstName =
      AdfmfJavaUtilities.getValueExpression(
                    "#{bindings.firstName.inputValue}", String.class);
String firstName =
      (String)veFirstName.getValue(AdfmfJavaUtilities.getAdfELContext());
if(firstName.equalsIgnoreCase("Wrong name"){
   veFirstName.setValue(AdfmfJavaUtilities.getAdfELContext(),"Right name");
}
```

Invoking Methods

The framework not only allows you to work with attributes programmatically, but you can also execute methods on the binding container from within Java code. For this, the MethodExpression object must be used. First, you need to invoke the getMethodExpression() method in the AdfmfJavaUtilities class to get a MethodExpression object. You must use the EL expression that evaluates to the method binding. Finally, you call the invoke() method on the method expression in order to execute the action binding.

```
MethodExpression me =
    AdfmfJavaUtilities.getMethodExpression("#{bindings.Next.execute}",
                                    Object.class, new Class[] {});
me.invoke(AdfmfJavaUtilities.getAdfELContext(), new Object[] {});
```

Summary

The binding layer is one of the most important layers in an Oracle MAF application. It abstracts business service implementation from the user interface and enables developers to work with business services in a declarative way. The API also enables developers to work with bindings programmatically. In this chapter you learned

- To understand the individual parts of the binding layer
- To understand the data control and its parts
- How to implement data-bound AMX pages
- How to implement simple validations
- To understand the different kinds of data controls in the framework
- How to work with the binding layer programmatically

CHAPTER
6

Application Features

M ost mobile applications consist of multiple functionalities that users select to perform a specific task. Within MAF, these parts can be developed separately as application features. Features are a core architectural element of an MAF application and are reusable across MAF applications. An example is a "Manage Employees" feature as a functional part of an HR mobile application that allows you to browse and edit employees. Features can be chained in that navigation can be performed between features as well as within features. MAF enables you to create features and display entry points to these features on a springboard or on a navigation bar.

Oracle Mobile Application Framework Feature and Application Configuration Files

When you create a new Mobile Application Framework application, you will see that there are several files created for you. There are two files involved in application configuration and feature definition (see Figure 6-1). Those files are maf-feature.xml, also known as the feature definition file, and maf-application.xml, also known as the application definition file.

Both files are discussed in the following sections.

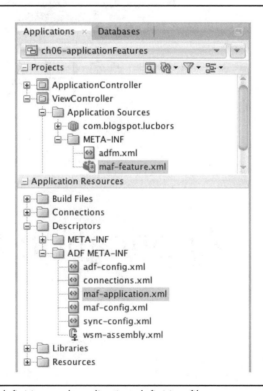

FIGURE 6-1. *Feature definition and application definition files*

The Application Configuration File

The maf-application.xml configuration file is located in Application Resources | Descriptors | ADF META-INF within the JDeveloper Application Navigator. This file enables you to set the basic configuration of the MAF application and has a number of responsibilities. First, the file is used to designate the application's display name. This can be defined on the Application tab. This tab also is used to supply a unique application ID to prevent naming collisions. It is recommended that you use the Java convention of reversing an owned domain for application IDs. For example, since Google owns the domain "google.com," the names of all applications should start with "com. google." It's important to follow this convention in order to avoid conflicts with other developers.

Finally, the Application tab enables you to define the behavior of the navigation bar and the springboard.

The Device Access tab in the maf-application.xml configuration panel allows you to control whether or not features have access to device features like the camera or GPS. The Device Access setting is configured in two files, the maf-application.xml file and the maf-feature.xml file. The device access setting in the maf-features.xml file defines the device access requirements for a specific feature but doesn't grant the access. The Device Access tab on the maf-application.xml file is where the application developer grants the device permission for the feature.

The third configuration tab, Feature References, configures which of the available application features defined in the maf-feature.xml file or an imported library is displayed as the content of the mobile application springboard (the equivalent of a home page on a smartphone) and the navigation bar.

The fourth tab, called Preferences, is used to create the user preferences for the mobile application that the user can configure via the device's settings. These are discussed in Chapter 17.

Application security, including authentication and access control, is configured using the Security tab. This is discussed in depth in Chapter 10.

A last tab, Cordova Plugins, allows you to configure plugins you develop with platform-specific languages, like Objective C for iOS, to extend the default MAF framework functionality, for example, to access barcode scanners.

The Feature Configuration File

Each mobile application must have at least one application feature. In the maf-feature.xml file, you define all features that are available in your MAF application. Because each application feature can be developed independently from one another (and also from the mobile application itself), the overview editor for the maf-feature.xml file enables you to define the child elements of <adfmf:features> to differentiate the application features by assigning each a name, an ID, and setting how their content can be implemented. Using the overview editor for application features, you can also control the runtime display of the application feature within the mobile application and designate when an application feature requires user authentication.

Define Application Features

Application features are defined in the maf-feature.xml file. If you need to add new features to an MAF application, you need to open the maf-feature.xml file. The easiest way to add new features is by using the green plus icon on the maf-feature.xml overview tab, as you can see in Figure 6-2.

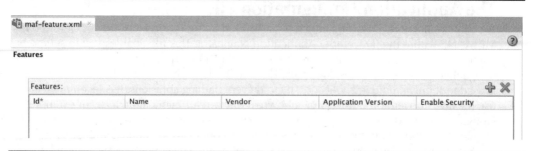

FIGURE 6-2. *Create features in the maf-feature.xml file.*

When you click this icon to create a new application feature, JDeveloper shows you a Create MAF Feature dialog window (Figure 6-3). In this window, you define a feature name, a feature ID, and a directory in which the feature's content is stored. You will also see a check box that, when checked, instructs JDeveloper to add a feature reference to the application configuration.

This means that the feature is added as an application feature and therefore is available for display on the springboard and/or navigation bar.

NOTE
As with other configuration files, JDeveloper can render the XML source, as well as an overview of the maf-feature.xml file. Changing these configuration files can be done in both views. Sometimes, for instance, when adding new features, it is easier to make changes in the overview. On other occasions, directly editing the XML source can be quicker and more convenient. For beginners, the overview editor is the recommended choice.

Features that you define in the maf-feature.xml need to be implemented as part of the MAF project the feature is defined in. The technology used to implement the features in the MAF application is also within the responsibilities of the maf-feature.xml and is defined using the Content tab of the feature definition file.

FIGURE 6-3. *Create MAF Feature dialog*

Defining Oracle Mobile Application Framework Feature Content

The content of a feature defines the client logic and the user interface for a MAF application. The Content tab of the overview editor, shown in Figure 6-4, provides you with drop-down lists and fields for defining the content-related configuration. In this tab you can specify the content type, the condition (constraint) under which content is shown or hidden, feature-level preference settings, and security requirements for each feature.

Each content type has its own set of parameters. If you pick the MAF AMX page or task flow for the application features that you implement, you must specify the file location. In addition, you can optionally select a CSS file to give the application feature a look and feel that is distinct from other application features (or the MAF application itself), or select a JavaScript file that controls the actions of the MAF AMX components.

The three types of content, as shown in Figure 6-5, are discussed in the next sections.

Oracle Mobile Application Framework Feature Content

If you choose MAF AMX, the application feature will be implemented as an MAF AMX page or as a task flow. The easiest way to create a new AMX mobile page is by using the green plus icon on the Content tab for the File section as you can see in Figure 6-6.

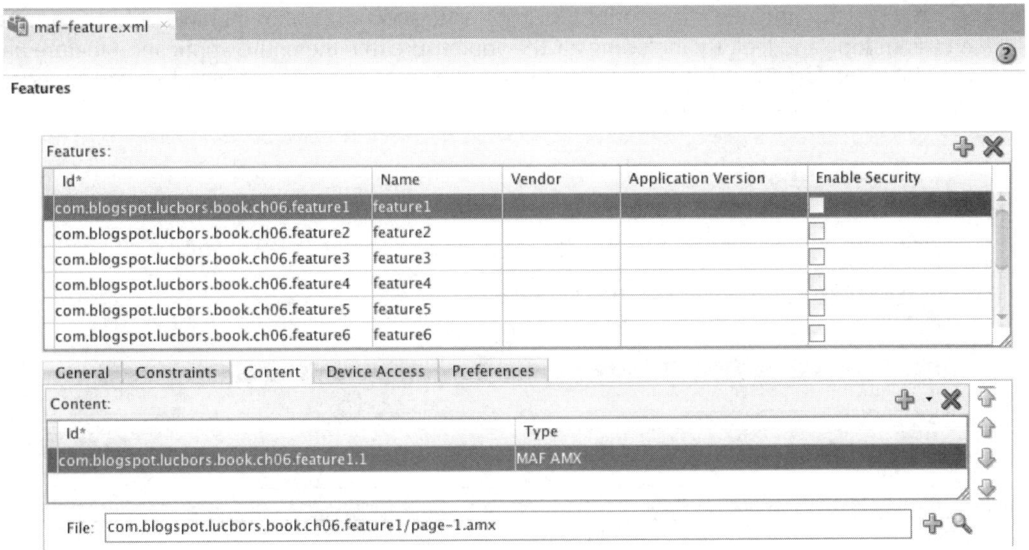

FIGURE 6-4. *The Content tab in the overview editor*

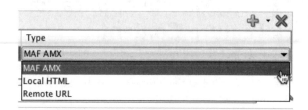

FIGURE 6-5. *Available types of content*

NOTE
You can also create MAF AMX pages by invoking the wizards in the New Gallery. Access to these wizards is available by first highlighting the view controller project in the Application Navigator and then choosing New. You can also create an MAF AMX page using the context menu that appears when you right-click the view controller project in the Application Navigator and then choose New. The MAF AMX pages that are created like this need to be manually added to a feature or task flow.

You will be presented with a Create MAF AMX Page dialog as displayed in Figure 6-7, where you can enter the file name and file location (directory) for the newly created page.

You can also include a JavaScript file and a style sheet (CSS) that includes selectors to specify a custom look and feel. By including a CSS, you ensure that the entire application feature has its own look and feel. This chapter will not go into specific details of the "includes" and "constraints." Both will be discussed in a later chapter in this book.

FIGURE 6-6. *Create a new MAF AMX page.*

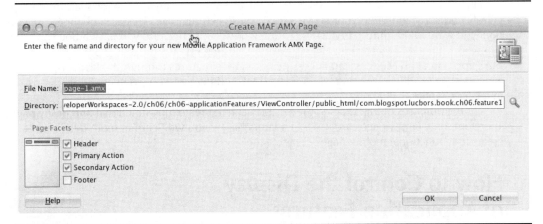

FIGURE 6-7. *Creating a new MAF AMX page as content for a feature*

NOTE
There is a difference between adding a constraint to the content of a feature or the feature itself. For example, a constraint for content may be to implement a wizard-style form input for smartphones and a single-form file entry on tablets. The feature constraints make sense where, for example, you want to make a remote URL available when there is network connectivity and otherwise show an MAF AMX page with access to local SQLite. Another good reason to use a feature constraint is to hide or show features based on security settings.

Remote URL and Local HTML

Remote URL content is actually a reference to a web application. Remote content can complement MAF AMX and local HTML content by providing server-side data and functionality. The remote URL implementation requires a valid web address pointing to a hosted web application. This web application can consist of pages that might be a JavaServer Faces page authored in Apache Trinidad for smartphones, or can consist of ADF Faces components for applications that run on tablet devices. You could use a remote URL when there is already a mobile-enabled page available that suits your needs and there is no need for disconnected access or device access. If this is the case, there is no need to redevelop the functionality as an MAF AMX page. You can simply use the existing remote application.

NOTE
The hosted web application does not necessarily need to be a mobile web application. However, it is good or even best practice to only use hosted web applications that are optimized to use in mobile browsers.

Finally, MAF enables you to use Local HTML to implement an application feature. With Local HTML, you can hand-build your HTML files or reuse existing ones. This is something you would do if you want to use third-party HTML5 frameworks, either because you have a developer who can work with it or because you already have an existing HTML5 file that you want to use in your MAF app. Local HTML files can access device-native features through the JavaScript APIs supported by Cordova. Working with Local HTML and Remote URL content will be discussed in a later chapter.

For the purposes of this chapter, there is no need to create fully functional and flashy pages. Therefore, only empty pages are used. In a later chapter you will learn in more detail how to create fully functional mobile pages.

How to Control the Display of Application Features

The display of application features on the springboard is a responsibility of the application definition file. In order to explain how this works, a fictional MAF application is used. This application contains nine features that are clearly recognizable by their names. You can find an overview of these features in Figure 6-8.

All nine features also have a corresponding image that will be displayed on the navigation bar and the springboard. You can provide these images in the maf-feature.xml on the General tab as you can see in Figure 6-9.

Id*	Name	Vendor	Application Version	Enable Security
com.blogspot.lucbors.book.ch06.feature1	feature1			☐
com.blogspot.lucbors.book.ch06.feature2	feature2			☐
com.blogspot.lucbors.book.ch06.feature3	feature3			☐
com.blogspot.lucbors.book.ch06.feature4	feature4			☐
com.blogspot.lucbors.book.ch06.feature5	feature5			☐
com.blogspot.lucbors.book.ch06.feature6	feature6			☐
com.blogspot.lucbors.book.ch06.feature7	feature7			☐
com.blogspot.lucbors.book.ch06.feature8	feature8			☐
com.blogspot.lucbors.book.ch06.feature9	feature9			☐

FIGURE 6-8. *The maf-feature.xml with nine features*

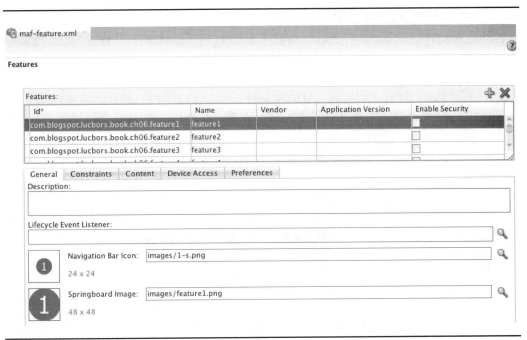

FIGURE 6-9. *Feature images to be displayed on springboard and navigation bar*

In the next sections you will learn how to control the display of these features on springboards and navigation bars in order to provide your application's users with quick access to the functionality in these features.

Working with Springboards and Navigation Bars

MAF enables you to create springboards on which you can display icons for all available features in your MAF application. Springboards are the application menu and they act as an entry point for the features in your MAF application. The maf-application.xml is the file where you can configure springboard and navigation bar behavior. Features can also be accessed via the navigation bar that is usually displayed at the bottom of your screen. The default feature of an MAF application and the order of features on the navigation bar and springboard are determined based on the order of feature references in the application configuration file. When to use a springboard and when to use a navigation bar or both is more or less a matter of taste. Both are used to provide access to features. If you only have a small number of features, a navigation bar would be sufficient, but usually, your application design will tell which method of access needs to be used.

The Navigation Bar

First, let's take a look at the navigation bar (Figure 6-10). The navigation bar is configured in the maf-application.xml.

By default, the navigation bar is displayed on application launch, and you will also see a navigation bar toggle button that enables you to show and hide the navigation bar at run time. These default settings are shown in Figure 6-11. Unchecking the check boxes changes default display behavior for the navigation bar, which is shown by default unless otherwise specified by the application feature.

The navigation bar is shown at the bottom of the application. At run time, this results in the navigation bar being displayed as in Figure 6-10.

FIGURE 6-10. *Default navigation bar*

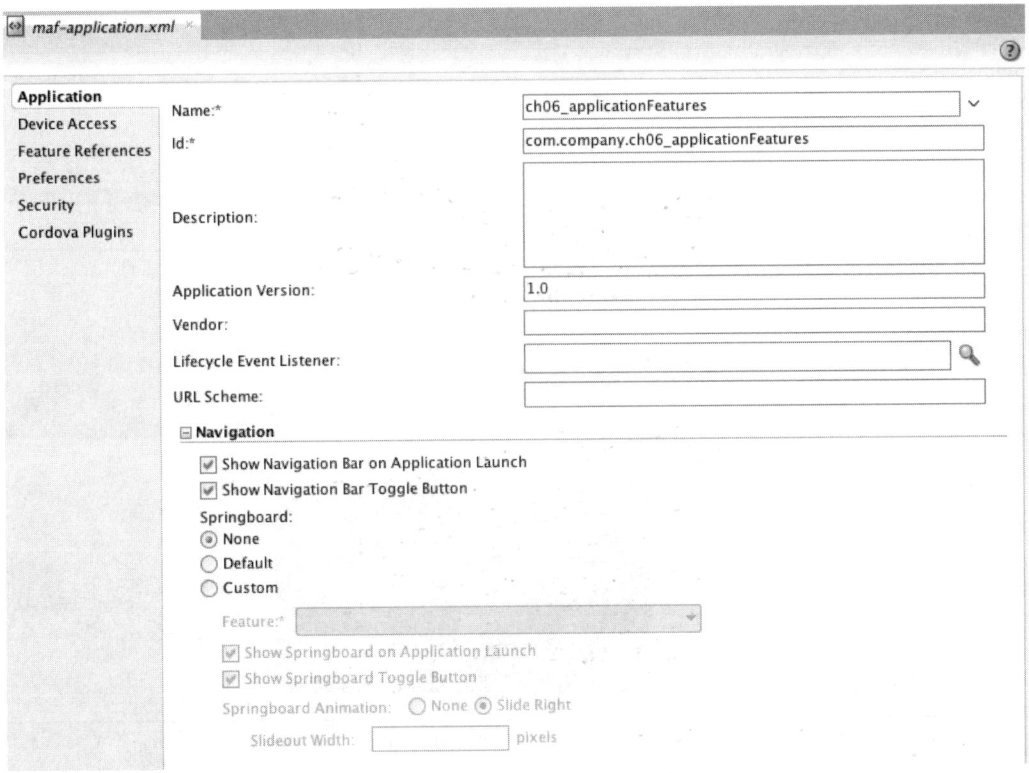

FIGURE 6-11. *Default setting for navigation bar in the maf-application.xml file*

As you can see in Figure 6-10, there is a More icon on the right side of the navigation bar. When you tap this icon, all features that do not fit on the navigation bar are displayed in a list. Invoking one of the list items results in opening the corresponding feature (Figure 6-12).

The "show navigation bar toggle" creates functionality to hide the navigation bar. When you invoke the application menu on your device, you will be given the choice to hide (Figure 6-13) or show (Figure 6-14) the navigation bar. This enables you to use all the available real estate on the device for application functionality.

FIGURE 6-12. *Displaying features in the "More" section of the navigation bar.*

FIGURE 6-13. *Hide Navigation*

FIGURE 6-14. *Show Navigation*

Springboard Navigation

Springboards act as an entry point for the features in your MAF application. When you create a new MAF application, JDeveloper creates the maf-application.xml file. In this file you can define how navigation to and from application features in the MAF application is implemented. In this section you will learn how to use the maf-application.xml to implement springboard navigation and the effect of the different options. By default (Figure 6-15), there is no springboard in your MAF application.

NOTE
Because of the default settings (as displayed in Figure 6-15), the springboard should not be displayed, but you will notice that there is a Show Springboard icon on the navigation bar. Invoking this icon doesn't result in showing the springboard, because no springboard is defined in your application. Preventing the springboard icon from showing up can be achieved by making a small adjustment in the actual XML code of the maf-applications.xml. Adding the following line of code makes sure the springboard icon doesn't show up:

```
<adfmf:navigation>
  <adfmf:springboard enabled="false"/>
</adfmf:navigation>
```

TIP
To get this setting, you can also select the Default radio button and then the None button in the maf-application.xml overview editor.

☐ **Navigation**

☑ Show Navigation Bar on Application Launch
☑ Show Navigation Bar Toggle Button

Springboard:
◉ None
○ Default
○ Custom

    Feature:* [_____ ▼]
    ☑ Show Springboard on Application Launch
    ☑ Show Springboard Toggle Button
    Springboard Animation: ○ None ◉ Slide Right
    Slideout Width: [_____] pixels

FIGURE 6-15. *Default maf-application.xml with no springboard*

When no springboard is used in the application, the application opens the first page of the first feature that is defined in the maf-feature.xml. In the example, this means that the application opens page-1.amx. After that, access to the different features is enabled via the navigation bar.

The second option is to use the default springboard that is automatically generated by JDeveloper at deployment time.

When selecting the Default springboard option (Figure 6-16), MAF renders a springboard as a list (Figure 6-18). There are two check boxes that enable you to show or hide the springboard on application launch and to have a toggle springboard button on the navigation bar.

This results in the following piece of XML in the maf-application.xml:

```
<adfmf:navigation>
    <adfmf:springboard enabled="true"
                       showSpringboardAtStartup="true"
                       displayGotoSpringboardControl="true"/>
    ..........
</adfmf:navigation>
```

The option to hide or show the springboard enables you to make optimal usage of the mobile device's real estate. You also see the Springboard Animation setting. With this setting you enable the springboard to slide from the right. This setting also changes how the springboard is displayed. If Springboard Animation is set to slide right, the springboard would only occupy a portion of the screen. If not, then it takes up the entire screen.

When you toggle the springboard icon (Figure 6-17), the application's springboard is displayed, showing all available features in a list, enabling you to start any of these features. When you invoke any of the list items in the springboard (Figure 6-18), the corresponding feature is activated and the springboard disappears.

Finally, MAF enables you to create custom springboards. These springboards are based on either an HTML page or a custom AMX page, both of which must be available as an application feature in the maf-feature.xml.

FIGURE 6-16. *Configuration to use the default springboard*

FIGURE 6-17. *The Springboard button in the applications menu*

In all situations where the default springboard is not what you are looking for, you would consider implementing a custom springboard. A custom springboard enables you to create an application springboard that exactly fits your needs. These custom springboards are based on either an HTML page or a custom AMX page, both of which must be available as an application feature in the maf-feature.xml.

Using an AMX Page as a Custom Springboard

The previously discussed default springboard implements the List Navigation pattern. This List Navigation is a very common UI pattern where the springboard displays a list of available features. When you tap such a list item, the feature is invoked. However, for implementing the most common UI pattern for navigation, the Grid Springboard, you need to create a custom springboard. Grid Springboards display application features in a grid layout, for instance, in a 2 × 2 or 3 × 3 grid.

FIGURE 6-18. *Default springboard*

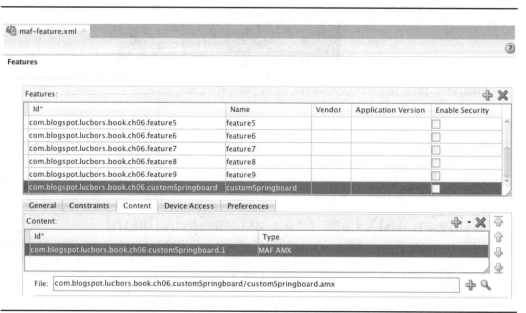

FIGURE 6-19. *Custom springboard feature definition*

The first step in the process is to create a brand-new AMX page. This AMX page contains the layout containers for rendering the grid that contains the springboard features. The custom springboard in this case must be defined as an MAF feature that gets its content from an AMX page as displayed in Figure 6-19.

The actual creation of a custom springboard is discussed in Chapter 12 where the springboard of the sample application is explained. In this chapter, you will learn some of the basic concepts of creating a custom Grid Springboard. The following code sample shows how to set up the basic custom springboard that, per feature, displays an image embedded in a command link. Clicking the link sets a pageFlowScope variable indicating the feature that should be invoked.

```
<amx:iterator var="row" value="#{bindings.features.collectionModel}"
              id="i1">
  <amx:panelGroupLayout id="plam2" halign="center" valign="middle"
                        inlineStyle="width:33%;display:inline-block;">
    <amx:tableLayout id="tl2">
      <amx:rowLayout id="rl2">
        <amx:cellFormat id="cf2" halign="center" valign="middle">
          <amx:commandLink id="cl3"
                           actionListener="#{bindings.gotoFeature.execute}" >
            <amx:image id="i2" source="/images/#{row.name}.png"
                       inlineStyle="width:36px;height:36px"/>
            <amx:setPropertyListener type="action" from="#{row.id}"
                                     to="#{pageFlowScope.FeatureId}" />
          </amx:commandLink>
        </amx:cellFormat>
      </amx:rowLayout>
    </amx:tableLayout>
```

```
        </amx:panelGroupLayout>
</amx:iterator>
```

You notice the <amx:iterator/>, which is created by dragging and dropping the features collection from the ApplicationFeatures data control (Figure 6-20). This collection contains all the features of the MAF application and is used in the custom springboard to create entries for all these features by simply iterating this collection.

You can also use the ApplicationFeatures data control to add components that can be used to navigate from the springboard to a feature. In the ApplicationFeatures data control, you find the goToFeature() operation (Figure 6-21), which, when invoked, navigates to the corresponding feature.

The gotoFeature() method can be dragged from the ApplicationsFeatures data control and dropped onto the MAF AMX page to create a commandLink. This commandLink can embed images to display the image that you want to show for the corresponding feature.

This drag-and-drop action will also create a binding in the PageDefinition file of the springboard page. The value that is used to execute the method is derived from a pageFlowScope variable. This variable contains the ID of the feature that needs to be invoked from the springboard. In the code of the Springboard AMX page, you notice a setPropertyListener that takes the ID of the current row and puts that ID into a pageFlowScope variable called FeatureId.

```
<methodAction id="gotoFeature" RequiresUpdateModel="true"
              Action="invokeMethod"
              MethodName="gotoFeature"
              IsViewObjectMethod="false"
              DataControl="ApplicationFeatures"
              InstanceName="data.ApplicationFeatures.dataProvider">
    <NamedData NDName="featureId"
               NDValue="#{pageFlowScope.FeatureId}"
               NDType="java.lang.String"/>
</methodAction>
```

FIGURE 6-20.   *The Features collection on the ApplicationFeatures data control*

FIGURE 6-21. *GotoFeature method*

Finally, the new MAF page needs to be linked to the applications as a springboard. This setting is part of the maf-application.xml file. When you define a custom springboard, the MAF application needs to know which feature implements that custom springboard. In this example, it is the feature called "customSpringboard" (Figure 6-22).

The feature that implements the springboard should not be visible on the navigation bar, nor within the springboard of the MAF application. Therefore, both "Show on Navigation Bar" and "Show on Springboard" must both be set to false in the maf-application.xml as you can see in Figure 6-23.

Now that the new custom springboard has been completely built and configured, it will look like a "real" grid-like springboard, as you can see in Figure 6-24.

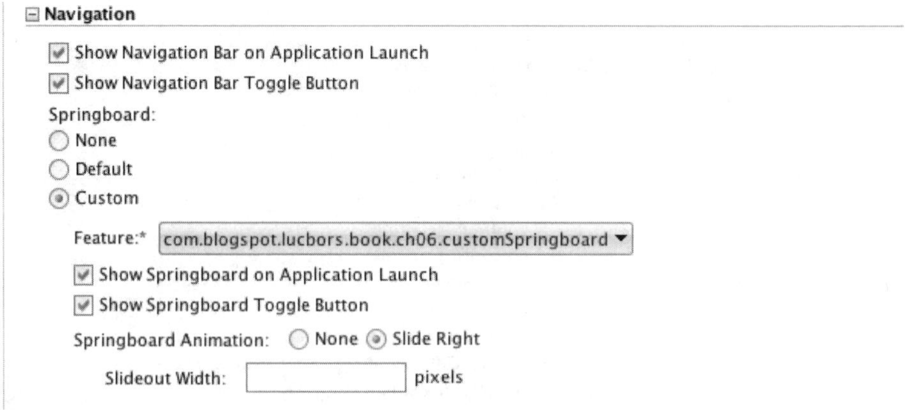

FIGURE 6-22. *Configuration to use a custom springboard*

maf-application.xml

Id*	Show on Navigation Bar	Show on Springboard
com.blogspot.lucbors.book.ch06.feature1	<default> (true)	<default> (true)
com.blogspot.lucbors.book.ch06.feature2	<default> (true)	<default> (true)
com.blogspot.lucbors.book.ch06.feature3	<default> (true)	<default> (true)
com.blogspot.lucbors.book.ch06.feature4	<default> (true)	<default> (true)
com.blogspot.lucbors.book.ch06.feature5	<default> (true)	<default> (true)
com.blogspot.lucbors.book.ch06.feature6	<default> (true)	<default> (true)
com.blogspot.lucbors.book.ch06.feature7	<default> (true)	<default> (true)
com.blogspot.lucbors.book.ch06.feature8	<default> (true)	<default> (true)
com.blogspot.lucbors.book.ch06.feature9	<default> (true)	<default> (true)
com.blogspot.lucbors.book.ch06.customSpringboard	false	false

Application
Device Access
Feature References
Preferences
Security
Cordova Plugins

Feature References:

FIGURE 6-23. *Disable the display of custom springboard on springboard and navigation bar.*

FIGURE 6-24. *The custom springboard in action*

Summary

MAF applications can consist of multiple functional parts called features. The features are defined in the maf-feature.xml file. Applications' access to these features is configured in the maf-application.xml. This is also the place to configure springboard and navigation bars.

MAF enables you to create custom springboards in order to give your users a completely customized entry point to features in your MAF application.

In this chapter you have learned to

- Configure features in the feature definition file
- Configure a navigation bar in the application definition file
- Configure a springboard in the application definition file
- Create a custom springboard with MAF

CHAPTER
7

Using Web Services
and the Local Database

Whathat is an app without its data? Usually data provides information in context, and thus an application without data is an application without any useful information to share. The Mobile Application Framework offers several ways of retrieving and working with data. In this chapter you will learn how to get data into your application by calling web services, and how to work with an on-device database to store the data to survive application restarts. Finally, you will be introduced to the concept of property change events and provider change events that can be used to make the application's UI respond to data change events.

Using Web Services

When you have an enterprise back-end system and its services that you want to disclose to a mobile application, you would typically do this using web services. With web services, there are several options. You have to choose between SOAP and REST web services. If you pick SOAP services, you are then tied into an XML payload. If you pick REST web services, there are two options for the payload: XML and JSON. Although the framework supports both SOAP and REST, and for REST both XML and JSON, the use of REST-JSON is recommended.

RESTful services are easy to create and simple to use. The JSON format is also less verbose than XML, creating smaller payloads and, therefore, is more efficient when transmitted across a network. As speed and performance are all-important for mobile applications, it is a common choice for mobile communications.

NOTE
Future versions of JDeveloper will offer enhanced support of REST-JSON. There will be a REST data control, and you will also be able to create REST-JSON web services on top of ADF Business Components to directly consume server-side ADF Business Components. Until then, you use the REST adapter to expose JAX-RS REST resources with a JSON payload.

When you look at the MAF architecture (Figure 7-1), there are many components involved.
Web services are not part of the framework's architecture itself, but they play a very important role in the overall solution architecture.

The most common way of using web services in an MAF application is by using a data control that will wire up the web service to the application without much development work required. Web service data controls are available for both SOAP and REST web services. In the following sections you will learn more about the SOAP and REST services and how to use them in an MAF application.

SOAP-XML vs. REST-JSON

There are many reasons why REST-JSON is preferred over SOAP-XML. First, there is the speed of deserialization, essentially converting it from the JSON payload to native data types. For JSON response, this is much faster than for XML responses, as typically the payloads are smaller, and smaller payloads are faster to transmit. Then there is simplicity. Generally, REST-JSON web services are easier to work with on the client, and the REST verb-based API is usually easy for developers to work with. However, the choice isn't always yours to make. Sometimes a SOAP-XML web service is what you get and, if so, you have to work with it. Luckily, the framework supports

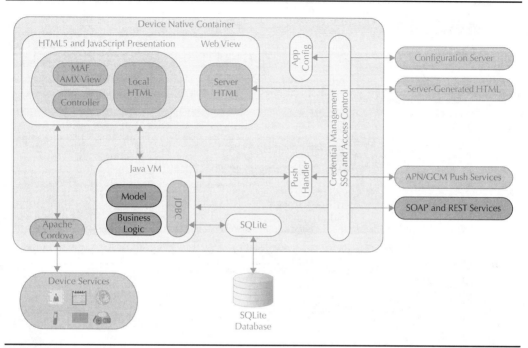

FIGURE 7-1. *Web services and the Mobile Application Framework*

all of this. In the next sections you will learn how to use both SOAP-XML and REST-JSON services.

SOAP-XML Services

SOAP-XML services provide a formal way of communication. A SOAP web service and the corresponding online Web Service Description Language (WSDL) file specify all the available operations and data that can be exchanged with the service. This has several advantages. Because of the strongly typed interaction, the consumer knows exactly what type of data to expect. In addition, as the WSDL clearly articulates the web service API, it is easy for third-party tools to interrogate this structure and call it on the developer's behalf. The contract-based and formal approach with the XML payload comes with the drawback of overhead and size, which in mobile environments is a disadvantage. However, in some situations, it may be the only type of web service available to you, so MAF takes care to integrate all types of web services, giving you flexibility in defining your mobile application.

If you want to use a SOAP-XML web service in your mobile application, you can create a web service data control. Let's look at a simple SOAP-XML service that provides country information. The description of this web service can be found here:

```
http://www.webservicex.net/country.asmx?WSDL
```

This WSDL URL must be entered on the first page of the Create Web Service Data Control wizard (Figure 7-2).

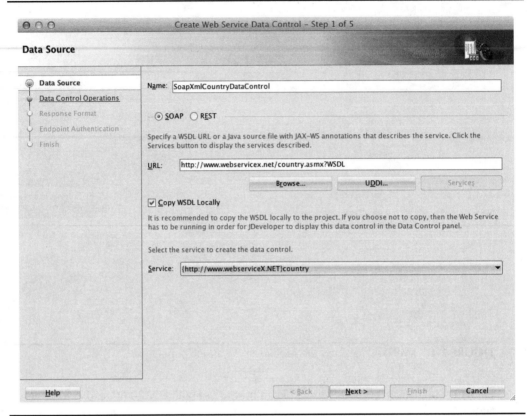

FIGURE 7-2. *Enter the WSDL URL in the SOAP Web Service Data Control wizard.*

TIP
It is recommended to leave the Copy WSDL Locally check box checked. It enables the Data Control Panel to display objects from the web service without being connected to the web service.

On the second page (Figure 7-3), you can select the web service operations that you want to expose in the data control. You can select as many of the available operations as you need. They will all show up in the generated data control.

The result is a web service data control that exposes the available operations, as you can see in Figure 7-4.

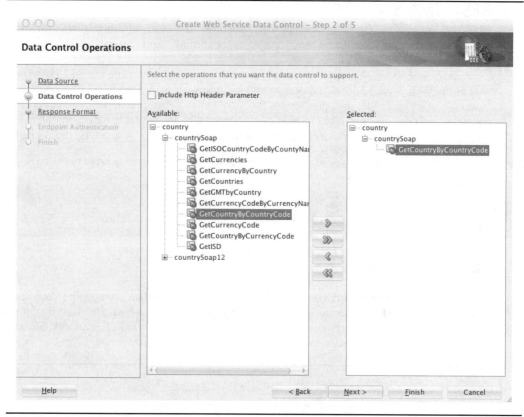

FIGURE 7-3. *Select the operations in the SOAP Web Service Data Control wizard.*

NOTE
Once the data control is created, you can use it in your MAF application. One way to do this is to drag and drop collections and operations from the data control on an AMX page. This works fine, but is less flexible than working with the data control from within Java code. You will learn how to work with the data control from within Java code later on in this book.

FIGURE 7-4. *The SOAP-XML Web Service data control*

REST-XML Services

REST-XML uses an XSD to define the payload structures. Therefore, at design time, you know exactly what the data formats are for each and every attribute, and you can use this information for building your mobile application.

A REST-XML service can be called from an MAF application by using the URL data control as well as the Web Services data control. You will learn how to work with a REST-XML web service based on an example that uses geonames. The GeoNames geographical database covers all countries and contains over eight million place names that are available for download free of charge. The URL to the CountryInfo service, including the required parameters, looks like this:

 `http://api.geonames.org/countryInfo?country=US&username=demo&style=full`

NOTE
The GeoNames API provides a username "demo" that can be used for demonstration purposes. If you use this, be aware that there is a limit of 30,000 calls. You can create your own user account at the web site of the GeoNames database.

To call out to this web service, you can use the Web Service data control. The Web Service data control for REST services uses a connection to the web service URL that must be defined in the connections.xml file. Such a connection can be created from within JDeveloper (Figure 7-5).

○ ○ ○	Create URL Connection

Configure a new URL connection. Choose Application Resources to add this connection to the current application. Choose Resource Palette if you don't want a single application to own it.

Create Connection in: ⦿ Application Resources ○ IDE Connections

Name:

> CountryRestXmlConnection

URL Endpoint:

> http://api.geonames.org/countryInfo

Authentication Type:

> None ▼

Username

Password

Realm

Test Connection

Status:

> The connection successfully established.

Help | OK | Cancel

FIGURE 7-5. *URL connection for the CountryInfo REST XML service*

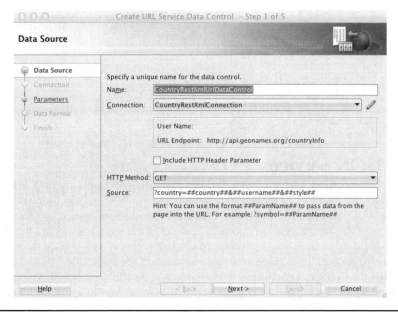

FIGURE 7-6. *Specifying the connection in the Create URL Service Data Control wizard*

JDeveloper separates the connection from the URL data control so that the same connection can be used in multiple data controls. A URL connection can be created as an IDE-level connection. This makes the connection available for multiple applications in JDeveloper. If you create the connection within an application (JDeveloper workspace), the connection is only available in that specific application.

Now you can create a URL data control that uses this connection. You have to specify this connection on the first page of the Create URL Service Data Control wizard (Figure 7-6). Note that the required parameters can be entered in the Source field; use the format "?symbol=##ParamName##".

If there is a single service that supports multiple methods, you should select the same endpoint and just keep adding methods to it—DO NOT generate separate data controls for each method. The parameters that you need in this call are defined on the second page of the wizard (Figure 7-7).

Again, once the data control (Figure 7-8) is created, you can use it in your MAF application, for instance, by dragging and dropping operations and collections.

Provide parameter value to test whether the URL and source are valid.

Parameters	Values
country	US
username	demo
style	full

FIGURE 7-7. *The URL parameters for the URL Service data control*

FIGURE 7-8. *The REST XML Web Service data control*

REST JSON Services

The data controls (both URL and Web Service) currently only support SOAP and REST-XML. If you want to call the REST-JSON service from within your MAF application, you must use the RestServiceAdapter interface and call it from Java. The RestServiceAdapter interface that is part of the framework lets you trigger execution of web service operations without the need to create a Web Service data control. You don't have to interact with the web service directly either, thus preventing tight coupling between the web service and the Java code.

All that the RestServiceAdapter interface needs is a valid connection; this connection can be created in exactly the same way as you did previously for the REST-XML service. The example in Figure 7-9 shows a URL connection to the GeoNames database, which also exposes a REST-JSON web service. The full URL including the URI is

```
http://api.geonames.org/countryInfoJSON?country=US&username=demo&style=full
```

In the URL connection you only need to enter the URL. The URI, the other part, is needed later, in the actual call to the service.

The call to the Country Info JSON service needs some extra information. This is called the request URI and it takes the necessary parameters. It is beyond the scope of this chapter to explain the individual parameters. More info on the API can be found on the geonames.org web site.

```java
public static String invokeRestService(){
    RestServiceAdapter restService = Model.createRestServiceAdapter();
    restService.clearRequestProperties();
    restService.setConnectionName("CountryRestConnection");
    restService.setRequestType(RestServiceAdapter.REQUEST_TYPE_GET);
    restService.setRetryLimit(0);

    String requestUri =
        "countryInfoJSON?formatted=true&country=US&username=demo&style=full";

    restService.setRequestURI(requestUri);
    String response = "";
    try{
        response = restService.send("");
        return response;
    }
    catch (Exception e){
        // something went wrong
    }
}
```

FIGURE 7-9. *Create URL Connection wizard*

The response of the service call can now be processed to show the data on an MAF AMX view. The processing of such a JSON result String is explained in detail in Chapter 15, where the result of a call to the Google Places API is processed and used in the mobile application.

Using the Local Database

If an application needs to work with data and store it on the device, or when the application needs to work with data when disconnected or restarted, it can use the on-device SQLite database to persist the data. When you look at the MAF architecture (Figure 7-10), there are lots of components involved. SQLite is an embedded database engine that is well suited for mobile applications. SQLite support is embedded in the iOS and Android operating systems. However, because it lacks encryption support, MAF also embeds SQLite support with the encryption extension.

Oracle provides a Java API on top of the SQLite database. When you use the local database in your Java code, you are actually doing straight JDBC calls. This enables you to reuse your Java coding skills.

SQLite allows you to manage any number of databases on the device, typically tied to one application each. Those databases can be encrypted if security of the data on the device is

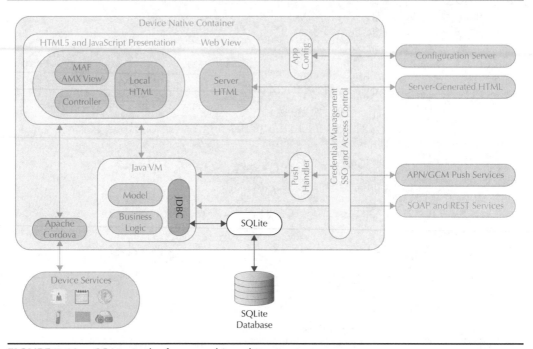

FIGURE 7-10. *SQLite in the framework's architecture*

critical. Usually, encryption is recommended. If for any reason your device is lost or stolen, the data on it cannot be accessed.

SQLite is fully transactional and it supports the ACID semantics. That means that a transaction is always atomic, consistent, isolated, and durable. Even if the transaction is interrupted by system crashes or power failures, your data won't be corrupted.

SQLite is self-contained and, therefore, there are no external dependencies to include in your JDeveloper projects. It is already a part of the Mobile Application Framework. There is no need to add a JAR file to your applications. Figure 7-11 shows the SQLite logo.

FIGURE 7-11. *SQLite logo*

The SQLite database is a server-less database. This means that there is no server process that runs in the background. This reduces scalability to exactly one user, which arguably is not a problem on a mobile device.

From a development perspective, SQLite runs with no configurations at all. The developer just needs to open the database and make JDBC calls.

Why Use the SQLite Database?

After reading the previous sections, you should be convinced of the power of SQLite. But why should you use a SQLite local database in your mobile application? Mostly, the mobile app will use web services in order to read and write data on the remote server. There are, however, several use cases for the on-device SQLite database.

The first one is when you want to create an application that should work whether there is a network and Internet connection or not. If you use the SQLite database, your application will be able to work even when fully disconnected. The data it needs is stored in the SQLite database and this is accessible.

Another reason to work with the SQLite database is to cache remote data for performance reasons. The mobile networks are getting more and more reliable, but sometimes they are still unreliable or very slow. Besides that, bandwidth on mobile networks is very expensive. Therefore, it would be a good idea to cache some of the data that was retrieved by a web service call to the remote server. Think of static data or data that is not likely to change frequently. Also, users may query lookup data that they won't update, which also is a candidate for locally stored data.

The third reason to use the SQLite database is when you need a transactional buffer. Consider the scenario where the user types in some data and, after submitting the application, issues a web service call to change some data on the remote server. When you do a web service call, the mobile application has no control of the transaction. You cannot be sure that the web service call actually works. Therefore, in some situations, it can be a good idea to store the data in the local database until you are sure that the web service call was successful. In that way, if the web service call fails, you can use the locally stored data to try again later. This prevents the user from having to enter the data again whenever a web service call fails.

These are just three main reasons to use the SQLite database. There are probably more reasons, but it depends on the specific use cases.

There is also one thing that the local database should not be used for. You should not store user preferences in the SQLite database. There is no need for that. The framework offers functionality to manage user preferences. You will learn more about this later on in this book.

How to Use the SQLite Database

Now you know what the SQLite database is and you know several good reasons to use it. The next question is: how do I use the SQLite database? The first step, even before starting to use the database, is to create the database by using JDBC.

In SQLite, each database is contained in its own file, and this file is managed by the SQLite back-end. There are two ways to create a SQLite database. The first way is to simply issue DML statements via JDBC, such as create table or create index.

The second way is to use a preseeded database file. This file is packaged with your mobile application code. It must be stored in a specific location in order for your application to load it.

There are tools available to get you started with the creation of a preseeded database. These tools, such as MesaSQLite, SQLiteManager, and SQLiteDatabase Browser, give you all the functionality you need to create a preseeded database for your mobile application.

TIP
You can also use JDeveloper to do the same, by downloading and using the Zentus JDBC driver, and then set up a DB connection in JDeveloper to "connect" to a database file. You can actually use the database creation/modification capabilities in JDeveloper.

Whatever way you choose, to actually make the database ready for use by your mobile application, you must execute code from an application life cycle listener. You will learn about the life cycle listener later on in this book.

Connecting to the SQLite Database

To connect to the SQLite database from within your mobile application, you can use JDBC calls.

The first step is to actually find where the database is located on the device. There is no need to hardcode the path to the database file. In fact, hardcoding is bad practice. The framework has a utility class (AdfmfJavaUtilities) that contains a getDirectoryPathRoot(). This method enables access to files on both iOS and Android systems. You can use this method to access the location of the temporary files, application files (on iOS systems), and the cache directory on the device using the TemporaryDirectory, ApplicationDirectory, and DeviceOnlyDirectory constants, respectively.

Because the database file is deployed together with the mobile application, it is stored in the ApplicationDirectory. Finding the path to the database can be done according to the following code sample. This path, combined with the database file name, can now be used to create and connect to a new JDBC data source. The method in this sample would typically be part of a DBConnectionFactory class that you implement in the ApplicationController. This method will be used throughout the remaining part of the chapter to set up a connection to the database.

```
public class DBConnectionFactory {
    public DBConnectionFactory() {
        super();
    }
    protected static Connection conn = null;
    public static Connection getConnection() throws Exception {
        if (conn == null) {
            try {
                String root = AdfmfJavaUtilities.getDirectoryPathRoot(
                                AdfmfJavaUtilities.ApplicationDirectory);
                String database = root + "/book.db";
                conn = new SQLite.JDBCDataSource(
                                "jdbc:sqlite"+database).getConnection();
            } catch (SQLException e) {
                //handle error here
                System.err.println(e.getMessage());
            }
        }
```

```
        return conn;
    }
}
```

NOTE
If the database does not exist, SQLite will automatically create it when the SQLite JDBC connection is created.

Encrypting the SQLite Database

As mentioned earlier, SQLite offers encryption of the database. Encryption, and decryption, is very simple. If you want to encrypt the database, you only need a password. For encrypting, the AdfmfJavaUtilities class has the encryptDatabase() method. It takes the connection and the password as arguments.

```
String pwd = "bookPassword";
AdfmfJavaUtilities.encryptDatabase(connection,pwd);
```

Decrypting the database works the same. However, you need to obtain a connection to the encrypted database, using the password that was used to encrypt it, before you can decrypt it.

```
Connection = new SQLite.JDBCDataSource(
                        "jdbc:sqlite"+database).getConnection(null,pwd);
AdfmfJavaUtilities.decryptDatabase(connection);
```

NOTE
Beware not to open an encrypted database incorrectly. If you happen to do so and decide to encrypt the database again, you are in trouble. There is no way that the old correct password, the invalid password, or the new password can unlock the database, resulting in the irretrievable loss of data. The catch is that SQLite does not display any error messages if you open an encrypted database with an incorrect password. In other words, be very careful!

Limitations of SQLite

SQLite is a very powerful database, but there are a couple of limitations.

The first limitation is related to concurrency. You can have multiple read-only connections to the database at the same time, but you can only have one single read/write connection. This is only a challenge if your mobile application is multithreaded.

Another limitation is that, although SQLite is SQL92-compliant, it does not support full outer join and right outer join statements. Also, SQLite does not support user privileges. There is no way to grant or revoke roles to users. Once a user has access to the database, the user can do anything.

SQLite supports data types for table columns. When you issue a create table statement, you can specify a data type for each column. This is great, but at run time, there is no check of the data type of the inserted or updated values against the data type of the column. That means that you can put a String into an Integer field. So be careful to check all values before the update or insert statement is issued. SQLite will not warn you if you've done it incorrectly. The following example explains this in more detail.

First create a simple table with two columns:

```
create table Test (I int, S varchar);
```

Next insert a row with correct values and data types:

```
insert into Test values(10, 'foobar');
```

Then try the same with incorrect types.

```
insert into Test values('foobar', 10);
```

Unlike most database systems, in SQLite, performing such a statement will successfully insert the data without any error.

Besides these limitations, there are also some limitations to transaction support in SQLite. SQLite does not support nested transactions. When you issue a commit, there is a single read/write connection. You already know this from the first limitation, which was about concurrency. When you have several open connections and each of them issues a commit, only the first transaction is actually committed successfully to the SQLite database. All other connections will switch to read-only mode and the commit statement they issued will fail.

Finally, the SQLite database supports the rollback statement, but it will fail if there are open ResultSets.

All the limitations mentioned in this section are limitations that you need to take care of when designing your mobile application. One thing you can do is use a SQL connection factory that is a singleton and ensures there is not concurrency in accessing the database. For preventing wrong types in an insert statement, you could create helper classes that expose an API for the Java programmer to update a specific table instead of composing the SQL update statement himself.

The SQLite VACUUM Command

When records are deleted from a SQLite database, its size does not change. This leads to fragmentation after records are deleted and, ultimately, results in degraded performance. You can avoid this by periodically running the VACUUM command. There is, however, a more convenient option.

This is to use auto_vacuum mode.

The default setting for auto_vacuum is 0 or "none." The "none" setting means that auto_vacuum is disabled. When auto_vacuum is disabled and data is deleted from a database, the database file remains the same size. Unused database file pages are added to a "freelist" and reused for subsequent inserts. So no database file space is lost. However, the database file does not shrink. In this mode, the VACUUM command can be used to rebuild the entire database file and thus reclaim unused disk space.

When the auto_vacuum mode is 1 or "full," the freelist pages are moved to the end of the database file and the database file is truncated to remove the freelist pages at every transaction commit. Note, however, that auto_vacuum only truncates the freelist pages from the file. Auto_vacuum does not defragment the database nor repack individual database pages the way that the VACUUM command does. In fact, because it moves pages around within the file, auto_vacuum can actually make fragmentation worse.

Auto-vacuuming is only possible if the database stores some additional information that allows each database page to be traced backward to its referrer. Therefore, auto-vacuuming must be turned on before any tables are created. It is not possible to enable or disable auto_vacuum after a table has been created.

It is recommended that every database with moderate transaction rate be occasionally vacuumed manually, even if auto_vacuum is enabled. This to prevent performance degradation due to high levels of fragmentation. So unless you have very good reasons to use auto_vacuum, it is best to use the default, which is set auto_vacuum mode to NONE.

```
String root = AdfmfJavaUtilities.getDirectoryPathRoot(
                  AdfmfJavaUtilities.ApplicationDirectory);
String database = root + "/book.db";
Connection = new SQLite.JDBCDataSource(
                    "jdbc:sqlite"+database).getConnection();
Stmt = connection.preparedStatement("PRAGMA auto_vacuum=FULL;");
Stmt.executeUpdate();
```

SQLite Creation of Database Objects

So far we have been looking at how the database can be created and encrypted and how to do some housekeeping to reclaim unused disk space. Now it is time to look into the creation of database objects in the SQLite database.

Let's assume that we want to create an entire new database for the mobile application and not use a preseeded one. Typically, you can use a SQL script that executes when the application starts.

myNewDatabase.sql

This script drops the table, then creates it again, and finally has some insert statements to put data into the table. For this sample we use a simple table called CHAPTERS containing columns for chapter number, chapter name, and number of pages.

```
DROP TABLE CHAPTERS;

CREATE TABLE CHAPTERS
(
NR NUMBER(4) NOT NULL,
NAME VARCHAR2(64),
PAGES NUMBER(4),
DEADLINE date
);

INSERT INTO CHAPTERS (NR, NAME, PAGES, DEADLINE)
            VALUES(1, 'Chapter One', 10 , sysdate);
INSERT INTO CHAPTERS (NR, NAME, PAGES, DEADLINE)
```

```
                VALUES(2, 'Chapter Two', 20 , sysdate);
INSERT INTO CHAPTERS (NR, NAME, PAGES, DEADLINE)
                VALUES(3, 'Chapter Three', 30 , sysdate);
INSERT INTO CHAPTERS (NR, NAME, PAGES, DEADLINE)
                VALUES(4, 'Chapter Four', 40 , sysdate);
```

If you want to use this script in your mobile application to create a database, you must add it to your ApplicationController project as a resource.

Now that the script is finished, we need to create a method that actually reads the script and executes the lines of SQL code in order to create the database and its objects. This method contains the following steps:

1. Find the ApplicationDirectory.

2. Set the database name.

3. Check if the database already exists, because if it does, there is no need to create it.

4. If the database does not exist, create it. This can be done by creating a SQLite JDBC connection to the non-existing database.

5. Get the myNewDatabase.sql file as a Stream so we can read it line by line.

6. Execute all SQL statements as they come in.

7. Finally, commit the transaction.

NOTE
SQLite ignores any commit statement. Each statement is committed as soon as it is executed against the database. This auto-commit functionality is provided by the SQLite database by default. The auto-commit can be disabled to improve your application's performance. To do this, use the Connection's setAutoCommit(false) method.

```
private static void initializeDatabaseFromScript() throws Exception {
    InputStream scriptStream = null;
    Connection conn = null;
    try {
        // ApplicationDirectory returns the private read-write area of the
        // device's file system that this application can access.
        // This is where the database is created
        String docRoot = AdfmfJavaUtilities.getDirectoryPathRoot
                                (AdfmfJavaUtilities.ApplicationDirectory);
        String dbName = docRoot + "/book.db";
        // Verify whether or not the database exists.
        // If it does, then it has already been initialized
        // and no further actions are required
        File dbFile = new File(dbName);
        if (dbFile.exists())
            return;
```

```
        // If the database does not exist, a new database is automatically
        // created when the SQLite JDBC connection is created
        conn = new SQLite.JDBCDataSource("jdbc:sqlite:" + docRoot +
                                    "/book.db").getConnection();

        // To improve performance, the statements are executed
        // one at a time in the context of a single transaction
        conn.setAutoCommit(false);

        // Since the SQL script has been packaged as a resource within
        // the application, the getResourceAsStream method is used
        scriptStream = Thread.currentThread().getContextClassLoader().
                    getResourceAsStream("META-INF/ myNewDatabase.sql");

        BufferedReader scriptReader = new BufferedReader
                                    (new InputStreamReader(scriptStream));
        String nextLine;
        StringBuffer nextStatement = new StringBuffer();
        // The while loop iterates over all the lines in the SQL script,
        // assembling them into valid SQL statements and executing them as
        // a terminating semicolon is encountered

        Statement stmt = conn.createStatement();
        while ((nextLine = scriptReader.readLine()) != null) {
            // Skipping blank lines, comments, and COMMIT statements
            if (nextLine.startsWith("REM")      ||
                nextLine.startsWith("COMMIT")   ||
                nextLine.length() < 1)
                continue;
            nextStatement.append(nextLine);
            if (nextLine.endsWith(";")) {
                stmt.execute(nextStatement.toString());
                nextStatement = new StringBuffer();
            }
        }
    conn.commit();
    }
    finally {
        if (conn != null)
            conn.close();
    }
}
```

This method, combined with the myNewDatabase.sql script, will create an on-device database called book.db.

TIP
The samples that ship with the Mobile Application Framework contain an HR sample application. This has some excellent examples of how to work with the SQLite database.

Data Selection and Manipulation with SQLite

The database is created, and the data is in it. Now it is time to read the data from the database and to do some data manipulation. If you are familiar with plain JDBC, this should not be a problem. If not, you will learn how to work with JDBC to read and write data.

Reading data from the SQLite database is not difficult. You write the query that you want to perform and create a JDBC prepared statement based on that query. After executing the query in code, you loop through the result set and create a new POJO object based on the data in the result set. In the following sample, we select all chapters from the CHAPTERS table, create a chapter object for all of them, and add all of these chapter objects to an object (java.util.List) called s_book.

```
Public void retrieveChaptersFromDB(){
    try{
        Connection conn = DBConnectionFactory.getConnection();
        s_book.clear();
        conn.setAutoCommit(false);
        PreparedStatement stmt = conn.prepareStatement(
                            "SELECT * FROM CHAPTERS");
        ResultSet rs = stmt.executeQuery();
        while (rs.next()){
            int nr = rs.getInt("NR");
            String name = rs.getString("NAME");
            int pages = rs.getInt("PAGES");
            Date deadline = rs.getDate("DEADLINE");
            Chapter chptr = new Chapter(nr, name, pages, deadline);
            s_book.add(chptr);
        }
        rs.close();
    }......... .
```

Updating data in a SQLite table is just as easy. The update SQL statement is passed as a string to a JDBC prepared statement that can be executed on the SQLite database. Note that SQLite does not have support for Oracle named bindings in the JDBC statement. All parameters used in the update statement must use the positional binding syntax. That means that when you set the value of any of these parameters, you need to specifically assign it to a numbered position. In the following sample, the value that is assigned to the "?" next to NAME should be assigned to position 1.

```
public void updateChaptersInDB(){
    try {Connection conn = DBConnectionFactory.getConnection();
        conn.setAutoCommit(false);
        String stmt=
            "UPDATE CHAPTERS SET NAME=?,PAGES=?,DEADLINE=? WHERE NR=?";
        PreparedStatement pStmt = conn.prepareStatement(stmt);
        pStmt.setString(1,chapter.getName());
        pStmt.setInt(2,chapter.getPages());
        pStmt.setDate(3, emp.getDeadline());
        pStmt.setInt(2,chapter.getNr());
        pStmt.execute();conn.commit();
```

```
    }
    catch (SQLException e) {
        // something went wrong
    }
}
```

Deleting is just as easy. Write the delete statement, parse it to create a preparedStatement, and execute it. There is no need to put a complete code sample here.

```
Connection conn = DBConnectionFactory.getConnection();
conn.setAutoCommit(false);
String stmt = "DELETE FROM CHAPTERS WHERE NR=?";
PreparedStatement pStmt = conn.prepareStatement(stmt);
pStmt.setInt(1, nr);
pStmt.execute();
conn.commit();
```

The Concept of Property Change Events

In the previous sections you learned how to work with web services and with the local database. In Chapter 5 you also were introduced to the binding layer, also known as Model, where you learned how to use POJOs as the data holders for the user interface. This all plays a role in getting data from any kind of data source to the mobile application's user interface. There is one more thing that is very important in order to have a responsive and interactive mobile application, and that is the page refresh. If the data in your POJO changes, you might want to refresh the corresponding page accordingly.

The concept of AJAX to support partial page refresh in web applications is not available in the Mobile Application Framework. The way to refresh the user interface based on a value change event is different.

To simplify data change events, MAF uses the property change listener pattern.

You will learn how this works based on a simple example; a calculator that adds up two numbers and shows the result (Figure 7-12).

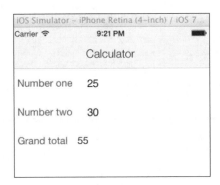

FIGURE 7-12. *A simple calculator to add up two numbers*

The calculator uses a simple Java class with three properties and is exposed as a managed bean. The three properties are one for each number, and a third one for the total.

```java
public class MobileCalc {
    private int numberOne;
    private int numberTwo;
    private int result;
}
```

When you generate accessors for this class, you can also instruct JDeveloper to generate the necessary code to source notifications from your bean's property accessors by selecting the "Notify listeners when property changes" check box in the Generate Accessors dialog, as you can see in Figure 7-13.

The PropertyChangeSupport object is generated automatically, with the calls to firePropertyChange in the generated setter method. Additionally, the addPropertyChangeListener and removePropertyChangeListener methods are added so property change listeners can register and unregister themselves with this object. The PropertyChangeSupport class implements this change notification in a thread-safe manner. The event-receiving part implements the PropertyChangeListener interface, which also is implemented by MAF.

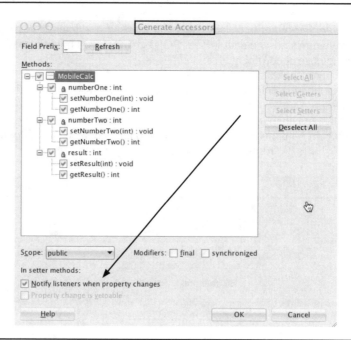

FIGURE 7-13. *Generate accessors and propertyChangeListeners*

This is what the getter for NumberOne looks like after the accessors and listeners have been created:

```
public void setNumberOne(int numberOne) {
    int oldNumberOne = this.numberOne;
    this.numberOne = numberOne;
    propertyChangeSupport.firePropertyChange(
                        "numberOne", oldNumberOne, numberOne);
}
```

So whenever the setter is fired, the firePropertyChange method is invoked, with the property name and both the old and new value as arguments. This is the way for the framework to catch changes in the data and to notify the user interface layer that data has been changed.

The addPropertyChangeListener and removePropertyChangeListener methods are created so property change listeners can register and unregister themselves with this object.

```
public void addPropertyChangeListener(PropertyChangeListener l) {
    propertyChangeSupport.addPropertyChangeListener(l);
}

public void removePropertyChangeListener(PropertyChangeListener l) {
    propertyChangeSupport.removePropertyChangeListener(l);
}
```

In order for the calculator to work, you need to add a call to setResult() in the setter of both the numbers:

```
setResult(numberOne + numberTwo);
```

With this change, the calculator class is finished and you can use it in a simple AMX page. Simply create two input components and one output component for the result. There is no need to add a button to do the calculation. The bean immediately processes any changes. When you change the value of either input component, the calculation takes place and the result is displayed.

```
<amx:inputText label="Number one" id="it1"
                value="#{pageFlowScope.mobileCalcBean.numberOne}"/>
<amx:inputText label="Number two" id="it2"
                value="#{pageFlowScope.mobileCalcBean.numberTwo}"/>
<amx:panelLabelAndMessage label="Grand total" id="plam1">
    <amx:outputText id="it4"
                    value="#{pageFlowScope.mobileCalcBean.result}"/>
</amx:panelLabelAndMessage>
```

This was a simple example of how to work with propertyChangeEvents based on individual properties. Now what if you are working with collections? You can respond to changes in collections in a similar way. Instead of property Change Events, you must use provider Change Events. To explain this, we will take a look at two classes, Chapter and Book.

```
Public class Chapter{
    private int nr;
```

```
private String name;
private int pages;
private Date deadline;
```

The Book class contains functionality to add chapters to the book and to remove and reorder chapters. I wish it were this easy in real life. In the constructor of this class, some chapters are added to the book. Furthermore, there are methods to add and remove chapters, one to reorder chapters, and finally one that gets the entire book. The latter returns the collection that can be used in the user interface. Note the ProviderChangeSupport object. This will be used to inform the user interface about changes in the book.

```
Public class Book{
private List s_chapters = null;
    private transient ProviderChangeSupport providerChangeSupport =
            new ProviderChangeSupport(this);
    Public Book(){
    // constructor; create the initial book; that is, add some chapters
    If (s_chapters ==null){
        s_chapters = new ArrayList();
        addChapter (new Chapter(0, "Chapter One"   , 10 ,)) ;
        addChapter (new Chapter(1, "Chapter Two"   , 20 ,)) ;
        addChapter (new Chapter(2, "Chapter Three" , 30 ,)) ;
        }
    }

    public Chapter[] getBook() {
        //This Method gets a list of the chapters
        Chapter[] chapters = null;
        chapters = (Chapter[]) s_chapters.toArray(
                                new Chapter[s_chapters.size()]);
        return chapters;
    }
    public synchronized void addChapter (Chapter c) {
        s_chapters.add(c);
        providerChangeSupport.fireProviderCreate("book", c.getNr(), c);
    }

    public synchronized void removeAchapter() {
        // hardcoded remove number 4
        for (int i = 0; i < chapters.size(); i++) {
            Chapter c = (Chapter)s_chapters.get(i);
            if (p.getNr() == 4) {
                c = (Chapter)s_chapters.remove(i);
                providerChangeSupport.fireProviderDelete("book", c.getNr());
            }
        }
    }

    public synchronized void sortChapters() {
        Collections.sort(s_chapters);
        providerChangeSupport.fireProviderRefresh("book");
    }
```

Provider change events are available for creation of a row and deletion of a row. In those cases, row currency is retained. Note that in the addChapter method, the fireProviderCreate method is called in order to inform the application about the fact that a new chapter was added to the book.

```
providerChangeSupport.fireProviderCreate("book", c.getNr(), c);
```

In the deleteAchapter method, the fireProviderDelete method is fired.

```
providerChangeSupport.fireProviderDelete("book", c.getNr());
```

However, when the complete collection is refreshed, the corresponding iterator is refreshed and the row currency is lost. The latter happens, for instance, when the contents of the list are reordered, as you can see in the sortChapters() method.

```
providerChangeSupport.fireProviderRefresh("book");
```

Finally, there is one more method that you should become familiar with, and that is the flushDataChangeEvent. If you use a background thread and you want to communicate any data changes to the AMX page, you can use flushDataChangeEvent. This method is part of the AdfmfJavaUtilities class, which forces the queued data changes to the client.

Summary

An application without any data usually is of no value at all. Applications run in the context of data. Mobile applications can be used to view data that is relevant to the device's context, such as location, but they can also be used to enter or modify data. In order to work with data, a mobile application can either use web services or the on-device SQLite database. In this chapter you learned

- How to create a Web Service data control
- How to invoke web services using a data control
- How to call REST-JSON services from Java
- Some of the core concepts of the SQLite database
- How to create an on-device database
- How to work with the on-device database in Java code
- The concept of property change listeners

CHAPTER

8

Device Interaction

A smartphone (or tablet for that matter) is called "smart" for a reason. It's not just a phone. It has numerous integrated features beyond just a browser and an Internet connection that you can use. Both have cameras, GPS locators, gyros, accelerometers, address books, and much more. It's these features coupled with the ability for you to write your own mobile applications that provide very exciting opportunities for creating solutions that your business has never realized before. Your imagination here is the limit—no longer are your applications bound to a PC; they're free to roam, take photos, and check their location, all while being connected to your HQ systems. This can be a very valuable extension of your mobile application. Imagine that you are able to integrate these services into your MAF application.

MAF makes full use of these device features, providing the mobile application programmer both a declarative data control–driven and programmatic API–driven approach to calling these services. Under the covers, MAF makes use of the Apache Cordova open source JavaScript APIs to allow your MAF application to make use of these services regardless of whether you're running on iOS or Android. Do you need to know how to use Apache Cordova? Not necessarily. To guard you from learning Cordova, MAF introduces a declarative device data control as well as Java and JavaScript APIs that wrap the underlying Apache Cordova implementation. The Oracle MAF Java and JavaScript APIs perform the same function, and also allow Oracle to absorb changes to the Apache Cordova APIs by hiding the changes under the Oracle Java/JavaScript APIs if they do occur. Besides the Apache Cordova functionality, the device data control also gives the developer declarative access to device features such as e-mail, SMS, and displaying a file.

The Concepts of Device Interaction

As described, there are three ways of interacting with device services, namely through the declarative data control or the programmatic MAF Java API and JavaScript APIs. There is also a fourth way to access device features, which isn't designed to invoke the services but rather test their availability and their status, by using Expression Language.

Let's take a look at how these mechanisms work.

Using the DeviceFeatures Data Control

In the context of JDeveloper and MAF, data controls are one of the significant productivity boosters for developers. Rather than forcing developers to write their own code to access operations and data structures, which in many cases look very similar, JDeveloper plugs these constructs into a declarative data control, which provides a set of abstract, standardized controls. The pure power of this solution is that at design time, JDeveloper allows programmers to drag and drop the contents of the data control onto pages, and JDeveloper will take care of creating UI controls and back-end code to call the data control services on the programmer's behalf, just with a few mouse clicks.

In the context of MAF, the DeviceFeatures data control, which is implicitly available for MAF applications, provides a number of operations to call the underlying Apache Cordova APIs as shown in Figure 8-1.

As can be seen from Figure 8-1, the DeviceFeatures data control contains operations for interacting with the contacts on the device, using the camera, sending e-mails and text messages, and displaying files and using the device's GPS facilities. Using such an operation is actually very

FIGURE 8-1. *DeviceFeatures data control*

straightforward. Simply drag an operation from the DeviceFeatures data control and drop it on your AMX page. There is no need to do any coding to invoke the API or to add the components to the page. JDeveloper and MAF handle it all. For instance, take a look at the sendSMS operation on the DeviceFeatures data control in Figure 8-2.

When this operation is dragged and dropped on the page as an " MAF Parameter Form," everything that is needed to invoke the operation, that being UI components and the code to invoke the SMS service, is created for you. First, you will see a popup in which you can change the components that are created for you on the AMX page. Figure 8-3 shows the Edit Form Fields popup for the sendSMS. You will see two components: one for the "to" and a second one for the "body" of the text message.

Next the Edit Action Binding dialog appears to allow you to edit the default values for both parameters as shown in Figure 8-4.

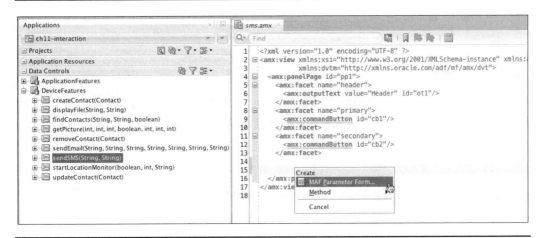

FIGURE 8-2. *sendSMS drag and drop from DeviceFeatures data control*

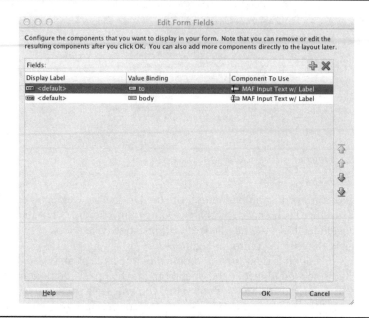

FIGURE 8-3. *Edit Form Fields popup for the sendSMS parameter form*

FIGURE 8-4. *The Edit Action Binding dialog*

FIGURE 8-5. *Grant SMS Access prompt*

Finally, if this is the first time you've integrated the SMS service into your application, JDeveloper will ask you if it should add the required permissions to your application to allow it to call the SMS services on your phone, as shown in Figure 8-5. Device permissions will be further covered in Chapter 10.

When you select the OK button, you will get a button to invoke the sendSMS operation and input components for each and every parameter that the operation needs, as you can see in this code sample:

```
<amx:panelFormLayout id="pfl1">
     <amx:inputText value="#{bindings.to.inputValue}"
                    label="#{bindings.to.hints.label}" id="it1"/>
     <amx:inputText value="#{bindings.body.inputValue}"
                    label="#{bindings.body.hints.label}" id="it2"/>
</amx:panelFormLayout>
<amx:commandButton actionListener="#{bindings.sendSMS.execute}"
                   text="sendSMS"
                   disabled="#{!bindings.sendSMS.enabled}" id="cb3"/>
```

As you'll note, the inputText and commandButton UI controls make use of EL expressions to call the underlying data control sendSMS operation and supply its parameters. In order to make this functionality work at run time, JDeveloper also creates entries in the relating PageDefinition file to define which operations the UI components will make use of—think of this as the Java code you used to have to write to access APIs, but JDeveloper is doing it all declaratively. As an example, in the following code sample, you see the sendSMS_to and sendSMS_body variables for each argument of the sendSMS method. Next, you see a method action called sendSMS, which is more or less telling the application that there is an action called sendSMS that is linked to the sendSMS method of the DeviceFeatures data control. The method action binding also defines the two arguments "to" and "body," both of type String, that take their values from the defined variables. Finally, you notice two attribute bindings. These are used to link the input components on the page to the pageDefinition, as you can see in this code fragment:

```
<?xml version="1.0" encoding="UTF-8" ?>
<pageDefinition xmlns="http://xmlns.oracle.com/adfm/uimodel"
version="12.1.3.10.41" id="smsPageDef"
                 Package="com.blogspot.lucbors.book.ch11.sms">
  <parameters/>
  <executables>
    <variableIterator id="variables">
```

```
          <variable Type="java.lang.String" Name="sendSMS_to"
                    IsQueriable="false"/>
          <variable Type="java.lang.String" Name="sendSMS_body"
                    IsQueriable="false"/>
      </variableIterator>
    </executables>
    <bindings>
      <methodAction id="sendSMS" RequiresUpdateModel="true"
                    Action="invokeMethod" MethodName="sendSMS"
                    IsViewObjectMethod="false" DataControl="DeviceFeatures"
                    InstanceName="data.DeviceFeatures.dataProvider">
        <NamedData NDName="to" NDType="java.lang.String"
                   NDValue="${bindings.sendSMS_to}"/>
        <NamedData NDName="body" NDType="java.lang.String"
                   NDValue="${bindings.sendSMS_body}"/>
      </methodAction>
      <attributeValues IterBinding="variables" id="to">
        <AttrNames>
          <Item Value="sendSMS_to"/>
        </AttrNames>
      </attributeValues>
      <attributeValues IterBinding="variables" id="body">
        <AttrNames>
          <Item Value="sendSMS_body"/>
        </AttrNames>
      </attributeValues>
    </bindings>
</pageDefinition>
```

The concept of dragging and dropping a method from the DeviceFeatures data control to the page is the same for all available device interactions.

Figure 8-6 displays the resulting MAF AMX page at run time. There are input components for all the necessary arguments, in this case "to" and "body." Next there is a button that, when pressed, invokes the sendSMS method action in the PageDefinition.

So whenever you use the DeviceFeatures data control for device interaction, a lot of programming magic occurs on your behalf! And only little to no coding is involved.

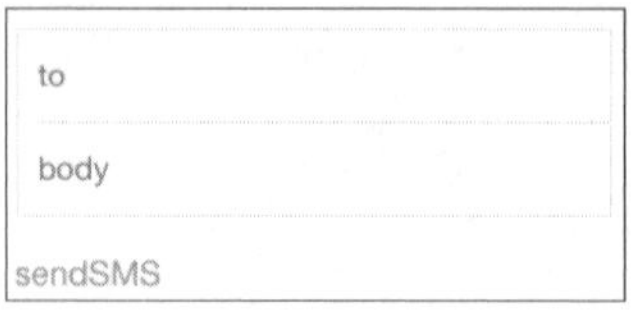

FIGURE 8-6. *Default UI for sendSMS*

Using the Java APIs

Luckily, your job as a programmer hasn't been made redundant.

If you need more control or flexibility when interacting with the device's services, you can use the Java API to accomplish this. By using the Java API, you can directly access device services from your own managed beans. As an extension to the data control approach, the Java APIs return the result of calling each service. This gives you programmatic control to work with the results and also any errors that occur. From that perspective, the data control approach is more of a fire-and-forget approach to invoking these services, and this reveals why it provides the least flexible solution.

From the MAF Java APIs, the DeviceManager is the singleton that enables you to access device functionality. You can get a handle on this object by calling DeviceManagerFactory .getDeviceManager. So whenever you use this, you need to import the DeviceManagerFactory class as depicted in Figure 8-7.

The DeviceManager, like the data control, provides the functions for calling the device services. These methods are discussed in the later sections. A typical code sample for using the device API to invoke the camera looks like this:

```
DeviceManager dm = DeviceManagerFactory.getDeviceManager();
dm.sendSMS("123-456-7890", "Hi there, this is a test");
```

Using the JavaScript APIs

As you learned previously, MAF applications can also use non-AMX pages, such as local HTML5 pages. Whenever these pages need to access device services, you can use the MAF JavaScript API for device interaction, which, under the covers, directly accesses the Apache Cordova API. Arguably, you could call the Apache Cordova JavaScript APIs directly, but Oracle's wrapping JavaScript APIs are designed to isolate MAF developers from any changes in the Apache Cordova APIs.

A typical JavaScript call in your own local HTML page would look as follows:

```
adf.mf.api.sendSMS({to: "1234567890", body: "Hi there, this is a test"});
```

Because in this case you are actually using Cordova more or less directly, you might want to look into the Cordova API. More information can be found at http://cordova.apache.org/docs/en/2.2.0/.

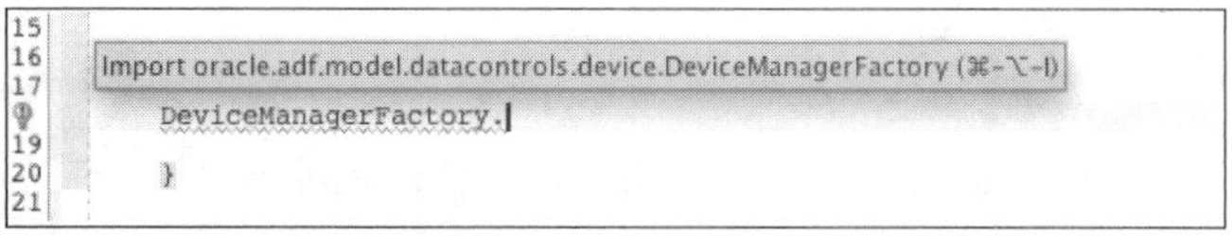

FIGURE 8-7. *Importing the DeviceManagerFactory class*

The DeviceScope Object

Besides the "real" interaction with the device features, MAF also provides the possibility to drill into the features to discover read-only information about them at run time, so you can pragmatically change the behavior of your application. As an example, you can check whether the mobile application currently has a network connection before sending an e-mail. Alternatively, you can query what the screen width is in order to determine whether you have room to show all the UI components. Another example: you can ask what platform your application is running on. To access these properties of your device and its features, MAF provides a DeviceScope object that is accessible via both an implicit EL managed bean of the same name and the relating DeviceManager singleton in Java. Table 8-1 shows what the properties include, among others.

As an example, the typical syntax of an EL expression for finding if the device has an onboard camera or not is

```
#{deviceScope.device.hasCamera}
```

Type	Property
Device	Model
	Name
	OS
	Phonegap
	Platform
	Version
Hardware	hasAccelerometer
	hasCamera
	hasCompass
	hasContacts
	hasFileAccess
	hasGeolocation
	hasLocalStorage
	hasMediaPlayer
	hasMediaRecorder
	hasTouchScreen
	networkStatus
	screen (diagonalSize, availableHeight, availableWidth, height, width, dpi, scaleFactor)

TABLE 8-1. *Available Properties*

This kind of expression can easily be used to, for instance, enable or disable device features. You can hide or show a button to invoke the camera based on the availability of the camera:

```
<amx:commandButton rendered="#{deviceScope.device.hasCamera}"/>
```

Whenever you need this information in Java, you can access the properties via the DeviceManager. As in the previous EL example, if you need to take a picture but you don't know if the device actually has a camera, you can now check via the DeviceManager.hasCamera method if a camera is available, and you might take the images from the device's album whenever there is no camera available.

```
public int getImageSource() {
    DeviceManager dm = DeviceManagerFactory.getDeviceManager();
    if(dm.hasCamera()){
        source = DeviceManager.CAMERA_SOURCETYPE_CAMERA;
    }
    else{
        source = DeviceManager.CAMERA_SOURCETYPE_PHOTOLIBRARY;
        }
        return source;
}
```

Implementing Device Interaction

Now that you have been introduced to device interaction using the data control, the Java APIs, and the JavaScript API, it is time to take a look at what specific feature operations are available. Rather than discussing the operations from the perspective of the data control, Java APIs, and JavaScript APIs separately, as the operations are pretty much the same across all three, from here on in we'll discuss the Java APIs and only deviate from this if there's a significant difference between the operations.

Interacting with the Contact List

Do you recognize this problem? You likely have several different address books containing contact information, such as that stored on your phone, your enterprise database, business cards (rolodex for that matter), contacts in the cloud—contacts, contacts everywhere! It would be extremely useful if our mobile applications allowed us to synchronize all these sources so they're all kept up to date, rather than many out-of-date disparate copies. The single source of truth in this case would be the device's contact list. Contacts from all other sources can be added to, updated, or removed from the device's contact list. This section reveals the concept of giving facilities to work with the on-device address book and explains how you can create contacts, find contacts, update contacts, and also delete contacts.

Creating Contacts

The Java API for this interaction looks like this:

```
DeviceManager dm = DeviceManagerFactory.getDeviceManager();
Contact createdContact = dm.createContact(newContact);
```

The createContact method, given a brand-new Contact object, inserts the Contact object into your device's address book, and then returns a reference to the resulting contact as it exists in the address book, including a contact ID.

The Contact object contains a number of fields, including a contactName, as well as contactFields storing phone numbers, e-mail addresses, physical addresses, and more. The following code sample shows how you can create a new contact object:

```
DeviceManager dm = DeviceManagerFactory.getDeviceManager();
Contact createdContact = dm.createContact(aContact)
```

The createContact method generates and returns a new Contact object, populated with the information that was provided when creating the new Contact.

You notice that the createContact method uses a Contact object in order for a real contact to be created. This Contact object contains a contactName, contactFields, such as phone numbers and e-mail addresses, and Address fields. The following code sample shows how you can create a new Contact object:

```
/* * Create a new contact */
Contact newContact = new Contact();
ContactName name = new ContactName();
name.setFamilyName("Doe");
name.setGivenName("John");
newContact.setName(name);
ContactField phoneNumber = new ContactField(); phoneNumber.setType("mobile");
phoneNumber.setValue("123-456-7890");
phoneNumbers = new ContactField[] { phoneNumber };
ContactField email = new ContactField();
email.setType("home");
email.setValue("john.doe@home.org" );
emails = new ContactField[] { email };
ContactAddresses address = new ContactAddresses();
address.setType("home");
address.setStreetAddress("400 Streetway");
address.setLocality("City");
address.setCountry("Netherlands");
addresses = new ContactAddresses[] { address };
newContact setNote("Extra note to be added to this address");
newContact.setPhoneNumbers(phoneNumbers);
newContact.setEmails(emails);
newContact.setAddresses(addresses);
DeviceManager dm = DeviceManagerFactory.getDeviceManager();
Contact createdContact = dm.createContact(newContact);
}
```

Finding Contacts

If you want to use contact information in your MAF application and you need to get this information from the device's address book, then you can use the findContacts method. The findContacts method requires three arguments. The first is a comma-separated list of contact fields to match. For instance, if you only want to search in the e-mails and phone numbers of a contact, you would specify "emails, phoneNumbers." The second argument is the search criterion, that is, what you are searching for, such as "John Doe," for example. The third argument specifies whether you want the first result (false) or multiple (true) matching results. By default, the method only returns the first match found.

```
findContact(){
   DeviceManager dm = DeviceManagerFactory.getDeviceManager();
   Contact[] foundContacts = dm.findContacts("emails, phoneNumbers"
                                        ,"John Doe"
                                        , false);

}
```

Updating Contacts

Updating the contact can be done in a similarly simple way. First, you need to find the contact that you want to update. Let's assume that you want to change the phone number of "John Doe." The code sample from the previous section returns one contact. Now you can work with this contact to change the phone number. After changing the phone number, call the updateContact() method to actually update the contact.

```
DeviceManager dm = DeviceManagerFactory.getDeviceManager();
foundContacts[0].getPhoneNumbers()[0].setValue("123-456-7890");
Contact updatedContact = dm.updateContact(foundContacts[0]);
```

Removing Contacts

Finally, MAF allows you to delete contacts from the address book on your device. For that, you can use the removeContact() method. The removeContact() method removes the contact that you supply.

```
DeviceManager dm = DeviceManagerFactory.getDeviceManager();
dm.removeContact(foundContacts[0]);
```

Interacting with the Camera

Nowadays virtually every mobile device comes with an onboard camera that is able to take high-quality pictures, and it provides an excellent opportunity in your mobile applications to capture images and attach them to the application's workflow, rather than just taking happy snaps of your kids. The MAF DeviceManager provides the getPicture() method.

If you use the data control and drag the getPicture operation onto your page, you will get a page that looks like the one in Figure 8-8. MAF creates input components for all of the arguments.

FIGURE 8-8. *Default getPicture screen*

The getPicture() method doesn't actually take the picture, but rather, it calls the device's picture application to do this. This is similar for the SMS and e-mails integration services too. The API for this interaction looks like this:

```
DeviceManager dm = DeviceManagerFactory.getDeviceManager();
dm.getPicture(int quality,
              int destinationType,
              int sourceType,
              boolean allowEdit,
              int encodingType,
              int targetWidth,
              int targetHeight)
```

The getPicture() method returns a String representing either base64 image data or a file URI to where the image is stored on the device, depending on the value of the destinationType parameter. Typically, if you're going to export the image over some web service, it's easier to have the data in a base64-encoded string to transmit. Alternatively, if the images will only sit on the device, then accessing them from the file URI is sufficient.

Depending on the sourceType parameter, the image is obtained by either selecting a saved image from the photo library or photo album, or from the device's camera by taking a picture itself. The method in the following code sample can be called from the command button, resulting in the camera being invoked and the image saved to the local filesystem:

```
public void getPicture(ActionEvent actionEvent){
DeviceManager dm = DeviceManagerFactory.getDeviceManager();
if (dm.hasCamera){
  String theImage = dm.getPicture(
                  100
                  ,DeviceManager.CAMERA_DESTINATIONTYPE_FILE_URI
                  ,DeviceManager.CAMERA_SOURCETYPE_CAMERA
                  , false
                  ,DeviceManager.CAMERA_ENCODINGTYPE_PNG
                  ,1000
                  ,1000);
    }
}
```

If you use DESTINATIONTYPE_DATA_URL, you will get the image as a base64-encoded string. This enables you to send the image to a remote server using a web service.

Memory Considerations

The image quality of pictures taken using the camera on newer devices is quite good, and images from the photo album will not be downscaled to a lower quality, even if a quality parameter is specified. *Encoding such images using Base64 has caused memory issues on many newer devices. Therefore, using FILE_URI as the Camera.destinationType is highly recommended.*

Taking big pictures can cause memory issues. On iOS, you should set the quality parameter to a value less than 50 to avoid memory issues. On Android, when destinationType DATA_URL is used, large images can exhaust available memory, producing an out-of-memory error, and will typically do so if the default image size is used. All parameters of the getPicture method require values except targetHeight and targetWidth, which can be null. When these are empty (or "0"), the picture is captured in its full resolution. These two parameters have the greatest impact on image size, and taking pictures with full resolution would frequently result in out-of-memory errors, even when saving to a file. Therefore, it is recommended not to leave the value for these parameters as "0." Set the targetWidth and targetHeight to constrain the image size to the lowest acceptable value. If you only need a 1-MP resolution, simply set targetWidth and targetHeight to 1000, 1000. There are many other documented quirks that can be found in the Apache Cordova documentation.

Sending Text Messages

MAF also allows you to send text messages from within your mobile application. You simply supply the phone number and the text you want to use in the message. Calling sendSMS invokes the device's SMS service with prepopulated fields for SMSto and SMSbody.

```
// Send an SMS to the phone number "1234567890"
DeviceManager dm = DeviceManagerFactory.getDeviceManager();
dm.sendSMS("1234567890", "Testing SMS functionality");
```

Sending E-mails

Sending e-mails is another option you have from within MAF. You can use all the options you have in plain e-mails, even bcc and attachments. The API for sending e-mails is, again, very straightforward. Simply supply addresses, subject, the e-mail body, and optionally, attachments. With this information, call the API, and the e-mail client on your device is invoked.

```
DeviceManager dm = DeviceManagerFactory.getDeviceManager();
dm.sendEmail(
          java.lang.String to
         ,java.lang.String cc
         ,java.lang.String subject
         ,java.lang.String body
         ,java.lang.String bcc
         ,java.lang.String attachments
         ,java.lang.String mimeTypes)
```

All parameters are Strings, but you can use a comma-separated list of addresses or attachments to use multiple addresses or to send multiple attachments. An example of a method that constructs the e-mail and then invokes the e-mail client of the mobile device is given in the following code sample. This method can be invoked from a command button.

```
public void sendEmail(ActionEvent actionEvent){
    DeviceManager dm = DeviceManagerFactory.getDeviceManager();
    String content = "I wish you all the best for next year.";
    dm.sendEmail("my.mail@company.org"
             , null
             , "Merry Xmas"
             , content
             , bcc
             , null
             , null);
```

Later in this chapter you learn how to send an e-mail with attachments.

Integrating with GPS

Location-based information is a very important feature available to mobile apps. Devices can have a GPS locator, and MAF enables you to acquire GPS information such as the device's current position. To get the current position of the device, you need to invoke the getCurrentPosition() method. Again, the device data control comes with a clear API method. This method requires two parameters. The first one is the maximum age in milliseconds for the obtained location; the second one is a Boolean indicating whether or not to use the most accurate possible method of obtaining a location fix.

```
public Location getPosition(){
    DeviceManager dm = DeviceManagerFactory.getDeviceManager();
    Location currentPosition = dm.getCurrentPosition( 60000
                                                    , true);

    return currentPosition;
}
```

The returned Location object of this method call contains information such as longitude, latitude, altitude, and speed. You can access that information in Java via the following methods:

```
currentPosition.getLatitude();
currentPosition.getLongitude();
currentPosition,getLatitude();
currentPosition.getSpeed();
```

NOTE
You can use a geolocation service like Google to convert the coordinates to an address. In Chapter 15 you will learn how to use these coordinates with Google's GeoLocation service to perform a vicinity search.

Tracking Movement
The current position is a nice thing to have, but sometimes you really need to track movement of the device. And yes, even this can be achieved with MAF.

```
DeviceManager dm = DeviceManagerFactory.getDeviceManager();
dm.startUpdatingPosition(20000, true, "MyGPSSubscriptionID", new GeolocationCallback (){
    public void locationUpdated(Location position) {
      // any kind of logic here….
}
```

The startUpdatingPosition() method is invoked and updates every 20 seconds with high accuracy. The String "MyGPSSubscriptionID" is set to identify this tracking session and can be used to stop subscribing to location updates. Finally, a GeoLocationCallback is invoked. When the device's location changes, the locationUpdated() method specified in the callBack will be invoked.

With this information, you can actually do a lot more than just plotting points.

File Display
The DeviceFeatures data control includes the displayFile method, which enables you to display files that are local to the device. Depending on the platform, application users can view PDFs, image files, Microsoft Office documents, and various other file types. The displayFile method is

only able to display files that are local to the device. This means that remote files first have to be downloaded. The following code sample shows how to download a remote file, write it to the device's application directory, and open it using the displayFile() method. The method can be invoked from a command button or command link.

```java
public void remotePreview(ActionEvent e){
    URL remoteFileUrl;
    InputStream is;
    FileOutputStream fos;
    try{
        // open connection to remote PDF file
        remoteFileUrl = new URL(
                "http://ilabs.uw.edu/sites/default/files/sample_0.pdf");

        URLConnection connection = remoteFileUrl.openConnection();
        is = connection.getInputStream();
        // we write the file to the application directory
        File localFile = new File(
            AdfmfJavaUtilities.getDirectoryPathRoot(
                    AdfmfJavaUtilities.DownloadDirectory) +
                        "/downloadedPDF.pdf");
        fos = new FileOutputStream(localFile);
        int x;
        int read = 0;
        while ((x = is.read()) != -1)
        {
            ++read;
            fos.write(x);
        }
        is.close();
        fos.close();

        // displayFile takes a URL string which has to be encoded.
        // Call a method in a utility class to do the encoding of the String

        String encodedString = MyUtils.EncodeUrlString(localFile);

        // create URL and invoke displayFile with its String representation
        URL localURL = new URL("file", "localhost", encodedString);

        DeviceManager dm = DeviceManagerFactory.getDeviceManager();
        dm.displayFile(localURL.toString(), "Preview Header");
    }
    catch (Exception f)
    {
        System.out.println("MDO - exception caught: " + f.toString());
    }
}
```

NOTE
On iOS, the application user has the option to preview supported files within the MAF application. Users can also open those files with third-party applications, e-mail them, or send them to a printer. On Android, all files are opened in third-party applications. In other words, the application user leaves the MAF application while viewing the file.

The code for the utility used in this example is as follows:

```
Public String EncodeUrlString(File localFile)
      // displayFile takes a URL string which has to be encoded.
      // iOS does not handle "+" as an encoding for space (" ") but
      // expects "%20" instead.  Also, the leading slash MUST NOT be
      // encoded to "%2F".  We will revert it to a slash after the
      // URLEncoder converts it to "%2F".
      StringBuffer buffer = new StringBuffer();
      String path = URLEncoder.encode(localFile.getPath(), "UTF-8");
      // replace "+" with "%20"
      String replacedString = "+";
      String replacement = "%20";
      int index = 0, previousIndex = 0;
      index = path.indexOf(replacedString, index);
      while (index != -1){
        buffer.append(path.substring(previousIndex,
                                      index)).append(replacement);
        previousIndex = index + 1;
        index = path.indexOf(replacedString,
                              index + replacedString.length());
      }
      buffer.append(path.substring(previousIndex, path.length()));
      // revert the leading encoded slash ("%2F") to a literal slash ("/")
      if (buffer.indexOf("%2F") == 0)
      {
        buffer.replace(0, 3, "/");
      }
    return buffer.toString();
```

Implementing Common Use Cases

Now that we know how device interactions are implemented within our MAF applications, let's investigate how to implement some common use cases.

Use Case 1 for Device Interaction: E-mail with Photo Attachment

Local citizens are always sending in e-mails, pictures, and poorly worded descriptions of pollution and litter in their local national park. These collections of information that are often received separately are hard to collate and report in the local government incident report system, and often take days to get reported. Now with your newfound MAF development skills, you can see a great opportunity to provide a mobile application allowing the general public to very quickly submit all this information through a single nifty application.

As the MAF developer, you analyze the requirements and realize you'll need to integrate the following device features: Get Picture, Get Location, and Send E-mail. Also, the words "very quickly" need to be taken into account. It would be nice if the app had just one single button or link to access all of these features. In this case, using the DeviceFeatures data control to call each feature isn't appropriate, as the user will need to touch several buttons and invoke the relating feature. In this case, to provide a quick and efficient application from the user's perspective, we need to just create a Java class and use the DeviceManager to call each method in one operation. Let's start with the first action: taking a photo of the specific area.

Take a Picture

In the section about interacting with the camera, you already learned how to invoke the camera via the Java API. Now we will use this API to take the picture. Because this picture will be attached to an e-mail, in this case, there is no need to use the DESTINATIONTYPE_DATA_URL. We need only the file location of the picture, not the String representation of the picture. It has to be a high-quality, noneditable image taken with the camera.

The getPicture() code sample given in the section "Interacting with the Camera" implements exactly these requirements. This method returns a String containing the absolute path to the file containing the picture. Later we will use this to attach the image to the e-mail.

Getting the Coordinates

The use case requires including the GPS coordinates of the area. For that, we can simply call out to the getCurrentPosition() method. No need to make this more difficult at all.

```
public Location getPosition (){
    DeviceManager dm = DeviceManagerFactory.getDeviceManager();
    Location currentPosition = dm.getCurrentPosition(60000, true);
    return currentPosition;
}
```

So with this method returning the current position, we can now use all this information in the e-mail.

Send an E-mail with Attachment

Sending the e-mail with the attachment and geolocation is something we can also do from within Java code. For that, we use a method that takes two arguments. The first is the URL of the image. The second is the current location. From the location, both latitude and longitude can be derived.

```
public void sendEmail(String attachment, Location here){
    String mailTo = "John.Doe@home.org";
    String subject = "Email with attached image and GPS coordinates" ;
    String content = "The picture was taken at the following coordinates:" +
                     " latitude=" + here.getLatitude() +
                     ", longitude=" + here.getLongitude();
    DeviceManager dm = DeviceManagerFactory.getDeviceManager();
```

```
dm.sendEmail(mailTo
            , null
            , subject
            , content
            , null
            , attachment
            , "image/jpg");
}
```

Now you need to make sure that there is one method that hooks this all up: taking the picture, deriving the location, and sending the e-mail. This method can then be invoked from the user interface.

```
public void executeLogic(ActionEvent actionEvent) {
    String att = getPicture();
    Location whereAmI = getPosition();
    sendEmail(att, whereAmI);
```

Finally, we need to enable users to call out to this method from within the MAF app itself. For that purpose, we use a command button and have the actionListener property refer to the executeLogic method described earlier.

```
<amx:commandButton text="Take Picture and send Email"
            id="cb3"
            actionListener="#{pageFlowScope.interactionBean.executeLogic}"/>
```

Now it is there. If you need to report an incident, you can open the app and immediately send an e-mail with an image attached by using a single button in the MAF app (Figure 8-9).

So to wrap it all up, when the user pushes the button, the camera is opened in order to take a picture. After taking the picture, the e-mail client is opened with addressees, subject, body, and attachment already filled out, and the user can send the e-mail without any further actions, as shown in Figure 8-10.

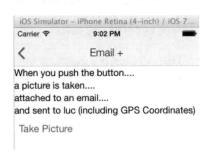

FIGURE 8-9. *Screen to invoke send e-mail*

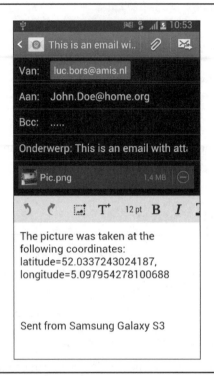

FIGURE 8-10. *Completely prepared e-mail*

Use Case 2: Tracking Your Daily Workout Session

With mobile devices that have a GPS service, you can use GPS for several purposes. One of these purposes could be tracking and tracing where the user and mobile device are located. That information can be used to track your daily workout session, so you know exactly where you ran (or skated or whatever exercise you did) and how fast you were. When you implement a track and trace solution, there are a couple of things you need to know, but the most important is location information. To be more specific, you need location information about the current position, and in order to do the actual tracking, all previous positions in the current track and trace session. The first step in implementing this use case is to find the location at a given point in time. This is not very difficult and can be achieved by invoking the startLocationMonitor method (Figure 8-11).

When you drop this method from the data control on an MAF AMX page, a methodAction binding is created in the PageDefinition file. When the user invokes this method at run time, the location monitor is started. The update interval parameter defines how often the location information is updated. One other thing that needs to be set up is a method that can be used as a location listener. This location listener is fired whenever the update interval expires. This method is implemented in a custom Java class called locationTrackingBean and hooked to the locationListener via the page definition file.

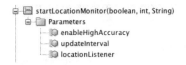

FIGURE 8-11. *StartLocationMonitor on the DeviceFeatures data control*

```xml
<methodAction id="startLocationMonitor" RequiresUpdateModel="true"
    Action="invokeMethod"
    MethodName="startLocationMonitor" IsViewObjectMethod="false"
    DataControl="DeviceFeatures"
    InstanceName="data.DeviceFeatures.dataProvider">
    <NamedData NDName="enableHighAccuracy"
            NDValue="#{pageFlowScope.locationTrackingBean.highAccuracy}"
            NDType="boolean"/>
    <NamedData NDName="updateInterval"
            NDValue="#{pageFlowScope.locationTrackingBean.updateInterval}"
            NDType="int"/>
    <NamedData NDName="locationListener"
            NDValue="pageFlowScope.locationTrackingBean.locationUpdated"
            NDType="java.lang.String"/>
</methodAction>
```

NOTE
NDValue is usually set based on EL expressions. The preceding code sample shows that all NDValue settings use an EL expression, except for locationListener, which does not use an EL expression. There is no obvious reason for this. At the time of writing, a bug has been filed and the issue should be resolved in future versions.

The startLocationMonitor is invoked via a button on the page. If you click the button, the tracking starts. When you run the app and start the GPS Locator for the first time, you need to allow the app to use your current location. On iOS, this shows up as a message, as displayed in Figure 8-12.

> "ch11GPS" Would Like to Use
> Your Current Location
>
> Don't Allow   OK

FIGURE 8-12. *Allow access to GPS*

When the update interval expires, the new GPS information is forwarded to the locationUpdated method, which stores the location information in memory.

The locationListener method takes the current location as an argument.

```
public void locationUpdated(Location currentLocation) {
    this.setLatitude(currentLocation.getLatitude());
    this.setLongitude(currentLocation.getLongitude());
    this.setSpeed(currentLocation.getSpeed());
    this.setWatchId(currentLocation.getWatchId());
    MethodExpression me = AdfmfJavaUtilities.getMethodExpression(
                          "#{bindings.ExecuteGetPosition.execute}",
                          Object.class, new Class[] {});
    me.invoke(AdfmfJavaUtilities.getAdfELContext(), new Object[] {});
}
```

Once you start moving, you will see the changes of coordinates and speed displayed on the page (Figure 8-13).

FIGURE 8-13. *Current location and speed*

For storing the coordinates and speed in memory, a custom object called CustomLocation is used. This class contains *x* and *y* coordinates as well as speed.

```
public class CustomLocation {
    double x = 5.10;
    double y = 52.00;
    double speed=0;
    ......
```

When the interval expires, a new location is added to a map of points, containing all the points in the current trace session.

```
public void Execute() {
    CustomLocation p = new CustomLocation();
    ValueExpression lat = AdfmfJavaUtilities.getValueExpression(
            "#{pageFlowScope.LocationTrackingBean.latitude}", Double.class);
    double y = ((Double)lat.getValue(
                    AdfmfJavaUtilities.getAdfELContext())).doubleValue();
    ValueExpression lng = AdfmfJavaUtilities.getValueExpression(
            "#{pageFlowScope.LocationTrackingBean.longitude}", Double.class);
    double x = ((Double)lng.getValue(
                    AdfmfJavaUtilities.getAdfELContext())).doubleValue();
    ValueExpression sp = AdfmfJavaUtilities.getValueExpression(
            "#{pageFlowScope.LocationTrackingBean.speed}", Double.class);
    double speed = ((Double)sp.getValue(
                    AdfmfJavaUtilities.getAdfELContext())).doubleValue();
    p.setX(x);
    p.setY(y);
    p.setSpeed(speed);
    points.add(p);
}
```

At the end of the tracking session, all points of the trip are available and can be plotted on a map (Figure 8-14) so you can see exactly where you were and how fast you were traveling. If you want to stop tracking, which you should do after a while to prevent your device from going flat, you can call clearWatchPosition():

```
DeviceManagerFactory().getDeviceManager().clearWatchPosition(getWatchId());
```

NOTE
Obviously, this only works if there is GPS available. If there is no GPS available, the user should be informed to either activate the GPS feature via their device's setting or not to use this functionality. This can be achieved to call the method from Java instead of invoking it directly from the button. So instead of coding
```
actionListener="#{bindings.startLocationMonitor.execute}"
```
you would use something like
```
actionListener="#{pageFlowScope.LocationTrackingBean
.startGPSifAvailable}"
```
Another option is, of course, to disable the button if there is no GPS available.
```
disabled="#{!deviceScope.device.hasGeoLocation}"
```

FIGURE 8-14. *Points plotted on a map*

Use Case 3 for Device Interaction: Creating a Custom Contacts App

When you have all your contacts in the device's contacts database, you need to open the contacts application on your device each and every time you want to access contact data. It would be more convenient to have access to these contacts directly from within your MAF app. In the MAF app, you want to have access to all contacts, search within the contacts, and display these contacts in a list. After selecting one of the contacts, you want to see all details. Given the use case, you need to create a list, displaying all contacts on your device, with the possibility to search. On selecting one of the found contacts, we want to navigate from the list to a detail page where you can browse the address details of a selected contact.

Creating the Search Page

Searching contacts is fairly easy and can be implemented by invoking the findContacts method. You can drag and drop this method on an MAF page. When you drop it as a parameter form (Figure 8-15), you already end up with a working search page. You have a button to execute the findContacts, and there are input components for search criteria and contact fields.

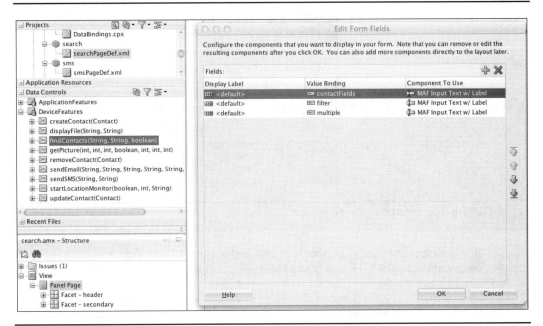

FIGURE 8-15. *Creating the search contacts page*

To store search criteria in memory in order to have them available in all pages of this contact app, you can create a pageFlow scoped bean. That bean contains variables for all search criteria used in the app.

```
public class ContactBean {
    String contactFields = "birthday,displayname,id,nickname,note,addresses,ca
tegories,emails,ims,
name,organizations,phoneNumbers,photos,urls";
    String filter = "";
    boolean multiple = true;
```

Now instead of retrieving and setting the value via the binding layer, we use the variable in the managed bean. So the search page now ends up looking like this. Note the references to the pageFlowScope variables.

```
<amx:panelFormLayout id="pfl1">
    <amx:inputText label="Contact Fields" id="confields"
                   value="#{pageFlowScope.ContactBean.contactFields}"
                   hintText="List the contact fields returned"/>
    <amx:inputText label="Filter" id="filter"
                   value="#{pageFlowScope.ContactBean.filter}"
                   hintText="String to search for"/>
    <amx:selectBooleanSwitch label="Multiple" id="multiple"
                             value="#{pageFlowScope.ContactBean.multiple}"
                             offLabel="No" onLabel="Yes"/>
</amx:panelFormLayout>
```

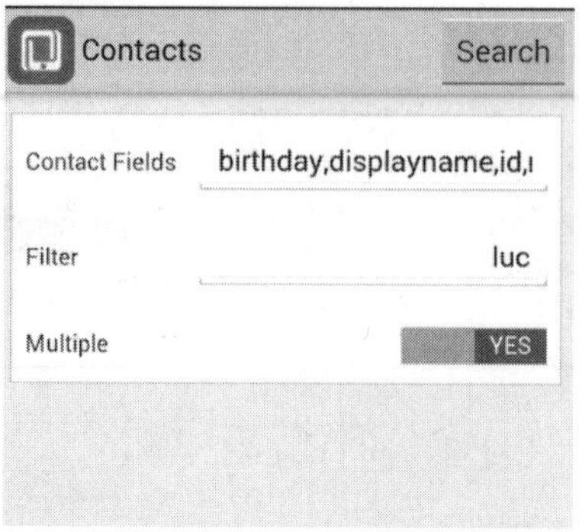

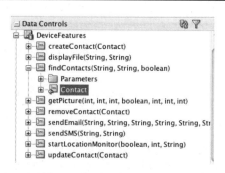

FIGURE 8-16. *Search contacts for "luc"*

That is all that's needed to be able to search and retrieve all your device's contacts in your MAF application. Figure 8-16 shows an MAF application that enables you to search contacts containing the string "luc."

Next we can create the list page displaying the search results. It is very simple. Just drag the result of the findContacts operation (which is Contact, as you can see in Figure 8-17) and drop it on the list page.

When you drop the operation and select the List View, you will be prompted to provide values for the parameters of the operation. By setting these to the pageFlowScope variables (Figure 8-18), we make sure that the results page uses exactly the same parameters as the ones that were entered on the first page.

After pressing OK in the Edit Action Binding dialog, you will then be prompted via the Edit List View dialog to select which elements to show in the list (Figure 8-19).

Ensure that the Single Item option for the List Item Selection radio group is also selected. Upon selecting OK, you will then be prompted to confirm the device permissions for the application to access the device's contacts (Figure 8-20).

FIGURE 8-17. *Drag and drop the result.*

FIGURE 8-18. *Setting the search parameters*

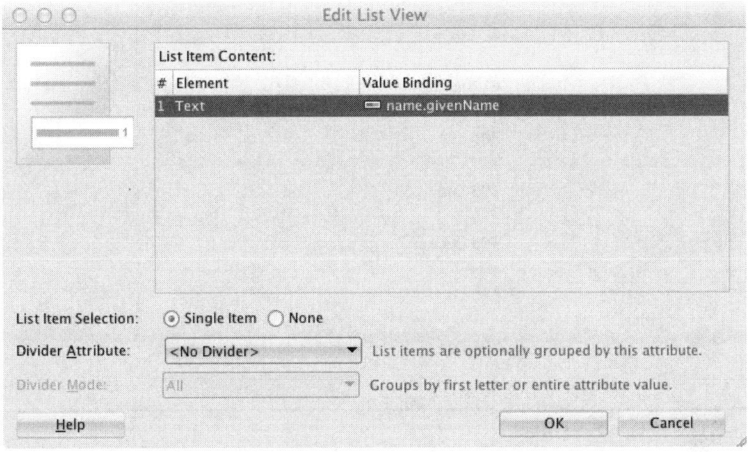

FIGURE 8-19. *Edit Contacts List View*

FIGURE 8-20. *Granting access to contacts*

When you open the results page, the expected search results are shown (Figure 8-21) because the findContacts operation was invoked using the parameters entered on the search page.

The final step is to create a page containing details for the selected contact. This actually works more or less the same as with the search results page. There are two small differences. Let's take a look.

The first difference is that we do not want to display the selected contact as a list, but as a single contact. So we do not drop the contact from the data control on to the page as a list, but one by one we add the fields as simple input text components. Again, when you drop the first field, MAF needs you to enter the argument values for the findContacts operation. This can be done exactly the same as previously (see Figure 8-18). Other information, such as e-mail addresses, which are a collection, can be dropped as a list. Because these are a result of the already configured findContacts operation, there is no need for extra configuration.

	Results
23 Luc	
61 luc	
300 Luc	
495 Luc	
496 Lucas	
585 Luc	
586 Luc	

FIGURE 8-21. *Search results*

The second difference is that we do not want to be on the first row of the search results. We only want to display that one single contact that was selected from the list page.

```
<amx:listView var="row" value="#{bindings.Contact.collectionModel}"
               fetchSize="#{bindings.Contact.rangeSize}"
               selectedRowKeys="#{bindings.Contact.collectionModel.selectedRow}"
               selectionListener="#{bindings.Contact.collectionModel.makeCurrent}"
               showMoreStrategy="autoScroll"
               bufferStrategy="viewport" id="lv1">
    <amx:listItem id="li1">
       <amx:outputText value="#{row.name.bindings.givenName.inputValue}" id="ot2"/>
    </amx:listItem>
</amx:listView>
```

The SelectionListener will make sure that the selected row is made the current row in the Contact iterator. If the details page uses the same iterator, it shows exactly the same contact that was selected on the list page. When the details page (Figure 8-22) is opened, the details of the selected contact are displayed.

You have created your own address book inside your MAF app.

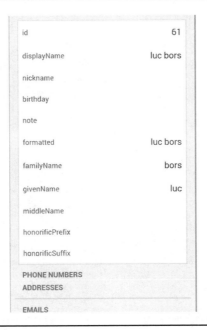

FIGURE 8-22. *Contact details*

Summary

Using device interaction enables you to really make the app stand out from what you would have done with a regular desktop application. With MAF, you are able to reach out to the device and use the services available, to allow the user to get contextual information on where they are, take pictures, share and access contacts, send e-mails and SMS, and more. By knowing and using the APIs, you have full control and flexibility on how and when you want to interact with the device and how to handle errors or other unexpected situations. Note that MAF ships with a deviceDemo sample app that you can reference for additional samples.

In this chapter you have learned how to

- Understand the available mechanisms to implement device interaction
- Use the device data control
- Use the APIs
- Recognize common use cases for device interaction and implement them with MAF

CHAPTER
9

Debugging and Testing Oracle Mobile Application Framework Applications

Testing and debugging your newly developed MAF application is probably one of the most important keys to success. Although testing can be expensive and time-consuming, it is definitely needed to ensure that your consumers have a positive user experience when they use your app. Mobile users are notoriously fickle, and if your application fails or crashes, you may simply lose them forever as they vent their frustrations by deleting your app and moving to a competitor's.

The actual testing process of a mobile application is a process by which the mobile app is tested for its functionality, usability, and consistency.

This chapter describes the techniques you can use to test and debug your MAF application

Testing Strategies for Mobile Applications

The biggest mobile testing challenge is that there are many different devices that could use your app, and all of them must be considered when testing your mobile application. Whenever you choose to reduce the number of devices, you are taking a chance that your application might not work on a device, locking out a number of potential groups of users. To handle the device challenge, you have two options: You can test using real devices, or you can test using emulated devices.

Testing on Real Devices or Using Emulators/Simulators

The advantages of using real devices for testing are obvious. Real devices have all of the limitations and quirks present in the actual client hardware. Also, it is possible to work with hardware exceptions such as low battery, power-offs, insufficient memory, and others.

There are, however, some disadvantages. Testing with real devices can be very expensive. Imagine that you have to buy all the devices that your app supports. Also, real devices are not

Difference Between Simulator and Emulator

You might have noticed we have the iOS Simulator and the Android Emulator. What's the difference between a simulator and emulator? From your point of view as a mobile developer, not a lot. They are both designed to allow you to test your applications on your PC or Mac without requiring a real mobile device to deploy to.

There are some distinct differences under the hood between Apple's simulator and Android's emulator. As mentioned in earlier chapters, the Android Emulator is incredibly slow unless you install the Intel HAXM drivers. This is because Google has designed the emulator to not cheat at all; it runs your application's Android code on the full Android stack, the Linux kernel, Android system image, and more on top of the QEMU emulator running ARM code translated back into instructions for your PC or Mac.

Conversely, when deploying to the iOS Simulator, the application is compiled not in iOS bytecode, but recompiled to native x86 code to run on your PC or Mac. As the code is natively compiled for your PC or Mac, it runs much faster than the Android Emulator equivalent.

Which is better for testing purposes? Well, we want testing to be as fast as possible, so the iOS Simulator wins. But we want the tested code to be tested on a platform that matches the end-device platform as closely as possible, so Android wins. As you can see, it's swings and roundabouts; both have advantages over the other, and the end result is that you test on both.

In Chapter 2 you already learned how to install and configure Android-Emulated devices and the iOS Simulator.

designed with testing in mind. Due to their limited processing power and storage, this does not always allow on-board diagnostic software to be loaded.

Device emulation also has several advantages. Emulated devices are easier to manage, and it is simple to switch between device types by simply loading a new device profile or selecting a new simulated device. Usually, emulators run on more powerful machines and emulators are designed with testing in mind. Emulation is also very cost-effective. There is no need to buy the actual device if you can simulate it. Obviously, the big disadvantage of emulated devices is the lack of the quirks and faults that only the real device can provide, and you can only work with hardware exceptions to some extent. In addition, many device services such as cameras cannot be fully emulated.

Because of the advantages and disadvantages of both options, typically, a combination of both approaches yields the best results.

Testing an Oracle Mobile Application Framework Application

Testing typically involves several stages. First, you as a developer will have to test the application technically in order to make sure there are no obvious bugs in the application before you release it for functional testing. In this stage, you can use unit testing. During functional testing, the app will be deployed to multiple devices, either real or emulated/simulated, in order to make sure that the app has no platform-specific bugs. Finally, you can choose to distribute the app to a group of users specifically selected to perform the final acceptance testing. Usually, this last kind of test should not produce any more big issues, and you should be able to publish your app soon after this stage has finished.

Unit Testing Oracle Mobile Application Framework Applications

Unit testing typically involves the creation and running of Java test code that invokes the actual Java code that is part of your MAF application. Creating and running unit tests contributes to code quality and helps you to build stable and reliable MAF applications. You can use the JDeveloper "Check for Updates" feature to download and install the JUnit Integration extension.

Once the extension is installed, you can create new unit tests for the Java classes in your MAF application.

NOTE
When you create a new unit test, make sure that you select JUnit 3.8x as test type. This is a requirement because JUnit 4.0 requires JDK 5.0 and MAF at the moment this book is released uses Java 1.4.

After your unit tests have been created, you can run the tests and check the outcome in the JDeveloper JUnit Test Runner Log console.

Debugging an Oracle Mobile Application Framework Application

During the testing of the MAF application, you will probably find several bugs. Remember, the goal of testing is to find bugs in order to make your application more stable. The goal of testing certainly isn't to prove that your application has no bugs; that's just blinding you to the job of finding bugs.

Once you identify a bug, typically you then need to analyze the bug and your code to work out what's going wrong with your application. To assist you with this process, JDeveloper provides the ability to debug your MAF applications with a modern debugger built into the IDE.

In order to debug an MAF application, it must be deployed in debug mode. This is because debug mode allows for inclusion of special debugging libraries and symbols at compile time that the IDE can connect to and interpret.

Configure Debug Mode

In order to debug your MAF application, you must directly debug against the Java Virtual Machine (JVM) that runs the MAF application. The JDeveloper debugger can be used to connect to the JVM instance on a mobile device or simulator and control the Java portions of your deployed MAF application.

In order to actually debug the application, you must change some settings in the JVM configuration file. This file, cvm.properties, can be used to configure the application startup and heap space size, as well as Java and JavaScript debugging options.

The file can be found in the application resources' META-INF directory as you can see in Figure 9-1.

When you open this file, you will see the setting for Java debugging. The "debug.enabled" setting should be set to true if you want to be able to debug the application.

```
# Java debugging settings
java.debug.enabled=true
```

There is a second debug-related setting in this file. This setting can be used to set the port number that should be used for debugging. This setting defaults to 8000.

```
# Specifies the integer value of the port to use during debugging
java.debug.port=8000
```

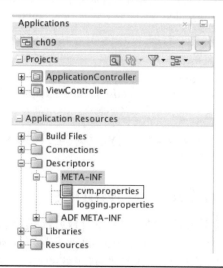

FIGURE 9-1. *The location of the cvm.properties file*

The specified port number should match the one that is set in the "run configuration" settings. Those settings can be accessed in the Project Preferences under the Run/Debug node. You can enter the Edit Run Configuration dialog (Figure 9-2) where you can set the port number. When you change the port number in either file, make sure that you adjust it in the other file.

In addition, there are other important settings to configure.

The selected protocol defines whether you want to listen to or to attach to JDPA.

NOTE
A JPDA Transport is a method of communication between a debugger and the virtual machine that is being debugged (hereafter the target VM). The communication is connection-oriented—one side acts as a server (our MAF application in this case) and listens for a connection. The other side acts as a client (the JDeveloper IDE in our example) and connects to the server. JPDA allows either the debugger application or the target VM to act as the server. Transport implementations can allow communications between processes running on a single machine, on different machines, or either.

For debugging MAF applications, you want to attach to the JVM that is part of your MAF application. This JVM will be listening for JDeveloper to attach. Once that process is completed, you can start debugging.

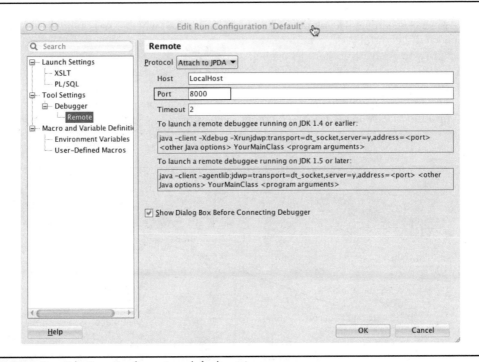

FIGURE 9-2. *Edit Run Configuration default settings*

The host refers to the address of the server that hosts the JVM. For emulation and simulation, this is Localhost, or the corresponding IP address. If you want to debug an application that is running on an actual device, you must enter the device's IP address. The timeout setting specifies the timeout, in seconds, to wait for the debugger to attach. The check box Show Dialog Box Before Connecting Debugger speaks for itself.

Start a Debug Session

When all configurations are in place, you can now start a debug session. In order to do this, you must first deploy the MAF application in debug mode. If the deployment is complete, you can start debugging.

The first step in a debug session is to open the application that you want to debug on the device or in a simulator/emulator. The JVM is started and will wait for the debugger to attach. The next step is to start a debug session in JDeveloper by invoking the debug icon from the toolbar as you can see in Figure 9-3, or by starting a debug session from the Run menu.

If the check box Show Dialog Box Before Connecting Debugger in the run configuration was checked, JDeveloper shows you a dialog (Figure 9-4) when you try to connect to the debugger. In this debugger you can change the settings that were configured in the Edit Run Configuration dialog.

After you click OK, the debug session is started.

NOTE
A timeout can occur on either side. If you wait too long with attaching to the JVM, the JVM will time out. If you wait too long with starting the MAF application on the device, the debugger in JDeveloper will time out.

You can see in the JDeveloper Log console (Figure 9-5) whether or not the debugger connected successfully.

Now you are ready to start debugging.

TIP
An MAF application that is running in debug mode can be recognized by a red triangle in the upper-left corner (Figure 9-6).

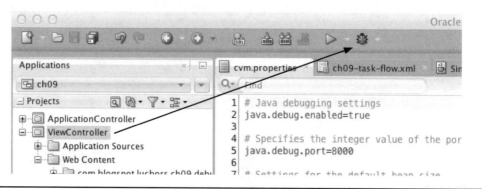

FIGURE 9-3. *Starting the debugger*

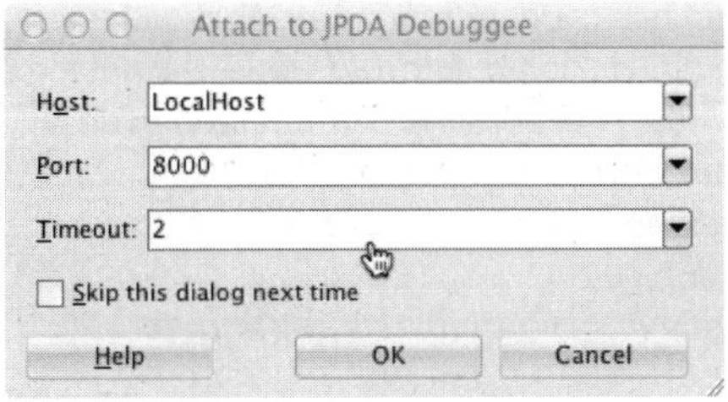

FIGURE 9-4. *Attach to JPDA Debuggee dialog*

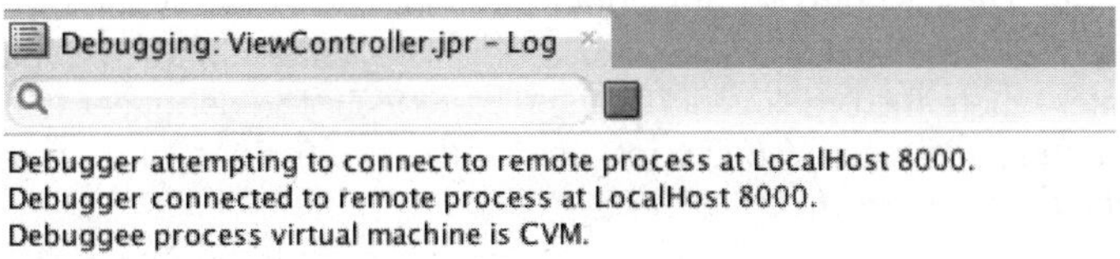

FIGURE 9-5. *Debug Log console*

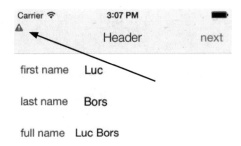

FIGURE 9-6. *A red triangle visible in debug mode*

NOTE
If you want to debug Java code, either on an Android-powered device connected through USB or on an Android-powered device emulator, you need to forward the TCP port. This can be achieved by executing the following command on a terminal.
For the device debugging, you must use option -d:
```
adb -d forward tcp:8000 tcp:8000
```
For the emulator debugging, you must use option -e:
```
adb -e forward tcp:8000 tcp:8000
```

Using Breakpoints to Debug Java Code

When the debug session is running, you can use the app at your convenience. The actual debugging depends on the breakpoints you set in JDeveloper.

You can set a breakpoint at a line of Java code by clicking in the left margin of the code editor window. The line of code will be highlighted in pink, and a red dot appears in the left margin.

JDeveloper enables you to set breakpoints in your Java code. When running in debug mode, program execution proceeds up to the breakpoint. The red dot in the left margin of the source editor indicates where the break is occurring (Figure 9-7). The debugger window opens and displays the debugging trace. You can inspect values, expressions, and find other information relevant to the debug session.

```java
package com.blogspot.lucbors.ch09.view.beans;

import ...;

public class SimpleBean {

    private String firstName;
    private PropertyChangeSupport propertyChangeSupport = new PropertyChangeSupport(this);

    public void setFirstName(String firstName) {
        Trace.log(Utility.ApplicationLogger,
                Level.INFO,
                SimpleBean.class,
                "setFirstName",
                "firstName= "+firstName);

        String oldFirstName = this.firstName;
        this.firstName = firstName;
        propertyChangeSupport.firePropertyChange("firstName", oldFirstName, firstName);

        setFullName(this.firstName + " "+ this.lastName);

    }
```

FIGURE 9-7. *Execution stops at a breakpoint.*

You can use JDeveloper to step through the code line by line and also step into the code of called Java methods in other classes. This enables you to get full insight into the execution of your Java code.

The Oracle JDeveloper Debugger

When you use the debugger in JDeveloper, you have many options to step through code, inspect values, and work with breakpoints. As you can see in Figure 9-8, the debug toolbar contains several buttons that can be used during debugging. The most important buttons in the context of MAF debugging are

- **3 Step over** The called method will be executed, but the debugger will continue at the next line of code in the caller.

- **4 Step into** The debugger opens the called method on the current line, and you will be able to step through the code of the called method in turn.

- **5 Step out** The debugger completes the current method and steps out of the method and resumes execution at the line immediately after the method call in the caller.

- **6 Step to end** Executes the current method entirely, but stops at the last line so you can see the result.

- **7 Resume** Resumes program execution until the next breakpoint.

During a debug session, you can inspect values of properties in the Java class. When you hover the mouse over the property as shown in Figure 9-9, the value of the property will be shown.

One other way to inspect values is to use CTRL-I. This opens a popup where you can enter the name of the property whose value you want to inspect.

TIP
The debugger can be configured in the JDeveloper Preferences, in the Debugger node.

Refer to the JDeveloper help for more details on how to use the debugger in JDeveloper.

Debug JavaScript

The cvm.properties file can also be used to enable and configure JavaScript logging.

First, you need to set javascript.debug.enabled: This setting enables or disables JavaScript debugging when the application is running in the device simulator. Valid values are true and false.

The next setting is the javascript.debug.feature: This specifies the application feature that is to trigger the activation of JavaScript debugging in MAF. The format of the value is featureId:port. The port must be specified (it is initially set to a placeholder value).

FIGURE 9-8. *The JDeveloper debug toolbar*

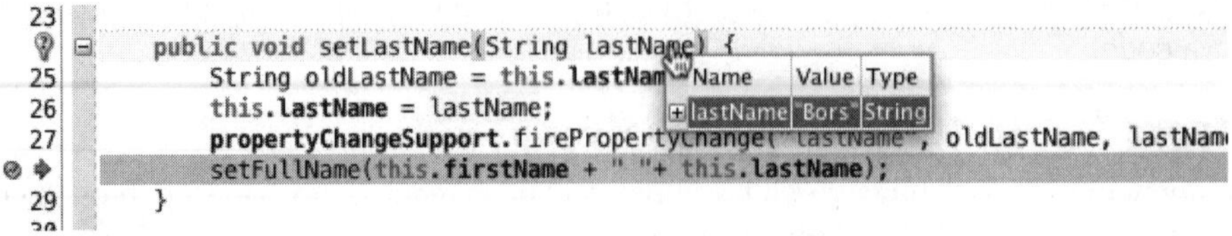

```
23    public void setLastName(String lastName) {
25        String oldLastName = this.lastName;
26        this.lastName = lastName;
27        propertyChangeSupport.firePropertyChange("lastName", oldLastName, lastName
          setFullName(this.firstName + " "+ this.lastName);
29    }
```

| Name | Value | Type |
| lastName | Bors | String |

FIGURE 9-9. *Inspect values by hovering.*

For the sample app in this chapter, the valid settings would be:

```
javascript.debug.enabled=true
javascript.debug.feature=com.blogspot.lucbors.ch09.debugFeature:9999
```

After configuring the MAF application for JavaScript debugging, you need to set up the tools that you can use for the actual JavaScript debugging. This is different for iOS and Android, and in the next sections you will learn how to make the configurations that help you with JavaScript debugging on both platforms.

JavaScript Debugging on iOS

If you are working with the iOS 6 platform, you can use the Safari 6 browser to debug JavaScript. To do so, open the Safari preferences, select Advanced, and then enable the Develop menu in the browser by selecting the "Show Develop menu in menu bar" check box, as shown in Figure 9-10.

FIGURE 9-10. *Enable the Safari Develop menu in Advanced Preferences.*

FIGURE 9-11. *Access the Developer tools from Safari.*

If you now start the MAF application to the iOS Simulator, you can access the Developer tools (Web Inspector) to debug the MAF application from the Safari Develop menu (Figure 9-11). Select either iPhone Simulator or iPad Simulator, depending on which device simulator is launched. Simply select a UIWebView that you are planning to debug.

The select UIWebView opens in the Web Inspector where you have access to CSS, HTML, and JavaScript. You can select the JavaScript file that you want to debug and set breakpoints in the code. Next, simply open the debugger by clicking the Debugger icon as shown in Figure 9-12, and step through the code to debug it.

JavaScript Debugging on Android

Google, like Apple, has similar debugging capabilities and, as with Apple, where you need to use Safari to connect to the iOS Simulator, Android developers need to use Chrome. Using "chrome:// inspect" (Figure 9-13), developers can gain access to the running emulators or connected devices.

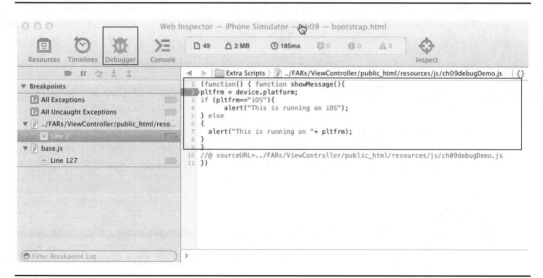

FIGURE 9-12. *Debugging JavaScript on iOS using the Web Inspector debugger*

FIGURE 9-13. *Using Chrome://inspect to get emulated and connected devices*

It even simplifies setting up port forwarding if you want to debug your application by providing direct access to the Android Debug Bridge (adb) forward tcp option, which can be changed in the browser. The full documentation can be found at the Google developers' web site, https://developers.google.com/chrome-developer-tools/.

With this set up, you can debug the JavaScript of a running MAF application from within the Google Chrome browser. Simply deploy and launch your application on the device or emulator, start Google Chrome, and navigate to chrome://inspect. This will bring up the DevTools main page, from where you can select devices and check "Discover USB devices" for actual device debugging.

NOTE
If the device asks to allow access to the Development PC, confirm this and continue.

Once you get DevTools connected to your application, you will see the list of emulators or devices and the current list of views that can be inspected. Select "inspect" for the page you want to debug, and now you can debug the HTML, CSS, and also the JavaScript, as you can see in Figure 9-14.

Logging

The concept of instrumenting your code, that is, adding explicit code to produce logs, is an important aid to debugging applications, including mobile applications. Too often, logging is only added to an application when it is too late. It is better to make the implementation of logging part of your development process. It helps you in two ways. First, it is very valuable during debugging. You can run your code without the need of breakpoints, and after the run, you can analyze your log to get an overview of all called classes and methods. It also allows you to pinpoint possible

FIGURE 9-14. *Debugging JavaScript on Android*

areas where problems occur. The second important aspect of logging is monitoring. MAF ships with several logger utilities that you can use for this purpose.

Configure and Using Logging in MAF

The class oracle.adfmf.util.Utility in the Utils package of the MAF API provides the key logger and the name to instantiate a logger.

```
Logger logger = Utility.ApplcationLogger ;
String logger name = Utility.APP_LOGNAME ;
```

There are three packages available for the logger. Their names already tell the purpose of these loggers:

- **oracle.adfmf.application**   Application Logger: Used for MAF application logging.
- **oracle.adfmf.framework**   Framework Logger: Displays log entries that are executed while running MAF features.
- **oracle.adfmf.performance**   Performance Logger: This logger is used to measure values, such as execution time of a method.

These three loggers are very useful and can be configured differently in the logging.properties file. The file can be found in the Application Resources (Figure 9-15), and holds configurations for what console handler is used and for what level logging is performed.

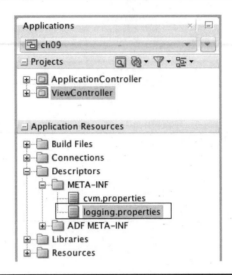

FIGURE 9-15. *The logging.properties file in Application Resources*

The logging.properties file is added to your MAF application automatically. The default contents of this file are displayed in the following code sample:

```
# default all loggers to use the ConsoleHandler
  .handlers=com.sun.util.logging.ConsoleHandler
# default all loggers to use the SimpleFormatter
  .formatter=com.sun.util.logging.SimpleFormatter
# default ConsoleHandler logging level to SEVERE
  oracle.adfmf.util.logging.ConsoleHandler.level=SEVERE
  oracle.adfmf.util.logging.ConsoleHandler.formatter=
                  oracle.adfmf.util.logging.PatternFormatter
  oracle.adfmf.util.logging.PatternFormatter.pattern=
              [%LEVEL% - %LOGGER% - %CLASS% - %METHOD%] %MESSAGE%

#configure the framework logger to only use the adfmf ConsoleHandler
  oracle.adfmf.framework.useParentHandlers=false
  oracle.adfmf.framework.handlers=oracle.adfmf.util.logging.ConsoleHandler
  oracle.adfmf.framework.level=SEVERE
#configure the application logger to only use the adfmf ConsoleHandler
  oracle.adfmf.application.useParentHandlers=false
  oracle.adfmf.application.handlers=oracle.adfmf.util.logging.ConsoleHandler
  oracle.adfmf.application.level=SEVERE
```

There is one more class that you can use for logging in MAF. This is the oracle.adfmf.util .logging.Trace class. It takes in the overloaded method log (...), a logger, and the information for the log entry and performs logging. An example for the use of the Trace class can be found in the following code sample. It holds an entry for INFO level and SEVERE level. Depending on the configuration of the ConsoleHandler level in the logging.properties file, these log entries will appear in your log file.

```
public void setFullName(String fullName) {
    Trace.log(Utility.ApplicationLogger,
            Level.INFO,
            SimpleBean.class,
            "setFullName",
            "fullName= "+fullName);
        String oldFullName = this.fullName;
        this.fullName = fullName;
        propertyChangeSupport.firePropertyChange("fullName", oldFullName, fullName);
        if (this.lastName==null){
            Trace.log(Utility.ApplicationLogger,
                    Level.SEVERE,
                    SimpleBean.class,
                    "setFullName",
                    "lastName is empty" );
    }
}
```

NOTE
When selecting the amount of verbosity for a logging level, keep in mind that increasing the verbosity of the output at the SEVERE, WARNING, and INFO levels negatively affects performance of your application.

View Logging Output

There is a difference in how to view logging on iOS and Android. Accessing log files on both platforms is explained in the next two sections.

Viewing the iOS Log   When you use the iOS Simulator on Mac OS X, your log file is typically found at the following location:

```
/Users/<userid>/Library/Application Support/iPhone
Simulator/<version>/Applications/<AppID>/Documents/logs/application.log
```

You can open and inspect the log file from within a terminal window (Figure 9-16).

TIP
If you use a terminal window to navigate to this location, you must use either double quotes (") or single quotes ('). Otherwise, the spaces in /Application Support/iPhone Simulator/ prevent you from opening this location.

```
○ ○ ○                           logs — vim — 105×16
2014-07-18 10:57:18.111 ch09[27554:e03] Redirected stderr to: /Users/lucbors/Library/Application Support/
iPhone Simulator/7.1/Applications/com.company.ch09/Documents/logs/application.log
2014-07-18 10:57:18.115 ch09[27554:e03] Reachability Flag Status: -R -----l- networkStatusForFlags
2014-07-18 10:57:18.360 ch09[27554:70b] Multi-tasking -> Device: YES, App: YES
2014-07-18 10:57:18.736 ch09[27554:70b] [LOG] Back Channel Hidden Feature: Received Event: deviceready
2014-07-18 10:57:18.738 ch09[27554:70b] [LOG] Back Channel Hidden Feature - Startup is complete.
2014-07-18 10:57:18.747 ch09[27554:70b] Multi-tasking -> Device: YES, App: YES
Jul 18, 2014 10:57:38 AM com.blogspot.lucbors.ch09.view.beans.SimpleBean setFullName
SEVERE: lastName is empty
Jul 18, 2014 10:58:13 AM com.blogspot.lucbors.ch09.view.beans.SimpleBean setFullName
SEVERE: lastName is empty
2014-07-18 10:59:59.357 ch09[27554:70b] active
~
~
~
```

FIGURE 9-16. *Viewing the iOS Simulator log*

As you can see from the first line in the preceding log file example, the log statements are redirected to the application.log file.

Using Xcode to Prevent Redirecting the Log   There is also the possibility to view the log statements in the console. This, however, is not default behavior. To achieve this, you must use Xcode.

First, you must open your Xcode project called Oracle_ADFmc_Container_Template .xcodeproj. This project is created during deployment to the iOS Simulator and can be found in your deployment directory as can be seen from Figure 9-17.

When you double-click this project, Xcode opens your app and you can inspect it. The next step is to change the scheme settings for your application in Xcode so that log statements are no longer redirected to a log file, but displayed in the console in real time.

From the Product menu | Scheme | Edit Scheme add the following argument to be passed on launch:

```
-consoleRedirect=FALSE
```

FIGURE 9-17.   *The temporary Xcode project in the deploy folder*

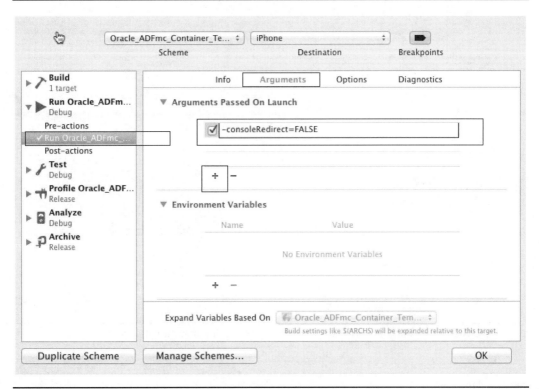

FIGURE 9-18.   *Changed scheme in Xcode to no longer redirect output*

Figure 9-18 shows the Xcode setting.

When you now run the app from within Xcode, the log messages are visible in the console in Xcode.

Viewing the Android Log   When you use Android, the log can be analyzed using the debug monitor. The debug monitor can be started by invoking the "monitor" executable. The monitor is found in the android-sdk\tools directory. You can use the monitor to inspect log files of both connected devices and emulated devices. Figure 9-19 shows the monitor displaying the log for the demo application of this chapter.

The monitor enables you to filter log files for specific strings, process IDs, or other identifiers. These filters can be saved and applied at your convenience.

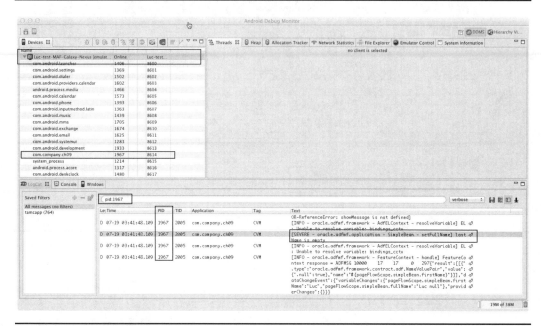

FIGURE 9-19. *The Android debug monitor showing log message for an MAF application*

TIP
You can optionally set your application as a "Debugging Application" by going to your device Settings | Developer options | Select debug app, and then selecting the Oracle MAF application you want to debug. All applications compiled in debug mode will show up here. This will allow you to select the MAF application process in the Android Debug Monitor application and perform additional debugging. This most likely will provide you with much more info than you will ever want (or care) to know.

JavaScript Logging
You can also instruct MAF to produce a JavaScript log statement. You can use the following statement in your JavaScript function to write a log message to the log file:

```
console.log("<your log message here>")
```

This produces a log message. Other options are console.error, console.warning, and console .info to produce messages with a specific severity. You can also produce log statements that provide more info and are configurable through the logging.properties file.

To make use of these properties defined in the logging file, you need to use the adf.mf.log package and the application logger that it provides. You can then issue log statements pretty much the same way as explained previously for the Java logging.

```
adf.mf.log.Application.logp(adf.mf.log.level.WARNING,
                           "<JavaScriptFile>",
                           "<JavaScriptFunction>",
                           "<Specific message text>");
```

Summary

Testing and debugging of an MAF application is probably one the most important keys to success. A thoroughly tested application will result in happy users. The process of testing and debugging involves several phases. These can be executed on either real devices or simulated/emulated devices. During this testing, log statements can provide valuable information for developers to debug their application.

In this chapter you learned

- How to test your MAF application
- How to debug your MAF application
- How to work with logging
- How to use the Android Emulator
- How to use the iOS Simulator

CHAPTER
10

Security and Deployment

In the previous chapters you learned to understand the different parts of the Mobile Application Framework, and by now you know how to develop a mobile application with MAF. Two important concepts of MAF have not been discussed yet. The first is security. A mobile application without security is like leaving your doors unlocked and open to burglars. Oracle MAF provides you with several mechanisms to easily secure your application in mostly declarative ways, thus ensuring only authorized use of the app and its corresponding data. Security is a wide topic that deserves a book on itself. In this book, you will learn how to set up security in the MAF application. Note that security usually also needs a server-side implementation. This is out of the scope of this book. The first part of this chapter explains how to secure your mobile application.

The second concept is deployment. After building and securing an app, it needs to actually get deployed to the physical mobile device. You will learn how to deploy applications in the second part of this chapter.

Oracle Mobile Application Framework Security Concepts

In this section you will learn how to secure MAF applications, using three concepts. First, you will see how to work with user credentials to authenticate users accessing your MAF application and control the authority of who has access. After that, web service security in relation to MAF will be discussed. Finally, you will learn how access to device features can be restricted in MAF at the application feature level.

Let's compare securing an Oracle MAF application to getting on a flight to San Francisco. When you arrive at the airport of departure, you can enter that airport without a problem. This is a public area. Only after you have checked in with a valid ID and have a valid boarding pass are you allowed to continue to the boarding area. Depending on your destination, you are either allowed to the domestic terminals or the international ones. Before entering either terminal, you have to pass the luggage check-in. This is a typical area where you are not allowed to take any pictures.

All of these concepts can be translated to a MAF application: Enter the public area (login page), show your ID (enter credentials), get your boarding pass (roles), and continue to the restricted areas (secure features). There might be areas (features) where you are not allowed to take pictures (no device access allowed).

Let's see how this can be implemented in an Oracle MAF application.

Implementing Login

Authentication in an Oracle MAF application is implemented at the feature level. Whenever a user tries to activate a secured application feature, MAF wants to authenticate the user; that is, whenever the feature is about to be displayed in the web view or when the mobile operating system returns the feature to the foreground, Oracle MAF checks whether or not the feature requires authentication and, if so, displays a login page. The user needs to enter the username and the password. Once the user submits the login form, the credentials are sent to the server. Only after successful authentication will Oracle MAF render the requested feature.

To understand how authentication works, you must first know the set of options that are available.

Oracle MAF supports four distinct authentication technologies, each suited to a different use case. Although MAF can work with all these technologies, you as a developer have to configure which one will be used. This configuration, at the MAF Login Server connection, will be explained later.

The first supported technology is Federated SSO or web SSO through which authenticated users of your organization will seamlessly gain access to the applications and services by sharing identity information across their security domains.

Second is mobile and social authentication, which enables MAF applications to benefit from the full feature set of Oracle's Identity Management Solutions. For example, if the OAMMS server is integrated with Oracle Access Manager and Oracle Adaptive Access Manager, you can offer multistep authentication to MAF applications and uniquely identify each connecting device, also known as device fingerprinting.

Third, MAF applications can use the OAuth protocol to authenticate against APIs that support OAuth. OAuth is an open standard for authorization. It can be used to log in users using, for example, their Facebook, Twitter, or Google account. Using OAuth requires a server-side implementation of Oracle Mobile and Social server.

Finally, there is HTTP Basic, which is supported by nearly any web server. This ensures MAF applications can authenticate against any authentication server that supports authentication of credentials over HTTP and HTTPS. Because of this, in the remainder of this chapter, we will use HTTP Basic authentication to explain how to implement authentication in MAF applications. This includes Identity Management Servers (IDM) such as the Oracle Access Management (OAM) Identity Server. Besides OAM, Oracle MAF can use any basic authentication server.

NOTE
It is recommended that authentication information always be sent across encrypted networks.

Basic authentication is an HTTP standard authentication method designed to allow a client to provide credentials—in the form of a user ID and password—when making a request to a server system. Basic authentication is supported by the majority of web clients and is the authentication mechanism that can be implemented with the least additional effort.

Another option is to simply use a secured resource behind an application server, such as a web application page that is secured with a web.xml constraint.

NOTE
Typically, an application would only use one login server. However, you can also have multiple login servers per application if that is required, each mapped to a single feature. A feature itself only supports one login server. You would typically use multiple login servers when data sources require different authentication credentials.

Understanding the Authentication Flow

When a user tries to activate a secured feature, MAF presents the user with a login page. After the user enters their credentials, the Oracle Mobile and Social SDK APIs, which are embedded in MAF, handle the authentication. The Oracle Mobile and Social SDK is responsible for packaging and sending the user's credentials to the authentication server. The SDK is part of Oracle's Access Manager for Mobile and Social (OAMMS) Suite.

You can benefit from declarative and wizard-driven implementation of the security when building a MAF application. There is little or no need to write custom security code.

NOTE
Using OAMMS in the Oracle MAF application does not mean that you need a server that is running Oracle IDM. MAF has the embedded SDK for free, enabling MAF developers to use it. OAMMS can also work with other third-party identity services.

Depending on the success or failure of the authentication, the IDM Mobile SDK's APIs return either a failure or a valid user object to MAF. If the login fails, the login page remains, thereby preventing users from continuing until they enter the correct credentials.

Security Considerations

Before you can implement security, there are some things to consider. An MAF app can consist of multiple features. Do they all need to have security enabled? You might decide to enable security only on those features that need to be protected with credentials and/or that need to access (secured) back-end services. It is also possible to configure multiple sets of login credentials. One application may be configured to access one or more login servers. A feature can only point to one login server. Finally, you need to decide whether or not the app has to operate offline and, if so, if there are any secured features that need to be configured to use the local credential cache for authentication. Local and hybrid connections are only available for basic authentication and authentication to Oracle Access Management Mobile and Social (OAMMS). Because OAuth and Federated SSO use remote authentication, application users cannot log back into an application unless they authenticate successfully.

If security is a concern, it is recommended that you configure a connection to the login server using the OAuth or Web SSO connection type. OAuth and Web SSO require authentication against a remote login server and do not allow users to authenticate on the device from a local credential store. This gives you full server-side control on what devices and/or users can access your MAF application, and the corresponding data services and access for individual users and devices can be revoked.

NOTE
You can also create a MAF login connection to create a named connection during development and populate the login attributes to fully define the connection at run time. This can be useful when not all connection details are known at design time. Developers must use AdfmfJavaUtilities.updateSecurityConfigWithURLParameters() to define the details of the connection.

Configuring Authentication

In order to make the MAF application show a login page, you need to enable security at the feature level. This can be done in the feature configuration file (maf-feature.xml) as shown in Figure 10-1.

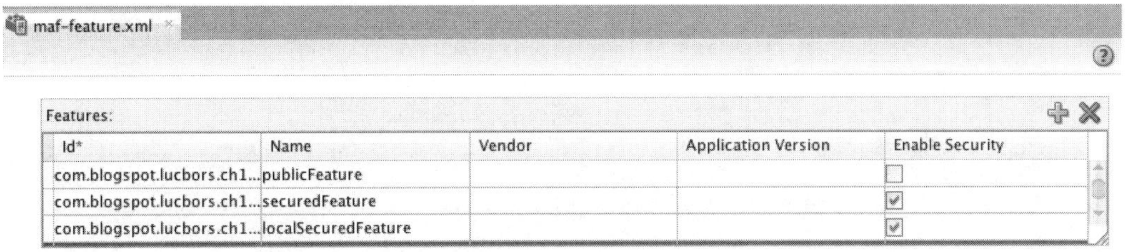

FIGURE 10-1. *Configure feature-level security.*

After enabling security at the feature level, you must further configure security at the application level in the maf-application.xml file. Features with security enabled show up on the Security tab in the application configuration file, as you can see in Figure 10-2.

The next step is to create a MAF login connection that can be used by secured features. You can do this by either invoking the New Gallery and choosing New MAF Login Server Connection or by creating it directly from within the application configuration file. The Create MAF Login Connection wizard opens at the General tab (Figure 10-3). Here you can set the Authentication Server Type and enter the connection name. For this example, we use HTTP Basic. Note that Oracle Mobile-Social, OAuth, and Federated SSO are also valid options. On the specific tab (in this example, HTTP Basic), you can enter the values for the login and logout URL.

You must also indicate if you always want to use the remote login server or if you want to store the credentials locally on the device. If you choose the Local option, the initial authentication is done against the remote authentication server; however, the username and password are also stored locally on the device. This means that subsequent authentication can be

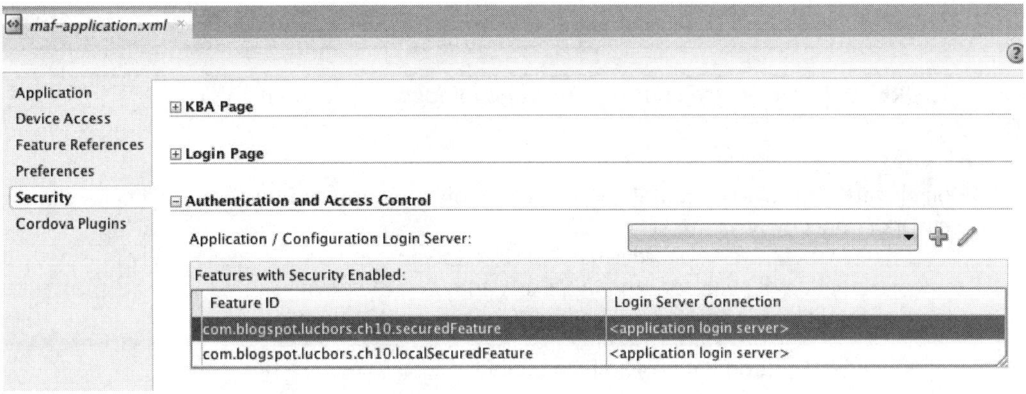

FIGURE 10-2. *Security settings at the maf-application.xml*

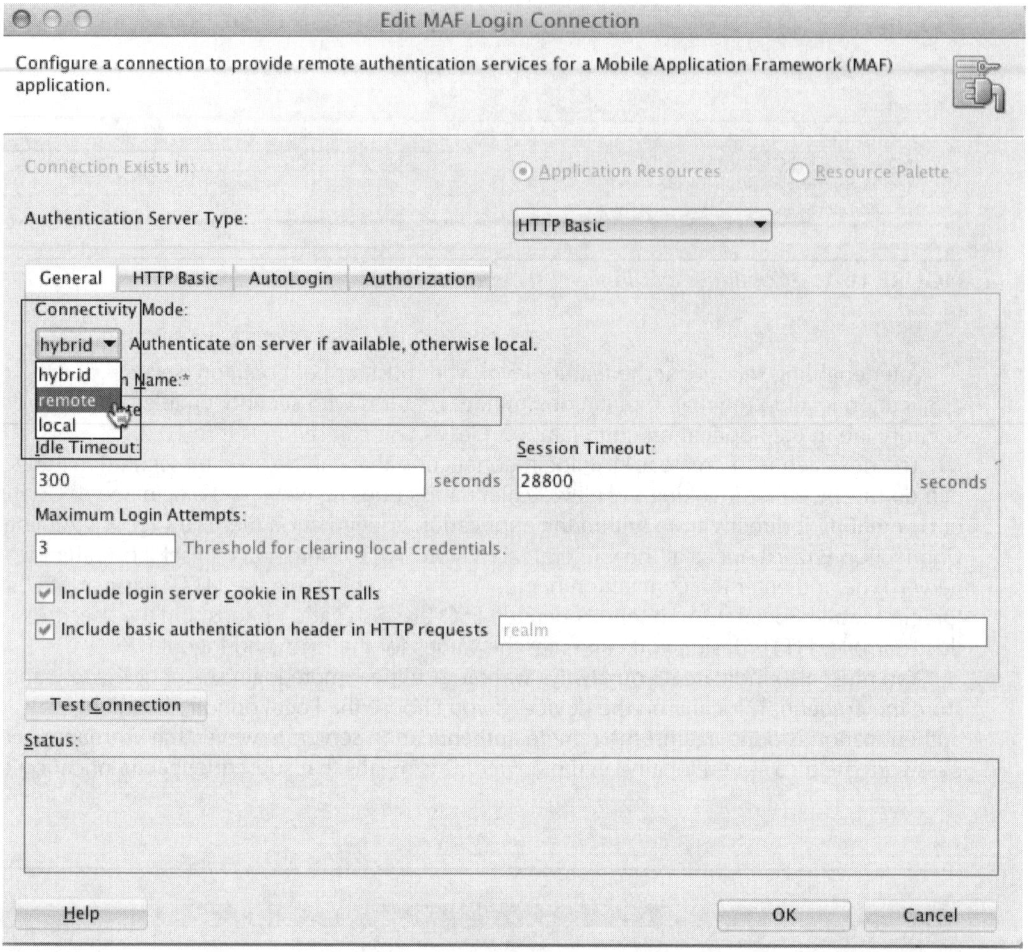

FIGURE 10-3. *Select the connectivity mode for login connection.*

done locally. This is important if you need to allow your application to authenticate regardless of network connectivity.

The device's native keystore is used to store the encrypted credentials safely in exactly the same way that credentials for other apps are stored on the device.

Note that in the example application, we have three features:

- **publicFeature:** with no authentication
- **securedFeature:** with remote authentication
- **localSecuredFeature:** with local authentication

The actual configuration of the login server and adding login servers to secured features must be done at the application level. For this, you can use the application configuration file (maf-application.xml). This file also has a security section, which can be edited in the Security tab of the overview editor. This tab shows all features that have security enabled. All these secured features need to be configured with a specific authentication server. You have two options here: either create a new login server connection or use an existing one.

Let's assume that there is no existing login server connection and that a new one must be created (Figure 10-4). The login server connection needs a name, and you must provide the URL for the login and logout server. If you are using Oracle Access Manager for Mobile and Social, then you will need to enter login and logout URLs based on how you have configured the OAMMS. If you are using just your own authentication URL, then the login and logout URLs are the same. The login server connection needs a name, and you must provide the URL for the login and logout server. You must also provide values for Idle Timeout and Session Timeout. These values indicate the time after which a user needs to reauthenticate. This enables you to take care of the scenario where a user is fired and their enterprise account is disabled but the mobile app has the credentials stored locally.

The Idle Timeout indicates how long a feature can remain idle. After this period expires, the user is timed out of all the application features that are secured by the login connection and must log in when the feature is reactivated. The Session Timeout indicates the time that a user can remain logged in to a feature without hitting the server to access secured resources. This prevents server-side timeout from kicking in and causing unpredictable results. Therefore, always set Session Timeout to a value that's slightly less than the server-side timeout for these secured resources.

Note that when the Session Timeout expires, the user is prompted to log in again only if the Idle Timeout is not expired.

The cookie field is used by the MAF application to retrieve and also send cookies that contain user credentials. For example, if the authentication URL server returns credentials in a cookie

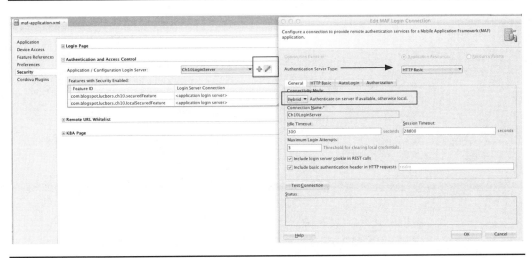

FIGURE 10-4. *Creating a new mobile login connection*

called JSESSIONID, then you must specify this cookie when you configure security. The same cookie is used when accessing remote URL resources.

When you run the application, the framework will prompt you to log in when you access a secured feature. Initial authentication is against a remote server. For the "localSecuredFeature," subsequent authentication is against the local credential store. This means that even if there is no network connection available, the application will be able to authenticate the user and the user will be able to use the feature.

Mobile Application Framework and Authorization

After the user is authenticated, we need to look at what the user is allowed to do in the mobile application. This is called authorization, and in the Mobile Application Framework, this is achieved by using the user's roles and privileges. To put this in the context of the trip to San Francisco, a user would have the role "passenger" and the privilege "domestic" to gain access to the domestic terminals. To get the user's roles and privileges, Mobile Application Framework uses an Access Control Service (ACS). The Access Control Service is a REST JSON service that is invoked to download the roles and privileges assigned to the user, which are then fetched in a single HTTP POST. The URL for the ACS can also be configured in the login connection (Figure 10-5).

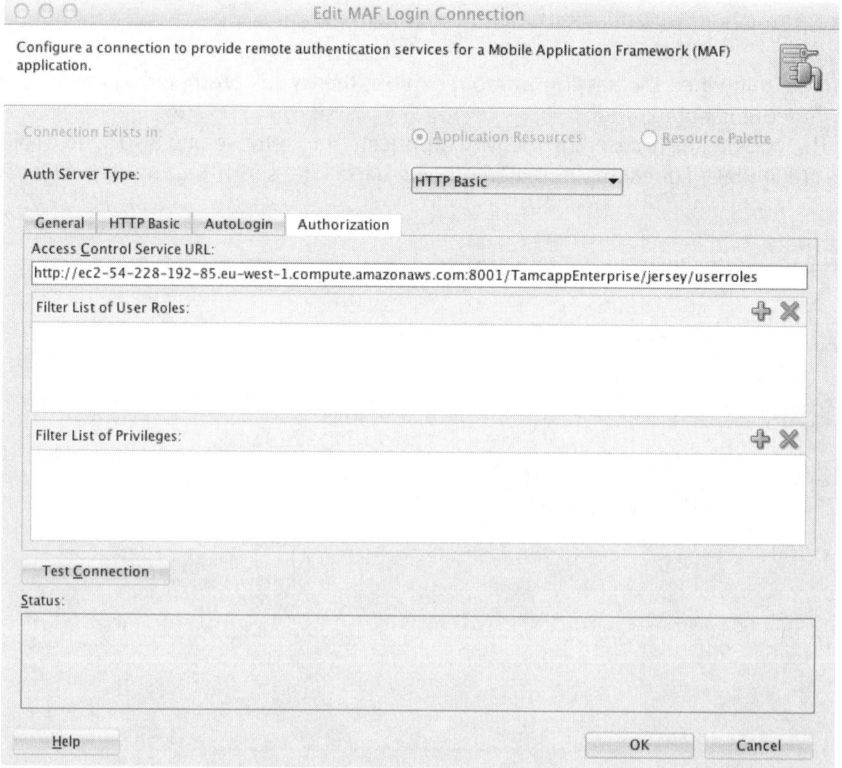

FIGURE 10-5. *Configure the Access Control Service URL.*

The ACS can also return specific roles and privileges by providing lists of roles and privileges that are applicable to the mobile application, as a user may have many more roles and privileges that are not used by the MAF application. These specific roles and privileges can be configured by adding user roles and privileges to the filter list on the Authorization tab of the connection (Figure 10-6). This is the same for all four available authentication technologies.

This prevents the application from downloading all roles that are assigned to the user, and the application will only get the roles it is interested in.

This could result in the following POST:

```
Protocol: POST
Authorization: Basic xxxxxxxxxxxx
Content-Type: application/json
{"userId": "passengerOne",
    "filterMask": ["role", "privilege"],
    "roleFilter": ["passenger", "visitor"],
    "privilegeFilter": ["international", "domestic", "checkin"]
}
```

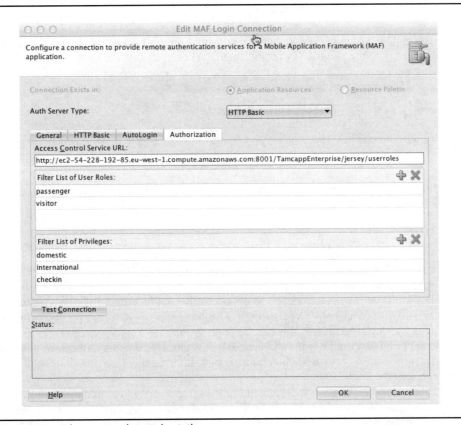

FIGURE 10-6. *Filter user roles and privileges*

The POST indicates that we are only interested if user "passengerOne" has roles "passenger" or "visitor" and if he has privileges "international", "domestic," or "checkin."

Typically, such a POST could result in the returned JSON object looking like this:

```
Content-Type: application/json {
    "userId": " passengerOne ",
    "roles": ["passenger"],
    "privileges": ["domestic"]
}
```

> **NOTE**
> *The ACS needs to be implemented by the developer, as it is not part of the Mobile Application Framework. When you create the ACS, you must make sure that headers meet the following requirements. The request header must contain the following fields: If-Match, Accept-Language, User-Agent, Authorization, Content-Type, and Content-Length. The response header must include the following fields: Last-Modified, Content-Type, and Content-Length. If you are integrating with Oracle Applications, please also check product information web pages for these applications, as certain applications will be publishing services that comply with the MAF ACS format.*

The assigned roles and privileges can be used to restrict access to certain parts of the application or to toggle visibility of user interface components. You can either check if the user has a specific role or if a specific privilege is granted to the authenticated user. This is done by means of EL expressions that use the securityContext object.

```
"#{securityContext.userInRole['passenger']}"
```

And if indeed it is a passenger, you can also check if this user has a specific privilege.

```
"#{securityContext.userGrantedPrivilege['domestic']}"
```

These expressions both evaluate to true or false and can be used in the rendered property of User Interface components.

```
<amx:commandButton id="bt1" action="goToTerminal"
                   rendered="#{securityContext.userInRole['passenger']}">
```

You will learn more on using securityContext in Chapter 16.

There is one more authorization aspect to discuss and that is device access. Oracle Mobile Application Framework enables you to declaratively enable and disable device access. The feature called "noImagesAllowedFeature" is a feature where we want to prevent the user from invoking the device's camera. This can be done by not checking the Request Access check box for Camera Permission on the feature's Device Access tab. This will prevent access to the camera.

The other option is to actually request access to the Camera, as shown in Figure 10-7, but not to grant it at the application level.

All the checked boxes are delegated to the application configuration file where you need to explicitly grant access to the device. So if we choose to request camera access at the feature level, the feature shows up at the application-level Device Access tab (Figure 10-8). If you uncheck the

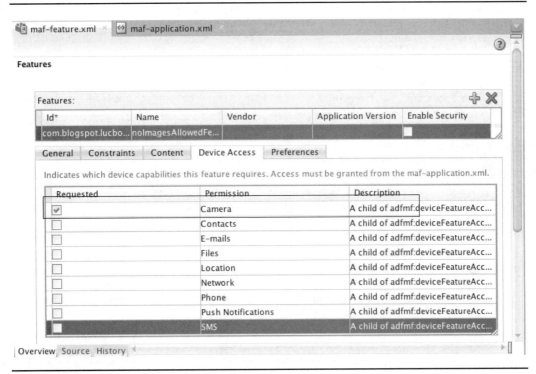

FIGURE 10-7. *Request feature-level device access.*

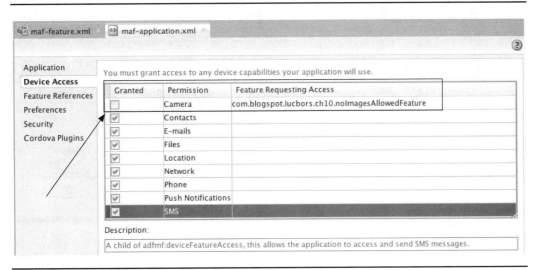

FIGURE 10-8. *Application-level access to device capabilities*

"Granted" check box at the application level, the application has full control. If the application does not grant access to a device, the features don't have access.

Using Secured Web Services

In the previous sections, you learned how to secure the mobile application and parts within the application. In this section, you will learn how to call out to secured web services. If you need to call web services that are secured, you can benefit from the fact that both REST and SOAP services use HTTP and HTTPS as a transport protocol.

NOTE
Setting up server-side web services and web service security is beyond the scope of this book. You will need to be able to recognize and understand these policies in order to configure secure web service calls from within your Oracle Mobile Application Framework application.

Oracle Mobile Application Framework supports several security policies. Which policy needs to be applied to the service call totally depends on what is implemented server side in the web service. Once you know what policy to apply, it is very simple to configure this in Oracle Mobile Application Framework. You can simply invoke the Data Control Policy Editor from the context menu on the data control definition by clicking Define Web Service Security as displayed in Figure 10-9.

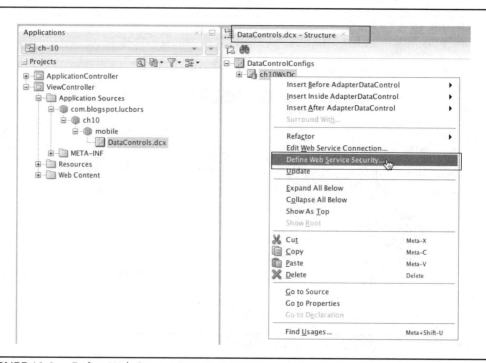

FIGURE 10-9. *Define Web Service Security in MAF*

In the Edit Data Control Policies editor, you need to pick the appropriate policy from the list of available policies (Figure 10-10).

When you call the secured web service, the Mobile Application Framework ensures that the username and password of the authenticated user are added to the web service call according to the policy. There is nothing more a developer needs to do.

Note, however, that the user has to be authenticated before a secured web service call can be executed successfully.

An application can have multiple login servers defined for different features. Therefore, the web service needs to know exactly which one of these to use. In order to configure this, the adfCredentialStoreKey entry of the login server connection must be added to the server connection in the connections.xml. This needs to be done manually, as there is no wizard or dialog for this particular task.

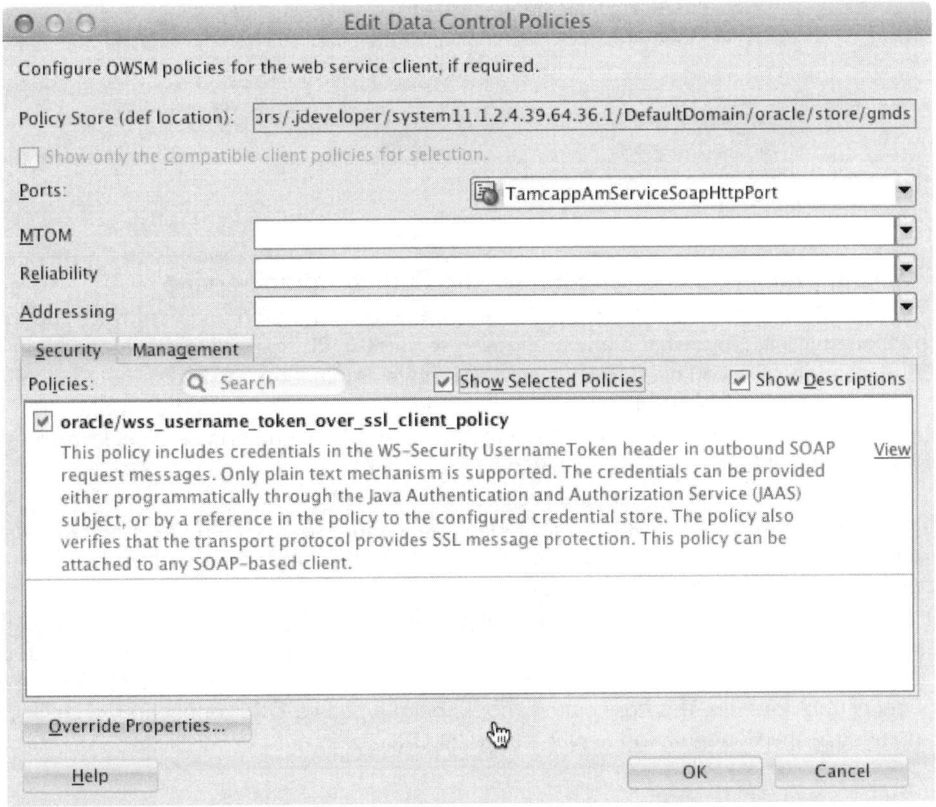

FIGURE 10-10.   *Select the security policy from a list.*

```
<?xml version = '1.0' encoding = 'UTF-8'?>
    <References xmlns="http://xmlns.oracle.com/adf/jndi">
        <Reference name="myWsDC" adfCredentialStoreKey="Authenticate"
            <Factory className="... .. .. WebServiceConnectionFactory"/>
            <RefAddresses>
                <XmlRefAddr addrType="WebServiceConnection">
                    <Contents>
                        ... ... ...
                    </Contents>
                </XmlRefAddr>
            </RefAddresses>
        </Reference>
        <Reference name="Authenticate"
                className="oracle.adf.model.connection.adfmf.LoginConnection"
                adfCredentialStoreKey="Authenticate" partial="false" xmlns=""
                manageInOracleEnterpriseManager="true" deployable="true">
            <Factory className=".. .. .. ..LoginConnectionFactory"/>
            <RefAddresses>
                <XmlRefAddr addrType="adfmfLogin">
                    <Contents>
                        .. .. .. .. ..
                    </Contents>
                </XmlRefAddr>
            </RefAddresses>
        </Reference>
    </References>
```

Making Connections Configurable: The Configuration Service

Now all security has been set up, the application has been tested and deployed, and the users are working with it. Now what if any of the web services' URL changes or any of the login servers' URL changes? Do you need to change your mobile application and redistribute it, which can be a difficult process if your users refuse to download the latest version of your application? To solve this problem, the framework provides a feature called Configuration Service. Its role and place in the overall architecture are displayed in Figure 10-11.

This Configuration Service enables you to download a new version of the connections.xml file and other configuration files to your mobile application, so there is no need to redeploy the application. You only need to make sure that the latest version of the configuration files are present at the configuration server.

If your mobile application uses a Configuration Service, you can either automatically check for new versions of the configuration files or create a custom user interface to check for new configurations. In both cases, you need to define the URL to the Configuration Service in the connections.xml file. This connection should be of type HttpURLConnection, with its URL value pointing to the Configuration Server end-point URL.

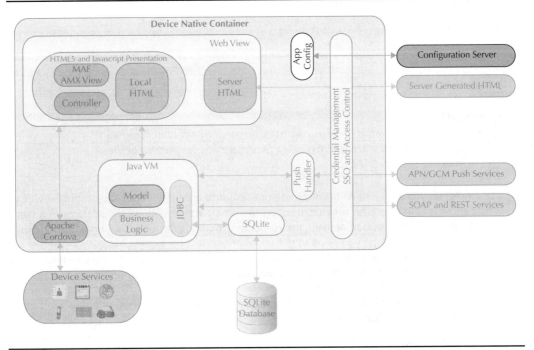

FIGURE 10-11. *The Configuration Server in the overall architecture*

```
<Reference name="cfgService"
          className="oracle.adf.model.connection.url.HttpURLConnection"
          xmlns="">
   <Factor
      className="oracle.adf.model.connection.url.URLConnectionFactory"/>
      <RefAddresses>
         <XmlRefAddr addrType="cfgService">
            <Contents>
            <urlconnection name="cfgService"
                           url="<theUrl to your configuration server>"/>
            </Contents>
         </XmlRefAddr>
      </RefAddresses>
</Reference>
```

At run time, the Mobile Application Framework constructs the complete URL to the Configuration Service. It consists of three parts:

■ The URL defined in the connections.xml file

■ The application bundle ID as defined in the adfmf-application.xml

■ The name of the file that needs to be downloaded, for instance: Connections.xml

This all adds up to the following URL:

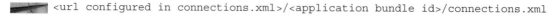

```
<url configured in connections.xml>/<application bundle id>/connections.xml
```

This approach enables you to use a single configuration server to host configuration files for many different applications. All your seeded configuration files must reside at exactly this location in order to download them.

NOTE
The same approach is used to construct the path to adf-config.xml and maf-config.xml that are the two other files that must be present at the configuration server's URL.

MAF provides a set of APIs within the oracle.adfmf.config.client.ConfigurationService class that allow you to check for new changes on the server and download the updates. You can use these APIs in a Java bean to activate the respective methods through the Configuration Service. Application feature. First you need to define what connection to the configuration server must be used. For this, the setDeliveryMechanismConfiguration() method can be used. Before actually downloading the new configuration files, you can check if a new configuration is available by invoking the isThereAnyNewConfigurationChanges() method. This will return true if a new configuration exists. Finally, with the stageAndActivateVersion() method, the new configurations are downloaded and activated.

```
if (cfgService == null) {
    cfgService = new ConfigurationService();
}
cfgService.addProgressListener(this);
cfgService.setDeliveryMechanism(_HTTP);
cfgService.setDeliveryMechanismConfiguration("connectionName",
                                            CFG_SERVICE_CONN_NAME);
cfgService.setDeliveryMechanismConfiguration(_ROOT, _sourceLocation);
if(cfgService.isThereAnyNewConfigurationChanges(<APPLICATION_ID>, <VERSION>)){

    cfgService.stageAndActivateVersion(<VERSION>);


}
cfgService.removeProgressListener(this);
```

Setting Up Secure Communication

To set up secure communication between the server and the mobile application, you can use SSL (Secure Sockets Layer) handshake or, by its new name, TLS (Transport Layer Security) handshake. Both are protocols that are designed to provide communication security. They use certificates and exchange a key to ensure message confidentiality and message authentication. In Figure 10-12 you see how such a secure communication is set up.

The trusted certificates and Certificate Authorities are stored in a cacerts file. When you create a new mobile application, JDeveloper creates the cacerts certificate file within the Application Resources Security folder (Figure 10-13).

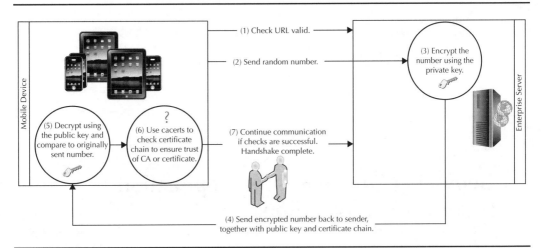

FIGURE 10-12. *Setting up secure communication*

This file identifies a set of certificates from a limited set of well-known and trusted sources (Certificate Authorities). For an application that requires custom certificates or simply less well-known certificates (certificates that are not in the default cacerts file), you will need to add these certificates by using the keytool. It is more likely than not that you will need to add your certificate, even if you are using a certificate from a typically well-known authority. A typical command to import such a certificate is shown in the following example, where the certificate with name maf_book_certificate is imported into the cacerts keystore.

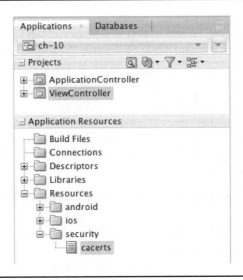

FIGURE 10-13. *The cacerts file*

```
keytool
    -importcert
    -keystore cacerts
    -file maf_book_certificate
    -storepass changeit
    -noprompt
```

NOTE
The default password of the cacerts is changeit.

Deploying Oracle Mobile Application Framework Applications

Once the mobile application is developed and secured, it must be deployed. An Oracle MAF application runs on a device or on a device simulator. In order to get an MAF application on a device or simulator, the application must be deployed. For this, you must create an iOS application bundle (.ipa and .app files) or Android application package (.apk) file.

NOTE
MAF creates an .ipa file when you select either the Deploy to Distribution package or Deploy to iTunes. It creates an .app file when you select the Deploy Application to Simulator option.

During deployment, the actual magic takes place and JDeveloper converts your source code to a platform-specific deployable and runnable format by using the platform-specific build tools. In Chapter 2 you already learned how to set up these platform-specific tools and how to configure JDeveloper to use them. In short, this is how deployment works:

The Mobile Application Framework executes the deployment of an application by copying a platform-specific template application to a temporary location, updating that application with the code, resources, and configuration defined in the MAF project. MAF then builds and deploys the application using the tools of the target platform.

Deployment Profiles

Deployment profiles are used to specify how the application is packaged into the platform-specific archive that is used to deploy the application to the device.

When you create a new MAF application, default deployment profiles are created for you for all supported mobile platforms. These profiles can be used right away to deploy the application. It is, however, recommended that you make some changes to these profiles. In this section, you will learn more about the deployment profiles and the changes you need to make.

Deploying for the Different Platforms

Oracle MAF applications can be deployed to multiple platforms. As you can imagine, all of these platforms have their own needs regarding the application. These specific requirements for each platform can be configured in the deployment profile, essentially a named configuration set. The default iOS and Android deployment profiles for a MAF application can be changed to suit your own needs, but you can also create new deployment profiles. The deployment profiles can be created and accessed from within the application's properties (Figure 10-14).

There are several options that can be configured in the deployment profile. One of these options is the configuration of the application images. Application images are used by the application for splash screens, application icons, and more specifically for iOS, the artwork that is used in iTunes to advertise your application if you choose to go that route. Those images have to meet specific requirements that are defined by both Apple for iOS and Google for Android. These requirements are often subject to change by the respective device vendors. Refer to the platform-specific web sites for the latest information.

For iOS applications you can also define the device orientations that are supported by the application (Figure 10-15) such as landscape or portrait.

Specific Android Deployment Options

For Android there are several specific options that can be configured, as you can see in Figure 10-16.

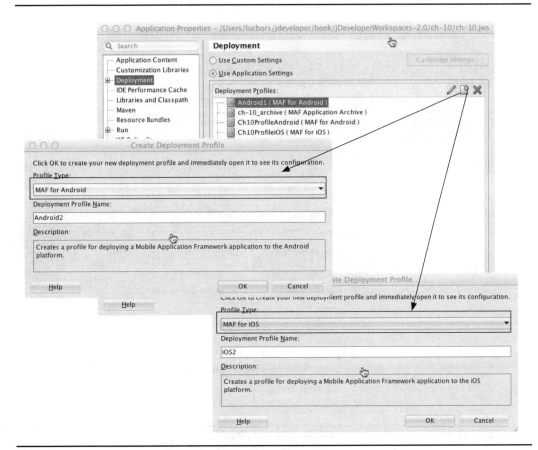

FIGURE 10-14. *Create and edit deployment profiles.*

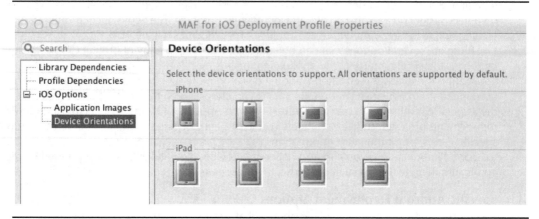

FIGURE 10-15. *Supported device orientations for iOS deployment*

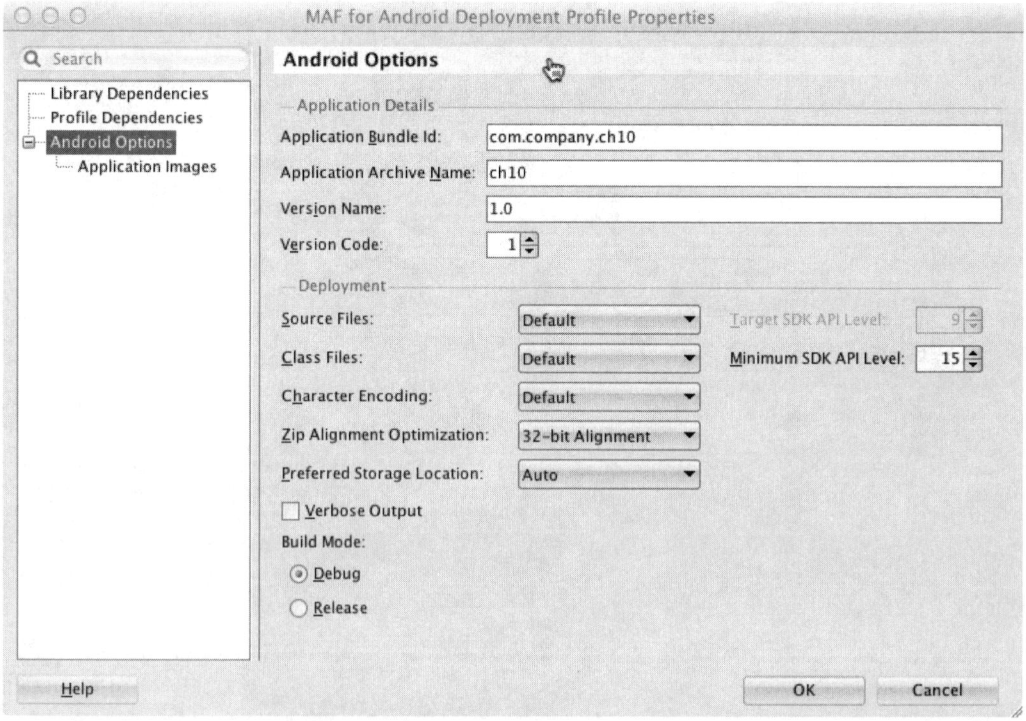

FIGURE 10-16. *Specific Android deployment profile properties*

All of these settings are required for publishing Android applications and they match the Android-specific settings and go into the manifest of the Android application. The application archive name is the name that will be used for the application archive. This setting defaults from the application ID as set in the maf-application.xml file.

MAF Deployment Property	Android Property	Description
Application Bundle ID	Android:package	The package name serves as a unique identifier for the application.
Version Name	Android:versionCode	An integer value that represents the version of the application code, relative to other versions.
Version Code	Android:versionName	A string value that represents the release version of the application code, as it should be shown to users.
Minimum SDK API level	Android:minSdkVersion	The minimum version of the Android platform on which the application will run, specified by the platform's API level identifier
Target SDK API level	Android:targetSdkVersion	Specifies the API level on which the application is designed to run

NOTE
The application bundle ID may contain uppercase or lowercase letters ("a" through "Z") and numbers. However, individual package name parts may only start with letters. Also note that Google Play accepts underscores ("_"), but in JDeveloper's deployment profile, you will get an error if you use underscores.

The other settings that are used for the build tools to create the actual deployable artifact are more or less compiler directives and normally there is no need to change these settings:

- **source files and class files**   What JDK version the compiler should use
- **character encoding**   Tells the compiler how to handle characters beyond the ASCII character set
- **zip alignment**   Whether to use 32-bit or 64-bit zip alignment

Finally, you need to indicate whether or not this is a deployment for debugging or a real production release. Applications that are deployed for debug mode will have the android:debuggable in the manifest file and its value will be true. These applications cannot be published to Google Play, but it allows you to use debugging tools like Android Monitor to perform deep analysis of the MAF application. If you select "release," the android:debuggable attribute is not added to the manifest, which results in an application that can be published to Google Play.

TIP
Make multiple deployment profiles per supported platform during application development. At least have one for both debug and release mode. This allows you to quickly switch from debug mode back to release mode. The same tip applies to iOS deployment. Also note that an application created under release mode would roughly be 50 percent of the size of the debug version. Furthermore, an application deployed in release mode runs a lot faster.

NOTE
In order to deploy an Android application in release mode, you must create a Java keystore first. You will then need to configure the location and passwords of this Java keystore in JDeveloper | Tools | Preferences | MAF | Android. You cannot use a debug keystore or leave the keystore blank.

Specific iOS Deployment Options

The iOS deployment profile also has several iOS-specific settings that can be changed (Figure 10-17).

The Application Bundle ID must be unique for each application installed on an iOS device and must adhere to the reverse-domain name style naming conventions. The Application Archive Name indicates the name of the deployed archive. It defaults to the application id attribute configured in the maf-application.xml file. For deployment, you also need to pick the minimum iOS version that your app supports.

When using a simulator, you must also pick the simulator target version. Usually, the default of "highest available" works fine, but if you want to test older versions, you should change the default.

TIP
Create specific deployment profiles for specific versions.

You must also indicate if your application supports iPhone, iPad, or both. Finally, select the appropriate build mode, which can be either debug or release.

NOTE
If you pick a specific version of the simulator, the MAF application would be deployed to that version as expected and to the instance of the simulator specified in the Tools | Preferences | MAF Settings. However, JDeveloper will always launch the most recent instance of the simulator, and the simulator version launched would be the last launched version. Therefore, if you cannot find the MAF application in the simulator that came up, double-check the simulator instance and versions.

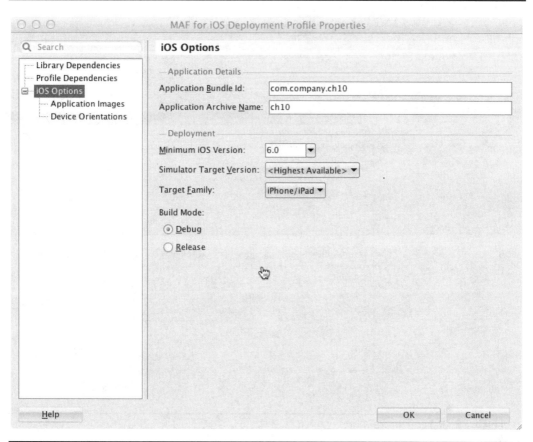

FIGURE 10-17. *Specific iOS deployment profile properties*

Deploying the Mobile Application to Android and iOS

JDeveloper offers functionality to deploy the mobile application from within the IDE. Let's first take a look at the deployment to the Android platform (Figure 10-18).

If you have an Android device connected to your development machine, you can deploy the application directly to the device by selecting "Deploy application to device."

This assumes that the Android device is tethered to your development machine and is being properly recognized. It also requires that you enable USB debugging and allows installation of application from unknown sources. These settings are enabled through the Android settings.

In the same way, you can deploy the application to an emulator by selecting "Deploy application to simulator." However, you would need to first launch the Android Emulator, as JDeveloper does not automatically try to launch the emulator for you.

If you want to publish the mobile application in Google Play, you need to deploy it as a package, an .apk file. After that, the .apk file can be uploaded to Google Play in the Google Developer Console. For that, you will need an Android Developer account.

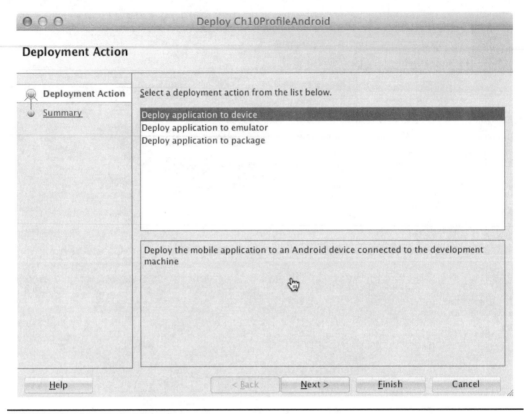

FIGURE 10-18. *Android deployment*

Of course, you can also deploy the application for the iOS platform from within JDeveloper (Figure 10-19).

For deploying to the simulator, you obviously select "Deploy application to simulator." The other two options create an .ipa file that is suitable for installation on an iOS device. If you select "Deploy application to iTunes," the .ipa file is created and deployed to iTunes. From within iTunes, the application can be synchronized to an iOS device.

If you want to distribute the mobile application via the Apple Store, you must deploy the mobile application to an .ipa file. This can be achieved by selecting "Deploy to distribution package." For deploying your mobile apps to your own iOS device or iTunes, you will need an iOS Developer account.

Whenever you want to deploy an app to an actual device, you would need to deploy to a .ipa file and sign it with appropriate certificates and distribution profiles. You can sign it with developer or distribution provisioning profile, and depending on the type of the profile and certificate, the app can be deployed to a developer device, to any device through the Apple App Store, or to any device within an enterprise. For details, please consult the Apple Developer Portal at developer.apple.com.

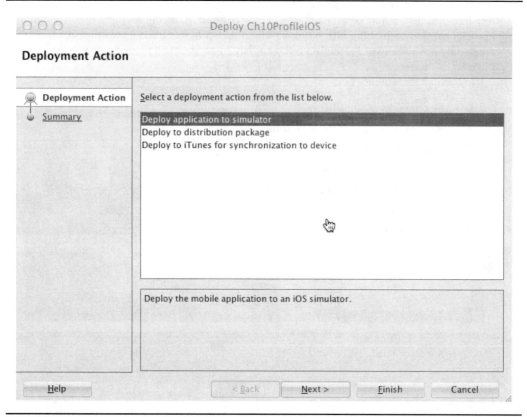

FIGURE 10-19. *iOS deployment*

NOTE
The actual deployment (or publication) in the Apple App Store or Google Play is beyond the scope of this book.

Summary

Security always is a big issue when building applications, and in a mobile context, this issue even becomes bigger. The Oracle Mobile Application Framework offers great support for building secure mobile applications. It also provides you with the concept of a configuration server that allows you to build a configurable mobile application.

Deployment to supported platforms also is a more or less declarative process. The specific requirements for the supported platforms can be defined in the deployment profiles, and the framework takes care of the rest. No earlier than at deployment, the platform-specific artifacts are created by the framework, shielding you from having to know all the ins and outs of the supported platforms.

In this chapter you learned

- The concepts of security
- How to secure a MAF application
- How to call secured web services
- How to authenticate and authorize users
- How to use a configuration service
- How to create deployment profiles
- How to deploy a MAF application

PART
II

Developing the
Sample Application

CHAPTER
11

Explaining the TAMCAPP
Sample Application

This book contains a lot of information and small code samples that will help build an Oracle MAF application. Yet it helps to build an end-to-end mobile application to learn many of the valuable lessons provided in this book so you garner experience in all parts of the development life cycle. To assist this learning process, let's introduce a sample application called TAMCAPP, which is short for "The Awesome Mobile Conference App." TAMCAPP is an interactive mobile application designed to be used by conference presenters, attendees, and the conference organizers (Figure 11-1 shows the logo).

TAMCAPP will cover many aspects of the Oracle MAF Framework, from setting up the basic application with features and pages to using more advanced features of the framework, such as device interaction, remote URLs, security, and preferences.

From a data perspective, the information about the conference sessions will be fetched from data sources based on SOAP XML web services and REST-JSON web services, and stored in the mobile's local database. At initial startup, the local database will be created and a web service call is executed to retrieve the data that needs to be stored in the local database such that the user has meaningful conference details to work with. As long as there is a network connection, changes in the schedule are stored both on-device and in the enterprise database.

If there is no connection available, changes will be stored locally. Once the device is back online, a web service is automatically called to synchronize the data with the enterprise database. This mechanism is explained in Chapter 18.

The primary functionality TAMCAPP will provide to conferences attendees is as follows:

- Register for the conference
- Change personal information
- Add other attendees to the on-device contacts
- Build their conference schedule
- Browse a conference venue map
- Browse session abstracts and speakers
- Perform session evaluation

FIGURE 11-1. *The TAMCAPP application logo*

Besides that, they can

- Access social media such as Twitter
- Use the app to locate local points of interest such as landmarks, restaurants, hotels, and museums

Speakers can also

- Browse session evaluations for sessions they conducted

The conference organizers can

- Push a notification to all users whenever a session is cancelled or the schedule changes
- Send e-mails to maintenance personnel to report broken inventory such as projector and/ or microphones
- Check the headcount in a session for those who turned up

The Data Model

The TAMCAPP application uses both a remote enterprise database and a local on-device database. This enables the user to have access to certain features even in a disconnected mode.

The Enterprise Data Model

In order to be able to store the data necessary for the conference, there is a server-based database. A diagram for this database is shown in Figure 11-2. The database contains multiple tables, but the most important ones are the ones for PRESENTATIONS and ATTENDEES. These tables are joined in an ATTENDANCES table that is used for both schedule building and session evaluations. The other tables, COUNTRIES, ROOMS, SLOTS, TOPICS, and TRACKS, are lookup tables that are not directly of great importance to the Oracle MAF application.

The On-Device Data Model

On the device there will be one table called mySchedule to store the user's schedule so the user can even access their schedule in disconnected mode. It's a frustrating issue at most conferences that the Wi-Fi often goes down, so it's essential the user can access their schedule disconnected.

The on-device table also allows users to do offline evaluations of the presentations they attended. After getting back online, the changes in the schedule and the conducted evaluations are synchronized with the enterprise database. The mySchedule table is a copy (or duplicate) of the Attendances table with some extra lookup information such as presenter name, session title, and session dates and contains only attendances for the attendee that is the owner of the device.

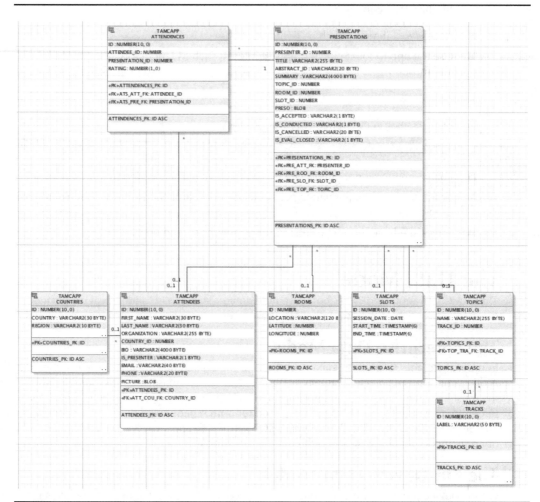

FIGURE 11-2. *The enterprise data model*

The Web Services

The enterprise data model will predominantly be exposed as a set of web services deployed through the enterprise's servers. This will include the following discrete SOAP web service operations to supplement the mobile app's functionality:

- Register attendee
- Edit attendee
- Edit schedule
- Search sessions
- Evaluate session

- Browse evaluations
- Submit headcount

TAMCAPP will also integrate a single REST-JSON web service, a Google service that provides information about local points of interest to the conference center, such as restaurants.

This book does not cover the development and implementation of these web services to our enterprise's servers. For all intents and purposes, they can be regarded as black boxes beyond the data and APIs they provide. In my opinion, in real life you should also see web services as black boxes, with a given interface definition and functionality.

It's worth noting that the type of web service, be it a SOAP or REST web service, will have a large impact on how these web services are invoked from within the Oracle MAF application.

At any point in this book where a web service is invoked, an API is provided so you will know how the web service is called and what the result of such a call can be.

TAMCAPP Application Design and Flow

TAMCAPP will use a custom skin to implement the specific TAMCAPP look and feel with its own background colors, font sizes, and images.

Only registered users are able to use the TAMCAPP application. In order to register to use the application, after installing the app and running it for the first time, the registration feature is invoked. During the registration process, not only is the user registered, but the device is also registered in the enterprise database. This device registration is necessary in order to support push notifications of session and schedule changes during the conference.

The Features

The functionality in TAMCAPP is grouped into several features. These are the features in the application:

- Registration
  - Register user
- Attendees
  - Browse attendees
  - Edit attendee
- Sessions
  - Search sessions
  - Detailed session information
  - View evaluations
- Schedule
  - My schedule
- Social media
  - Twitter
- Maps

- ■ Points of interest
- ■ Venue maps
- ■ Organization
  - ■ Report technical issue

In the TAMCAPP app, a navigation bar and springboard are used to navigate to and from features.

Registration and Login

After downloading and installing the TAMCAPP app, the user needs to register in order to receive a password for the application. This password is needed to log in and use all the secured application features. Registration is done at the registration page, which is shown in Figure 11-3. Registration not only registers the user, but also registers the device. The device needs to be registered in order

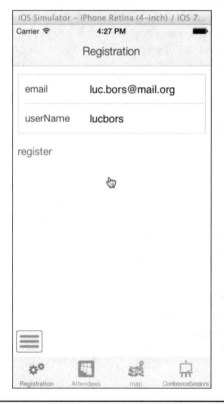

FIGURE 11-3. *The Registration page*

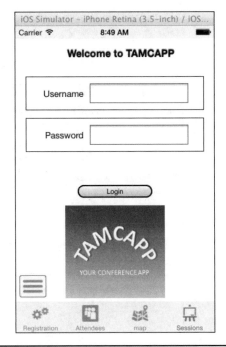

FIGURE 11-4. *The Login page*

to receive push notifications that are sent out by the conference organizers on changes to the conference schedule.

On subsequent application launch, the user is prompted to enter the username and password on the login page (Figure 11-4).

The Springboard

After a successful login, the application will show the springboard. The springboard will allow access to the application's available features, as well as a logoff button that shuts down the app.

The springboard (Figure 11-5) will be implemented as a custom springboard and displays all the available features for the logged-in user. From the springboard, a user also has the possibility to log off from the application.

The implementation of the springboard is discussed in Chapter 12.

FIGURE 11-5. *The springboard*

Attendees

The Attendees feature contains a list of all attendees (Figure 11-6), and an attendee can change personal information (Figure 11-7) such as name, phone, and e-mail address. The selected attendee can be called and e-mailed from within this list. An attendee can also change their picture by either using an existing one on the device, or taking a new picture using the device's camera. Other attendees' details can be copied from this list to the on-device contact list.

A picture of the attendee can be taken from within the application and uploaded to the enterprise database. This is all explained in Chapter 14.

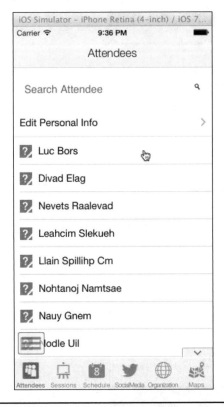

FIGURE 11-6. *The Attendee page*

FIGURE 11-7. *The Edit Attendee page*

Social Media

Via the Social Media feature, attendees can access the TAMCAPP Twitter account and read the tweets of @tamcappconf, as you can see in Figure 11-8. In Chapter 15, you will learn two methods to implement the interaction between Oracle MAF and Twitter.

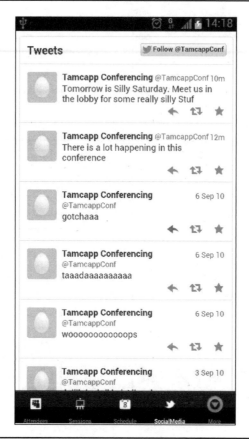

FIGURE 11-8. *Embedding a Twitter feed*

Maps

The Maps feature enables users to display a map of the conference venue (Figure 11-9). All conference rooms on the map have a "hotspot" where, if you move your finger over it, information is displayed in a hint text. When you tap a hotspot, a popup is displayed, containing all kinds of relevant information about the specific location such as sessions in that room and how many attendees the room can hold.

The Maps section also contains a map with local places of interest. The point of interest page shows the user what the points of interest are nearest to his current location, as you can see in Figure 11-10. These points are plotted on a geographical map. The points are retrieved by calling a Google REST-JSON web service, which returns the points based on coordinates, type, and radius.

You will learn how to implement this map functionality in Chapter 15.

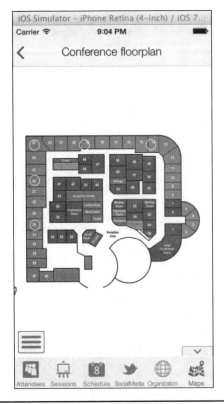

FIGURE 11-9. *The conference floor plan*

FIGURE 11-10. *Points of interest*

Conference Sessions

The Conference Sessions feature contains both a list of sessions and a detailed view of each session, including a session evaluation page where speakers can view their session evaluations. The feature uses role-based security to distinguish between speakers and regular attendees. Only speakers have access to the "session evaluations" page, whereas regular attendees cannot access it.

The conference session feature starts with a list view containing all the sessions divided by separate days of the conference, as displayed in Figure 11-11. These sessions can then be searched and filtered by entering a search string in the search box. The browser session page has

FIGURE 11-11. *The Browse Conference Sessions page*

functionality to add a selected session to the user's schedule. For that the user simply invokes the "add" button, and the session is automatically added to his schedule.

In the list you can select a session and open the details of the particular session, as you can see in Figure 11-12. The detail page shows time, place, and presenter for the given session and also displays the session abstract. There is also the possibility to download the presentation paper and to view it on the device (Figure 11-13).

Finally, a user can rate a conference session by means of a star rating between 1 and 5. After submitting the rating, evaluations for this session are disabled.

FIGURE 11-12.   *The Session Details page*

FIGURE 11-13.   *The Session Paper viewer*

My Schedule

My Schedule contains all the conference sessions that were added to the schedule of the user (Figure 11-14). From within My Schedule a user can delete sessions from their schedule by swiping to the right. Also, the user can invoke the Conference Sessions feature to look at the details of a selected session.

Speakers

Besides all the functionality that regular attendees have, speakers also have access to the evaluations of their sessions. The session evaluation is displayed on a dashboard containing several graphs and gauges. An example for a single conference session is shown in Figure 11-15. If a speaker has multiple sessions, a drop-down is rendered so the speaker can change the session for which he wants to access the evaluation by selecting the particular conference session from the drop-down.

This functionality is described in Chapters 13 and 16.

FIGURE 11-14. *The My Schedule page*

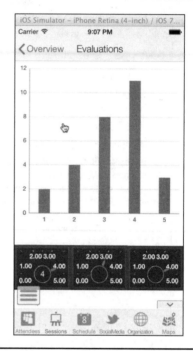

FIGURE 11-15. *The Session Evaluation page*

Organization

Members of the organization committee have several features available to do administrative tasks such as recording session headcounts and reporting technical issues at the conference. Issue reporting consists of taking a picture and sending it to the support department via e-mail as displayed in Figures 11-16 and 11-17.

A headcount in a session is implemented as a kind of "digital clicker" (Figure 11-18). The user taps a button for each and every attendee that enters the room. After all have entered and the session starts, the total is submitted.

Finally, the organizing committee is able to send out push notifications to all the users of TAMCAPP to notify them of changes to the schedule. Notifications are sent from a server-side application. All devices that have TAMCAPP installed are registered in the enterprise database. This registration occurs during the first start of the application where the user registers themselves.

FIGURE 11-16. *The Report Issues page*

FIGURE 11-17. *Invoke e-mail client*

FIGURE 11-18. *The Digital Clicker page*

FIGURE 11-19. *The Banner Notification alert*

The notification will show up on the device either as a banner (Figure 11-19) or as an alert (Figure 11-20), and also in the Notification Center. After clicking the notification, the TAMCAPP application is opened and the changes are displayed. This behaves differently between iOS and Android. The differences will be explained in Chapter 17.

On iOS devices, the push notifications are visualized by badging the application icon.

Implementation of push notifications in the TAMCAPP Oracle MAF app is also explained in Chapter 17.

FIGURE 11-20. *Notifications in the Notification Center*

Tablet Layout

So far the functionality described was designed and built for smartphones. If TAMCAPP runs on a tablet, the layout will be different. The overall functionality is the same, but because on a tablet you have more real estate available, the application looks different. The tablet layout is discussed in Chapter 18.

Summary

This chapter describes the sample application TAMCAPP, which consists of several features that all together cover the possibilities that you have with the Oracle MAF Framework. This chapter has given you a glimpse of the functionality contained in TAMCAPP. In the next chapters you will learn how to implement this functionality.

CHAPTER
12

Developing the Springboard

I n the previous chapter we reviewed the entire TAMCAPP application. From this we know what the springboard looks like and what features are in the application. Now it is time to start building the TAMCAPP Oracle MAF application. Building an Oracle MAF application starts with creating a new application and defining the features used in the app. In this chapter you will learn how to set up the TAMCAPP application and how to build the custom springboard that is used in this app.

Creating the Application

The first step in creating the TAMCAPP MAF application is to use JDeveloper and create a new Oracle MAF application. The only thing you might want to consider is the application package prefix that will be used to organize artifacts throughout the application. The creation of a new MAF application by default will create two projects in JDeveloper. The first project, ApplicationController, will be used later. The second project, ViewController, is the one that is needed to create the features.

The maf-feature.xml, highlighted in Figure 12-1, is the file where all the features of an Oracle MAF application are defined.

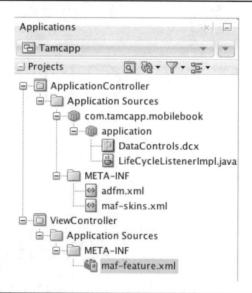

FIGURE 12-1. Default project setup

Defining the Features of the TAMCAPP Application

As described in the previous chapter, the TAMCAPP application consists of the following features:

- **Attendees**   The feature that implements all functionality needed to browse and edit attendee data
- **Sessions**   The feature that implements all functionality needed to browse sessions, read session-related papers, set up the schedule, and look into session evaluations
- **Schedule**   The feature that implements all functionality to view your schedule
- **Organization (on-device)**   The feature that implements all functionality necessary for the organizing committee
- **Maps**   The feature that implements functionality to browse maps of the conference venue and maps of the immediate vicinity
- **Social media**   The feature that implements functionality to show the conference's Twitter feed
- **Organization (remote)**   The feature that implements functionality necessary for the organizing committee and that is available as an existing application on a remote server

Before implementing features, which will be covered in the next chapter, you first need to define them in the maf-feature.xml file as shown in Figure 12-2.

When defining features, you need to configure whether they will be implemented with a single Oracle MAF AMX page, an Oracle MAF bounded task flow containing multiple AMX pages, an HTML page, or a remote URL. The Attendees, Sessions, Schedule, OrganizationLocal, and Maps features use AMX-type technology. Whenever the feature has some kind of flow

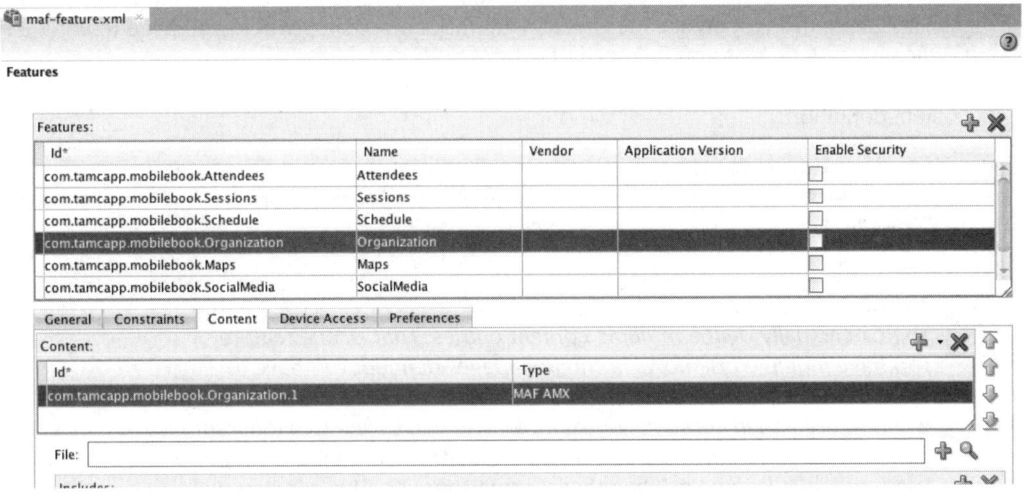

FIGURE 12-2.   *MAF AMX features in the TAMCAPP application*

consisting of multiple pages, you would use an Oracle MAF mobile bounded task flow. If there is only one single page in the feature, an AMX page will do.

When you define a new feature, the MAF feature definition file will store its configuration as an <adfmf:feature /> tag:

```
<adfmf:feature id="com.tamcapp.mobilebook.Attendees" name="Attendees"
                icon="images/Myspace.png"
                image="images/Myspace.png">
   <adfmf:constraints/>
   <adfmf:content id="com.tamcapp.mobilebook.Attendees.1">
      <adfmf:amx/>
   </adfmf:content>
</adfmf:feature>
```

Note that the <adfmf:amx/> is empty. As soon as you define a file that implements the feature, that file is referenced here.

TIP

If you are starting with an Oracle MAF application and need to create multiple features with the same content type (such as AMX), the XML view of the maf-feature file offers a quick solution. Instead of using the overview editor to create all the features declaratively, simply create the first one declaratively and after that use the XML view to copy this first feature and paste it as many times as you need. You need to manually change id, name, and content id, but still, this can be a faster way to set up multiple features from scratch.

Let's continue with the creation of the Attendees feature. The Attendees feature is based on a task flow. On the Content tab, you need to invoke the plus icon at the File reference. When you pick task flow, this will invoke the Create MAF Task Flow dialog where you need to enter a name for the new task flow as you can see in Figure 12-3.

After you click OK, the feature definition now contains a reference to the task flow in the content definition.

```
<adfmf:content id="com.tamcapp.mobilebook.Attendees.1">
   <adfmf:amx file="com.tamcapp.mobilebook.Attendees/AttendeeTaskFlow.xml#AttendeeTaskFlow"/>
</adfmf:content>
```

NOTE

You can actually define multiple content entries. That is, one feature can have multiple task flows or multiple pages defined. You have to use the constraints section on the content section in order to define when to use which content. For example, you can define two different task flows for one single feature. Based on a constraint, one would be used for tablet layout and the other for smartphones. This concept will be explained in more detail in Chapter 18.

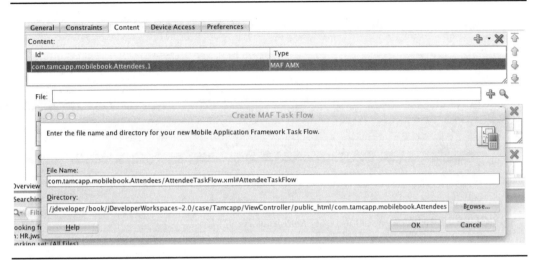

FIGURE 12-3.   *Create the Attendees feature as a mobile task flow.*

Continue to create the content for all other features based on AMX. All will use task flows as content type. In a later stage, you will also implement a feature that is not based on a task flow, but directly on an AMX page.

Working with Feature Archives

In the previous section all features were added to the maf-feature.xml. Although this works fine, there is another solution. To enable reuse by MAF ViewController projects, application features are bundled into an archive known as a Feature Archive (FAR). A FAR is a JAR file that contains the application feature artifacts that can be consumed by mobile applications. Such an approach would typically lead to multiple small MAF application workspaces with one or a few features, instead of one big MAF application workspace with many features.

All features in a FAR can be used in a MAF application by adding them as feature references in the maf-application.xml.

In order to create a FAR and use the features contained in the FAR in a consuming application, you must take three simple steps. The first is the creation of a new Feature Archive deployment profile on the ViewController project that you want to deploy as a FAR by invoking the context menu on the ViewController and choosing Deploy | New Deployment Profile. In the Create dialog you must select MAF Feature Archive.

With the deployment profile in place, you can now deploy the ViewController project as a FAR. The FAR will be saved on the file system and is ready to be used in other MAF applications.

In order to use the FAR in an application, you must have a File System Connection in JDeveloper that points to the location where the FAR was saved. If you don't have such a connection, you must create one. Open the Resources window, choose New, then IDE Connections, and then choose File System and enter the location where the Feature Archive is saved. If all is configured correctly, you

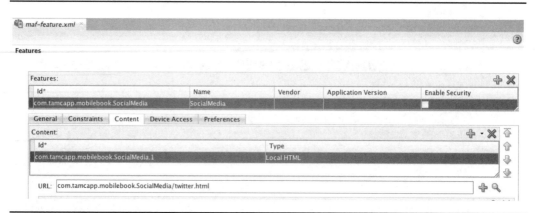

FIGURE 12-4. *Define social media feature as Local HTML.*

should now be able to find the FAR in the Resource window. Now you can right-click the Feature Archive file and choose "Add to Application As" and then choose Library.

All features in the FAR are now available for use in the consuming MAF application and can be added as feature references to the maf-application.xml file.

Local HTML: The Social Media Feature

For the Social Media feature, the Local HTML content type will be used. This enables you to create your own HTML page.

Setup for the Local HTML is very easy, as shown in Figure 12-4. At the feature level on the Content tab, simply select Local HTML as type. JDeveloper now enables you to either create a new HTML file or to browse to an existing file on your filesystem. Click the plus icon, and enter the name of the local HTML file, in this case, twitter.html.

The real content of this page will be created in Chapter 15.

Remote URL: The Organizations Remote Feature

The Organizations feature to send out push messages is implemented as a remote URL. Remote URL content is actually a reference to a web application. Remote content can complement AMX and Local HTML content by providing server-side generated HTML content. The remote URL implementation requires a valid web address as well as a hosted web application. The hosted web application does not necessarily need to be a mobile web application. However, it is good or even best practice to only use hosted web applications that are optimized to use in mobile browsers. It is obvious that remote URL content requires a network connection and therefore is not accessible in disconnected mode.

Setup for the remote URL is very easy as shown in Figure 12-5. At the feature level on the Content tab, simply select Remote URL as type. JDeveloper now shows you the Edit URL Connection dialog box, which you will learn about later. Also, you can instruct Oracle MAF to show browser navigation buttons. These buttons would allow you to go back, forward, and refresh the remote URL content.

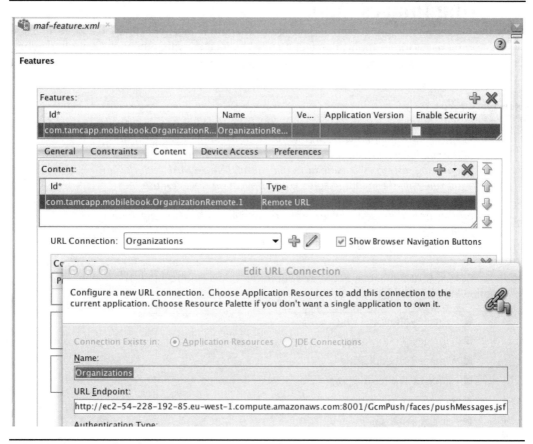

FIGURE 12-5. *Define the Organizations Remote feature as a remote URL.*

When you define a new URL connection to invoke a remote URL, JDeveloper adds the reference to the features definition file. The connection that JDeveloper created is now also available as an application resource (as you can see in Figure 12-6), so it can be used in other features in the mobile application.

FIGURE 12-6. *The URL connection for the Organizations Remote URL*

Using Images

The images on the springboard and navigation bar are in fact application feature-level resources. Custom images for an application feature must be located within the ViewController\public_html directory. If possible, create a subdirectory called images so that you have the images in a separate folder.

NOTE
Oracle MAF does not support resources referenced from another location, meaning that you cannot, for example, enter a value outside of the public_html directory using ../ as a prefix. To safeguard against referencing resources outside of public_ html, Oracle MAF includes an audit rule called File that ensures your application does not use files not in the public_html directory. You can access the Oracle MAF audit profiles from the Audit Profiles node in Preferences by choosing Tools | Preferences | Audit | Profiles. When this profile is selected, JDeveloper issues a warning if you change the location of a resource.

For TAMCAPP the images are in a subfolder under public_html. The features use the following images:

- images/attendees.png
- images/sessions.png
- images/schedule.png
- images/Twitter-Bird.png
- images/organization.png
- images/maps.png

NOTE
If an application feature uses custom images for the navigation bar and springboard rather than the default ones provided by Oracle MAF, you must create these images to the specifications described by Android and iOS separately. For Android, this is specified on the Android Developers web site. For iOS, this is covered in the chapter entitled "Custom Icon and Image Creation Guidelines" in the iOS Human Interface Guidelines, which is available from the iOS Developer Library.

To define the icon to use for a feature on the navigation bar and separately the springboard, these need to be defined under the relating fields of the General tab for the corresponding feature. Figure 12-7 shows an example of this for the Social Media feature.

There is also an option to define images on the Content tab of the corresponding feature. The default setting here is to take the image that is defined on the General tab. However, you can overwrite this behavior by defining a specific image on the Content tab. You would use this in the

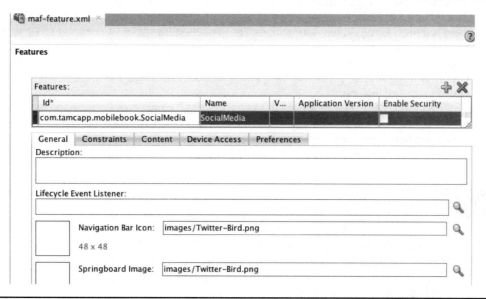

FIGURE 12-7. *Springboard and navigation bar images for the Social Media feature*

scenario where you have multiple contents for different form factors, mobile OS, or any other device characteristics.

Creating the TAMCAPP Custom Springboard

A springboard is a very common navigation control on mobile apps. Some of them have the very common "list-like" springboards, which is the same as the Oracle MAF default springboard. Others have very fancy springboards in a matrix layout or any other kind of layout.

As mentioned, a detailed description of how to implement all the features is provided in the next chapters of the book. The features can be invoked from the springboard. As you learned in Chapter 7, a springboard is automatically created for you, but you can also create a custom springboard. In the next section, you will learn how to create a custom springboard.

TIP

If you want to see how Oracle MAF implements the default springboard and benefit from this, you can look at the source of the default springboard. The default springboard is an AMX page that is bundled in a Feature Archive (FAR) JAR file and deployed with other FARs that are included in the Oracle MAF application. This JAR file includes all of the artifacts associated with a springboard, such as the DataBindings.cpx and PageDef.xml files. This file is only available after you select Default as the springboard option in the maf-application .xml file. You can open the FAR and have a look at the springboard.amx file yourself.

Oracle MAF enables you to create custom springboards and use them in the MAF application. As mentioned in Chapter 6, the default Oracle MAF springboard uses the List layout. For TAMCAPP, there is a need for a grid-like springboard. For implementing the most common UI pattern for navigation, the grid springboard, you need to create a custom springboard. Grid springboards display application features in a grid layout, for instance, in a 2 × 2 or 3 × 3 grid. When creating a custom springboard, an additional Oracle MAF feature containing the springboard needs to be added to the application.

This Oracle MAF feature is used to implement the springboard. Because the feature represents the springboard, it must be configured so it doesn't show up at the springboard or on the navigation bar. These configurations are part of the maf-application.xml file. Later in this chapter you will learn more about this.

TIP
You can also decide to create images that already have the text of the feature embedded. This way, the creation of the matrix layout, or any other, is easier. Bear in mind, though, that there is no easy way to change this text. As a matter of fact, you will have to create new images whenever the text changes. Another disadvantage is that you cannot use a resource bundle for multiple languages. But if it is only the layout that worries you, the images are an easy solution.

The first step in the process is to create a new AMX page. This AMX page contains the layout containers to render the grid that contains the springboard features. The custom springboard in this case must be defined as an Oracle MAF feature that gets its content from an AMX mobile page as displayed in Figure 12-8. This page is created just like any other AMX page. It will display icons for each feature of the application.

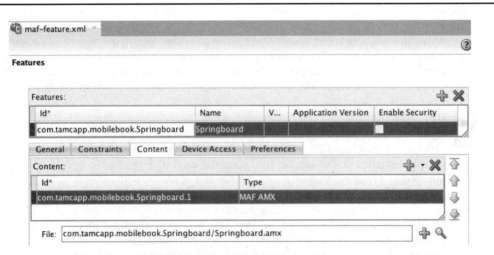

FIGURE 12-8. *Custom springboard feature definition*

When laying out the springboard in a 3 × 2 matrix, you can use a table component, with rows and cells contained within a panelGroupLayout component whose inline style width property is set to 33 percent. In this way, three of those components will add up to take 100 percent (actually 99 percent) of the available width.

```
<amx:panelGroupLayout id="plam2"
    inlineStyle="width:33%;display:inline-block;"
    halign="center" valign="middle">
```

The page renders the springboard based on a table layout whose real content is derived from an iterator. Within this iterator the panelGroupLayout component is used. In order to create a springboard with three columns, the iterator stamps out one panelGroupLayout component per entry in the iterator.

```
<amx:iterator var="row"
                value="#{bindings.features.collectionModel}"
                id="i1">
    <amx:panelGroupLayout id="plam2"
                    inlineStyle="width:33%;display:inline-block;"
                    halign="center" valign="middle">

... ... ...
```

The <amx:iterator/> component is created by dragging and dropping the features collection from the ApplicationFeatures data control (Figure 12-9). This collection contains all the features of the MAF application (with property show on Springboard = true) and is used in the springboard to create entries for all these features by simply iterating this collection.

You can also use the ApplicationFeatures data control to add components that can be used to navigate from the springboard to a feature such as the gotoFeature() (Figure 12-10) operation, which, when invoked and supplied with a feature name, navigates to the corresponding feature.

You can drag-and-drop the gotoFeature() method from the ApplicationsFeatures data control into the cellFormat to create a commandLink. A commandLink can embed, which makes it ideal for showing an icon for a feature it may invoke.

FIGURE 12-9. *The Features collection on the ApplicationFeatures data control*

FIGURE 12-10. *gotoFeature*

This drag-and-drop action will also create a MethodAction binding in the PageDefinition file of the springboard page. The MethodAction binding has a NamedData section that contains NDName, NDType, and NDValue attributes to define the parameter that is used to invoke the gotoFeature method, namely in this case, the feature name to navigate to. By default, the NDValue is empty, so you need to supply it with a valid feature name as a string.

This value would typically be the Id of the feature that needs to be invoked from the springboard. In the code of the springboard AMX page, you notice a setPropertyListener that takes the Id of the current row ("#{row.id}") and puts that into a PageFlowScope variable called FeatureId.

```
<amx:setPropertyListener type="action"
                         from="#{row.id}
                         to="#{pageFlowScope.FeatureId}" />
```

This pageFlowScope variable can now be used in the NDValue of the MethodAction binding. The ADF binding framework will handle the proper invocation for you.

```
<methodAction id="gotoFeature" RequiresUpdateModel="true"
              Action="invokeMethod"
              MethodName="gotoFeature"
              IsViewObjectMethod="false"
              DataControl="ApplicationFeatures"
              InstanceName="data.ApplicationFeatures.dataProvider">
    <NamedData NDName="featureId"
               NDValue="#{pageFlowScope.FeatureId}"
               NDType="java.lang.String"/>
</methodAction>
```

The final thing to do is to provide the complete code sample for the final version of the Grid Springboard.

```
<amx:tableLayout id="tl1" inlineStyle="width:100%;">
    <amx:rowLayout id="rl1">
        <amx:cellFormat id="cf1" height="10" inlineStyle="width:100%;"/>
    </amx:rowLayout>
    <amx:rowLayout id="rl4">
        <amx:cellFormat id="cf4" inlineStyle="width:100%;">
            <amx:panelGroupLayout id="pgl1" layout="wrap" halign="center">
                <amx:iterator var="row"
                              value="#{bindings.features.collectionModel}"
                              id="i1">
                    <amx:panelGroupLayout id="plam2"
                                  inlineStyle="width:33%;display:inline-block;"
                                  halign="center" valign="middle">
                        <amx:tableLayout id="tl2">
                            <amx:rowLayout id="rl2">
                                <amx:cellFormat id="cf2" halign="center"
                                                valign="middle">
                                    <amx:commandLink
                                    actionListener="#{bindings.gotoFeature.execute}"
                                    id="cl3">
                                        <amx:image id="i2" source="#{row.image}"
                                               inlineStyle="width:44px;height:44px"/>
                                        <amx:setPropertyListener type="action"
                                                from="#{row.id}
                                                to="#{pageFlowScope.FeatureId}" />
                                    </amx:commandLink>
                                </amx:cellFormat>
                            </amx:rowLayout>
                            <amx:rowLayout id="rl3">
                                <amx:cellFormat id="cf3" halign="center"
                                                valign="middle">
                                    <amx:commandLink id="cl2"
                                    actionListener="#{bindings.gotoFeature.execute}">
                                        <amx:outputText value="#{row.name}" id="ot2"/>
                                        <amx:setPropertyListener type="action"
                                                from="#{row.id}"
                                                to="#{pageFlowScope.FeatureId}"/>
                                    </amx:commandLink>
                                </amx:cellFormat>
                            </amx:rowLayout>
                        </amx:tableLayout>
                        <amx:spacer id="s2" height="25"/>
                    </amx:panelGroupLayout>
                </amx:iterator>
            </amx:panelGroupLayout>
        </amx:cellFormat>
    </amx:rowLayout>
</amx:tableLayout>
```

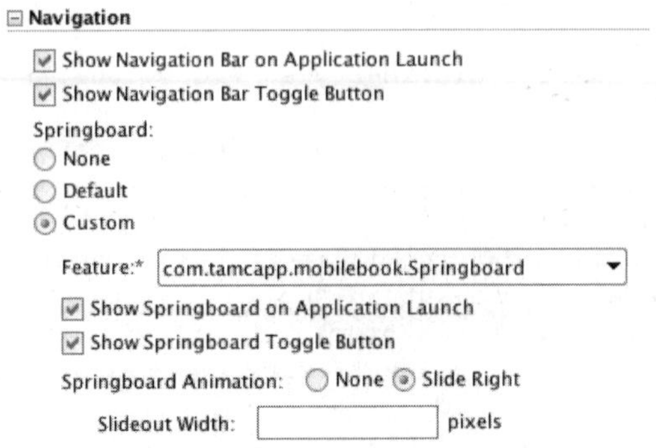

FIGURE 12-11. *Configuration to use a custom springboard*

Finally, the newly created AMX page needs to be linked to the applications as a springboard. This setting is part of the maf-application.xml file. When you define a custom springboard, Oracle MAF needs to know which feature implements that custom springboard. For TAMCAPP, you will use the designated springboard feature called "Springboard" (Figure 12-11).

The feature that implements the springboard should not be visible on either the navigation bar or within the springboard of the Oracle MAF application. It is invoked by the toggle Springboard button. Therefore, both "Show on Navigation Bar" and "Show on Springboard" must both be set to false in the maf-application.xml, as you can see in Figure 12-12.

Now that the new custom springboard is completely built and configured, it will look like a "real" grid-like springboard, as you can see in Figure 12-13.

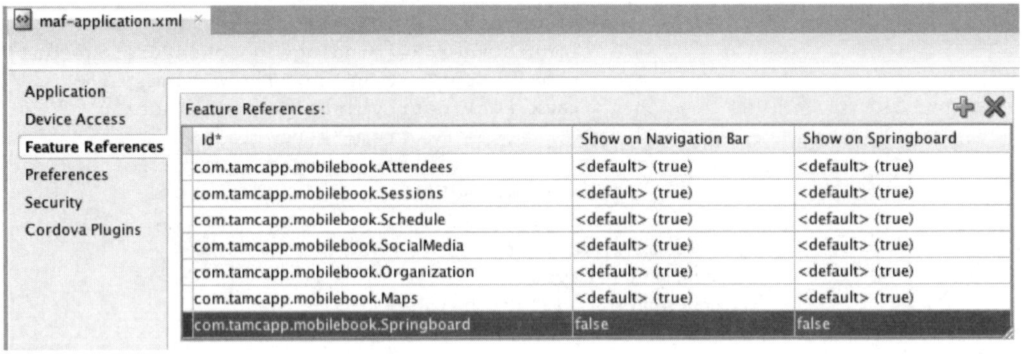

FIGURE 12-12. *Disable the display of custom springboard on springboard and navigation bar.*

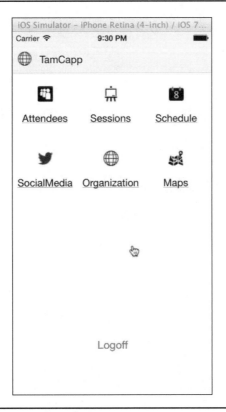

FIGURE 12-13.   *The custom springboard in action*

Summary

The TAMCAPP application is now set up, and the springboard is created. All features are defined. Now you are ready to learn how to implement the real functionality of TAMCAPP. In this chapter you learned how to set up an Oracle MAF application and how to create a dynamic custom springboard. Also, you learned

- How to find all features that are displayed on the springboard
- How to invoke features using the binding framework
- How to use propertyListeners to supply values to MethodActions

CHAPTER
13

Building the Conference
Session Feature

D uring a conference you definitely want to have all information about conference sessions available at any time and any place. For the TAMCAPP application, this functionality is implemented in the Conference Session feature. The feature provides access to all session information; you can see the sessions grouped by track, and you are able to filter and search for sessions and even build your own conference schedule. Besides that, if you are a speaker, you are able to see evaluations of your sessions. Therefore, the Conference Session feature is more or less the most important feature of the TAMCAPP app.

From a development perspective, the Conference Session feature contains many aspects of the Oracle Mobile Application Framework. The Conference Session feature is implemented by a task flow (Figure 13-1). This task flow contains view activities for browsing the sessions, looking at a selected session in detail from the browse screen, and the session evaluations required for speakers, all of which are accessible from the start activity. However, when you are not a speaker, you will not see this start activity and you will be routed directly to the session list in the Browse Sessions AMX page.

Besides the visible content, the Conference Session feature also contains functionality such as navigating from a List AMX page to a Detail AMX page and adding conference sessions to a personal schedule that is stored in the on-device SQLite database while offline, and synchronized to the enterprise database when online. The view activities in the task flow are implemented as Oracle MAF AMX pages. The next sections describe how these view activities are implemented. Let's start with the Browse Sessions AMX page.

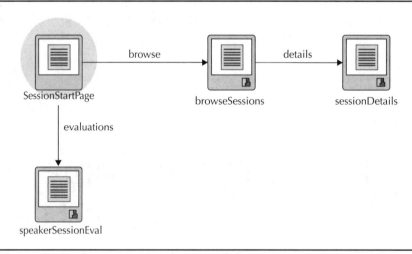

FIGURE 13-1. *The Conference Sessions feature task flow*

Implementing Browse Conference Sessions

The Browse Conference Session AMX page (Figure 13-2) shows all sessions that are available during the conference. The information on this page is derived from a SOAP web service. On entering the Browse Session AMX page, all available conference sessions are fetched and displayed in a list view. From within this list, you can add sessions to your schedule and navigate to the Session Details page. The technical implementation of the Browse Conference Sessions list consists of three parts starting with a web service data control. This data control is then used in a Java class called ConferenceSessions. This Java class has its own data control that delivers its data to the Conference Session List AMX page via a PageDefinition file.

Connecting to the Data

Calling out to a web service retrieves the information on the Conference Sessions list. The web service that is used for this is a SOAP XML web service. Specific implementation details for the web service are beyond the scope of this book. The web service provides several operations, but for the Conference Sessions feature, only a couple of them are relevant:

- **searchSessions**   Based on a search String, returns all conference sessions meeting the search criteria.

- **updateAttendances**   This operation is used to send conference session evaluations to the server.

- **createAttendances**   This operation is used to create a session attendance when a conference session is added to the user's personal schedule.

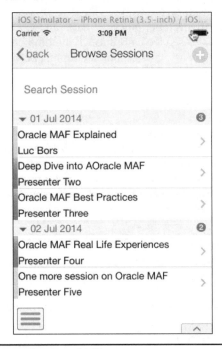

FIGURE 13-2.   *The Conference Sessions AMX page*

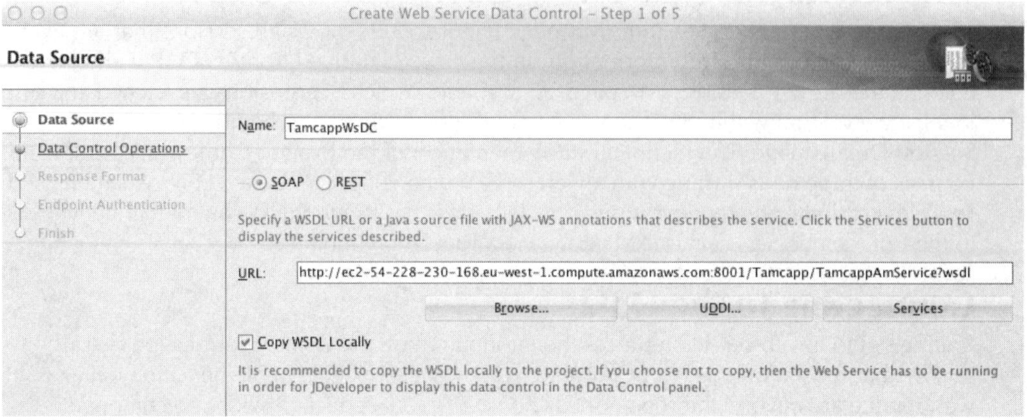

FIGURE 13-3. *Creating the WebService data control*

Because the web service is a SOAP web service, the TAMCAPP application can invoke the web service by using a web service data control. Within JDeveloper the web service data control uses the SOAP web service's WSDL at design time to define what operations are available for the MAF application to consume (Figure 13-3).

As described earlier in Chapter 5, it's tempting to use JDeveloper's easy drag-and-drop features to create pages based on the web service data control operations straight from the Data Control panel. In this way JDeveloper quickly creates all the AMX page components and wires them up to the back-end web service calls through the binding layer, with little coding effort.

Yet this approach, while easy, creates a tight coupling between your AMX page and the external web service. If the web service changes in any way, this will instantly break the page and you'll have to re-create it from scratch. This approach also doesn't allow for many other useful features like caching, data filtering, and additional aggregation such as combining the results of several web service calls.

An alternative approach, and a best practice not only with Oracle MAF, is to create an abstraction layer between the web service and the MAF AMX page. This abstraction layer is best implemented by a Java bean that calls the web service programmatically. We then expose the Java bean through a POJO data control. The general name for this approach is Bean Data Control Service object pattern. This pattern can be visualized by the image as displayed in Figure 13-4, and we'll investigate it further in the following sections.

Creating the Conference-Session Bean

The Conference-Session bean, or Conference-Session Service object if we stick to the pattern name, is the class that calls the web service. As explained in Chapter 5, for this, Oracle MAF can use the invokeDataControlMethod() method from the AdfmfJavaUtilities class. This method enables developers to call out to a method on a data control directly, without using a pageDefinition. This means that without having an MAF AMX page, developers are still able to work with data control operations.

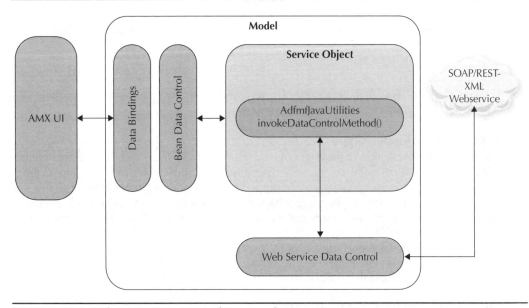

FIGURE 13-4.   *The Bean Data Control Service object pattern*

NOTE
The data control containing the method MUST be available in the databindings.cpx file. If not, the invokeDataControlMethod() method cannot find it and throws an exception. There are several ways to get the data control in the databindings.cpx file. It can be added manually, but it can also be added by dropping one of the data control's operations on an MAF AMX page. Dropping from the data control will add the entry to the databindings.cpx, as well as change the AMX file and the corresponding pageDefinition file. You need to manually remove these changes from the AMX file and pageDefinition file, whereas the entry in the databindings.cpx must be saved.

```
GenericType result = (GenericType)AdfmfJavaUtilities.invokeDataControlMethod("
TamcappWsDC", null,
"searchSessions", pnames, params, ptypes);
```

This call is part of the searchConferenceSessions() method in the ConferenceSessions class. The result (a GenericType) of this method call can now be processed and turned into the ConferenceSession object to be explained later.

```
int x = result.getAttributeCount();
for (int i = 0; i < x; i++) {
    GenericType infoResult = (GenericType)result.getAttribute(i);
```

```
ConferenceSession cs = new ConferenceSession ();
cs = (ConferenceSession)
      GenericTypeBeanSerializationHelper.fromGenericType(
    ConferenceSession.class, infoResult);
addSearchResult(cs);
}
```

Note that this code snippet uses GenericType and GenericTypeBeanSerializationHelper. Both will be explained next.

Explaining the GenericType

The internal representation of the data payload returned by both the web service data control and URL (or REST) data control is not strongly typed. Internally, the Oracle MAF implementation uses a class known as GenericType, a simple property map containing name/value pairs to store individual payload elements, in a larger hierarchical structure to represent the hierarchical structures often returned in web services. GenericType includes methods like getAttribute, where you supply the index of the attribute or its string property name, and it returns the matching value. As seen from the preceding example, the invokeDataControlMethod returns a GenericType object, and developers either need to parse these GenericType objects themselves or use the GenericTypeBeanSerializationHelper, MAF Frameworks helper class for this.

GenericTypeBeanSerializationHelper

The GenericTypeBeanSerializationHelper class is a helper class for developers to aid in marshaling and unmarshaling the data contained within the GenericType. Rather than you having to programmatically take each element from the GenericTypes structure and then instantiate your own objects and populate the attributes one by one, which can be quite error-prone and laborious, the helper class will do the complete conversion for you en masse from the GenericType to your specified POJO structure, and back again where necessary.

To satisfy converting from the GenericType to your own POJOs, the helper class provides the fromGenericType method. This method takes as a parameter the class of the Java object you wish to return and the GenericType as parameters. The method instantiates instances of your Java object for you, then reads through each attribute in the GenericType and uses reflection to set that same attribute in the Java class. Finally, the method returns the instance of the class you specified as a parameter.

The reverse method, toGenericType, is also available when you want to go the other way. In this case, you supply the string that represents the package location in the data control definition (example: "MyDC.myParams.MyCollection") and then pass in the Java object you have that holds the data, and a GenericType is returned to you. Again, it will use reflection to calculate the attributes that match between the Java class and the GenericType and call the getters/setters on those.

Creating the Conference Session POJOs

Usually, the result of a web service call does not have the exact same data structure that the mobile application needs. To be in full control of the data structure, the result of the web service call is transformed to the application's specific data model, represented by one or more POJOs.

For the TAMCAPP app, the session POJO is described in the following code sample. Note that the Slot object is not a simple data type; it represents an object, the actual timeslot in which the Conference-Session is planned, containing both a start and stop date and time.

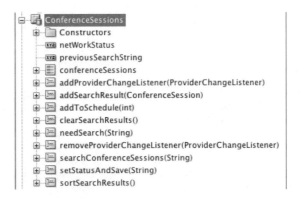

FIGURE 13-5.   *The ConferenceSessions data control*

```
public class ConferenceSession {
    int id;
    String presenterName;
    String title;
    String sessionAbstract;
    String topic;
    String room;
    Slot slot;
```

Creating the Bean Data Control

Once we have our basic Java class that we want to expose to the AMX UI through a data control, creating a data control for the Java class is simple. Just right-click on the Java class in the Application Navigator and select Create Data Control. For the ConferenceSessions class, the data control is displayed in Figure 13-5.

When you take a close look at this data control, you see that it resembles the structure of the ConferenceSessions class. In the next sections you will learn more about this class and its methods. All methods from the ConferenceSessions Java class are available as operations on this data control. These operations have results that are represented by collections that can be dragged from the data control onto the page. This functionality enables developers to create MAF AMX pages very quickly, as you will learn in the next sections.

Building the Conference Session List AMX Page

Creation of the List View starts with the creation of a simple MAF AMX page. This AMX page is created by double-clicking the corresponding view activity on the task flow diagram. The next step is to drag and drop the conferenceSessions collection from the data control on the AMX page as a "List View" as displayed in Figure 13-6.

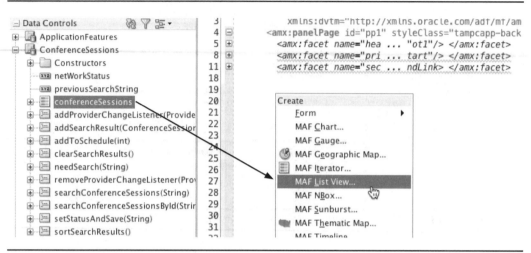

FIGURE 13-6. *Drop collection as List View*

After dropping the collection as a List View, JDeveloper prompts you to select one of the available predefined layouts. After you choose the appropriate one, the list attributes need to be set and also a divider attribute can be configured. The divider attribute is used by Oracle MAF to group the list entries. For the Conference Sessions feature, the Date is a perfect divider attribute because it will show all conference sessions per date (Figure 13-7).

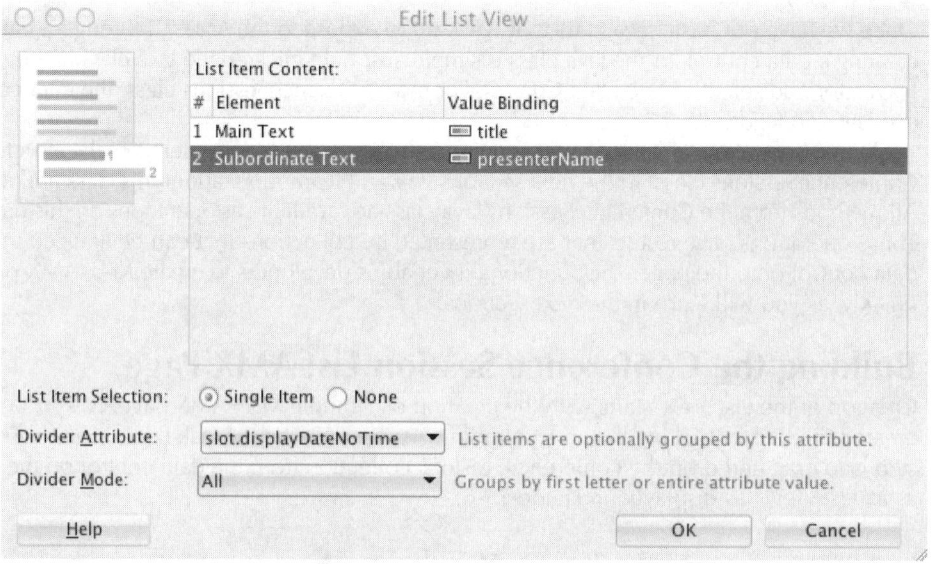

FIGURE 13-7. *List View configuration*

The final result is displayed in the following code sample:

```
<amx:listView var="row"
    value="#{bindings.conferenceSessions.collectionModel}"
    fetchSize="#{bindings.conferenceSessions.rangeSize}"
    dividerMode="all" id="lv1"
    dividerAttribute="slot.displayDateNoTime" collapsibleDividers="true"
    selectedRowKeys=
        "#{bindings.conferenceSessions.collectionModel.selectedRow}"
    selectionListener=
        "#{bindings.conferenceSessions1.collectionModel.makeCurrent}"
    showDividerCount="true" collapsedDividers='"02 Jul 2013" '>
  <amx:listItem id="li1" action="details">
     <amx:tableLayout width="100%" id="tl2">
        <amx:rowLayout id="rl2">
           <amx:cellFormat width="8px" halign="center" rowSpan="2" id="cf5"
                           valign="middle"/>
           <amx:cellFormat width="100%" height="28px" id="cf3">
              <amx:outputText value="#{row.title}" id="ot3"/>
           </amx:cellFormat>
        </amx:rowLayout>
        <amx:rowLayout id="rl3">
           <amx:cellFormat width="100%" height="12px" id="cf1">
              <amx:outputText value="#{row.presenterName}"id="ot2"/>
           </amx:cellFormat>
        </amx:rowLayout>
     </amx:tableLayout>
  </amx:listItem>
</amx:listView>
```

Note that the value for the listView is derived from an EL expression:

```
<amx:listView value="#{bindings. conferenceSessions.collectionModel}"
```

This EL expression evaluates to the tree binding called sessions in the PageDefinition of the MAF AMX page.

```
<tree IterBinding=" conferenceSessions Iterator" id=" conferenceSessions ">
   <nodeDefinition>
     …..
   </nodeDefinition>
</tree>
```

Implementing Search for Conference Sessions

By default, all available conference sessions are displayed in the list. The TAMCAPP application provides the possibility to search within the conference sessions. This search functionality is implemented by the same web service.

The method needed for searching is searchConferenceSessions. This operation can also be dragged/dropped onto the page (Figure 13-8). As the user will need a field to enter the search criteria and a button to invoke the search method, a parameter form is the best choice. This will

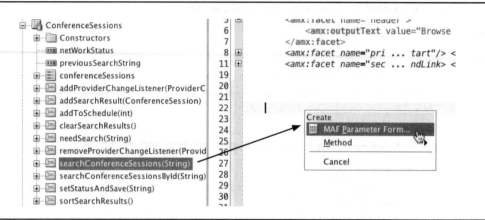

FIGURE 13-8. *Drag-and-drop parameter form*

create the necessary amx:inputText and amx:commandButton control and the associated bindings
to call the data control searchConferenceSessions method.

The corresponding MAF AMX page code is displayed in the following example:

```
<amx:tableLayout id="tl1" width="100%" shortDesc="Table">
  <amx:rowLayout id="rl1">
    <amx:cellFormat id="cf2" width="100%" shortDesc="Cell">
      <amx:inputText simple="true" id="inputText2"
                     value="#{bindings.searchString.inputValue}"
                     hintText="Search Session"/>
    </amx:cellFormat>
    <amx:cellFormat id="cf4" width="48px" halign="center" shortDesc="Cell">
      <amx:commandButton id="cb1a" shortDesc="Search Link"
             icon="/images/find.png"
             actionListener="#{bindings.searchConferenceSessions.execute}">
      </amx:commandButton>
    </amx:cellFormat>
  </amx:rowLayout>
</amx:tableLayout>
```

Invoking the button will call out to the searchConferenceSessions method and take the
searchString value as an argument.

```
public void searchConferenceSessions(String searchString) {
    // clear searchresults before starting a new search
    clearSearchResults();
    List pnames = new ArrayList();
    List params = new ArrayList();
    List ptypes = new ArrayList();
    pnames.add("findCriteria");
    ptypes.add(String.class);
    params.add(null);
    pnames.add("b_searchString");
    ptypes.add(String.class);
```

```
params.add(searchString);
pnames.add("findControl");
ptypes.add(String.class);
params.add(null);
try {
   // This calls the DC method and gives us the Return
    GenericType result =
       (GenericType)AdfmfJavaUtilities.invokeDataControlMethod("TamcappWsDC",
       null, "searchSessions", pnames, params, ptypes);
```

Preventing Unnecessary Web Service Calls

After the first call to the web service, the result is stored in memory in the ConferenceSessions class as a List of ConferenceSessions in the s_searchResults object. When navigating from the List page to the Details page and back again, by default, the web service would be called again, and not only is this not necessary if we've already fetched the data, but it will unnecessarily slow the application down and annoy the user!

Preventing the web service call is actually very easy and can be done from within the same Java code. We simply check if the search criteria have changed and if the Sessions collection is empty. If either condition is true, we then make the web service call; otherwise, there's no work to be done:

```
if (s_searchResults.isEmpty()){
    searchConferenceSessions(currentSearchString);
}
else {
  if (!currentSearchString.equalsIgnoreCase(previousSearchString)){
      searchConferenceSessions(currentSearchString);
      setPreviousSearchString(currentSearchString);
  }
}
```

Note that the binding layer itself does not cache data and thus the caching must be done in the model by the POJO service object. This, of course, only works as long as the bean that caches the data exists in memory. There are several scenarios where you might want to hold on to data for a longer time, such as when you have no network access or when you want to persist data even when the TAMCAPP app is closed or even while the device is shut down.

Later in this chapter you will learn how to use the local SQLite database to support these scenarios.

The Conference Session Detail Page

Now the Conference Session List page is complete. The next step in implementing the Conference Session feature is the creation of the Conference Session Detail page. The Conference Session Detail page (Figure 13-9) is a page where you can browse the specific details of a given session. This includes time, room, and abstract, but also you can download and view the session paper. Instead of using a List layout, this page uses a Form layout.

The page can be created in exactly the same way as the list page by dragging and dropping the Session collection from the Data Control panel (Figure 13-10). This time, it must be dropped as a form instead of a List View.

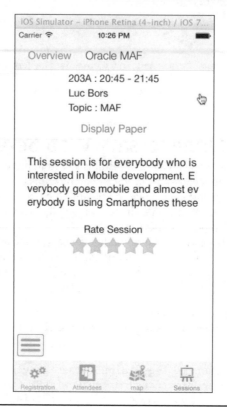

FIGURE 13-9. *The Conference Sessions Detail page*

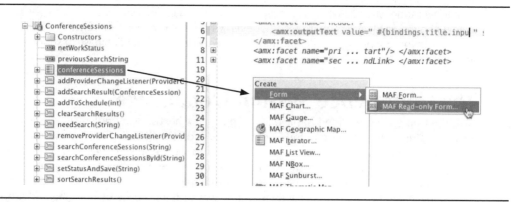

FIGURE 13-10. *Creating the Conference Session Detail page*

For the layout of the Conference Session Detail page, there is nothing really special. The only things worth mentioning are the grouping of the room, session start time, and session end time. By placing these three components in one cellFormat component, they are displayed in one line.

```
<amx:cellFormat id="cf2">
    <amx:outputText value="#{bindings.room.inputValue} : "
                    styleClass="tamcapp-smaller-text" id="ot7"/>
    <amx:outputText value="#{bindings.displayStartTime.inputValue} - "
                    styleClass="tamcapp-smaller-text" id="ot10
    <amx:outputText value="#{bindings.displayEndTime.inputValue}"
                    styleClass="tamcapp-smaller-text" id="ot10a"/>
</amx:cellFormat>
```

The session abstract text is displayed in a multiline box without a label. This is achieved by setting the rows attribute of the inputText component to a value greater than 1 and setting the simple property to true:

```
<amx:inputText value="#{bindings.sessionAbstract.inputValue}"
               styleClass="tamcapp-smaller-text" rows="4"
               simple="true" id="ot11"/>
```

Navigating from the List to the Details

If you are in a List View, it makes sense that you want to touch on one of the items in the list and open corresponding details. It is very common that when you navigate from a page that contains a table to a page with a corresponding form, the currently selected row is retained and on the form page that same row is displayed. Of course, this only works when the table and form are based on the same iterator and data collection. Luckily, in Oracle MAF, the current row in a collection is retained when navigating from one page to another, so there is nothing special that you need to do except for using the same iterator and data collection on the List and Details page.

Viewing the Conference Session Paper

A special feature on the Conference Session Detail AMX page is the display of the submitted conference session paper. With the push of a button, the paper is downloaded to the device and displayed in a viewer. For this, the displayFile operation of the Device feature data control is used. This, however, can only display files that are local to the device. That is why documents need to be downloaded first. The downloading and displaying are invoked by one and the same command button that invokes an actionListener containing all necessary code:

```
<amx:commandButton text="Display Paper" id="cb3"
                   actionListener="#{showDocumentBean.remotePreview}"/>
```

In the remotePreview method of the showDocumentBean, the document is downloaded and saved to the local file system. The URL of the document is retrieved from the fileURL property of the Session object. For the Session detail page, this property can be found via the PageDefinition file of the page by using the following EL expression, which evaluates to the file URL:

```
#{bindings.fileURL.inputValue}
```

The expression is used with the getValueExpression() method, and the actual URL is then parsed to create a new URL object for downloading the file to the device:

```
public void remotePreview(ActionEvent e)
{
  URL remoteFileUrl;
  InputStream is;
  FileOutputStream fos;
  try
  {
    // open connection to remote PDF file
    ValueExpression ve =
        AdfmfJavaUtilities.getValueExpression("#{bindings.fileURL.inputValue}"
      , String.class);
    String inputpath =
        (String) ve.getValue(AdfmfJavaUtilities.getAdfELContext());
    if (inputpath != null && !"".equals(inputpath)) {
      remoteFileUrl =  new URL(inputpath);
    }
    URLConnection connection = remoteFileUrl.openConnection();
    is = connection.getInputStream();
    // we write the file to the application directory
    File localFile = new File(
        AdfmfJavaUtilities.getDirectoryPathRoot(
            AdfmfJavaUtilities.DownloadDirectory)
          + "/downloadedPDF.pdf");
```

The processing of the downloaded file is performed by the exact same logic as used in Chapter 8. Finally, the displayFile() method of the Device Features data control reads as follows:

```
// get the header text we want to display
ValueExpression ve1 =
        AdfmfJavaUtilities.getValueExpression(
            "#{bindings.headerText.inputValue}", String.class);
String headerText =
        (String) ve1.getValue(AdfmfJavaUtilities.getAdfELContext());
if (headerText == null || "".equals(headerText)) {
        headerText = "Remote File";
}
// create URL and invoke displayFile with its String representation.
// This String representation is in the buffer which is a StringBuffer
// containing the encoded URL string.
  URL localURL = new URL("file", "localhost", buffer.toString());
  DeviceManagerFactory.getDeviceManager().displayFile(
                                        localURL.toString(),
                                        headerText);
```

Creating Visible Track Indicators

The Conference Sessions List AMX page is now almost finished, though we'd like to include one last feature to help users. We'd like to include a visual color indicator for each session to distinguish between different tracks at the conference; often, conferences have multiple tracks covering different topics, so this is an important addition. For TAMCAPP, a colored bar is used in front of each session. This bar is implemented by using a combination of Expression Language and CSS.

In Oracle MAF, skinning can be used to apply certain CSS-defined styles to the application. Skinning of an Oracle MAF application is a mechanism that enables you to provide the application with a custom look and feel and was described in Chapter 4.

Setting the Indicator Color

The styles for the color indicators are defined in the tamcapp.css and use a gradient, but that, of course, is just a matter of taste. The greenCell and redCell are used in the MAF AMX pages as color indicators.

```
.greenCell{
  background-image: -webkit-gradient(linear, left bottom, left top,
                    color-stop(0, #00ff00),
                    color-stop(0.48, #52ff52),
                    color-stop(0.49, #63ff63),
                    color-stop(1.00, #73ff73));
}

.redCell{
  background-image: -webkit-gradient(linear, left bottom, left top,
                    color-stop(0, #ff0000),
                    color-stop(0.48, #ff2222),
                    color-stop(0.49, #ff3232),
                    color-stop(1.00, #ffb5b5));
}
```

It is very convenient to see different tracks with different colors. This enables you to see interesting sessions at a glance. For this, the styleClass property can be used. The styleClass property can be based on an EL expression. This EL expression checks what track the session is in, and based on that, a different style is applied to the appropriate component (Figure 13-11).

FIGURE 13-11. *The color indicators for conference session tracks*

```
<amx:cellFormat width="8px" halign="center" rowSpan="2" id="cf5"
        styleClass=" #{row.topic=='Oracle MAF' ? 'greenCell' : 'redCell' }"
        valign="middle">
</amx:cellFormat>
```

Evaluate Conference Sessions

Conference session evaluations provide valuable feedback for presenters. Based on these evaluations, presenters can see how the audience liked their presentations and if there is room for improvement.

In TAMCAPP, the evaluation of conference sessions is implemented on the Session Detail MAF AMX page. The evaluations can be done by means of a star-rating component. This component is part of the Oracle MAF mobile DVT component library and is exactly the component you need. It provides the possibility to enter a rating between 1 and 5 by selecting stars.

```
<dvtm:ratingGauge id="ratingGauge1" inputIncrement="half"
     emptyText="Evaluation Pending" maxValue="5"
     minValue="0" inlineStyle="height:50%;"
     value="#{bindings.conferenceSessionRating.inputValue}"
     valueChangeListener=
          "#{pageFlowScope.conferenceSessionBean.RateConfSession}"/>
```

The component has a valueChangeListener that is fired whenever the value of the component changes. These changes are immediately processed by the updateAttendences operation of the web service.

The operation (Figure 13-12) takes an Attendences object containing the rating among others.

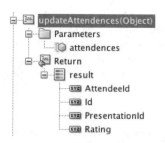

FIGURE 13-12. *UpdateAttendences operation*

View Conference Session Evaluations

If you are a presenter, you can view your conference session evaluations. These evaluations are displayed on a speaker dashboard. The dashboard shows a graph displaying the number of responses per rating and also some extra information, such as skills, materials, and added value, displayed in gauges. How this specific page is hidden from nonpresenters is explained in Chapter 16.

The MAF AMX page (Figure 13-13) with the evaluations can be created very easily. The Oracle MAF Data Visualization Components can be based on data-bound collections in exactly the same way as tables and forms. The collections and/or attributes can be dragged from the data control and dropped as a DVT component. For the bar chart with scores, this is displayed in Figure 13-14.

NOTE
For the purpose of the evaluation AMX page, a bean and a data control were created.

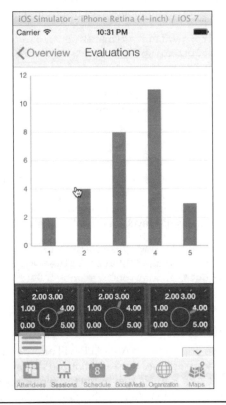

FIGURE 13-13. *Speaker Evaluations dashboard*

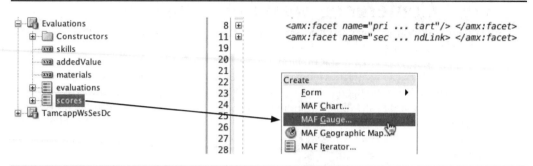

FIGURE 13-14. *Creating the Session Evaluations dashboard*

The Evaluations data control is based on the Evaluations class. This class contains methods getEvaluations() and getScores(). Describing the class, its methods, and how to create a data control from it would result in more of the same. Therefore, this is not explained again. Using the data control for drag-and-drop as a mobile chart results in the following AMX code:

```
<dvtm:barChart var="row" value="#{bindings.scores.collectionModel}" id="bc1"
               animationOnDisplay="auto" animationOnDataChange="auto"
               animationDuration="2500">
    <amx:facet name="dataStamp">
        <dvtm:chartDataItem group="#{row.score}" value="#{row.count}"
               series="#{bindings.scores.hints.count.label}" id="cdi1"/>
    </amx:facet>
    <dvtm:legend rendered="false" id="l1"/>
</dvtm:barChart>
```

On the lower part of the sessions evaluation AMX page, there are three gauges displaying ratings for skills, materials, and added value. The gauges are the same, except for the value attribute, which derives its value from three different attribute bindings: addedValue, Materials, and Skills; the code for Skills is displayed in the following code sample:

```
<dvtm:dialGauge minValue="0" maxValue="5" background="rectangleDarkCustom"
                indicator="needleDark" value="#{bindings.skills.inputValue}"
                id="dg1" animationDuration="2500">
```

The Schedule Builder

Like any good conference application, TAMCAPP will allow you to build your own schedule, essentially allowing you to register for sessions that you will attend during the conference. The schedule builder in TAMCAPP is integrated in the Conference Session List AMX page. The schedule is the only part of the TAMCAPP application that supports offline functionality. This means that the data is stored both locally on the device and remotely on the enterprise database.

As described in Chapter 7, the on-device SQLite database can be created on the fly. Data storage and retrieval from an application perspective is done by means of SQL statements.

To support both offline and online functionality, the pending transactions need to be recognized in order to send them to the enterprise database once there is a connection again. So whenever there is no connection, changes are marked as unsynchronized and stored in the local database.

Setting Up the Local SQLite Database

As explained in Chapter 7, Oracle MAF enables you to work with an on-device database. The "My Schedule" data is stored in this local on-device database in the MY_SCHEDULE table. The assumption is made that at initial startup there is not yet any data in "My Schedule" because usually you will not have created a personal schedule before installing the app. Therefore, the only thing needed at initial startup is the creation of the database and the MY_SCHEDULE table to store the future schedule the user will create. For that, we can use the application life cycle listener that resides in the ApplicationController project. This custom life cycle listener class implements the Oracle MAF LifeCycleListener interface and therefore has a start() method. This start() method can be used to install the table scripts at application startup. First, there is a check to see whether or not the database exists. This check is implemented by issuing a select statement on the table. If the statement fails, the assumption is made that the database does not exist and a method is called to create the database tables.

```
public void start(){
try {
    //Getting the connection to the database
     Statement stat = DBConnectionFactory.getConnection().createStatement();
     ResultSet rs = stat.executeQuery("SELECT * FROM MY_SCHEDULE;");
   } catch (SQLException e)
    { // probably means no database file is found
      initDB();
   }
   catch (Exception e) {
     e.printStackTrace();
 }
}
```

The initDB() method takes the tamcapp.sql script, which is deployed with the application, essentially a SQL script to create the MY_SCHEDULE table, opens it, and reads it line by line to execute the SQL statements.

```
/**
  * This method will read the sql file and
  * commit the SQL statements to the SQLite DB
  */
private void initDB() {
   try {
      // SQL script is packaged as a resource with the application,
      // so the getResourceAsStream method can be used
      ClassLoader cl = Thread.currentThread().getContextClassLoader();
      InputStream is = cl.getResourceAsStream(".adf/META-INF/tamcapp.sql");
      if (is == null) {
         System.err.println("Could not look up : .adf/META-INF/tamcapp.sql");
         return;
```

```
      }
      BufferedReader bReader = new BufferedReader(new InputStreamReader(is));
      List stmts = new ArrayList();
      String strstmt = "";
      String ln = bReader.readLine();
      // The while loop iterates over all the lines in the SQL script,
      // assembling them into valid SQL statements and executing them
      // when a terminating semicolon is encountered; skipping blank lines
      // and comments
      while (ln != null) {
         if (ln.startsWith("REM")) {
            ln = bReader.readLine();
            continue;
         }
         strstmt = strstmt + ln;
         if (strstmt.endsWith(";")) {
            stmts.add(strstmt); strstmt = "";
            ln = bReader.readLine(); continue;
         }
         ln = bReader.readLine();
      }
      // To improve performance, the statements are executed
      // one at a time in the context of a single transaction
      DBConnectionFactory.getConnection().setAutoCommit(false);
      for (int i = 0; i < stmts.size(); i++) {
         Statement pStmt =
               DBConnectionFactory.getConnection().createStatement();
         pStmt.executeUpdate((String)stmts.get(i));
      }
      DBConnectionFactory.getConnection().commit();
   } catch (Exception e) {
     e.printStackTrace();
   }
```

The contents of the corresponding tamcapp.sql file are displayed in this code sample:

```
CREATE TABLE MY_SCHEDULE (
   SESSION_ID          NUMBER(4) NOT NULL,
   PRESENTER_NAME      VARCHAR(30),
   SESSION_TITLE       VARCHAR(30),
   SESSION_ABSTRACT    VARCHAR(30) ,
   TOPIC               VARCHAR(30) ,
   ROOM                VARCHAR(30) ,
   SESSION_START       DATE,
   SESSION_END         DATE,
   SYNCHRONIZED        VARCHAR2(1) ,
   CONSTRAINT MY_SCHEDULE_PK PRIMARY KEY(SESSION_ID)
);
```

From within the Conference Session List, you can add conference sessions to your conference schedule. You simply tap the Add button, and the selected session is added to the schedule, or you can use a different but more common way of implementing this, which is using the tapHold gesture. The technical implementation of the schedule builder is described in the following section.

Adding a Conference Session to mySchedule

The way the adding works from within the Conference Session List AMX page is straightforward. The list item contains an amx:actionListener child component to call out to the addToSchedule() method. This needs a method binding that can be created by dragging and dropping the operation from the data control onto the page. An Edit Action Binding dialog (Figure 13-15) is displayed, and the value for the current session can be set to the previously discussed pageFlowScope parameter.

Now whenever the tapHold gesture is invoked, the addToSchedule is called and uses the current ConferenceSession as an argument.

```
<amx:actionListener id="al1"
                    binding="#{bindings.addToSchedule.execute}"
type="tapHold"/>
```

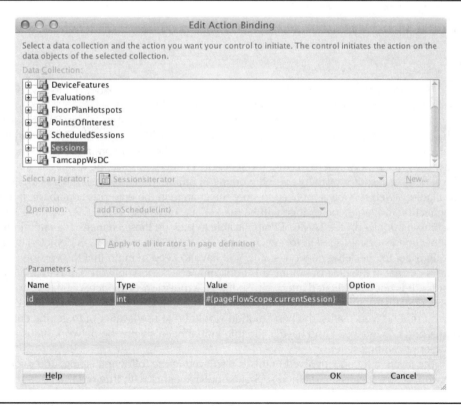

FIGURE 13-15.   *AddSession method binding*

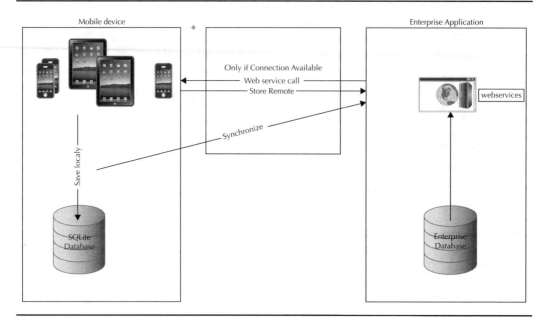

FIGURE 13-16. *Online/offline storage and synchronization*

The same method can be called from the Add button in the header of the Session List AMX page. As mentioned before, the real functionality is implemented in Java.

Adding a conference session to the schedule is actually creating a new ScheduledSession object and adding it to the ScheduledSessions collection. The word "table" is not used on purpose. This is because the entry is actually added to the collection, and behind the scenes, a Java class determines where to store the schedule change. To start, the change is stored in the local database, so it is available when working in offline mode. Next, if there is a connection available, a web service is invoked to store the change in the enterprise database. If there is no connection available, the change will be marked as "unsynchronized." By marking local changes as "unsynchronized," the TAMCAPP app is able to pick up these changes at a later time when a connection is reestablished to try synchronization again. This workflow is depicted in Figure 13-16.

In order to check the network status, you have to keep in mind that the version of Oracle MAF that is current at the time of writing this book only checks the network status at application startup. It is not re-evaluated after that. So the EL expression "#{deviceScope.hardware. networkStatus}" cannot be used when the app is running to get an accurate network status. To get the current network status, the best solution would be to use JavaScript to get the current network status and create a bean and have a variable in that bean signify the network status and have the JavaScript call that setter.

The JavaScript code involved in this is displayed in the following listing, and depending on the network status, it calls the method setStatusAndSave either with true or false.

```
(function () {
    if (!window.application)
        window.application = {
        };

    /**
     * Method to check the network status
     */
    application.checkConnection = function () {
        var networkState = navigator.network.connection.type;
        var states = {
        };
        states[Connection.UNKNOWN] = 'Unknown connection';
        states[Connection.ETHERNET] = 'Ethernet connection';
        states[Connection.WIFI] = 'WiFi connection';
        states[Connection.CELL_2G] = 'Cell 2G connection';
        states[Connection.CELL_3G] = 'Cell 3G connection';
        states[Connection.CELL_4G] = 'Cell 4G connection';
        states[Connection.NONE] = 'No network connection';
        if (networkState == Connection.NONE || networkState == Connection.UNKNOWN) {
            adf.mf.api.invokeMethod("com.tamcapp.mobilebook.mobile.model.Sessions",
                                "setStatusAndSave", "false", onSuccess, onFail);
        }
        else {
            adf.mf.api.invokeMethod("com.tamcapp.mobilebook.mobile.model.Sessions",
                                "setStatusAndSave", "true", onSuccess, onFail);
        }
    }
    function onSuccess(param) { }
    function onFail() {}
})();
```

The setStatusAndSave method in the ConferenceSessions class takes the networkStatus as an argument and puts this in an application scope variable so it is accessible throughout the application.

```
public void setStatusAndSave(String networkStatus) {
    ValueExpression ve = AdfmfJavaUtilities.getValueExpression(
        "#{applicationScope.networkStatus}", String.class);
    ve.setValue(AdfmfJavaUtilities.getAdfELContext(), networkStatus);
}
```

This all comes together in the addToSchedule method, which first checks the networkStatus and then performs the saving of the schedule change:

```
public void addToSchedule(int id){
    // First check to current Network status by calling the javascript function
        AdfmfContainerUtilities.invokeContainerJavaScriptFunction(
            "com.tamcapp.mobilebook.Sessions"
        , "application.checkConnection"
        , new Object[] { });
    String netWorkStatus = getNetWorkStatus();
    ScheduledSession s = getCurrentSession();
    // now depending on the networkstatus call out to the webservice
    if (netWorkStatus.equalsIgnoreCase("true")){
```

```
        // call Webservice
        GenericType result =
          (GenericType)AdfmfJavaUtilities.invokeDataControlMethod("TamcappWsDC",
                null, "saveMyScheduledSession", pnames, params, ptypes);
        // and after that
        // also save locally with synchronized indicator = "Y"
      s.setSyncrhonized("Y");
      AddSessionToDB(s);
    }
     else{
        //  save locally with synchronized indicator = "N".
        s.setSyncrhonized("N");
        AddSessionToDB(s);
      }
  }
}
/* * getNetworkStatus is able to get the networkstatus from the
 **  applicationscope because the applicationScope variable networkstatus
 **  was set when setStatusAndSave was called from the JavaScript function
 */
public String getNetWorkStatus() {
   ValueExpression networkStatusVal =
       AdfmfJavaUtilities.getValueExpression("#{applicationScope.networkStatus}",
                                  String.class);
   return (String)networkStatusVal.getValue(AdfmfJavaUtilities.getAdfELContext());
    }
```

Given that the save functionality is available (described in the final section of this chapter) and functioning, the next step is to implement the actual data synchronization. This can be done automatically, by means of a continuously running background process, which is described later in Chapter 18, after successfully writing a schedule change to the server database. The latter will be discussed in the next section.

NOTE
If the network status is always checked before saving, storing the network status in applicationScope for the purpose we described is not best practice. However, the background process that is implemented in Chapter 18 will check the network status continuously and store it in applicationScope. Therefore, the getNetworkStatus() method in the preceding code sample reads the network status from the applicationScope.

Synchronizing the Schedule Data

The local changes that need to be synchronized are all identified by the SYNCHRONIZED attribute having the value "N". All rows that meet this criteria need to be fetched and saved to the enterprise database, and after successful synchronization, these rows need to be updated to having SYNCHRONIZED = "Y". In fact, this is not really a very difficult task.

```
if (netWorkStatus.equalsIgnoreCase("true")){
        // call Webservice and after that
        // also save locally with synchronized indicator = "Y"
```

```
…. .…………
described earlier
……………
// Finally check for unsynchronized changes and if any are found
List unsynchronizedSessions = fetchUnsynchronized();
// call the webservice to synch and update locally to SYNCHRONIZED="Y"
int x = unsynchronizedSessions.size();
for (int i = 0; i < x; i++) {
  // callWebservice for Session s = (Session) unsynchronizedSessions
  GenericType result =
    (GenericType)AdfmfJavaUtilities.invokeDataControlMethod("TamcappWsDC",
         null, "saveSchedule",pnames, params, ptypes);
  // update synchronized attribute
   s.setSynchronized("Y");
   setSynchronized(s);
  }
}
```

Reading and Writing to the Local Database

For disconnected applications, your code is responsible for populating the local SQLite database. Then, the code that backs the user interface can retrieve data from the SQLite database instead of directly invoking web services, and also work against the SQLite database to store changes locally. All code used in the previous section is located in a class called MyScheduleDbAccessor, which is explained in this section. It contains methods to query the database with a dynamic where clause, to add new records to the database, and to update unsynchronized records to be synchronized.

```
public class MyScheduleDbAccessor {
    private String where;
    /**
      * Method will query the database and return
      * the result list
      */
    public List queryDb() {
    List s_myScheduledSessions = null;
    try {
        Connection conn = DBConnectionFactory.getConnection();
        conn.setAutoCommit(false);
        String statement = "SELECT * from MY_SCHEDULE" + getWhere();
        PreparedStatement stat = conn.prepareStatement(statement);
        ResultSet rs = stat.executeQuery();
        while (rs.next()) {
                int id = rs.getInt("SESSION_ID");
                String presenterName = rs.getString("PRESENTER_NAME");
                String title = rs.getString("TITLE");
                String sessionAbstract = rs.getString("SESSION_ABSTRACT");
                String topic = rs. getString ("TOPIC");
                String room = rs. getString ("ROOM");
                Date sessionStart = rs.getDate("SESSION_START");
                Date sessionEnd = rs.getDate("SESSION_END");
                String synchronized = rs. getString ("SYNCHRONIZED");
                Slot slot = New Slot (sessionStart, sessionEnd);
                ScheduledSession d = new ScheduledSession (id,presenterName,
```

```
                        title, sessionAbstract, topic, room,synchronized slot );
                s_myScheduledSessions.add(d);
            }
        rs.close();
        return s_myScheduledSessions;
        Trace.log(Utility.ApplicationLogger, Level.INFO, MyScheduleDbAccessor.class,
                    "Execute", "Exiting from queryDB Method");
    } catch (SQLException e) {
        System.err.println(e.getMessage());
    } catch (Exception e) {
        System.err.println(e.getMessage());
    }
}
public  List fetchUnsynched (){
    List s_myScheduledSessions = null;
    setWhere("WHERE SYNCHRONIZED='N'");
    s_myScheduledSessions  = queryDb();
    setWhere("");
    return s_myScheduledSessions;
}
  public void getWhere(){
        return this.where;}
  public String setWhere(String where){
            this.where = where;}
    /**
     * Method will commit the details of newly created Session object
     * @return
     */
    public boolean AddSessionToDB(ScheduledSession myScheduledSession) {
    boolean result = false;
        try {
            Connection conn = DBConnectionFactory.getConnection();
            conn.setAutoCommit(false);
            String insertSQL = "Insert into MY_SCHEDULE
            (SESSION_ID,PRESENTER_NAME, SESSION_TITLE, SESSION_ABSTRACT, TOPIC, ROOM,
SESSION_START, SESSION_END, SYNCHRONIZED) values (?,?,?,?,?,?,?,?,?)";
            PreparedStatement pStmt = conn.prepareStatement(insertSQL);
            pStmt.setInt(1, myScheduledSession.getId());
            pStmt.setString(2, myScheduledSession.getPresenterName ());
            pStmt.setString(3, myScheduledSession.getTitle());
            pStmt.setString(4, myScheduledSession.getAbstract());
            pStmt.setString(5, myScheduledSession.getTopic());
            pStmt.setString(6, myScheduledSession.getRoom());
            pStmt.setDate(7, myScheduledSession.getSlot.getSessionStart());
            pStmt.setDate(8, myScheduledSession.getSlot.getSessionEnd());
            pStmt.setString(9, myScheduledSession.getSynchronized());

            pStmt.execute();
            conn.commit();
            result = true;
        } catch (SQLException e) {
            System.err.println(e.getMessage());
        } catch (Exception e) {
            System.err.println(e.getMessage());
        }
        Trace.log(Utility.ApplicationLogger, Level.INFO, MySessionsList.class,
```

```
                    "AddSession", "Exiting AddSessionToDB");
            return result;
        }
   public boolean setSynchronized (ScheduledSession myScheduledSession) {
        boolean result = false
        try {
             Connection conn = DBConnectionFactory.getConnection();
             conn.setAutoCommit(false);
             String updateSQL =
                 "Update MY_SCHEDULE set SYNCHRONIZED='Y' where SESSION_ID = ?" ;
             pStmt.setString(1, myScheduledSession.getId());
             pStmt.execute();
             conn.commit();
             result = true;
          } catch (SQLException e) {
            System.err.println(e.getMessage());
          } catch (Exception e) {
            System.err.println(e.getMessage());
          }
        return result;
}
public class MyScheduleDbAccessor {
    private String where;
    /**
      * Method will query the database and return
      * the result list
      */
    public List queryDb() {
    List s_myScheduledSessions = null;
    try {
        Connection conn = DBConnectionFactory.getConnection();
        conn.setAutoCommit(false);
        String statement = "SELECT * from MY_SCHEDULE" + getWhere();
        PreparedStatement stat = conn.prepareStatement(statement);
        ResultSet rs = stat.executeQuery();
        while (rs.next()) {
                int id = rs.getInt("SESSION_ID");
                String presenterName = rs.getString("PRESENTER_NAME");
                String title = rs.getString("TITLE");
                String sessionAbstract = rs.getString("SESSION_ABSTRACT");
                String topic = rs. getString ("TOPIC");
                String room = rs. getString ("ROOM");
                Date sessionStart = rs.getDate("SESSION_START");
                Date sessionEnd = rs.getDate("SESSION_END");
                String synched = rs. getString ("SYNCHRONIZED");
                Slot slot = new Slot();
                slot.setStartTime(sessionStart);
                slot.setEndTime(sessionEnd);
                ScheduledSession d = new ScheduledSession (id,presenterName,
                        title, sessionAbstract, topic, room,synched slot );
                s_myScheduledSessions.add(d);
            }
        rs.close();
Trace.log(Utility.ApplicationLogger, Level.INFO, MyScheduleDbAccessor.class,
                    "Execute", "Exiting from queryDB Method");
} catch (SQLException e) {
```

```
            System.err.println(e.getMessage());
      } catch (Exception e) {
            System.err.println(e.getMessage());
        }
        return s_myScheduledSessions;
    }
  public  List fetchUnsynched (){
     List s_myScheduledSessions = null;
     setWhere("WHERE SYNCHRONIZED='N'");
     s_myScheduledSessions  = queryDb();
     setWhere("");
     return s_myScheduledSessions;
  }
  public String getWhere(){
        return this.where;}
  public void setWhere(String where){
         this.where = where;}
    /**
     * Method will commit the details of newly created Session object
     * @return
     */
    public boolean AddSessionToDB(ScheduledSession myScheduledSession) {
    boolean result = false;
        try {
            Connection conn = DBConnectionFactory.getConnection();
            conn.setAutoCommit(false);
            String insertSQL = "Insert into MY_SCHEDULE
            (SESSION_ID,PRESENTER_NAME, SESSION_TITLE, SESSION_ABSTRACT, TOPIC, ROOM,
SESSION_START, SESSION_END, SYNCHRONIZED) values (?,?,?,?,?,?,?,?,?)";
            PreparedStatement pStmt = conn.prepareStatement(insertSQL);
            pStmt.setInt(1, myScheduledSession.getId());
            pStmt.setString(2, myScheduledSession.getPresenterName ());
            pStmt.setString(3, myScheduledSession.getTitle());
            pStmt.setString(4, myScheduledSession.getSessionAbstract());
            pStmt.setString(5, myScheduledSession.getTopic());
            pStmt.setString(6, myScheduledSession.getRoom());
            pStmt.setDate(7, (Date)myScheduledSession.getSessionStartDateTime());
            pStmt.setDate(8, (Date)myScheduledSession.getSessionEndDateTime());
            pStmt.setString(9, myScheduledSession.getSynched());
            pStmt.execute();
            conn.commit();
            result = true;
        } catch (SQLException e) {
            System.err.println(e.getMessage());
        } catch (Exception e) {
            System.err.println(e.getMessage());
        }
        Trace.log(Utility.ApplicationLogger, Level.INFO, MyScheduleDbAccessor.class,
             "AddSession", "Exiting AddSessionToDB");
        return result;
    }
  public boolean setSynchronized (ScheduledSession myScheduledSession) {
      boolean result = false;
```

```
try {
    Connection conn = DBConnectionFactory.getConnection();
    conn.setAutoCommit(false);
    String updateSQL =
        "Update MY_SCHEDULE set SYNCHRONIZED='Y' where SESSION_ID = ?" ;
    PreparedStatement pStmt = conn.prepareStatement(updateSQL);
    pStmt.setInt(1, myScheduledSession.getId());
    pStmt.execute();
    conn.commit();
    result = true;
} catch (SQLException e) {
    System.err.println(e.getMessage());
} catch (Exception e) {
    System.err.println(e.getMessage());
}
    return result;
}
```

The A-Team Mobile Persistence Extension for Oracle MAF

Throughout this chapter you learned how to synchronize data between the on-device SQLite database and the enterprise database. This works fine and is something that you can implement in Java code. If you have multiple tables that you want to support offline and synchronize with the enterprise database, you will soon find that this can be laborious. The amount of code you have to write quickly increases, and while programming, you probably realize that you are repeating the same coding patterns for each web service that you want to call to read or write data. In order to make this task an easier task, you can use the Mobile Persistence Extension.

The Mobile Persistence Extension is created by the Oracle Fusion Middleware Architects team ("the A-team"). It is a lightweight persistence and synchronization framework. It is built on top of generic Java code that is used to invoke web services and to perform CRUD operations against the on-device SQLite database. If you are to build more and more Oracle MAF applications, you will soon find that you are repeating some laborious steps over and over again. These steps are usually related to creating POJO models, writing SQL statements, and mapping continuously between web services, POJOs, and SQL statements. Besides that, you have to create custom code that keeps track of the changes that are out of sync.

The Mobile Persistence Extension provides a solution for these challenges related to data persistence and synchronization in mobile applications. The Mobile Persistence Extension is currently available as an extension to JDeveloper and can be downloaded from the A-team's weblog:

http://www.ateam-oracle.com/a-team-mobile-persistence-extension-for-oracle-maf/

Summary

The reason people attend conferences is to attend the sessions presented by speakers. For a conference app to be considered any good by the conference attendees, the session information is a critical piece of functionality. Without session information, there is no way that an attendee can create a reasonable schedule, and the attendees will quickly become disillusioned with the app. It's also essential given the poor Wi-Fi and connectivity at most conference sites that the app provides the ability to access the session details offline. All this functionality is available in the TAMCAPP Conference Session feature and was implemented in this chapter. In this chapter, you learned

- How to create AMX pages based on SOAP web services
- How to implement the Bean Data Control Service object pattern
- How to work with Data Visualization Tools
- How to download and view documents
- How to work with the local database and synchronize with the enterprise database

CHAPTER
14

Building the
Attendees Feature

Wchen visiting a conference, it can be convenient to know who else is attending. This will enable you to find your peers and do some networking. For this purpose, TAMCAPP has the Attendees feature. The Attendees feature contains search functionality to find attendees and display a list of all found attendees, and the user can open attendee details. This Attendee Details AMX page is used to explain how to work with some of the device features. The TAMCAPP user can work with the attendees by adding them to the on-device contact list and getting in touch in several ways.

The user of TAMCAPP, an individual attendee, can change his or her own personal information such as a name, phone, and e-mail address in the Details AMX page and also change his or her picture by either using an existing one or taking a new one. A picture of the attendee can be taken from within the application and uploaded to the enterprise database. All AMX pages involved in this feature are displayed in Figure 14-1.

Functionality such as building lists and forms like AMX pages was already explained in the previous chapter and therefore will not be explained in detail in this chapter. This chapter will focus on implementing functionality such as programmatic navigation and "smart search," invoking the phone function, and using URL schemes. Also, you will learn how to work with the binding layer programmatically and how to upload an image to the server database.

In contrast to the Conference Session AMX pages, the Attendees AMX pages do not use the same data collection for both Attendee List and Attendee Details. This is done for reasons of efficiency. The first implementation (Conference Session, which uses a different collection) was explained in the previous chapter, and the second (Attendees) is explained in this chapter. The principle is the same. The main difference is that for Attendees, there must be a web service call when navigating from the List AMX page to the Details AMX page. This approach is used for a specific reason.

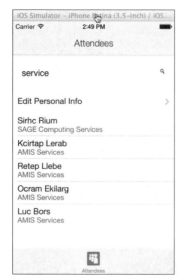

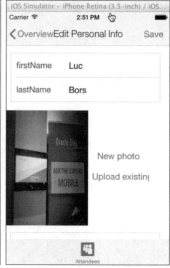

FIGURE 14-1. *Attendee List, Attendee Details, and Edit Personal Info*

Imagine a web service returning details on several hundreds of attendees who all have an image and other additional attributes. The amount of data that needs to be transferred from the server can add up very easily. Therefore, it can be more convenient to use two different web services: one that is used for the List page and that only returns data such as name and company, and a second one that is used for the Details page and returns additional data, such as a photo, but only for one attendee. This means an extra web service call, but usually, it is still a performance improvement, at least from the end user's perspective. The implementation is explained in the next section.

Implementing the Attendees List AMX Page

The Attendees List AMX page is a page containing search functionality for attendees, and after searching, the search result is displayed in a list of attendees. This is all very straightforward. A user can navigate from the list to the details. As stated earlier, when navigating to the details, a second web service is called in order to retrieve all information of the selected attendee.

Implementing Navigation to the Attendee Details AMX Page

Navigation from one page to another can be done in many different ways. Usually, some kind of command component is involved in navigating, or navigation is invoked on the list item directly. Both use the action attribute of the component that is used to invoke the corresponding navigation. Looking at mobile apps in general, there is an alternative way of navigating from a list, which is navigation from within a list by using the swipe left gesture. This is a very common pattern and can be implemented with Oracle MAF.

In Oracle MAF, the actionListener component can be used for this, by simply adding the actionListener component as child of the listItem and setting the type to swipeLeft. Note that there is also a setPropertyListener component that is used to put the rowKey (the Id of the selected Attendee) of the current row in a pageFlowScope variable.

```
<amx:listView var="row" value="#{bindings.attendees.collectionModel}"
               fetchSize="#{bindings.attendees.rangeSize}"
               selectedRowKeys="#{bindings.attendees.collectionModel.selectedRow}"
               selectionListener="#{bindings.attendees.collectionModel.makeCurrent}"
               showMoreStrategy="autoScroll" bufferStrategy="viewport"
               id="lv2">
  <amx:listItem showLinkIcon="false" id="li2">
    <amx:tableLayout width="100%" id="tl2">
      <amx:rowLayout id="rl2">
        <amx:cellFormat width="10px" rowSpan="2" id="cf6"/>
        <amx:cellFormat width="100%" height="28px" id="cf5">
          <amx:outputText value="#{row.firstName} #{row.lastName}"
                          styleClass="tamcapp-smaller-text" id="ot3"/>
        </amx:cellFormat>
      </amx:rowLayout>
      <amx:rowLayout id="rl3">
        <amx:cellFormat width="100%" height="12px" id="cf7">
          <amx:outputText value="#{row.organization}"
                          styleClass="adfmf-listItem-captionText" id="ot4"/>
        </amx:cellFormat>
      </amx:rowLayout>
    </amx:tableLayout>
```

```
<amx:actionListener id="al1" type="swipeLeft"
                    binding="#{pageFlowScope.attendeesBean.goDetails}"/>
<amx:setPropertyListener id="sp1" type="swipeLeft" from="#{row.rowKey}"
                         to="#{pageFlowScope.attendeesBean.currentAttendee}"/>
<amx:setPropertyListener id="sp17" type="swipeLeft" from="#{false}"
                         to="#{pageFlowScope.attendeesBean.me}"/>
    </amx:listItem>
</amx:listView>
```

The swipeLeft on the type attribute indicates that this listener fires whenever the user swipes to the left. After that, the method defined in the binding attribute kicks in. This method is responsible for invoking the programmatic navigation.

Looking at the task flow diagram (Figure 14-2), it is obvious that the navigation from List to Details is implemented by the control flow case "details." This is also visible from the XML fragment:

```
<control-flow-rule id="__1">
    <from-activity-id>AttendeeList</from-activity-id>
    <control-flow-case id="__2">
      <from-outcome>details</from-outcome>
        <to-activity-id>AttendeeDetail</to-activity-id>
    </control-flow-case>
</control-flow-rule>
```

The goDetails() method calls the doNavigation() method:

```
 public void goDetails(ActionEvent actionEvent) {
     TamcappUtils.doNavigation("details");
 }
```

The doNavigation method is defined in a utility class and takes the navigation case as an argument. In this way, programmatic navigation can be invoked in a flexible manner.

```
public static void doNavigation(String navCase) {
        AdfmfContainerUtilities.invokeContainerJavaScriptFunction(
                        AdfmfJavaUtilities.getFeatureName()
                        , "adf.mf.api.amx.doNavigation"
                        , new Object[] { navCase });
}
```

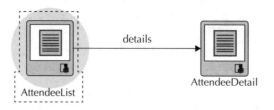

FIGURE 14-2. *Attendees task flow diagram with control flow*

Because of the navigation, the Attendee Details AMX page is called and the corresponding PageDefinition is instantiated. This PageDefinition has an invokeAction binding that calls the method binding for the searchAttendeesDetail method, which in turn calls the web service. The following code sample shows the entries in the PageDefinition:

```
<executables>
    <invokeAction id="autoQuery" Binds="searchAttendeesDetail"/>
</executables>
<bindings>
    <methodAction id="searchAttendeesDetail" RequiresUpdateModel="true"
                  Action="invokeMethod" MethodName="searchAttendeesDetail"
                  IsViewObjectMethod="false" DataControl="AttendeesDetail"
                  InstanceName="data.AttendeesDetail.dataProvider">
        <NamedData NDName="currentAttendee" NDType="java.lang.Long"
                   NDValue="#{pageFlowScope.attendeesBean.currentAttendee}"/>
    </methodAction>
```

In this case, each and every time navigation to the Attendee Details AMX page occurs, the web service is called with the appropriate Attendee Id, and the data of this attendee is displayed in the Details AMX page.

Smart Navigation

Imagine that when you search the attendees, only one attendee is returned. This will show up in the list, and after touching it, the user navigates to the Details AMX page. This is not really user-friendly, is it? The preferred flow would be that this one single attendee is displayed in the Details AMX page instead of in the List AMX page. It is pretty obvious that this is what the user will do anyway, so why not open the detail automatically right away? This means that both the search and the navigation need to be executed in one go. As explained in the previous section, Oracle MAF enables developers to use programmatic navigation, and this is also used to implement this smart search pattern.

NOTE
Whether or not a user likes this functionality is a matter of taste. In Chapter 16 you will learn how to use a preference to toggle between smart search and "normal" behavior.

The first step in this is, of course, invoking the searchAttendees operation on the web service. After successful invocation, the operation returns a result set. The number of attendees in this result set can now be determined, and if only one is found, the user navigates directly to the Details AMX page.

```
try {
    GenericType result =
      (GenericType)AdfmfJavaUtilities.invokeDataControlMethod(
        "TamcappWsAttDc", null, "searchAttendees",
          pnames, params, ptypes);
    int x = result.getAttributeCount();
    // process result
    ...
```

```
// end processing
// now check if there is only one result
if (x==1){
   prepareNavigation(attendeeId);
}
```

Note that if one result is found, the prepareNavigation() method is called with the attendeeId as an argument. This is needed because as opposed to navigation by means of a command component, programmatic navigation works in such a way that it does not invoke the setPropertyListener to set Attendee information in context. This needs to be done programmatically as well. This is what the prepareNavigation() method is used for. It takes that one single attendee from the search result and assigns that to the pageFlowScope variable containing the attendee to be shown on the Attendee Details AMX page before invoking the programmatic navigation.

```
public void prepareNavigation(int attendeeId) {
   ValueExpression ve = AdfmfJavaUtilities.getValueExpression(
            "#{pageFlowScope.attendeesBean.currentAttendee}", int.class);
   ve.setValue(AdfmfJavaUtilities.getAdfELContext(),
             new Integer(attendeeId));
   TamcappUtils.doNavigation("details");
   }
```

With the current attendee available in the pageFlowScope, we can now navigate across the flow in exactly the same way as if the Attendee Details AMX page was invoked from within the Attendees List AMX page: the Details AMX page is called, PageDefinition is instantiated, and the invoke action is executed with the "#{pageFlowScope.attendeesBean.currentAttendee}" as argument.

Implementing the Attendee Details AMX Page

Every now and then you run into a conference attendee whose information you would like to save for later use. The Attendee Details AMX page enables you to take the information of an attendee such as e-mail address, phone number, and other relevant information and save it to the on-device contact list, or send e-mails or text messages, or place phone calls. The main functionality responsible for this was already described in Chapter 8. However, the Attendee Details AMX page takes it one step further.

Working with the Attendee Information

The Attendee Details AMX page shows detail information of an attendee, but can also be used to edit the TAMCAPP user's own personal information and photo. To interact with the other attendees through calls, e-mails and so on, all these interactions are available from within a popup that shows when the users tapholds the Attendee Details information. The next sections explain how to implement the popup and the functionality for interacting with Attendees.

Implementing the Popup

A limitation in the current Oracle MAF version is that a showPopupBehavior is needed, but it doesn't provide all the functionality we want. Currently, MAF only supports showPopupBehavior on command elements and on the listView. It is not possible to add the showPopupBehavior as a child of any other layout container element such as panel form layout, panel group layout, table layout, row layout, or cell format.

Looking at the AMX source code in the Attendee Details AMX page, it is obvious that JDeveloper creates a PanelFormLayout with all the components that are selected during creation of the form layout. There is no obvious way that the showPopupBehavior can be added to this component. There is a trick, however. When all content on the page is surrounded by a List component, the showPopupBehavior can be added to this List component. Note that there is a styleClass defined on the listView component that makes the listView invisible.

```
<amx:listView id="lv1" styleClass="invisible">
    <amx:listItem id="lip1" shortDesc="Phone listItem" showLinkIcon="false">
        <amx:tableLayout id="tl1" width="100%">
            <amx:rowLayout id="rl1">
                .........
            </amx:rowLayout>
        </amx:tableLayout>
        <amx:showPopupBehavior id="spb1" type="tapHold" popupId="actions"
                               align="overlapBottom" alignId="lv1"/>
    </amx:listItem>
</amx:listView>
```

Now when the taphold gesture is invoked on this AMX page, a popup is displayed containing links to invoke the device's contact list, to send text messages and e-mails to call an attendee, and even to invoke the Skype app on your device (Figure 14-3).

How this functionality is implemented is discussed in the next sections.

Adding to the Contact List

To add the attendee to the device's contact list, the DeviceFeatures data control is used. As with other data control usages, I prefer to invoke this from Java code, where the supplied API has more flexibility and control. In the popup, a commandLink is used to invoke the addToContacts method in the attendeesBean. Note that in order to make all commandLinks in the popup look the same, the commandLink has no text defined and there is an image as child attribute.

```
<amx:commandLink id="cb6"
                 actionListener="#{pageFlowScope.attendeesBean.addToContacts}">
    <amx:image id="i7" source="/images/contact.png"
               inlineStyle="height:36px; width:36px;"/>
    <amx:closePopupBehavior popupId="actions" id="cp6"/>
</amx:commandLink>
```

FIGURE 14-3. *Popup containing applicable actions*

When the method is invoked, the currently selected attendee in the TAMCAPP application must be added to the contacts. By reaching out to the binding container from within Java code, this attendee can be looked up. The getValueExpression().getValue() method can be used to find the attribute bindings and their values. Note that this is on the Details AMX page where only one attendee is selected. Therefore, there is no need to look up the current row in the iterator. The appropriate values can be derived from the attribute bindings directly.

```
public void addToContacts(ActionEvent ae){ (){
    PersonDetail prd = new PersonDetail();
    AdfELContext adfELContext = AdfmfJavaUtilities.getAdfELContext();
    ValueExpression veFn = AdfmfJavaUtilities.getValueExpression(
                "#{bindings.firstName.inputValue}", String.class);
    prd.setFirstName(veFn.getValue(adfELContext).toString());
    ValueExpression veLn = AdfmfJavaUtilities.getValueExpression(
                "#{bindings.lastName.inputValue}", String.class);
    prd.setLastName(veLn.getValue(adfELContext).toString());
    ValueExpression vePhone = AdfmfJavaUtilities.getValueExpression(
                "#{bindings.phone.inputValue}", String.class);
    prd.setPhone(vePhone.getValue(adfELContext).toString());
    ValueExpression veEmail = AdfmfJavaUtilities.getValueExpression(
                "#{bindings.email.inputValue}", String.class);
    prd.setEmail(veEmail.getValue(adfELContext).toString());
    ValueExpression veCountry = AdfmfJavaUtilities.getValueExpression(
                "#{bindings.countryName.inputValue}", String.class);
    prd.setCountryName(veCountry.getValue(adfELContext).toString());
    …..
```

From here on, this PersonDetail object is used to create the new contact by invoking the getters on the PersonDetail object and the setters on the new Contact. After the contact has been added, it can be looked up in the device's Contact application (Figure 14-4).

```
    ContactField[] phoneNumbers = null;
    ContactField[] emails = null;
    ContactAddresses[] addresses = null;
    /* Create a new contact */
    Contact newContact = new Contact();
    ContactName name = new ContactName();
    name.setFamilyName(prd.getLastName());
    name.setGivenName(prd.getFirstName());
    /* and more here….
        …. commented out here for brevity
        …. Finally invoke the deviceManager and create the contact
    */
    DeviceManager dm = DeviceManagerFactory.getDeviceManager();
    dm.createContact(newContact);
```

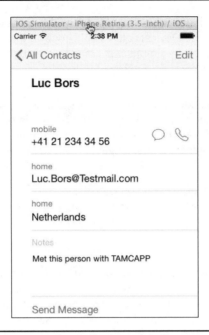

FIGURE 14-4. *The added contact on the device's contact list*

Sending Text Messages and E-mails

As with working with the contact list, sending out text messages and e-mails is also functionality provided by the DeviceFeatures data control, which TAMCAPP invokes from Java code:

```
public void sendEmail(ActionEvent ae) {
    AdfELContext adfELContext = AdfmfJavaUtilities.getAdfELContext();
    String subject = "Meeting during TAMCAPP event";
    DeviceManager dm = DeviceManagerFactory.getDeviceManager();
    ValueExpression veTo = AdfmfJavaUtilities.getValueExpression(
                "#{bindings.email.inputValue}", String.class);
    dm.sendEmail((String)veTo.getValue(adfELContext), null,
                subject, null, null, null, null);
}
```

And the same is used for sending text messages:

```
public void sendSms(ActionEvent ae) {
    AdfELContext adfELContext = AdfmfJavaUtilities.getAdfELContext();
    String body = "Want to have lunch ?";
    ValueExpression veTo = AdfmfJavaUtilities.getValueExpression(
                "#{bindings.phone.inputValue}", String.class);
    String to = veTo.getValue(adfELContext).toString();
    DeviceManager dm = DeviceManagerFactory.getDeviceManager();
    dm.sendSMS(to, body);
}
```

Calling an Attendee

The TAMCAPP application offers functionality to invoke the device's phone. This is something that cannot be done by using the DeviceFeatures data control. Instead, it uses the tel: URL scheme. The syntax for doing this is very simple and straightforward:

```
<a href="tel:+1234567890">Place call!</a>
```

In Oracle MAF a goLink component can be used in combination with the tel: URL scheme. The phone number to use can be retrieved from the binding layer by using an EL expression. In order to make the goLink look like a button, custom skinning can be used, but that is beyond the scope of this book. A simpler way to change the appearance of the goLink is to use an embedded image.

```
<amx:goLink id="gl1" shortDesc="Call Link"
            url="tel:#{bindings.phone.inputValue}">
    <amx:image id="i5" source="/images/call.png"
               inlineStyle="height:36px;width:36px"/>
</amx:goLink>
```

If the user activates a call link, he will receive a confirmation alert asking whether to place the call. I recommend using the phone number in the international format: the plus sign (+), the country code, the local area code, and the local number. There is no way we can really know where our attendees will be located. If they are in the same country, or even in the same local area, the international format will still work.

To take this one step further, TAMCAPP also has the functionality to invoke Skype from within the application. For that, the Skype URL scheme can be used. Skype has its own URL-scheme. To invoke Skype, TAMCAPP needs to supply the Skype username. Optionally, the "?call" parameter can be added to initiate a call immediately. Without it, the profile of the Skype user is displayed.

```
<a href="skype:skype_user?call">Skype me!</a>
```

For TAMCAPP, the assumption is made that the user's Skype name is a concatenation of the first name and last name. In real life, this is usually not the case, but for the purpose of this example, it works.

```
<amx:goLink url="skype:#{bindings.firstName.inputValue}
                      #{bindings.firstName.inputValue}?call"
            id="gl2" rendered="#{deviceScope.os=='iOS'}">
    <amx:image id="i6" source="/images/skype.jpg"
               inlineStyle="height:36px; width:36px;"/>
</amx:goLink>
```

Using URL-Scheme for SMS and E-mail

The e-mail and SMS solutions discussed in the previous section could also have been implemented using URL schemes, although this is not preferred. When using URL schemes, you cannot add attachments to an e-mail. Also note that when using the Java API, you will have maximum flexibility.

```
<amx:goLink url=" mailto:#{bindings.email.inputValue};subject= Meeting during
TAMCAPP event;body=just some text for the body" text="Send mail" </amx:goLink>

<amx:goLink url="sms: :#{bindings.phone.inputValue};body= Want to have lunch ? "
text="Send  SMS" </amx:goLink>
```

You can also use URL-scheme to invoke apps from an Oracle MAF application or even to call one Oracle MAF application from another MAF application. URL-scheme can also be used to exchange information between apps and, as such, between MAF apps. You will learn about this in Chapter 18.

Editing Personal Information

All TAMCAPP users are allowed to update their own information. This functionality is invoked by tapping the Edit Personal Info area on the Attendee List AMX page. This will navigate to the Details AMX page, setting the TAMCAPP user in context as being the currently edited Attendee. It will also set the pageFlowScope.attendeesBean.me property to true, thus opening the Attendee Details AMX page in edit mode. The user can now change contact information and upload a picture.

Saving the Changes

After changing information such as phone number or e-mail address, these changes must be saved to the enterprise database. Saving the changes is handled by the saveAttendee() method in the AttendeesDetail class. The changes to the personal information are being saved to the enterprise database by invoking the updateAttendees web service operation. Remember that when reading data from a web service, the fromGenericType method can be used. In the opposite situation, when writing data to a web service, the toGenericType method can be used. The toGenericType method of the GenericTypeBeanSerializationHandler will take each array element and append it to the toGenericType as an individual attribute.

Calling the web service operation with just any random object will not work. The data control expects an object of a very specific type, with attributes matching its own definition. It is possible to determine the name of the type expected by the data control by hovering above the parameter with the mouse pointer, as you can see in Figure 14-5.

So in order to transform an attendee from its Java structure to a generic type, the toGenericType requires an object of the type "TamcappWsAttDc.Types.updateAttendees.attendees":

```
GenericType gtAttendee = GenericTypeBeanSerializationHelper.toGenericType(
        "TamcappWsAttDc.Types.updateAttendees.attendees", attendee);
```

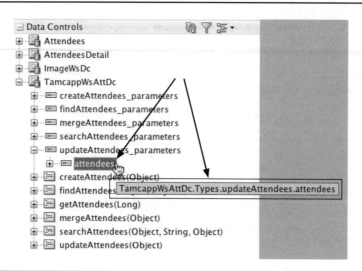

FIGURE 14-5. *Determine the name of the type expected.*

With this knowledge, the saveAttendee() method can now be completed. First, find the Attendee object whose information is being changed; next, transform this to a GenericType object; and finally, invoke the updateAttendees operation on the TamcaapWsAttDc data control. The complete code of the web service call to updateAttendees is shown in the following code sample:

```
public void saveAttendee(){
// we know that there is only one attendee in the search result because
// we invoke this saveAttendee from the details page
   PersonDetail attendee = (PersonDetail)s_searchResults.get(0);
   // Set attribute values
   List namesList = new ArrayList(1);
   List paramsList = new ArrayList(1);
   List typesList = new ArrayList(1);
   GenericType gtAttendee = GenericTypeBeanSerializationHelper.toGenericType(
                 "TamcappWsAttDc.Types.updateAttendees.attendees", attendee);
   namesList.add("attendees");
   paramsList.add(gtAttendee);
   typesList.add(Object.class);
   try {
      AdfmfJavaUtilities.invokeDataControlMethod(
                  "TamcappWsAttDc", null, "updateAttendees"
                  , namesList, paramsList, typesList);
   } catch (AdfInvocationException ex) {
      Trace.log(Utility.ApplicationLogger, Level.SEVERE,
          AttendeesDetail.class, "updateAttendees",">>>>>>" + ex.getMessage());
      AdfException e = new AdfException("Error Invoking Web Service. Try later",
                                  AdfException.WARNING);
      throw e;
   }
}
```

This saveAttendee() method is also available from the AttendeesDetail data control. After dragging and dropping as a commandButton on the Attendee Details AMX page, it can be invoked. Note that this button is only available if the attendee is changing his/her own information. For that, the previously explained "me" property is used.

```
<amx:facet name="secondary">
    <amx:commandButton id="cb2" text="Save"
                       styleClass="adfmf-commandButton-highlight"
                       actionListener="#{bindings.saveAttendee.execute}"
                       rendered="#{pageFlowScope.attendeesBean.me}" />
</amx:facet>
```

The Attendee Image

The image that is stored in the enterprise database is one of the attributes returned by the getAttendees operation of the web service. The image is returned as a String and can be displayed as an image by using the image Component.

```
<amx:image source="data:image/gif;base64,#{bindings.picture.inputValue}" />
```

All attendees can change their personal image if they use the TAMCAPP app. For taking a picture, the user can invoke a New Photo button from the Edit Personal Info MAF AMX page, and when he wants to upload an existing image, he can use the Upload Existing button. Both buttons use a method in the attendeesBean.

The uploadExisting uses the getFromFile() method, whereas the takePicture uses takePhoto(). Both methods are almost the same. The only difference is the source type. In one case, it is CAMERA_SOURCETYPE_PHOTOLIBRARY, whereas in the other case, it is CAMERA_SOURCETYPE_CAMERA. For reference, the takePhoto() method is shown in the following code. The call of the doUpload() method is actually the most important here. That method is explained in the next section.

```
public void takePhoto(ActionEvent ae) {
    DeviceManager dm = DeviceManagerFactory.getDeviceManager();
    if (dm.hasCamera()){
        String theImage = dm.getPicture(50
                    ,DeviceManager.CAMERA_DESTINATIONTYPE_DATA_URL
                    ,DeviceManager.CAMERA_SOURCETYPE_CAMERA
                    ,false,DeviceManager.CAMERA_ENCODINGTYPE_PNG ,400,200);
        // Only upload if the user did not cancel the camera.
        if(theImage!=null){
            doUpload(theImage);
        }
    }
}
```

After the image is taken or selected, it must be saved to the server. Uploading this image from the device to the server is something different. This involves a web service that takes the image as a String. This String should be a base64-encoded String representation of the image. In the takePhoto() method of the previous code sample, the destination type is set to CAMERA_DESTINATIONTYPE_DATA_URL, which is exactly what we want.

NOTE
These base64-encoded images can cause the application to run out of memory. The String size increases with increasing quality and image size. You have to find the optimal balance between image quality and memory usage by tweaking the quality, targetHeight, and targetWidth parameters as was explained in Chapter 8.

In the uploadImage() method, the imageSource is used as one of the arguments in the call of the saveImage web service operation. The two other arguments are the image type, in this case, png, and the Id of the current attendee. Note that for this web service, a data control (Figure 14-6) was created and that the saveImage() operation is invoked by using the invokeDataControlMethod. The complete code of the uploadImage() method is available in the following code sample:

```
public void uploadImage(Object imageSource) {
    String attendeeId = (String)AdfmfJavaUtilities.evaluateELExpression(
                        "#{pageFlowScope.attendeesBean.currentAttendee}");
    Integer id = Integer.valueOf(attendeeId);
    ArrayList parameterNames = new ArrayList();
    ArrayList parameterValue = new ArrayList();
    ArrayList parameterTypes = new ArrayList();
    parameterNames.add("arg0");//arg0 contains file content
    parameterNames.add("arg1");//arg1 contains file type e.g. jpg
    parameterNames.add("arg2");//arg2 contains the Id of the attendee.

    parameterValue.add(imageSource);
    parameterValue.add("png");
    parameterValue.add(id);
    parameterTypes.add(Object.class);
    parameterTypes.add(String.class);
    parameterTypes.add(Integer.class);
    try{
       AdfmfJavaUtilities.invokeDataControlMethod("ImageWsDc", null,
                     "saveImage",parameterNames, parameterValue,parameterTypes);
    } catch (AdfInvocationException e) {
      Trace.log(Utility.ApplicationLogger, Level.SEVERE,
           AttendeesDetail.class, " uploadImage ",">>>>>>" + ex.getMessage());
      AdfException e = new AdfException("Error Invoking Web Service. Try later",
                            AdfException.WARNING);
      throw e;
    }
}
```

FIGURE 14-6. *The Image Web Service data control*

After a successful upload, the image is stored in the database, and on every subsequent retrieval of this attendee's data, the new image is shown. For the attendee who took the picture and uploaded it, it makes no sense to call the web service again to retrieve the new image. The data of the new image is already on the device, so why not show it right away? This is actually a lot easier than it might seem. It is a few lines of code that need to be added right after the exception handler of the saveImage() method. This code will be executed only if there is no exception, meaning the picture upload was successful. In this code, just look up the current Attendee and change the value of the picture property using the exact same String that was used in the picture upload.

```
// Image upload; All is well;
// Now also update the photo in the current attendee in Memory
   PersonDetail prs = (PersonDetail)s_searchResults.get(0);
   prs.setPicture(imageSource.toString());
```

In the setter of the picture property, the firePropertyChange is invoked, thus informing the user interface that this property has been changed and displaying the new image.

```
public void setPicture(String picture) {
   String oldPicture = this.picture;
   this.picture = picture;
   propertyChangeSupport.firePropertyChange("picture", oldPicture, picture);
}
```

Summary

Just building a mobile app is one thing, but implementing it in a user-friendly way combined with common sense and recognizable UX patterns is something else. In this chapter, you learned some smart techniques for implementing user-friendly UX patterns for searching and navigating in an Oracle MAF application. You also learned how to

- Navigate programmatically
- Invoke the phone function and Skype
- Work with the binding layer programmatically
- Upload an image to the server database

CHAPTER
15

Developing the Maps
and Social Network

A s an expert in technology, you will probably travel a lot to visit conferences in many cities all over the world. You'll have lots of impressions you want to share, lots of questions about the new city. Try to imagine how to stay in touch with your friends and find your way around in an unknown city. Now try to imagine this again, but without using your smartphone... Difficult, right? A couple of years ago, we all managed to do this without the smartphone, but nowadays there are two things we cannot live without: location-based services and our social network interaction. Luckily, the TAMCAPP app comes to the rescue. The app supports both location-based services by means of maps and interaction with your social network using Twitter.

Implementing the Maps Feature

When going to a conference, you will sometimes end up in a city that is completely new to you. In order for you not to get lost, the TAMCAPP ships with a maps feature. This maps feature gives you both a map of the conference center with its rooms and a map with local points of interest such as restaurants and tourist attractions. The two maps are implemented in a different way. The first one is the conference center map. This map is implemented by using a customized Oracle MAF DVT thematic map component. The second one is the Points of Interest map. This map is implemented by using an Oracle MAF DVT map component. Both implementations are discussed in this chapter.

The maps feature is implemented as an Oracle MAF task flow as you can see in Figure 15-1.

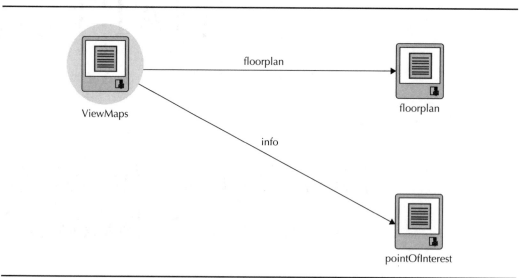

FIGURE 15-1. *The maps task flow*

The ViewMaps view contains a simple list view to invoke the different maps. Tapping a list item opens the corresponding map view.

```
<amx:listView var="row" id="lv1">
    <amx:listItem id="li1" action="floorplan">
        <amx:outputText value="Floor Plan" id="ot2"/>
    </amx:listItem>
    <amx:listItem id="li2" action="info">
        <amx:outputText value="Points of Interest" id="ot3"/>
    </amx:listItem>
</amx:listView>
```

The Venue Map

The venue map shows you an overview of the conference rooms. On this venue map (Figure 15-2), there will be hotspots that highlight and respond to the taphold gesture to show a popup containing information about the particular conference room. The venue map is based on a custom thematic

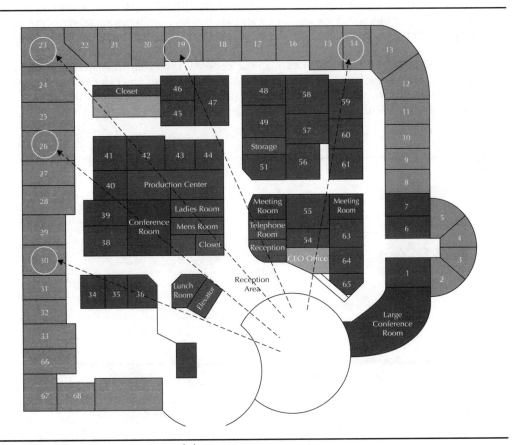

FIGURE 15-2.   *The venue map with hotspots*

map component. A thematic map is a map that focuses on a particular theme or special topic and does not just show natural features like rivers and cities. If these items are on a thematic map, they are background information and are used as reference points to enhance the map's theme. The Oracle MAF thematic map component is a component that supports a visualization of data against either a geographical map of a region or country, or a visualization of a custom map such as a floor plan, a park, or the theater seating plan or the layout of an airplane. Both predefined and custom markers can be positioned against the map. The implementation of this map consists of three main parts, all of which will be explained next:

- The custom image; an actual image containing the floor plan.
- An XML metadata file defining the layers and data points, which will be used as hotspots.
- The Oracle MAF DVT thematic map component itself.

The Oracle MAF thematic map component supports the use of a custom base map such as an image of a floor plan. To define a custom base map, you need to specify a background layer that refers to a custom image. On this image certain areas can be highlighted. To implement this, the thematic map uses data points. This is where the XML metadata file is used. The metadata file contains both the reference to the custom image and the data points.

Finally, this XML metadata file is referenced from within the actual MAF thematic map component. The MAF AMX file declares a custom area layer with named points. The MAF AMX file points to the metadata file shown by containing a list of points and their names. A schematic overview of the files involved is shown in Figure 15-3.

For the TAMCAPP app, a thematic map component is used with an image of the floor plan of the conference venue. At run time, the map will display hotspots for conference rooms. When the taphold gesture is invoked on one of these hotspots, a popup will show extra information about the session in that particular room. How all this is implemented is explained in the following sections.

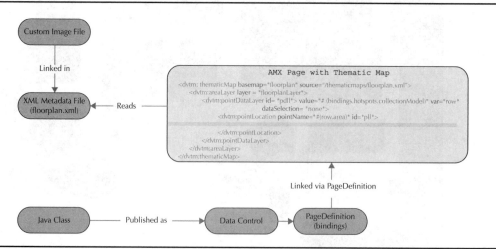

FIGURE 15-3. *Schematic overview of the files involved in a thematic map*

Adding and Configuring the Image

For this particular thematic map component, you need to have one or more images of the floor plans that make up the conference venue. These images need to be available within the application, not remotely. For the TAMCAPP app, an image named "floorplan.png" is used.

The configuration of the custom map is described in a metadata XML file (floorplan.xml). This file defines a basemap and a layer that contains the reference to the image. Both the basemap and the layer have an id that is used by the thematic map component to identify the appropriate basemap and layer. The other information defined in the XML metadata file is the points and their coordinates. The coordinates of the points will be used to plot the hotspots on the rendered map.

```
<basemap id="floorplan">
    <layer id="floorplanLayer">
        <image source="/thematicmaps/floorplan.png" width="762" height="650"/>
    </layer>
    <points>
        <point name="roomOne"   x="40"  y="40"/>
        <point name="roomTwo"   x="260" y="40"/>
        <point name="roomThree" x="40"  y="380"/>
        <point name="roomFour"  x="40"  y="190"/>
        <point name="roomFive"  x="550" y="40"/>
    </points>
</basemap>
```

NOTE
In the preceding example, there is one image defined for the floorplan layer. In this metadata file, you can specify different images for different screen resolutions and display directions. The thematic map chooses the correct image for the layer based on the screen resolution and direction.

Creating the Map

The Oracle MAF AMX page uses a thematicMap component to display the floor plan. Remember that, by default, the thematicMap component is based on a geographical map. This map is defined by the basemap attribute. The areaLayer in this example uses states.

```
<dvtm:thematicMap basemap="usa" id="tm2">
    <dvtm:areaLayer layer="states" id="al2"/>
</dvtm:thematicMap>
```

For the purpose of TAMCAPP, both the basemap and the layer need to be customized. To instruct the TAMCAPP thematicMap component to use a custom image, the basemap needs to point to the basemap id in the XML metadata file, and the area layer needs to point to the layer definition in the metadata file. Both the basemap and layer are read from the XML metadata file, in this case, the "thematicmaps/floorplan.xml." The pointDataLayer element of the thematicMap needs a data collection to plot the points on the map.

```
<dvtm:thematicMap basemap="floorplan" id="tm1"
                  source="/thematicmaps/floorplan.xml"
```

```
                           animationOnDisplay="alphaFade"
                           animationOnMapChange="cubeToLeft">
      <dvtm:areaLayer layer="floorplanLayer" id="al1" areaLabelDisplay="off">
         <dvtm:pointDataLayer id="pdl1" var="row"
                              value="#{bindings.hotspots.collectionModel}"
                              dataSelection="none">
    ....................
      </dvtm:pointDataLayer>
      </dvtm:areaLayer>
   </dvtm:thematicMap>
```

The data collection used by the datapoint layer is defined in the FloorPlanHotspots class, which will be explained later. This class defines a set of hotspots that is returned by a data service. For this class, a data control is created (Figure 15-4) that is used to drag and drop the thematic map and create the binding entries in the corresponding page definition file.

NOTE
Dragging and dropping based on a data service in the Data Control panel creates the thematic map component and also the necessary bindings. If the thematicMap component is created in this way, it can only be based on a predefined base map. That means that you need to change <dvtm:thematicMap/> and <dvtm:areaLayer/> manually to use your custom base map.

This FloorPlanHotspots class calls a data service. In this particular example, the data service is a method called initHotpots() in this Java class that creates a list containing a predefined hardcoded set of hotspots. The Hotspot object defines a hotspot.

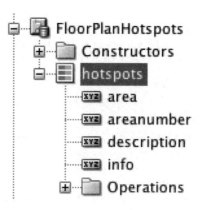

FIGURE 15-4. *FloorPlanHotspots data control*

```
public class Hotspot {
    private String area;
    private String info;
    private int areanumber;
    private String description;
private List s_searchResults = null;
public FloorPlanHotspots() {
    super();
    if (s_searchResults == null) {
        s_searchResults = new ArrayList();
        initHotspots();
    }
}
public void initHotspots() {
    s_searchResults.add((new Hotspot("roomOne", "Mobile Sessions", 1,
                "In this room there are about 10 sessions on Oracle MAF")));
    s_searchResults.add((new Hotspot("roomTwo", "Database Sessions", 2,
                "Database Sessions can be very interesting")));
    s_searchResults.add((new Hotspot("roomThree", "APEX Sessions", 3,
                "APEX is doing a good job. Just is not my thing")));
    s_searchResults.add((new Hotspot("roomFour", "PL SQL Sessions", 4,
                "PL SQL is way back for me")));
    s_searchResults.add((new Hotspot("roomFive", "Other Sessions", 5,
                "Need I say more")));
}
public Hotspot[] getHotspots() {
    Hotspot l[] = null;
    l = ( Hotspot[])s_searchResults.toArray(new  Hotspot[s_searchResults.size()]);
    return l;
}
```

This means that there are five predefined hotspots, all with their own area, info, areanumber, and description. This information can be used in the implementation of the actual hotspots. The coordinates of the hotspots are hardcoded in the floorplan.xml file. For example, a hotspot with area=roomOne will be plotted on *x*=40 and *y*=40 because in the floorplan.xml file, a datapoint is defined with the name roomOne.

```
<points>
    <point name="roomOne"    x="40"  y="40"/>
```

Defining the Hotspots

The datapoint layer of the thematic map is based on the #{bindings.hotspots.collectionModel}, which holds an array of hotspots and uses var="row" to stamp out the data points. This variable is used in the actual pointLocations and Markers. The pointLocation specifies the data that determines the location of the data points. These locations in the case of TAMCAPP are represented as *x* and *y* coordinates. The marker is used to stamp out a shape associated with data points on the map. The pointLocation uses #{row.area} to look up the corresponding coordinates in the XML metadata file by name (type="pointName") and plot the point on the defined location. On these locations, the markers are placed. The final result is displayed in Figure 15-5.

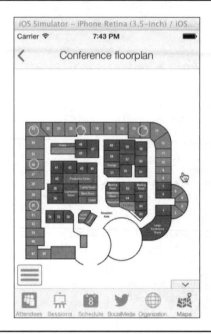

FIGURE 15-5.   *Showing the hotspots on the venue map*

```
<dvtm:pointLocation pointName="#{row.area}" id="pl1" type="pointName">
    <dvtm:marker id="marker1" value="#{row.areanumber}" fillColor="#636F57"
                opacity="0.0" scaleX="2"
                scaleY="2" shortDesc="#{row.info}" shape="circle"
                labelDisplay="on"
                labelPosition="center" labelStyle="font-size:0px;color:white;"
                gradientEffect="auto">
```

NOTE
The x and y coordinates have been hardcoded in the XML metadata file. They also could have been derived dynamically from the Hotspots collection. In order to do this, the Hotspots object needs attributes for both x and y coordinates and the pointLocation component's type must be set to "pointXY."

```
<dvtm:pointLocation id="pl1" type="pointXY"
                pointX="#{row.x}" pointY="#{row.y}" >
```

Invoking the Hotspot Popup

Finally, TAMCAPP displays a popup when one of the hotspots is tapped. This popup is invoked by an <amx:showPopupBehavior/> component. The information displayed in the popup is also retrieved from the row variable and put into pageFlowScope variables.

```
<dvtm:pointLocation pointName="#{row.area}" id="pl1">
    <dvtm:marker id="marker1" value="#{row.areanumber}" fillColor="#636F57"
                 opacity="0.0" scaleX="2"
                 scaleY="2" shortDesc="#{row.info}" shape="circle"
                 labelDisplay="on"
                 labelPosition="center" labelStyle="font-size:0px;color:white;"
                 gradientEffect="auto">
        <amx:setPropertyListener from="#{row.info}"
                                 to="#{pageFlowScope.hotspotsBean.info}"/>
        <amx:setPropertyListener from="#{row.areanumber}"
                                 to="#{pageFlowScope.hotspotsBean.areanumber}"/>
        <amx:setPropertyListener from="#{row.description}"
                                 to="#{pageFlowScope.hotspotsBean.description}"/>
        <amx:showPopupBehavior popupId="p1" align="overlapTop" alignId="tm1"/>
    </dvtm:marker>
</dvtm:pointLocation>
</dvtm:areaLayer>
</dvtm:thematicMap>
<amx:popup id="p1" autoDismiss="true" animation="slideRight"
           inlineStyle="padding:0px;">
    <amx:tableLayout id="tl1" width="75%" inlineStyle="width:300px;height:150px;">
        <amx:rowLayout id="rl911">
            <amx:cellFormat id="cf913" width="80%" valign="top" halign="start">
                <amx:outputText value="#{pageFlowScope.hotspotsBean.info}" id="ot41"/>
            </amx:cellFormat>
        </amx:rowLayout>
        <amx:rowLayout id="rl6">
            <amx:cellFormat id="cf99" width="80%" valign="top" halign="start">
                <amx:outputText value="#{pageFlowScope.hotspotsBean.description}"
id="ot91"/>
            </amx:cellFormat>
        </amx:rowLayout>
    </amx:tableLayout>
</amx:popup>
```

The Points of Interest Map

The points of interest map is implemented by an Oracle MAF DVT map component. This implementation consists of three main parts:

- A web service, which in this case is provided by Google
- A POJO supplying the data points
- A map component

The Google Places API

For the points of interest map, we are going to use the Google Places API. The Google Places API allows you to query place information on a variety of "places" (locations) including by category, such as establishments, prominent points of interest, geographic locations, and more. You can search for places either by proximity or a text string. A place search returns a list of places along with summary information about each place.

We will use the JSON-type response:

```
https://maps.googleapis.com/maps/api/place/nearbysearch/JSON?parameters
```

There are many parameters that can be used in the parameters section in the preceding sample URL. For the purpose of this book, we will only use the following:

- location=52.35985,4.88510 (will be derived from the GPS location of your device)
- radius=1000
- types (there are many types available, but for the example, just two are used)
  - food
  - art_gallery
- sensor=false
- key=<your google API key>

This will result in the following URL for the web service call:

```
https://maps.googleapis.com/maps/api/place/nearbysearch/
json?location=52.35985,4.8
8510&radius=1000&types=art_gallery&sensor=false&key=<your google API key>
```

Other parameters, and additional information, can be found at the documentation site of the Google Places API: https://developers.google.com/places/documentation/search.

When using the web service, Google returns the results as a JSON string:

```
"results" : [
    {
        "geometry" : {
            "location" : {
                "lat" : 52.363850,
                "lng" : 4.880790
            }
        },
        "icon" : "http://maps.gstatic.com/mapfiles/place_api/icons/cafe-71.png",
        "id" : "7e7aa85e3e8fb7436bf77647cecbc6ce80db0b4a",
        "name" : "American Hotel",
        "photos" : [
            {
                "height" : 858,
                "html_attributions" : [],
                "photo_reference" :
"CnRnAAAANnNEEbllpLaJOmSOpPbBY6yTKq7pX5ISR0SumPPjzCLoyMqAjLA5KSXX1WyHS6CzaeLloT3Ck
XjbpH5MOsHIXcMHY0IuvXjloK7ZSGnQPCSdcseeDz67n6P9xJjcHn_IQi_ofX6CYU8ep5d3Uww5FBIQ6TB
6XCXFelAUVw2hGDqZLRoUGv9owCeAoWlVUB-F753HUAcxgYA",
```

```
            "width" : 1280
          }
      ],
      "rating" : 3.60,
      "reference" : "CnRtAAAAw3CMp-foxCYu7Jz3AoVujavqDCaVCMSBin2Byjc-
gsOYR4b9R2WP64bTinDxnA1_gWfog9sVy5kJtj7dhCCefkcbBT-
nXR400EJekeDGAkaIPCpajV52u6rLd_9SRETAIMOTk3RE6eeXCM-
4Cop_NRIQemFOs_IWVK17667_0yitkxoUvAkxZbaAmwtqFXv3tQJb5jy88HQ",
      "types" : [ "cafe", "lodging", "food", "establishment" ],
      "vicinity" : "Leidsekade 97, Amsterdam"
    },
… next results……
```

NOTE
The reference and photo-reference information can be an expensive download. If you don't want to show the images, it is preferable to not download this information. Unfortunately, the Google Places API does not provide a way to exclude reference and photo-reference information. This means that even when you do not use this information, it will be downloaded to the app.

If you create your own points of interest map, you need to figure out what information is relevant for the map and will be used on the points of interest map. For the purpose of the TAMCAPP app, we will use the location values to plot the location against our maps, as well as the icon name, rating, and vicinity fields.

Invoking the Google Places Web Service

The Google Places web service is a REST-JSON web service. To handle the JSON response of the Google Places web service, you need to use the RestServiceAdapter and JSONBeanSerializationHelper classes. These classes are part of the Oracle MAF Framework and can be found in the "oracle .adfmf.*" package. In the current Oracle MAF releases, the only way to access REST-JSON services is manually through the RestServiceAdapter. To use the RestServiceAdapter interface in your MAF application, it needs a valid connection to the URL where the service is hosted. Make sure that there is a valid connection in the connections.xml, or simply create a new connection by invoking the New gallery in JDeveloper to create a new URL connection. The URL Endpoint defined in this connection refers to the root URL of the REST service. The actual request URI will be set in Java code, just before the service is invoked.

The URL connection does not define the URL parameters. Only the URL endpoint is needed. The RestServiceAdapter in the TAMCAPP application will construct the remaining part of the request.

NOTE
After you create the URL connection, it is recommended to restart JDeveloper. Unfortunately, due to a bug in JDeveloper, calling the web service without restarting JDeveloper can result in an error saying: "Failed to establish a URL connection. Please make sure a valid URL connection can be established." This happens even though the URL connection contains a valid connection. This bug probably will be fixed soon.

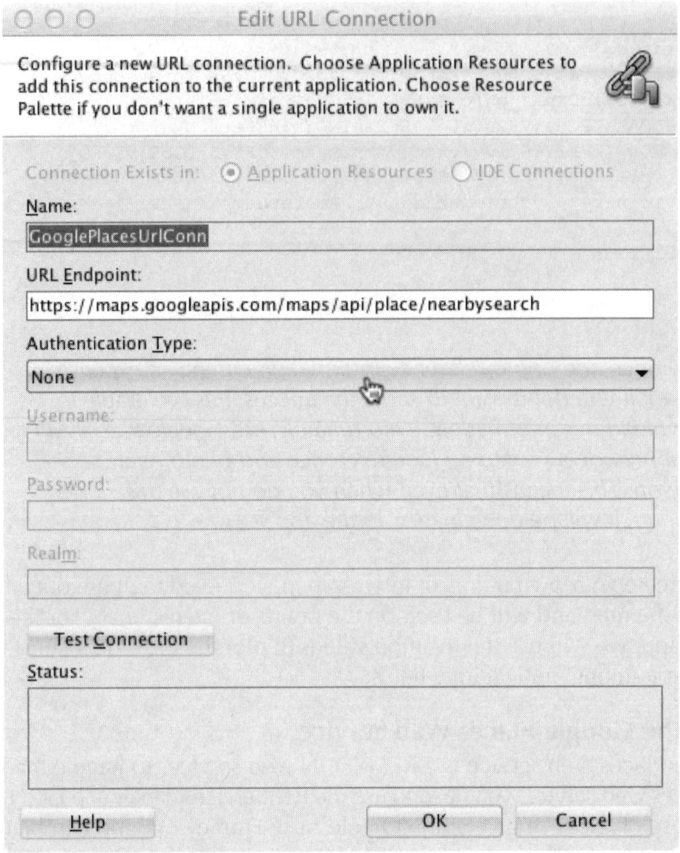

FIGURE 15-6. *Creating the URL connection*

To connect to a REST web service using the RestServiceAdapter, you need to define a URL endpoint connection, a request type (GET in this sample), and the request URI that contains information about the resource you attempted to query. The URL endpoint connection refers to the previously defined URL connection. The request type GET tells the RestServiceAdapter that we want to retrieve data. Finally, the RestServiceAdapter needs to know the request URI that tells the web service exactly what you are looking for. In the case of this example, the location, the radius, the type, and, of course, a valid Google API key are needed to construct the URI.

```
RestServiceAdapter restServiceAdapter = Model.createRestServiceAdapter();
// Clear any previous request properties
restServiceAdapter.clearRequestProperties();
// Set the connection name
restServiceAdapter.setConnectionName("GooglePlacesUrlConn");
```

```
// Specify the type of request
restServiceAdapter.setRequestType(RestServiceAdapter.REQUEST_TYPE_GET);
// Specify the number of retries
restServiceAdapter.setRetryLimit(0);
// Set the URI which is defined after the endpoint in the connections.xml.
// The request is the endpoint + the URI with query parameters
restServiceAdapter.setRequestURI("json?location=52.35985,4.88510&radius=1000&types=
food&sensor=false&key=<yourApiKey>");
String response = "not found";
try {
    response = restServiceAdapter.send("");
}
```

Working with the JSON-DATA

The response of the service call needs to be processed before we can use it in the TAMCAPP app. The result is a JSON structure. To work with this result, TAMCAPP uses the ServiceResult object, which mimics the JSON structure of the Google Places result. The result of the call to jsonHelper .fromJSON is to cast this to a ServiceResult object. From this point on, you can work with the result, which is now contained in a Java object.

```
public class ServiceResult {
    private String status;
    private String debug_info;
    private String html_attributions;
    private String next_page_token;
    private JSONArray results;
```

This ServiceResult object contains a JSONArray that cannot be used in this form by the TAMCAPP app. There must be some kind of transformation to the object model that defines a PlacesResult object in TAMCAPP.

```
public class PlacesResult {
    private String vicinity;
    private Double rating;
    private String name;
    private String types;
    private String icon;
    private PlacesGeometry geometry;
```

The first step in processing the JSON result is the deserialization from JSON to Java. For this purpose, MAF contains the JSONBeanSerializationHelper class. This does an excellent job in converting JSON to Java. The next code sample is the continuation of the sample where the request was constructed previously and focuses on deserialization of the response:

```
JSONBeanSerializationHelper jsonHelper = new JSONBeanSerializationHelper();
try {
    response = restServiceAdapter.send("");
    ServiceResult responseObject =
        (ServiceResult)jsonHelper.fromJSON(ServiceResult.class, response);
    if ( "OK".equalsIgnoreCase( responseObject.getStatus()) ) {
        placesResult = PlacesHelper.transformObject(responseObject).getResults();
    }
```

```
      this.result = responseObject.getStatus();
} catch (Exception e) {
  e.printStackTrace();
 this.result = "error";
}
```

The resultObject is transformed from a JSONArray to the TAMCAPP's object model's PlacesResult in a separate helper class called PlacesHelper. This class takes the JSONArray result Java object and, per result, creates an entry in a list of PlacesResult objects.

```
public static PlacesResponse transformObject(ServiceResult service) {
    PlacesResponse response = new PlacesResponse();
    response.setStatus(service.getStatus());
    PlacesResultList results = new PlacesResultList();
    response.setResults(results);
    JSONArray resultList = service.getResults();
       for (int i = 0; i < resultList.length(); i++) {
       try {
         PlacesResult placesResult = new PlacesResult();
         JSONObject result = resultList.getJSONObject(i);
         if (result.get("icon") != null) {
             placesResult.setIcon((String)result.get("icon"));
         }
    ......
```

The complete code sample for the method that invokes the web service can be found in the following sample:

```
public void searchAction() {
    this.result = "called";
    RestServiceAdapter restServiceAdapter = Model.createRestServiceAdapter();
    // Clear any previous request properties
    restServiceAdapter.clearRequestProperties();
    // Set the connection name
    restServiceAdapter.setConnectionName("GooglePlacesUrlConn");
    // Specify the type of request
    restServiceAdapter.setRequestType(RestServiceAdapter.REQUEST_TYPE_GET);
    restServiceAdapter.addRequestProperty("Content-Type", "application/json");
    restServiceAdapter.addRequestProperty(
                                "Accept","application/json;charset=UTF-8");
    // Specify the number of retries
     restServiceAdapter.setRetryLimit(0);
    // Set the URI which is defined after the endpoint in the connections.xml.
    // The request is the endpoint + the URI being set
    restServiceAdapter.setRequestURI("json?location=52.35985,4.88510&"
                    +"radius=1000&types=food&sensor=false&key=<yourApiKey>");
    String response = "not found";
    JSONBeanSerializationHelper jsonHelper = new JSONBeanSerializationHelper();
    try {
        // For GET request, there is no payload
        response = restServiceAdapter.send("");
        ServiceResult responseObject =
```

```
           (ServiceResult)jsonHelper.fromJSON(ServiceResult.class, response);
     if ( "OK".equalsIgnoreCase( responseObject.getStatus()) ) {
        placesResult = PlacesHelper.transformObject(responseObject).getResults();
     }
     this.result = responseObject.getStatus();
   } catch (Exception e) {
     e.printStackTrace();
     this.result = "error";
     }
 }
```

Now a data control (Figure 15-7) can be created from this class. This data control is used to create the map component. Simply drag and drop the placesResult collection from the data control onto the page as a geographic map. In the popup that JDeveloper shows you upon creation, you can use the address type map based on the vicinity.

```
<dvtm:geographicMap id="map1" zoomLevel="4" centerX="52.37323" centerY="4.89166">
    <dvtm:pointDataLayer value="#{bindings.placesResults.collectionModel}"
                      id="pdl2" var="row">
       <dvtm:pointLocation  id="ptl1" type="address"
                         pointName="#{row.name}" address="#{row.vicinity}">
          <dvtm:marker id="mrk1" source="#{row.icon}"/>
       </dvtm:pointLocation>
    </dvtm:pointDataLayer>
</dvtm:geographicMap>
```

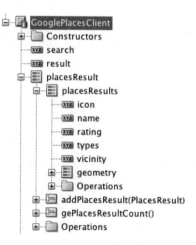

FIGURE 15-7. *GooglePlacesClient data control*

NOTE
The placesResult also contains the geometry with the exact x and y coordinates. Instead of the vicinity, these coordinates can be used if you need more accuracy. The maps component, however, is able to do a good job on geocoding based on the address contained by the vicinity.

Using the Device's GPS Coordinates

As you learned in the chapter about device interaction, Oracle MAF has access to the device's GPS. This information can be used in the points of interest map. For that purpose, the location parameter, which in the previously used code sample for the searchAction() uses a hardcoded value for the coordinates, needs to be created dynamically. So instead of using

```
location=52.35985,4.88510
```

the app will need to construct something like

```
location=<myLat>,<myLong>
```

In order to do that, the app needs to retrieve the current position of the device. The DeviceManager can do this for you.

```
public Location getPosition(){
    DeviceManager dm =DeviceManagerFactory.getDeviceManager();
    Location currentPosition = dm.getCurrentPosition( 60000, true);
    return currentPosition;
}
```

The returned Location object of this method call contains the information needed for the Google Places search: longitude and latitude. You can access that information in Java. Combining all this will lead to the following:

```
Location myPosition = getPosition();
String locationParameter = "location="+ myPosition.getLatitude();+","+
                    myPosition.getLongitude();
restServiceAdapter.setRequestURI(
"json?"+locationParameter+"&radius=1000&types=food&sensor=false&key=<yourApiKey>");
```

When the Google Places service is called now, it will return information on, in this case, food-related places in a 1,000-meter radius of the device's current location (Figure 15-8).

NOTE
In the chapter about enhancing the TAMCAPP app, you will learn a mechanism to invoke the Google Places search without having access to the GPS coordinates of the device.

FIGURE 15-8. *The icons on the map*

Switching Between Food and Leisure

It is very nice to have an overview of all nearby bars, restaurants, and other great places to get food. But during your stay in a new city, it would be nice to also visit some museums or theaters during your lazy Sunday or some of your very little time off during the conference. That is why the TAMCAPP application also provides the possibility to switch between food and leisure (Figure 15-9).

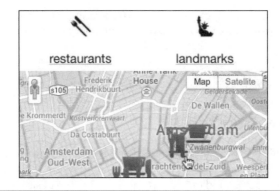

FIGURE 15-9. *Maps header to switch from restaurants to landmarks*

In order to do this, the points of interest map has a header section containing two buttons; one for restaurants and one for landmarks. When you invoke either one of the links, the map switches between the options. This is implemented by a combination of an actionListener and a setPropertyListener. The propertyListener sets the value of the currentMap type, and the actionListener invokes a method in a managed bean that calls the web service.

```
<amx:commandLink id="cl1 actionListener="#{pageFlowScope.mapsBean.switchMapMode}">
    <amx:image id="i1" source="/images/Fork and knife.png"/>
    <amx:setPropertyListener id="spl2" from="food"
                             to="#{pageFlowScope.mapsBean.currentMap}" type="action"/>
</amx:commandLink>
<amx:commandLink id="cl2"actionListener="#{pageFlowScope.mapsBean.switchMapMode}">
    <amx:image id="i2" source="/images/Statue Of Liberty.png"/>
    <amx:setPropertyListener id="spl2" from="museum|art_gallery|zoo|movie_theater"
                             to="#{pageFlowScope.mapsBean.currentMap}" type="action"/>
</amx:commandLink>
```

The Google Places API supports multiple types in one GET request. These types can be concatenated using a "pipe" symbol. This is demonstrated in the preceding code sample for the setPropertyListener "from" field of the second commandLink.

Whenever the user taps one of the icons, we want the web service to be reinvoked with the new parameters, and the new results will be displayed on the map. This is implemented in the mapsBeans' switchMapMode method, which calls the GooglePlacesClient searchAction, supplying this method with the appropriate map type. Note that the call is only executed when the map type actually changes.

```
public MapsBean() {
    poi = new GooglePlacesClient();
}
public void switchMapMode(ActionEvent actionEvent) {
    if (!currentMap.equalsIgnoreCase(previousMap)) {
        poi.searchAction(currentMap);
        setPreviousMap(currentMap);
    }
}
```

The searchAction method retrieves the mapType and uses it in constructing the requestURI. This requestURI now is pretty much dynamic, using the device's coordinates and the mapType set by the user.

```
restServiceAdapter.setRequestURI(
"?"+locationParameter+"&radius=1000&types="+mapType+"&sensor=false&key=<yorKey>");
```

Caching the Web Service Data

Now that you have implemented the points of interest map, you must realize that each and every time you change the type from food to leisure and back, the web service is invoked. This doesn't really make sense, because it is very possible that it will return the exact same results. What can you do to implement some kind of caching mechanism? The easiest way to implement this is to find out whether or not there is data in memory just before you call the web service.

For this purpose, two collections need to be created in the GooglePlacesClient class, one for each type of place:

```
private PlacesResultList foodPlaces = null;
private PlacesResultList leisurePlaces = null;
```

After calling the service the first time, put the result of the service call in the corresponding collection. Now when calling the web service the second time, find out if this call was executed before by checking if there is any data in the cache collection.

So in this case:

```
if (foodPlaces.getPlacesResultCount()>0){
  readFromCache();
}
```

You could also add an extra check, but only if your location has changed substantially so that you want to refresh the search results. With both checks in place, you are now pretty much sure not to call the web service too many times.

Embedding the Twitter Timeline

Being in a big city at a big conference with no access to social media is probably not a good thing. The least you need is news related to the conference. The TAMCAPP app has an embedded Twitter timeline for the Tamcapp Conference. It will show all tweets related to @tamcappConf, the Twitter account of the conference. Embedding Twitter can be done in different ways. The first is the Twitter REST API v1.1. This enables you to add a Twitter timeline to your Oracle MAF app. The GET statuses/user_timeline returns a collection of the most recent tweets posted by the user indicated by the screen_name or user_id parameters.

```
https://api.twitter.com/1.1/statuses/user_timeline.json?screen_name=<name>
```

This way of interacting has been explained in the previous section where the Google Places REST API was used to implement the points of interest map. This is also the mechanism that you must use when embedding a Twitter timeline in an Oracle MAF app for iOS. If you are only building for Android, you can use a different and much easier mechanism. You can use the Twitter Widget to implement the Twitter timeline. In the next section, you will learn how to use local HTML to embed the Twitter timeline in the TAMCAPP app.

Exploring the Twitter Widget

Just like timelines on twitter.com, embeddable timelines are interactive and enable your visitors to reply, retweet, and save favorite tweets directly from the TAMCAPP app. An integrated Tweet box encourages users to respond to or start new conversations, and the option to auto-expand media brings photos front and center.

These timeline tools are built specifically for the web, mobile web, and touch devices. It is in fact very easy to create a Twitter timeline widget on the Twitter web site (Figure 15-10). When you visit the settings page of your account and select "*widgets,*" you can create new widgets or edit existing ones.

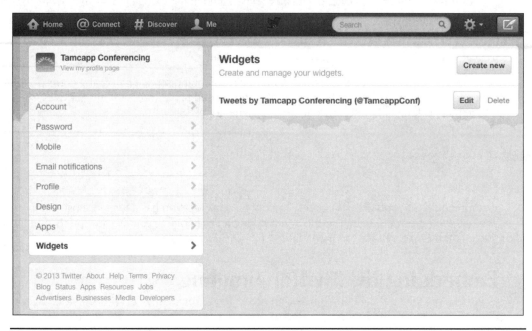

FIGURE 15-10. *The Twitter timeline widget*

Using the Widget in the Sample Application

To use the widget in TAMCAPP is actually very simple. You need to create an HTML page and paste the widget code generated by Twitter into the HTML page. And that really is all that is needed to show the Twitter timeline (Figure 15-11).

```
<!DOCTYPE HTML PUBLIC "-//W3C//DTD HTML 4.01 Transitional//EN" "http://www.w3.org/TR/
html4/loose.dtd">
<html>
   <head>
      <meta http-equiv="Content-Type" content="text/html; charset=ISO-8859-1">
      </meta>
   </head>
<body>
   <a class="twitter-timeline"  href="https://twitter.com/TamcappConf"  data-
      widget-id="yourData-Widget-Id"> Tweets by @TamcappConf</a>
   <script type="text/javascript">
!function(d,s,id){var js,fjs=d.getElementsByTagName(s)[0],p=/^http:/.test
(d.location)?'http':'https';if(!d.getElementById(id)){js=d.createElement(s);
js.id=id;js.src=p+"http://platform.twitter.com/widgets.js";fjs.
parentNode.insertBefore(js,fjs);}}
(document,"script","
twitter-wjs");
      </script>
   </body>
</html>
```

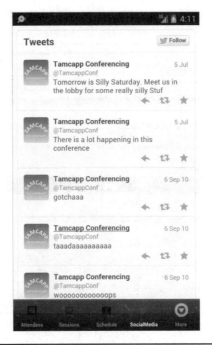

FIGURE 15-11. *The TamcappConf Twitter timeline*

Whitelisting the Twitter Domain

Because the Twitter widget uses a remote URL, Oracle MAF can only invoke this URL when you explicitly instruct the app that this is allowed. This process is called whitelisting. A URL or domain can be added to a whitelist in the application configuration file as displayed in Figure 15-12.

Entering the domain as shown in Figure 15-12 results in the following XML code:

```
<adfmf:remoteURLWhiteList>
    <adfmf:domain id="twitter">*twitter*</adfmf:domain>
</adfmf:remoteURLWhiteList>
```

NOTE
You can add multiple domains in the whitelist and even add a wildcard domain using an asterisk (*). This will result in all domains being allowed. Although this is a very easy way of doing this, you must realize that allowing access to all domains is a potential security risk.

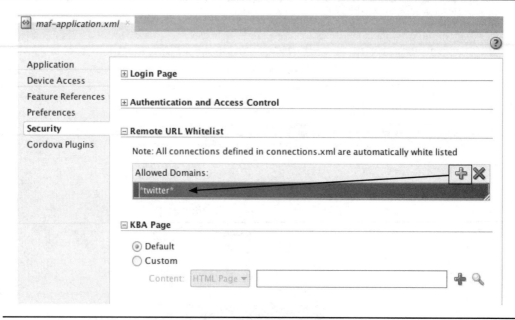

FIGURE 15-12. *Adding domains to the application's whitelist*

Summary

The TAMCAPP app enables you to find your way around at the conference site and in the conference city by means of maps. Also, you can read all tweets from the TAMCAPP account from within the app.

In this chapter you learned

- How to embed maps in your Oracle MAF application
- How to create a custom thematic map component
- How to use a REST-JSON web service and work with the results
- How to cache data
- How to use a geographical map
- How to embed a Twitter timeline using the Twitter widget

CHAPTER
16

Configuring Security
and Preferences

In the previous chapters, you learned how the functionality for the TAMCAPP application was developed. TAMCAPP is a great app for different groups of users. Both speakers and attendees can use the app, and members of the organizing committee can also use TAMCAPP. In this chapter, you will learn how to secure TAMCAPP and how to make TAMCAPP configurable by using preferences.

When the user installs the TAMCAPP app, it is not yet ready to use. As with many other apps, TAMCAPP needs to be configured. Security is used to shield TAMCAPP from unauthorized access. The user needs to have a username and password in order to log in to the application, and also for reasons such as push notifications (Chapter 17), some configuration must be performed. This is all taken care of at initial startup. The first time the user opens TAMCAPP, the user is directed to the Registration feature and is prompted to enter their e-mail address and a username. In this chapter, you will learn how to set up this registration and security functionality. In Chapter 10, you learned how Oracle Mobile Application Framework security works in general. In the following sections, you will learn how security is implemented for the TAMCAPP app.

In addition to security, this chapter goes into the use of application preferences, which the user can change to meet their needs. These preferences influence the behavior of the TAMCAPP application; they are stored with the app and can be changed by the TAMCAPP user. In the second part of this chapter, you will learn how to implement the preferences for TAMCAPP.

The Initial Registration Process

For a user to be able to log in to the TAMCAPP app, the user must have valid credentials. These credentials are provided by the TAMCAPP app at initial registration. To facilitate this, TAMCAPP has a Registration feature. This is the only feature in the TAMCAPP app that has no security enabled. So when the user opens the TAMCAPP app for the very first time, there are no features accessible except the Registration feature. The user is automatically directed to this Registration feature and is prompted to enter an e-mail address and username. After the user has invoked the Register button, this information is then sent to the TAMCAPP enterprise server where it is stored in the TAMCAPP "Subscriber" table. The enterprise application also creates a TAMCAPP user account that can be used to log in to the TAMCAPP application. The credentials, username and password, are returned by an e-mail. This information can be used to log in to the secured features of TAMCAPP, which obviously all require authentication. When the user tries to access such a secured feature, a login page is presented where the user can enter the username and password.

In Chapter 10, you already learned that Oracle MAF can authenticate against any basic authentication server. The TAMCAPP solution ships with its own authentication server.

Whenever the TAMCAPP user is challenged to provide credentials, these are sent to the authentication server. After successful login, the user's roles are determined, and returned to the TAMCAPP app. If the user is known as a speaker at the conference, he will get the role speaker; otherwise, the role attendee is assigned. These roles can now be used by the TAMCAPP app to display features the user is entitled to use. Also, specific page content such as buttons and input components can be hidden or displayed based on the user role.

The Logic Behind the Initial Registration

To invoke the registration at initial startup, the TAMCAPP app needs to be aware of the fact that this is the first time the user has started the TAMCAPP app. The way TAMCAPP determines this is by checking if the device is already registered in the enterprise database. If it is not, that means that this is the first time that TAMCAPP has been started on this device. This check is implemented in the start() method of the applicationLifeCycle listener of TAMCAPP:

```
public void start() {
    // Register application for push Notifications (explained in Chapter 17)
    EventSource evtSource =
            EventSourceFactory.getEventSource(NativePushNotificationEventSource.
                    NATIVE_PUSH_NOTIFICATION_REMOTE_EVENT_SOURCE_NAME);
    evtSource.addListener(new PushNotificationListener());

    // call Registration feature to check if device is registered
    AdfmfContainerUtilities.gotoFeature("com.tamcapp.mobilebook.reg.Registration");
}
```

In this method, the Registration feature is called. This feature has its own life cycle listener. In the activate() method of this listener, a web service is called to check whether or not the device is registered. If it is, the feature is deactivated again by navigating to the application's springboard. If it is not, the activation of the feature is continued and the registration page is shown so the user can register.

NOTE
The call to the Registration feature could have been implemented in the application life cycle listener directly. However, it is implemented in the features life cycle listener so the Registration feature is self-contained and can be reused.

```
public void activate() {
    String device = (String)AdfmfJavaUtilities.evaluateELExpression(
                            "#{applicationScope.deviceToken}");
    RegistrationService srv = new RegistrationService();
    userName = srv.getTamcappUserByDevice(device);
    if (userName.equalsIgnoreCase("NotRegistered")){
        // do nothing, just continue activating the feature.
    }
    else {
        // deactivate by going to springboard
        AdfmfContainerUtilities.gotoSpringboard();
    }
}
```

NOTE
The "#{applicationScope.deviceToken}" expression in the preceding code sample refers to the device-specific token, which is part of the information needed for push notifications. This will be explained in Chapter 17.

The actual registration process is facilitated by a web service. This web service takes a RegisteredUser object as parameter. This object contains all the information that is needed in order to register the user, including the information about the application and the device. The latter are being used for push notifications.

```
public class RegisteredUser {
    private String applicationId;
    private String deviceToken;
    private String deviceType;
    private String email;
    private String username;
    public RegisteredUser() {
      super();
    }
// getters and setters
}
```

The code that issues the call to the registration web service is shown next. This web service has an operation called "createTamcappUsers." It is responsible for storing the userId and the device information in a table and also makes sure that a user is created in the security realm. A security realm consists of a set of configured security providers, users, groups, security roles, and security policies.

```
public void register(String appId, String devToken, String devType, String email,
                     String userName) {
    RegisteredUser regUser = new RegisteredUser();
    regUser.setApplicationId(appId);
    regUser.setDeviceToken(devToken);
    regUser.setDeviceType(devType);
    regUser.setEmail(email);
    regUser.setUserName(userName);
    List pnames = new ArrayList();
    List params = new ArrayList();
    List ptypes = new ArrayList();
    GenericType gtRegUser = GenericTypeBeanSerializationHelper.toGenericType(
                "TamcappWsRegDc.Types.createTamcappUsers.tamcappUsers",regUser);
    pnames.add("tamcappUsers");
    params.add(gtRegUser);
    ptypes.add(Object.class);
    try {
     // This calls the DC method and gives us the Return
       GenericType result = (GenericType)AdfmfJavaUtilities.invokeDataControlMethod(
           "TamcappWsRegDc", null, "createTamcappUsers",pnames, params, ptypes);
    } catch (AdfInvocationException ex) {
     // If the web service is not available throw a nice exception
    }
}
```

The registered user receives an e-mail with credentials that can be used to log in to the TAMCAPP application. In the next section, you will learn how to implement the registration in the TAMCAPP app.

Implementing Security in TAMCAPP

All features in the TAMCAPP application are secure features, except for the Registration feature. The security for all other features is defined at the individual feature level. The maf-feature configuration file contains a security section for each feature. To enable security at the feature level, the check box Enable Security must be checked, as you can see in Figure 16-1.

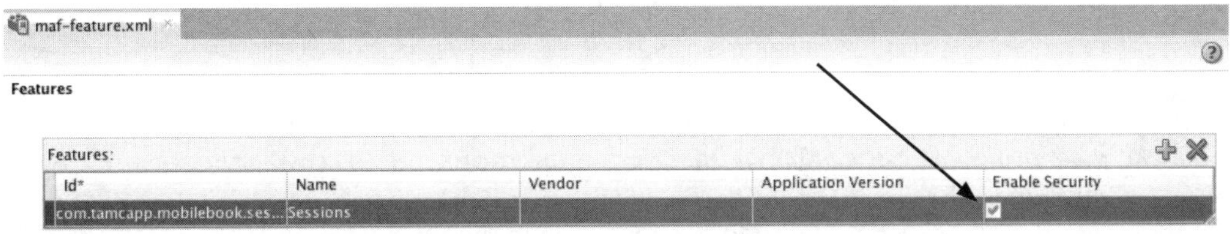

FIGURE 16-1. *Enable feature security.*

The next step is to create a login connection for this feature. This must be defined in the application configuration file. TAMCAPP uses HTTP basic authentication and a remote login server when available; otherwise, TAMCAPP will use local authentication. Therefore, on the General tab of the login connection, "Connectivity mode" should be set to "hybrid." The URL that is used for the basic authentication can be entered on the HTTP Basic tab, as you can see in Figure 16-2.

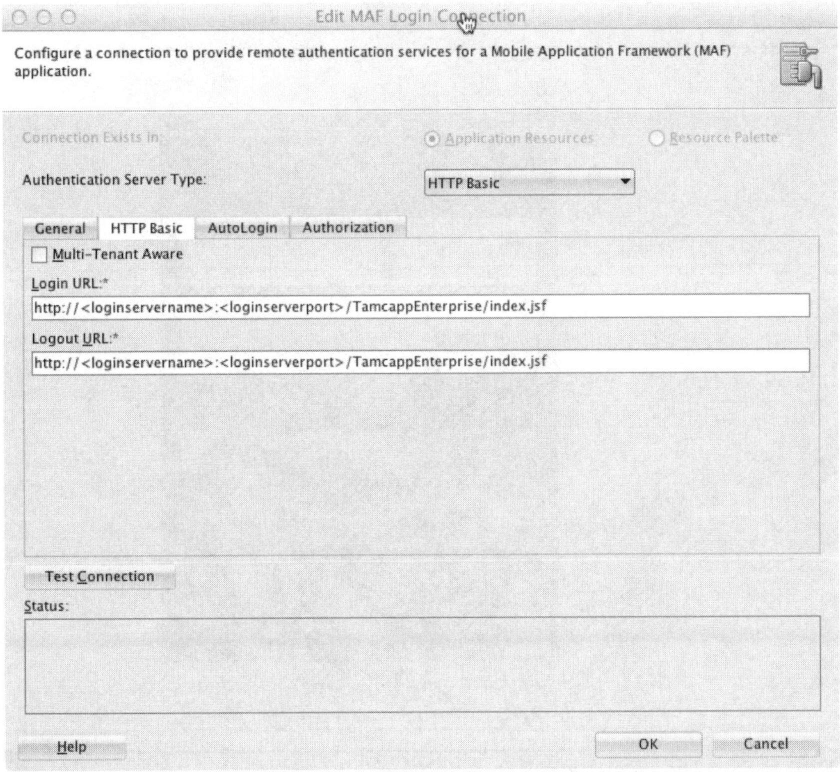

FIGURE 16-2. *The Edit MAF Mobile Login Connection dialog for TAMCAPP*

On the Authorization tab, the access control URL and the app's available roles can be configured. This will be explained later in this chapter.

NOTE
When the feature is deployed as Oracle MAF Feature Archive (FAR), the consuming app recognizes that the feature is secured. However, the consuming app needs to have a login server connection defined in order to assign this login server connection to the secured feature. If the login server is not defined in the consuming app, at run time, the app will not be able to find the login server.

TAMCAPP Login

When an Oracle MAF application is secured, it uses a default login page provided by the framework. Developers can design and build a customized login page. Oracle MAF presents users with a login page (Figure 16-3) when a secured application feature has been activated and the user is not yet authenticated, such as when it is about to be displayed within the web view or when the operating system returns the application feature to the foreground. In these instances, Oracle MAF determines whether access to the application feature requires user authentication and then challenges the user with a login page. Only when the user successfully enters valid credentials will Oracle MAF render the intended web view, UI component, or application page.

FIGURE 16-3. *The default login page*

By default, MAF only presents a login page to an unauthenticated user when it is required, either when an application feature requires security or when it includes constraints based on user roles or user privileges. If either of these conditions exists, then MAF presents users with the login page at the startup of the application and displays application features on the navigation bar accordingly.

Building a Custom Login Page for TAMCAPP

The default login page usually does the trick, but if there is need for extra functionality or maybe a customized look and feel, the framework offers the functionality to create a custom login page. The TAMCAPP app has such a custom login page that replaces the default one. Creating a custom login page is not straightforward. The easiest and preferred way to create a custom login page for an Oracle MAF app is to start with the standard login page. From there, it is easy to make adjustments and it is less likely that you will forget relevant components of the login process, such as JavaScript functions that need to be called.

To get the standard login page into the TAMCAPP app, you need to get hold of the standard login page. The preferred way to get it is to deploy the TAMCAPP app (or any other Oracle MAF app), and then enter the deploy directory on the file system. The default login page can be found on the file system. For iOS, it is called "adf.login.iphone.html" and will be found in the www directory under the temporary_xcode_project:

```
<jws-directory>/deploy/<deployment-profile-name>/temporary_xcode_project/www/adf.login.
iphone.html
```

For Android, it is called "adf.login.android.html" and can be found in the www directory inside the package (.apk) file:

```
<jws-directory>/deploy/<deployment-profile-name>/<deployment-profile-name>.apk/assets/
www/adf.login.android.html
```

Once you have located the standard login page, you need to copy and rename it to a location within the TAMCAPP application controller's public_html directory (Figure 16-4).

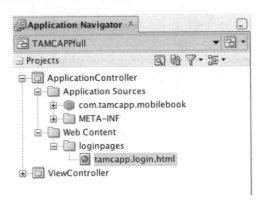

FIGURE 16-4. *The custom login page in the ApplicationController project*

FIGURE 16-5. *Assigning the custom login page*

Now the default login page can be adjusted to fit TAMCAPP's needs. For the purpose of this book, a custom image is added to the login page and its style is changed. This is not really a huge change, but at least it shows you the process of creating a custom login page. After the login page has been created, it needs to be assigned to the application. Assigning the custom login page to the TAMCAPP application is configured in the application configuration file, as you can see in Figure 16-5. In the security section of this file, "Custom" must be selected and the newly created tamcapplogin page must be assigned.

After this adjustment has been made, the XML of the maf-applications file looks like the following code sample:

```
<adfmf:login defaultConnRefId="Authenticate">
    <adfmf:localHTML url="loginpages/tamcapp.login.html"/>
</adfmf:login>
```

Whenever the user tries to access a secured feature, the custom login page (Figure 16-6) is rendered.

TIP
If you put the custom login page not directly under the public_html of the ApplicationController, but in a subfolder, you might find that the custom login page is not displaying in your application. To fix this behavior, you need to change the ApplicationController's deployment profile. In that deployment profile under File Groups | Features | Filters, check the folder containing the custom login page.

After successful login, the secured feature is opened. All information about the logged-in users' roles is now available in the TAMCAPP application.

The TAMCAPP Authorization Model
TAMCAPP uses a very basic authorization model. Each registered user has one or more application roles assigned, and these roles will be used in the TAMCAPP application. The available roles for the TAMCAPP application are

- Attendee
- Organizer
- Speaker

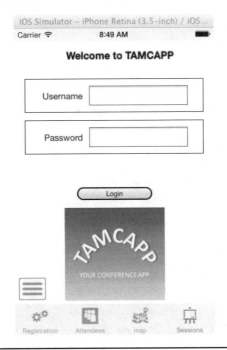

FIGURE 16-6. *The TAMCAPP custom login page in action*

In the login connection on the Authorization tab, the Access Control Service URL must be configured. This URL returns the roles for the logged-in user. Also, the user roles are filtered. The app is only interested in the roles that TAMCAPP uses, and all other roles are filtered out of the securityContext as displayed in Figure 16-7.

When the TAMCAPP user successfully logs in to the application, a JSON object is returned with the userId and all the assigned roles and privileges. The MAF framework evaluates the constraints configured for the application against the retrieved user roles and privileges and only makes the application features available to the user that satisfy all of the associated constraints.

In the following code sample, you see the result for an attendee (att1), a speaker (spe1), a member of the organizing committee (org1), and the administrator who has all roles assigned.

```
// att1
{"userId":"att1","roles":["Attendee"],"priviliges":[]}
// spe1
{"userId":"spe1","roles":["Speaker"],"priviliges":[]}
// org1
{"userId":"org1","roles":["Organizer"],"priviliges":[]}
// luc (administrator)
{"userId":"luc","roles":["Speaker","Attendee","Organizer"],"priviliges":[]}
```

Based on these responses, the securityContext of the TAMCAPP application is constructed. In the next section, you will learn how to use the securityContext in the TAMCAPP app.

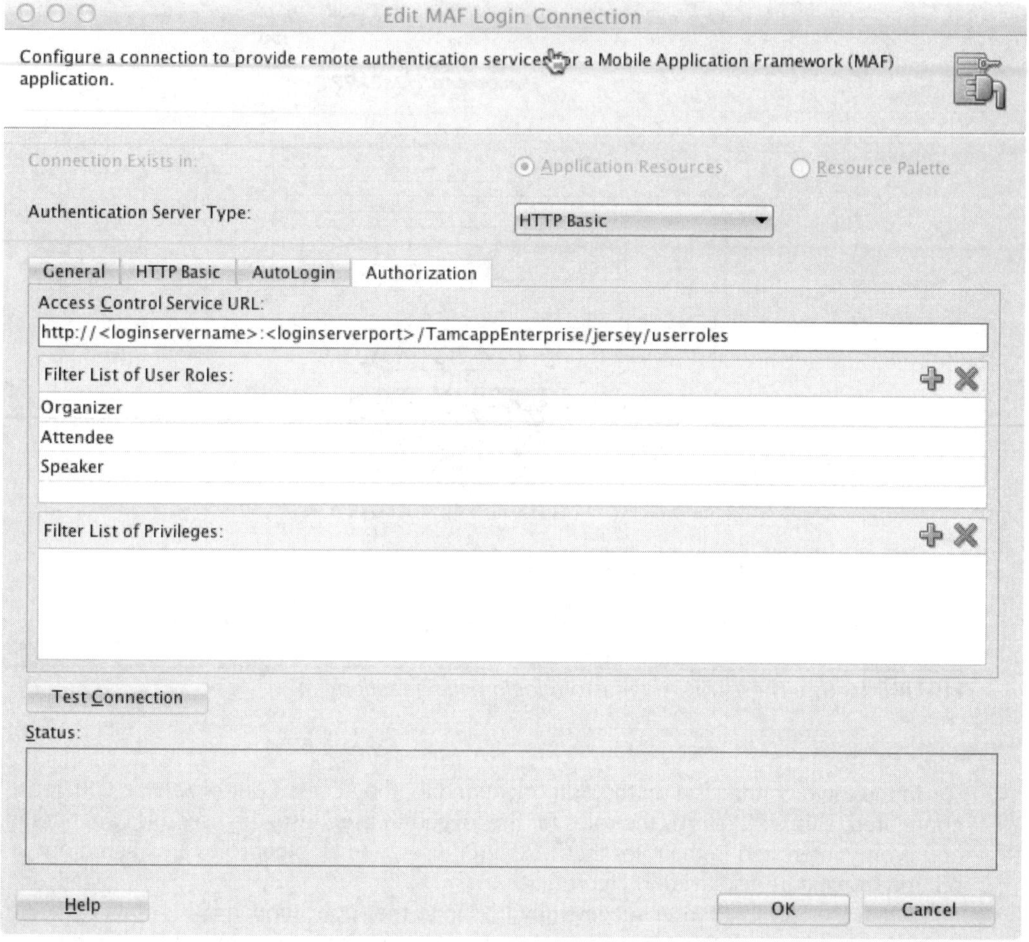

FIGURE 16-7. *Authorization configuration for TAMCAPP*

Hiding Content

So far, you have learned how to secure the features of an Oracle MAF app based on the roles of a user. You might be wondering if there is a way to use the security information in a more "granular" way such as disabling a button from accessing a page or hiding fields on the screen. The answer is yes. All information regarding security is available from within the securityContext that can be used in an EL expression. In TAMCAPP, this information is used to show or hide the evaluation's AMX page. The Conference Session feature contains an Evaluations AMX page. This page can be invoked from the session start AMX page, but is only available if the user is a speaker and thus has the role "speaker" assigned, as you can see in Figure 16-8.

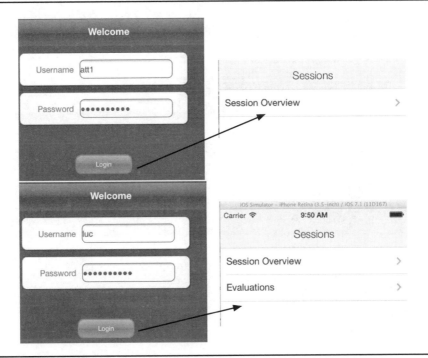

FIGURE 16-8. *Different users, different roles, different functionality*

In order to implement this, a simple EL expression is used. This expression checks if the user has the role "Speaker." If so, the item is rendered; if not, the item is not rendered.

```
<amx:listView var="row" id="lv1">
    <amx:listItem id="li1" action="browse">
       <amx:outputText value="Session Overview" id="ot2"/>
    </amx:listItem>
    <amx:listItem id="li2" action="evaluations
                  rendered="#{securityContext.userInRole['Speaker']}">
       <amx:outputText value="Evaluations" id="ot3"/>
    </amx:listItem>
</amx:listView>
```

NOTE
The EL expression used in the preceding XML code sample uses securityContext. This is not available from within autocomplete in the AMX code editor. If you do not know the exact expression that you need, you can invoke the Expression Builder to select the expression, as you can see in Figure 16-9.

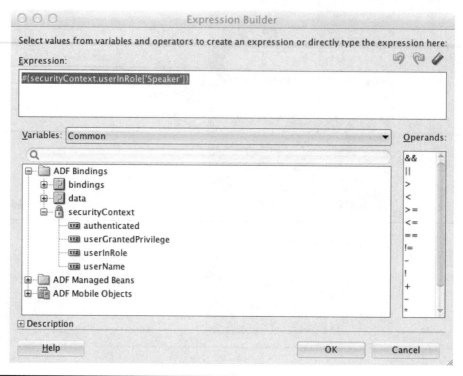

FIGURE 16-9. *Available securityContext expressions*

The securityContext is also available from Java. If you need to work with the securityContext from within Java, you can access it as shown in the following code sample:

```
SecurityContext sc = (SecurityContext)AdfmfJavaUtilities.evaluateELExpression("#{secur
ityContext}");

String inRole = sc.isUserInRole("Speaker");
String userName = sc.getUserName();
String hasPrivilege = sc.hasPrivilege("somePrivilege");
```

Application Preferences

Preferences are pieces of information that your application stores persistently and that can be used to allow the user to configure the app. Apps often expose preferences to users so that they can customize the appearance and behavior of the app. Preferences can store simple data types—strings, numbers, dates, Boolean values, URLs, data objects, and so forth—in a property list. Users can check and change preferences on both iOS and Android. On iOS, preferences are available from within the iOS settings application. Invoking Preferences from the Android application menu shows the preferences for an app on Android. You will see examples of this later in this section.

Preferences are different for each app, and it is up to you to decide what parts of your app you want to make configurable. Configuration involves checking the value of a stored preference from your code and taking action based on that value. Thus, the preference value itself should always be simple and have a specific meaning that is then implemented by your app. In Oracle MAF, preferences can be created at both application level and feature level. The maf-application.xml and maf-feature.xml files are responsible for defining the preferences.

Preference pages are defined with the <adfmf:preferences> element. This has a child, <adfmf:preferenceGroup>, and its child elements define the user preferences by creating pages that present options in various forms, such as read-only strings or drop-down menus. You can even create a separate page for preferences that you want to be grouped together.

The framework supports four kinds of preferences:

- List
- Boolean
- Text
- Number

An example of defined preferences, in this case, to configure how to display conference sessions, is displayed in Figure 16-10.

The following XML sample shows the same preferences:

```
<adfmf:preferences>
    <adfmf:preferenceList id="b" label="Show sessions by:" default="D">
        <adfmf:preferenceValue name="Day" value="D"/>
        <adfmf:preferenceValue name="Track" value="T"/>
    </adfmf:preferenceList>
</adfmf:preferences>
```

In the next section, you will learn how to create and use a preference in the TAMCAPP app.

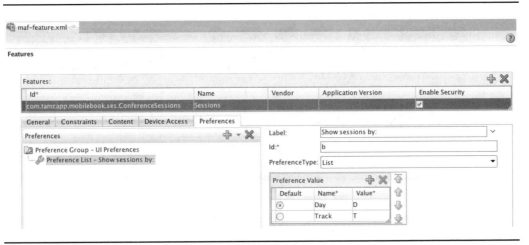

FIGURE 16-10. *A preference group for TAMCAPP*

Implementing the TAMCAPP Preferences

TAMCAPP ships with several preferences that allow users to influence the behavior of the
TAMCAPP application. The Smart Search functionality was implemented in Chapter 14. During
testing of the TAMCAPP application, the "user-friendliness" of this functionality was questioned by
several users, whereas others really liked it. In order to make TAMCAPP users decide whether or
not to use the Smart Search, a feature-level preference is introduced. This preference is a Boolean
preference. When the preference value is true, the application will use Smart Search, and when
the preference value is false, the application will fall back to the default behavior.

Creating a Feature-Level Preference to Toggle Between Regular and Smart Search

As mentioned earlier, preferences can be added at both application and feature level. The Smart
Search preference is a feature-level preference, and it is created in the Attendees feature.

NOTE
*If an application feature requires a specific set of user preferences
in addition to the general preferences defined for the consuming
application, you can define them in the feature configuration file.
This way, when you deploy the feature in a FAR, in the consuming
application, the preferences will also be available. In other words, by
defining the preferences at feature level, your feature is reusable.*

At the feature level, you can add as many preferences as you like. The creation of the
UseSmartSearch preference is pretty straightforward as you can see in Figure 16-11.

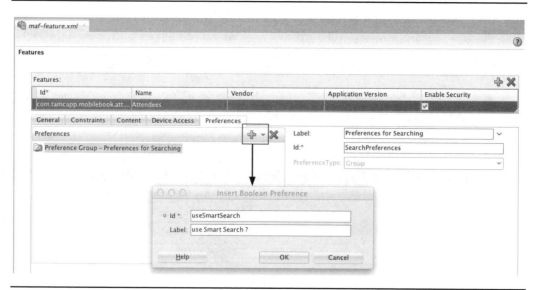

FIGURE 16-11.   *The creation of the UseSmartSearch preference*

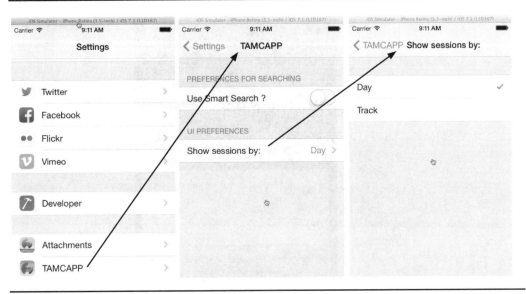

FIGURE 16-12. *TAMCAPP preferences on iOS*

Again, the corresponding XML is very simple:

```
<adfmf:preferences>
    <adfmf:preferenceGroup id="SearchPreferences"
                        label="Preferences for Searching">
      <adfmf:preferenceBoolean id="UseSmartSearch"
                             label="Use Smart Search ?"/>
    </adfmf:preferenceGroup>
</adfmf:preferences>
```

The preference can now be changed from within the application's preferences (Figures 16-12 and 16-13). The preferences on Android are available from within the TAMCAPP app by invoking the preferences. This is available from the Settings button on the Android device. On iOS, you must invoke the Settings app.

Using Preferences from Java Code

In the previous section you learned how to create a preference to influence the search behavior for TAMCAPP. Just setting the preference is one thing. Now it is time to learn how to use the preferences in the TAMCAPP application. The Smart Search functionality is implemented in Java code. If we want to use the preference to influence the search functionality, this preference must be available in Java. To be more specific, we need to access the preference value in the Java method that implements the Smart Search. For that, an EL expression can be used. The expression can be evaluated by calling the evaluateELExpression method in the AdfmfJavaUtilities class, as you will see later.

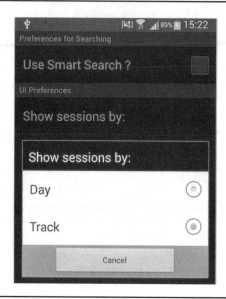

FIGURE 16-13. *TAMCAPP preferences on Android*

The EL expression is a little more complex than you might expect. In order to find the exact preference that we are looking for, you can invoke the EL Expression Builder (Figure 16-14). This also enables you to create the expression on the fly.

Now that the exact EL expression is determined, it can be used in Java code and adjust the behavior of TAMCAPP to enable and disable the Smart Search behavior.

```
public void prepareNavigation(int attendeeId) {
    Boolean useSmartSearch = (Boolean)AdfmfJavaUtilities.evaluateELExpression(
"#{preferenceScope.feature.com.tamcapp.mobilebook.att.Attendees.SearchPreferences.
UseSmartSearch}");
    // if smart search preference is true, use smart search and navigate
    if (useSmartSearch.booleanValue()){
        ValueExpression ve = AdfmfJavaUtilities.getValueExpression(
                "#{pageFlowScope.attendeesBean.currentAttendee}", int.class);
        ve.setValue(AdfmfJavaUtilities.getAdfELContext(), new Integer(attendeeId));
        TamcappUtils.doNavigation("details");
    }
    // else do nothing
}
```

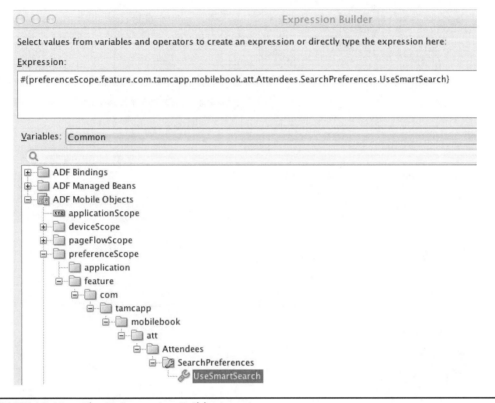

FIGURE 16-14. *The EL Expression Builder in action*

Summary

Security is very important in mobile apps. The Oracle Mobile Application Framework provides you with functionality that enables you to secure applications and features. Besides that, you can use Oracle MAF security to conditionally show and hide page content and to protect feature content from unauthorized access. Oracle MAF also enables you to define user preferences so that they can customize the appearance and behavior of the app.

In this chapter you learned

- How to implement security in TAMCAPP
- How to use securityContext to show and hide content
- How to use securityContext in Java code
- How to create a custom login page
- How to create preferences for the TAMCAPP app
- How to work with preferences from within Java

CHAPTER
17

Implementing
Push Notifications

Push notifications allow an app to notify users of new messages or events without the need to actually open the application, similar to how a text message will make a sound and pop up on your screen. This is a great way for apps to interact with users in the background, whether it be a game notifying the user of some event occurring in the game world or simply an e-mail application beeping as a new message arrives in the user's inbox. Similar to a mail application, the TAMCAPP application can notify users. Such a notification, for example, could be about a change in the conference session schedule or a notification to a speaker on a completed speaker evaluation.

In addition to pushing messages to the screen, iOS push notifications allow apps to display a number or "badge" on the app's icon, similar to an e-mail app that shows the number of unread messages.

The Oracle Mobile Application Framework (MAF) supports push notifications, and in this chapter you will learn how to implement this in the TAMCAPP app.

Understanding the Push Notification Architecture

When you want to implement push notification in an Oracle MAF app, part of the solution occurs server-side rather than just in the application. In order to support push notifications, you first need a server-side *push notification service*, which is typically supplied via either Apple or Google depending on the device you're building for. This notification service handles all aspects of queuing of messages and delivery to the target application running on the target device.

In addition, push notifications require a server-side application that is responsible for producing and sending the messages, and is typically referred to as the *provider*. Typically, you provide the provider application, installed at your own site.

Figure 17-1 shows an overview of all the components involved in the push notification architecture.

The usual flow in a push notification event is straightforward. When the MAF application starts, it issues a registration request (1) with the Push Notification Service. After successful registration, the Push Notification Service provides the app with a registration ID (2), a token that uniquely identifies the MAF app and the device.

NOTE
Registration occurs upon every start of the mobile application to ensure a valid token.

In order for the provider to send notifications to the device, the provider must know the device token. This is step 3, where after receiving the token, the device registers with the provider application. The provider stores the token for later use. Now the provider has all the information to send push notifications. Based on the token, push notifications can be targeted to a specific device. The provider does not send notifications directly to the device, but uses the notification services (4) provided by Google and Apple. These notification services finally send the notification (5) to the specific devices. In the next sections, you will learn how to set up the cloud services and the server application and also how to set up the TAMCAPP app to work with push notifications.

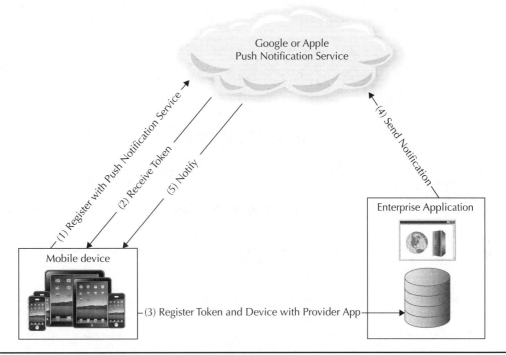

FIGURE 17-1. *Push notification architecture*

Setting Up the Cloud Services

As our Oracle MAF TAMCAPP app will support both Android and iOS devices, it will need to integrate with both Google and Apple's push notification services, referred to as the Google Cloud Messaging Service and Apple Push Notification Service, respectively.

Google Cloud Messaging

Google Cloud Messaging is configured via the Google Developer console accessible via Google's web sites.

In order to use the Google Developer console and the available services, you first need to create a valid Google account. A Google account can be created at:

```
https://accounts.google.com/SignUp
```

Next, you create a new Google Developer project to be able to use Google's publicly accessible APIs. The Google APIs enable developers to interact with Google Services such as Google Maps, Google Places, and more specifically for this chapter, Google's Cloud Messaging Service. When you create such a project, Google issues a project number. This number will be used as Sender Id/Authorization Id in the Oracle MAF app to identify the device so it receives the targeted notification.

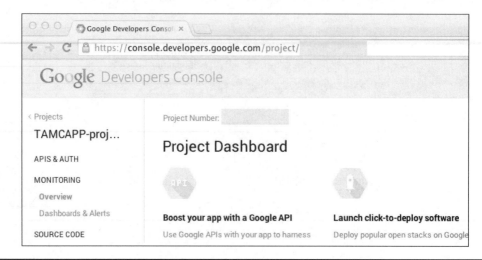

FIGURE 17-2. *Google Developer console for the TAMCAPP project*

After the cloud project is created, you can find the details of the project at the Google Developer console (Figure 17-2):

```
https://console.developers.google.com/console#/project/<YourProjectNumber>
```

Now Google Cloud Messaging can be enabled for this Google Developer project. Enabling Google Cloud Messaging is just a matter of switching a button (Figure 17-3).

The final step is to obtain an API key. This API key will be used for authentication when you are sending push requests from a server (provider) application to the GCM server. To obtain this

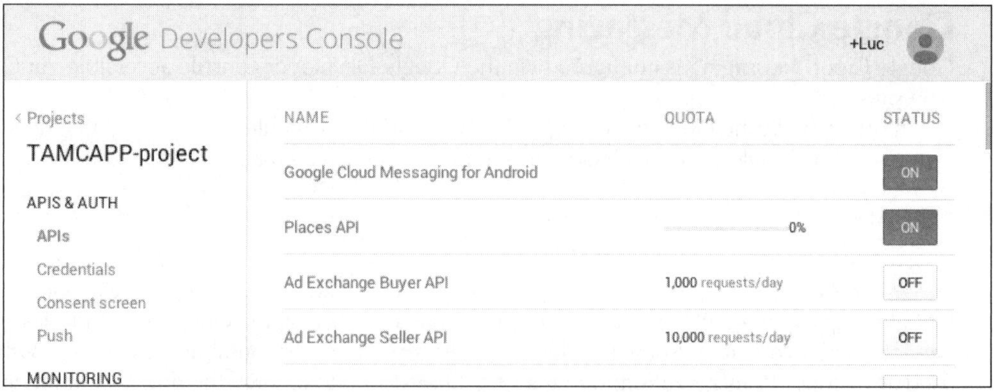

FIGURE 17-3. *Enable Google Cloud Messaging.*

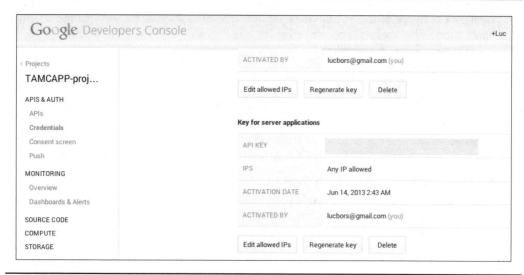

FIGURE 17-4. *The API key in the Google Developer console*

API key, you have to register the application. In the sidebar on the left, select "APIs & auth" and then "Credentials." Now under Public API access, click "Create new key," and in the "Create a new key" dialog, click "Server key."

After the app is registered, you can find the API key by clicking on "Credentials," and then select TAMCAPP (or your own app for that matter) and write down the API Key (Figure 17-4).

With all this in place, the configuration of the Google Cloud Messaging Service is done.

- The new Google Cloud project is created.
- The Google Cloud Messaging API is enabled.
- The API key is generated and ready to be used.

Setting Up Apple Push Notification Service

The configuration of the TAMCAPP app and Apple Push Notification Service is relatively more complex than Google Cloud Messaging. To send push notifications to the MAF app on iOS, you must register with Apple's Push Notification Service (APNS) and you'll need an iOS developer account. To register for an iOS developer account, visit the Apple Developer site at https://developer.apple.com/programs/ios/.

NOTE
Push notifications do work in the Android Emulator, but push notifications do not work in the iOS simulator. For testing push notifications on iOS, you will need to use an actual device.

To implement push notifications, Apple requires you to make a new App ID and provisioning profile for each app that uses push notifications, as well as an SSL certificate for the provider application. All of these can be created at the iOS Provisioning Portal: https://developer.apple.com/account/ios/profile/profileList.action.

In order to make push notifications work in the TAMCAPP app, TAMCAPP needs to be signed with a provisioning profile that is configured for push notifications. The provider application then needs to sign its push notifications to APNS with an SSL certificate.

The SSL certificate and provisioning profile are closely tied together and are only valid for a single App ID. This ensures that only the TAMCAPP provider application can send push notifications to instances of TAMCAPP and no other application can. Unfortunately, most of the problems with getting push notifications to work are due to problems with the certificates.

Generate an SSL Signing Certificate

An SSL signing certificate is required by APNS to create a .p12 certificate. To generate an SSL signing certificate, the following steps must be executed on your development machine (which must be a Mac).

First, launch the Keychain Access application from the applications/utilities folder on your development machine. Then from the Keychain Access menu, select Certificate Assistant | Request a Certificate From a Certificate Authority.

In the Certificate Information popup, enter a contact e-mail address and a name that you will use to sign the TAMCAPP app. Select "Saved to disk," and click Continue. You will be prompted to give the certificate signing request file a name, and you must enter a location where it will be saved. Any file name and location will do fine as long as you know where to find the file (Figure 17-5). For this sample, the name tamcappfull.certSigningRequest is used.

The Certificate Assistant popup can be closed after the certificate has been successfully saved.

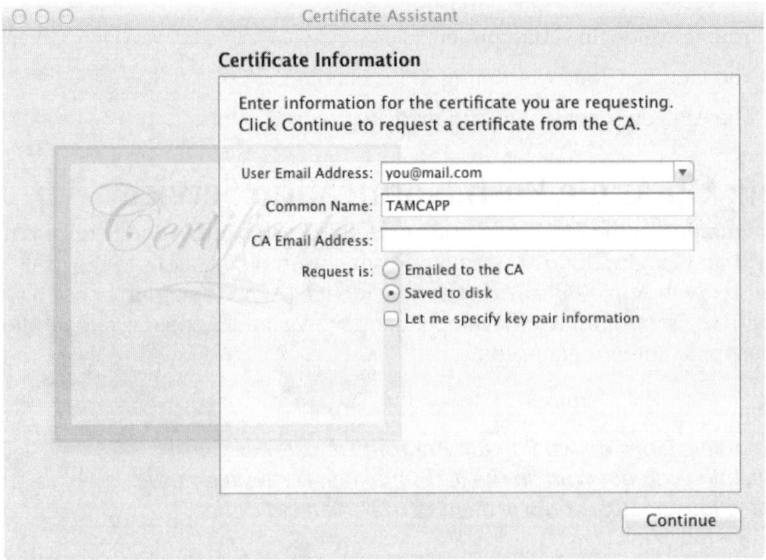

FIGURE 17-5. *Certificate Assistant popup*

Create an App ID for TAMCAPP

Next, an App ID for TAMCAPP must be created. This App ID will allow Apple APNS to identify the TAMCAPP app. The App ID must be created in the iOS Developer Portal: https://developer.apple.com/account/ios/identifiers/bundle/bundleList.action.

In the iOS Apps section, at the App Identifier Section, a new App ID can be created. The App ID string contains two parts separated by a period (.)—an App ID Prefix that is defined as your Team ID by default and an App ID Suffix that is defined as a Bundle ID search string. The following information must be entered:

- **App ID Description - Name**   A unique name that identifies the app, for example, TAMCAPPfull

- **App ID Prefix**   Select the appropriate value from the drop-down.

- **App ID Suffix**   Select Explicit App ID, and enter the desired App ID in reverse-domain format. For example, com.blogspot.lucbors.mobilebook.TAMCAPPfull.

- **App Services**   Select Push Notifications as depicted in Figure 17-6.

When all information is entered, you can click Submit to create the App ID. On the App ID page, the newly created App ID should now be visible (Figure 17-7).

NOTE
If you don't already have a provisioning profile, you must also create one for this App ID. To do this, in the iOS portal, choose the "Certificates, Identifiers & Profiles" link at the top left. On the next page, choose the "Provisioning Profiles" option near the bottom left. Next, you'll see a list of any provisioning profiles you have. Click the "plus" icon at the top right to create a new provisioning profile.

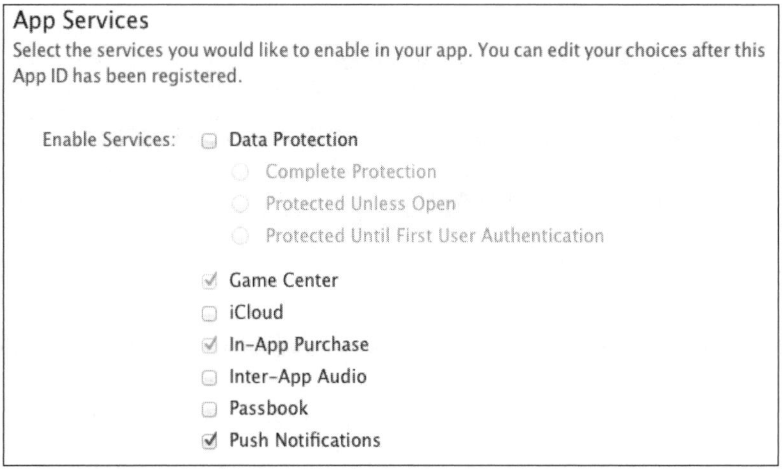

App Services
Select the services you would like to enable in your app. You can edit your choices after this App ID has been registered.

Enable Services: ☐ **Data Protection**
   ○ Complete Protection
   ○ Protected Unless Open
   ○ Protected Until First User Authentication

   ☑ **Game Center**
   ☐ iCloud
   ☑ **In-App Purchase**
   ☐ Inter-App Audio
   ☐ Passbook
   ☑ **Push Notifications**

FIGURE 17-6.   *Select Push Notifications in the App Services section.*

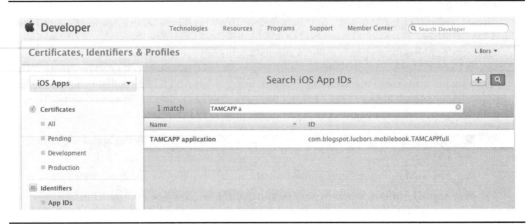

FIGURE 17-7. *The newly created App ID*

Generate a .p12 Certificate

Next, a .p12 certificate must be generated using the App ID and signing certificate you created in the previous steps. The .p12 certificate will be sent to Apple APNS with all push notification requests. The steps to create the .p12 certificate are listed next.

The first step is to create an SSL certificate for TAMCAPP. On the App IDs page in the iOS Developer Portal, select the App ID for TAMCAPP and click Edit. In the Push Notifications section, under the heading Development SSL Certificate, click Create Certificate (Figure 17-8).

FIGURE 17-8. *Create APNS SSL certificates.*

FIGURE 17-9. *Choose certSigningRequest and generate the certificate.*

To generate the certificate, the previously created tamcappfull.certSigningRequest file must be selected. After choosing the tamcappfull.certSigningRequest file, click Generate to generate the certificate (Figure 17-9).

Once the certificate generation is complete, the App ID settings window appears again and the certificate (aps_development.cer) can be downloaded to an appropriate location on the development machine (Figure 17-10).

The .cer file is ready to be added to the keychain on the development machine to actually associate the certificate with your private key that was used to create the certificate. This can be achieved by double-clicking the .cer file and clicking Add to install it in the keychain. The newly installed certificate will appear in the Keychain Access application under My Certificates with a name similar to "Apple Development iOS Push Services: <bundle identifier>" (Figure 17-11).

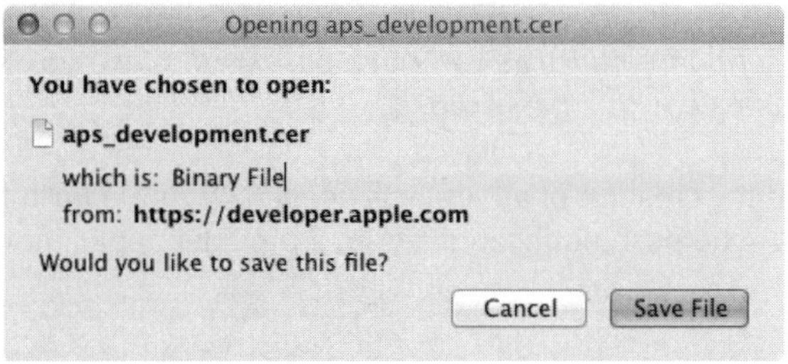

FIGURE 17-10. *Download the aps_development.cer file.*

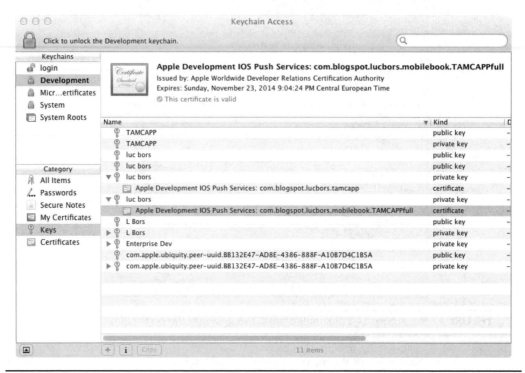

FIGURE 17-11. *Keychain Access overview*

The final step is to export the .p12 certificate by invoking the context menu on the certificate and selecting Export. Save the certificate to your desktop as a "Personal Information Exchange (.p12)" file, and enter a password in the password dialog.

NOTE
The provider application will use the .p12 certificate when sending notifications to the APNS. Blank or null passwords are in violation of the PKCS12 specifications. Furthermore, the Java platform's built-in PKCS12 implementation throws exceptions when trying to load a keystore with no password. The provider application uses Java, and Java does not support certificates without a password. Make sure you export the certificate with a password.

This completes the creation of all artifacts needed by Apple Push Notification Services in order to be able to send push notifications from a provider application via APNS to an iOS app.

Creating a Push Notification Provider Application

To actually send notifications to a mobile device, TAMCAPP uses a provider application to raise notifications and send them to the Push Notification Service from either Apple or Google.

The provider application can be written in any technology. For the TAMCAPP example in this book, the push notifications are sent via a Provider Application, which is a very simple Java web application that is created in JDeveloper. The next sections will not explain how to create such an application, but they will focus on how to implement the push notification functionality in a provider application.

Configuring the Provider Application

To send notifications using GCM, the Provider Application needs the gcm-server.jar library. The gcm-server library contains all classes needed for sending push notifications from the provider application to GCM. The library can be found in the android-sdk. Add gcm-server.jar from the Android SDK to the JDeveloper Project of the Provider Application (Figure 17-12).

For using APNS, the provider application can use the javaPNS library. This Java library is specifically designed to send notifications through the Apple Push Notification Service from a J2EE application. JavaPNS can be downloaded at the following link:

http://code.google.com/p/javapns/downloads/list

With both gcm-server and JavaPNS added to the application, the provider application is configured to send out push notifications. The provider application contains a single web page with a table that lists all subscribed devices, has a text box to compose a message, and finally a button to invoke Java logic that takes care of the actual pushing (Figure 17-13).

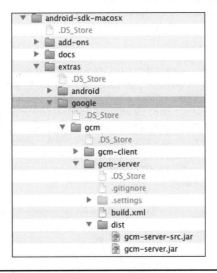

FIGURE 17-12. *Location of gcm-server.jar in the Android SDK*

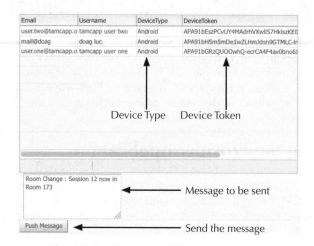

Email	Username	DeviceType	DeviceToken
user.two@tamcapp.o	tamcapp user two	Android	APA91bEszPCvUY4MAdrhVXwll57Hkls2KE0
mail@doag	doag luc	Android	APA91bHSmSmDe1wZLHmJdsn9GTMLC-lr
user.one@tamcapp.o	tamcapp user one	Android	APA91bGRzQUOOwhQ-ecrCA4F4av0bno6)

Device Type   Device Token

Room Change : Session 12 now in Room 173 ◄─── Message to be sent

Push Message ◄─── Send the message

FIGURE 17-13. *The provider application*

All information about the devices (deviceType and deviceToken) that is available in the provider application was actually provided when the TAMCAPP user registered at initial startup of the TAMCAPP app.

Creation of the provider application is beyond the scope of this book. The Java class, however, that provides the logic to send the actual push notification is a specific part of the push notification functionality. The Java class in this sample is called pushMessage.

The pushMessage class contains the logic that is needed to push the message. Note that the following method derives the deviceType and the deviceToken of the currently selected device and uses the deviceToken to target the notification to a specific device. The deviceType is used to invoke either a method for pushing to Android or a method for pushing to iOS.

```
public void pushNow() {
    DCBindingContainer bindings =(DCBindingContainer)
            BindingContext.getCurrent().getCurrentBindingsEntry();
    DCIteratorBinding iter =
            bindings.findIteratorBinding("GcmSubscribersIterator");
    Row curr = iter.getCurrentRow();
    String target = (String)curr.getAttribute("DeviceToken");
    String type   = (String)curr.getAttribute("DeviceType");
    if (type.equalsIgnoreCase("Android")) {
        pushMsgAmdroid(target, this.message);
    }
    else {
        pushMsgIos(target, this.message);
    }
}
```

Both platforms require a slightly different approach. These will be explained in the following two sections.

Pushing to Android

If a notification is pushed to an Android device, a Message object must be created. This Message object can contain several kinds of information. A very simple notification could be an alert with a message. This is shown in the following code sample.

NOTE
The Message class and Sender class are both available from the gcm-server library.

When sending the message, the sendNoRetry is invoked on sender, an instance of the Sender object. This instance is created using the API KEY created with Google Cloud.

```
private Sender sender = new Sender(<YOUR API KEY>);
Message message = new Message.Builder()
                    .addData("alert", msg)
                    .build();
result = sender.sendNoRetry(message, regId);
```

Besides this simple notification, the message can be extended with extra payload. In the following sample, the payload contains information on the feature that the Oracle MAF TAMCAPP app needs to activate and the sessionId it needs to show. This information will be used in a later section to explain how the TAMCAPP app can work with a custom payload.

```
String sound = "default";
Message message = new Message.Builder()
                    .addData("alert", msg)
                    .addData("sound",sound)
                    .addData("FeatureName", "Sessions")
                    .addData("SessionId", "12")
                    .build();

result = sender.sendNoRetry(message, regId);
```

Pushing to iOS

When using JavaPNS there are several options to send notifications. A simple one is to just push a message or a badging instruction. This can be achieved by a single line of code:

```
Push.alert(msg, KEYSTORE_LOCATION,KEYSTORE_PASSWORD , false, target);
```

or

```
Push.badge(3,  KEYSTORE_LOCATION,KEYSTORE_PASSWORD , false, target);
```

JavaPNS also contains a payload method in the Push class, which can contain a custom payload. In the following sample, the payload contains information on the feature that the Oracle MAF TAMCAPP app needs to activate and the sessionId it needs to show. This information will be used in a later section to explain how the TAMCAPP app can work with a custom payload. Also note that addBadge(1) is responsible for the badging of the application icon. Application icon badging is described in a later section of this chapter.

```
/* Build a blank payload to customize */
PushNotificationPayload payload = PushNotificationPayload.complex();
/* Customize the payload */

payload.addAlert(msg);
payload.addBadge(1);
payload.addCustomDictionary("FeatureName", "Sessions");
payload.addCustomDictionary("SessionId", "12");
Push.payload(payload, KEYSTORE_LOCATION, KEYSTORE_PASSWORD, false, target);
```

Implementing Push Support in TAMCAPP

In the previous section you learned how to create a simple provider application and how to write logic to send push notifications to the TAMCAPP users. The next, and final, step in implementing push notifications in TAMCAPP is to configure the TAMCAPP mobile app to receive push notifications. In order to support push notifications in the TAMCAPP app, the TAMCAPP app must register itself with the cloud services and with the enterprise application that is responsible for sending the messages. Registration of the TAMCAPP with both cloud services is mostly taken care of by the Oracle Mobile Application Framework automatically. There are just three minor manual steps involved.

The first step is to implement an applicationLifeCycleListener class and register that listener with the application. The registration must be done in the application configuration file maf-application.xml, as shown in Figure 17-14.

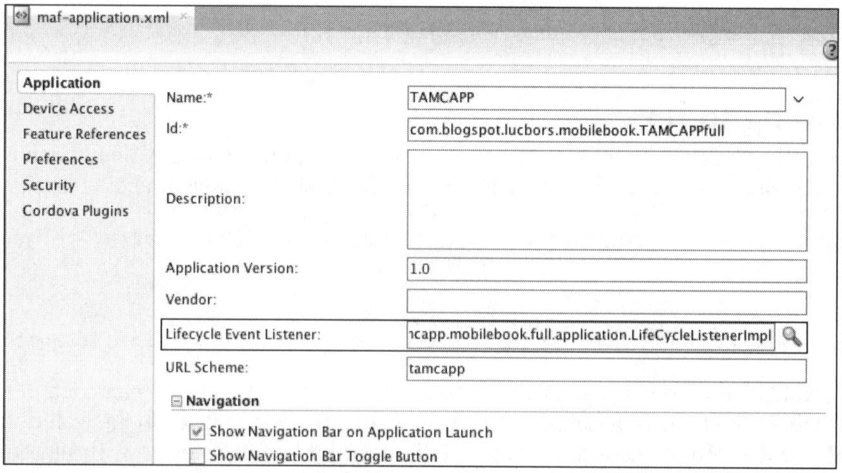

FIGURE 17-14. *Defining the Application Level Lifecycle Event Listener applicationLifeCycle*

The applicationLifeCycleListener must implement the oracle.adfmf.application
.PushNotificationConfig interface. This interface provides the registration configuration for
push notifications.

```
public class TamcappLifeCycleListenerImpl implements LifeCycleListener,
PushNotificationConfig {
    public TamcappLifeCycleListenerImpl() {
    }
...........// more
}
```

This life cycle listener class contains, among other things, the start() method. When the
TAMCAPP app starts, this start() method is invoked. In the start() method, the TAMCAPP app is
prepared to receive push notifications. That is why an EventSource object that represents the
source of a native push notification event is created. Also, an object of the push notification
listener class is created and added to the event source:

```
public void start() {
    EventSource evtSource = EventSourceFactory.getEventSource(
            NativePushNotificationEventSource.
                NATIVE_PUSH_NOTIFICATION_REMOTE_EVENT_SOURCE_NAME);
    evtSource.addListener(new PushNotificationListener());
}
```

The second step is to make sure that the application has permission to retrieve push
notifications. This is a setting in the application configuration file (Figure 17-15).

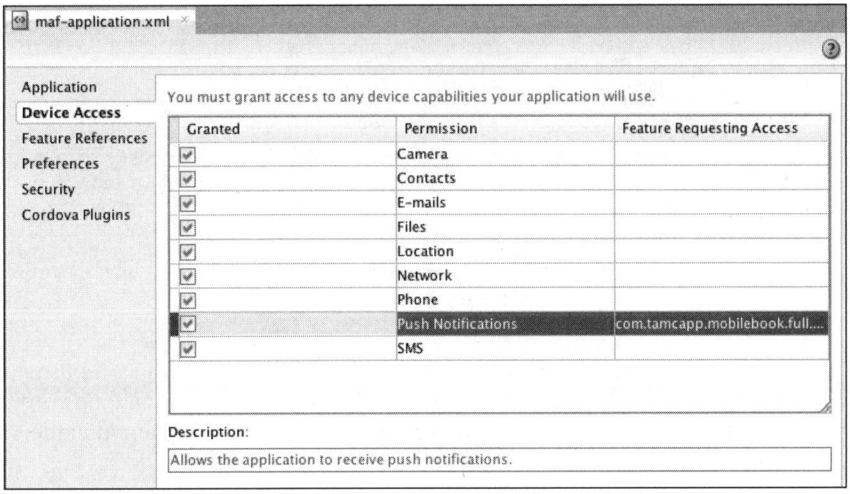

FIGURE 17-15. *Allow push notifications.*

The final step is the creation of an eventListener that is responsible for listening to pushNotification events. This eventListener is instantiated by the start() method of the TamcappLifeCycleListenerImpl class, as shown in the preceding code sample.

```
public class PushNotificationListener implements EventListener {
    public PushNotificationListener() {
        super();
    }
    public void onMessage(Event event) {
        ...more
    }
    public void onError(AdfException adfException) {
        ... more
    }
    public void onOpen(String token) {
        ...more
    }
}
```

The onOpen() method is the most important method for the configuration of the TAMCAPP app for push notifications. The onOpen() method is invoked when the Oracle MAF application successfully registers the device/application with the Push Notification service (APNs or GCMs). The method has a parameter called "token." The token is received from the notification services and uniquely identifies a device and application combination. In the onOpen() class, the token is stored in the ApplicationScope.

NOTE
The token is stored in the "ApplicationScope" of the TAMCAPP app such that we don't keep requesting a new token. Only if the TAMCAPP app is restarted will it request a new token.

```
public void onOpen(String token) {
    ValueExpression ve =
        AdfmfJavaUtilities.getValueExpression(
                "#{applicationScope.deviceToken}", String.class);
    if (token != null) {
        ve.setValue(AdfmfJavaUtilities.getAdfELContext(), token);
    } else {
        ve.setValue(AdfmfJavaUtilities.getAdfELContext(), "dummy Token");
    }
}
```

The PushNotificationListener class is also responsible for responding to push notifications. That is, Oracle Mobile Application Framework calls the onMessage() method with the notification payload whenever the application receives a notification. This is explained in the later section "Responding to Push Notifications."

Registering with the Provider Application

The retrieved token is sent to and stored in the provider application at initial registration. The provider application uses this token to target a notification to a specific device. TAMCAPP uses a web service that is called upon to do this when the TAMCAPP application is started and just after the token has been retrieved. This registration of the TAMCAPP user's device with the provider application is necessary in order to have the Device Identifier available in the enterprise application that is responsible for sending out push notifications. The provider application needs both the token and the operating system of the device. This registration is performed once, when the user registers and requests an account.

Configuring How Notifications Are Displayed

Depending on the mobile platform, notifications can be displayed in different ways. If TAMCAPP runs on Android, push notifications will be displayed in the message bar for a couple of seconds. After that, the app icon remains visible in the notification bar to inform the user that there is an unread notification. The whole message can be found in the Notification Center (Figure 17-16).

On iOS, push notifications can be displayed in several different ways. These options can be configured in the iOS settings application (Figure 17-17). This is standard iOS functionality and can be configured the way you like it.

When you use 'Alerts' as alert style, a notification shows up as a popup showing the message, and with a close and launch button (Figure 17-18).

In addition to notifications, Oracle MAF supports badging of the App icon. The application icon is badged with a number (Figure 17-19). Usually, the badge depicts the number of unread messages. The provider app can also provide the badging information. You can compare this to an e-mail app that displays the number of unread e-mails on the mail server. The TAMCAPP app badge shows the number of unread notifications.

FIGURE 17-16. *Notifications on Android (Notification Bar Message, Notification Bar Icon, and Notification Center)*

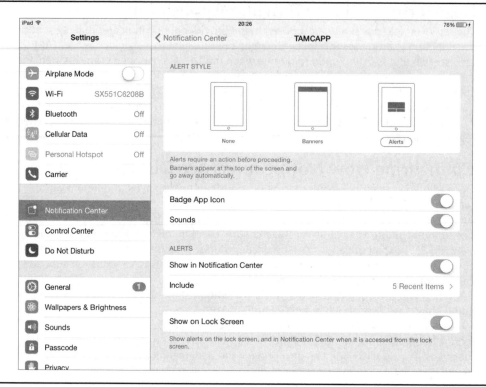

FIGURE 17-17. *The iOS Notification Settings for TAMCAPP*

NOTE
After "handling" a notification, TAMCAPP is able to change the badge number by using the setApplicationIconBadgeNumber() method from the AdfmfContainerUtilities class. Usually, one would also inform the server-side provider application that the notification has been handled. This would enable the provider application to change the number of unhandled notifications so that the next time a notification is sent, the badge number contains the exact right value.

FIGURE 17-18. *Notification popup on iOS*

FIGURE 17-19. *Application icon badging on iOS*

Responding to Push Notifications

The previous part of this chapter explained how to configure the Push Notification Services, the provider application, and how to set up TAMCAPP to receive push notifications. With all of that in place, it is now time to look at how TAMCAPP can actually respond to push notifications. When the message arrives at the device, the TAMCAPP user taps the message or touches the button, and the notification handler is invoked. This handler is the onMessage() method in the PushNotificationListener class. This method is able to see the payload and work with it.

NOTE
There are different situations as far as how an app can respond to push notifications. When the app is running and a notification is received, the app invokes the onMessage() method. If the app is running in the background, or not running at all, the message is displayed on the device. If the user taps the message, the Oracle MAF application opens and the onMessage() method is invoked. It is essential, however, to understand that the onMessage() method is called in all cases.

The notifications in TAMCAPP are all notifications regarding a specific conference session. Whenever a notification is received, the app should respond by navigating to the Conference Session feature and showing the details of the specific session. The steps involved in the implementation of this scenario are

- Ensure that the provider application passes a unique conference session identifier in the message payload

- In the onMessage method of the Application Lifecycle Event listener, parse the notification payload, and save it into applicationScope variables.

- Navigate to a particular feature, in this case, the Conference Session feature.

- In the default activity of the feature's AMX task flow, determine if the feature is invoked as the result of a push notification.

- If so, call a web service to retrieve the latest information for the given conference session based on the conference session ID that was part of the payload and that is stored in applicationScope.

- Finally, navigate to the Conference Session Detail AMX page and show the conference session information.

In order to achieve this, the Conference Session feature, created in Chapter 13, has to be modified.

There are two obvious changes:

- First, the feature can be activated based on a notification. For that, the feature needs to have a lifeCycleListener that in the activate() method contains the logic to respond to activation of the feature. Note that activation can be caused by notification and also when a user selects the application feature for the first time after launching an Oracle MAF application, or when the application has been reselected (that is, brought back to the foreground).

- Second, due to notifications, the feature has to invoke a different navigation route through the flow. Therefore, the task flow that implements the Conference Session feature has to be modified.

Both changes will be explained in the next few sections, but first, let's take a look at the onMessage() method that is responsible for handling the notification at the application level.

The onMessage() Method

The onMessage() method is called whenever TAMCAPP responds to a push notification. Remember that this is either when the TAMCAPP app receives a notification while being active, or when the TAMCAPP app receives a notification when it is not active and the user chooses to invoke the app due to the notification. In the onMessage() method we need to set some applicationScope information. This is because the notification is handled at the application level, whereas the functionality that we want to invoke is inside a feature. In order to share information throughout different features of the application, information can be stored in applicationScope variables.

The information needed is the notificationSessionId that represents the session that will be shown in the Conference Session feature and the "notified" variable, which indicates whether or not a notification caused the invocation of the feature. Finally, after setting these values in the application scope, the TAMCAPP app is instructed to invoke the Conference Session feature. This is achieved by simply calling the gotoFeature() method of the container utilities class.

```
public void onMessage(Event event) {
    AdfELContext adfELContext = AdfmfJavaUtilities.getAdfELContext();
    JSONBeanSerializationHelper jsonHelper = new JSONBeanSerializationHelper();
    try{
        PayloadServiceResponse serviceResponse =
            (PayloadServiceResponse)jsonHelper.fromJSON(
                PayloadServiceResponse.class, event.getPayload());
        String message = serviceResponse.getCustomMessage();
        ValueExpression notificationPayloadBinding =
            AdfmfJavaUtilities.getValueExpression(
                    "#{applicationScope.notificationSessionId}", String.class);
        ValueExpression ve = AdfmfJavaUtilities.getValueExpression(
```

```
                  "#{applicationScope.notified}", Boolean.class);
     ve.setValue(AdfmfJavaUtilities.getAdfELContext(), Boolean.TRUE);
     // also, let's decrease the application icon badge by one
     int currentBadge = AdfmfContainerUtilities.getApplicationIconBadgeNumber();
     if (currentBadge > 0){
         AdfmfContainerUtilities.setApplicationIconBadgeNumber(currentBadge - 1);
     }
     AdfmfContainerUtilities.gotoFeature(
                  "com.tamcapp.mobilebook.ses.ConferenceSessions");
  } catch (Exception e) {
     e.printStackTrace();
  }
}
```

In the preceding code sample, TAMCAPP works with the notification and finally invokes the Conference Session feature.

The Feature Life Cycle Listener

Based on the notification, the Conference Session feature can be activated. In order to respond to this activation, you would typically use a listener. For the TAMCAPP application, we previously created and registered an application life cycle event listener. This listener is available for the application. Such a life cycle event listener is also available for individual features and can be used to listen to activate and deactivate events. The listener is a Java class that implements the oracle.adfmf.feature.LifeCycleListener class. The class also has to be assigned to the Conference Session feature in order to work properly (Figure 17-20).

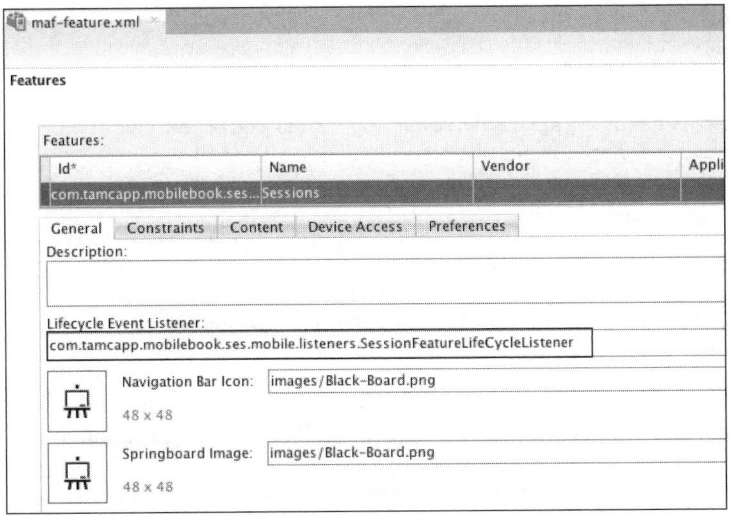

FIGURE 17-20.   *The definition of the Feature Life Cycle event listener*

In this life cycle listener, the activation event can be intercepted and logic can be added in order to respond to an activation event. If the activation was caused by a notification, we want to invoke programmatic navigation in order to invoke the Conference Session Detail AMX view with the appropriate session information. This navigation invokes the "featureActivated" navigation case. Note that the applicationScope variable that was set in the onMessage() method of the pushNotificationListener is now used to determine whether or not the activation was actually caused by a push notification.

```
public class SessionFeatureLifeCycleListener implements LifeCycleListener {
    public SessionFeatureLifeCycleListener() {
        super();
    }
    public void activate() {
        Boolean notified = (Boolean)AdfmfJavaUtilities.evaluateELExpression(
                            "#{applicationScope.notified}");
        if(notified.booleanValue()){
          AdfmfContainerUtilities.invokeContainerJavaScriptFunction(
                            AdfmfJavaUtilities.getFeatureName(),
                            "adf.mf.api.amx.doNavigation",
                            new Object[] { "featureActivated" });
        }
    }
    public void deactivate() {
    }
}
```

The invoked navigation case has to be a wildcard navigation. Wildcard navigation enables you to navigate from anywhere in the task flow. This navigation rule, called "featureActivated," navigates to a router activity in the task flow. This router has two outcomes based on whether or not the call was caused by a notification. The task flow is displayed in Figure 17-21.

```
<router id="router1">
    <case id="__9">
        <expression>#{applicationScope.notified}</expression>
        <outcome>notified</outcome>
    </case>
    <case id="__10">
        <expression>#{!applicationScope.notified}</expression>
        <outcome>notNotified</outcome>
    </case>
    <default-outcome>notNotified</default-outcome>
</router>
```

When a notification was involved, the flow continues to a method call activity that calls a web service operation (findSessionsById). This call retrieves the session information based on the session id that was in the notifications payload and that was stored in #{applicationScope .notificationSessionId}. This then is displayed in the SessionDetails AMX page.

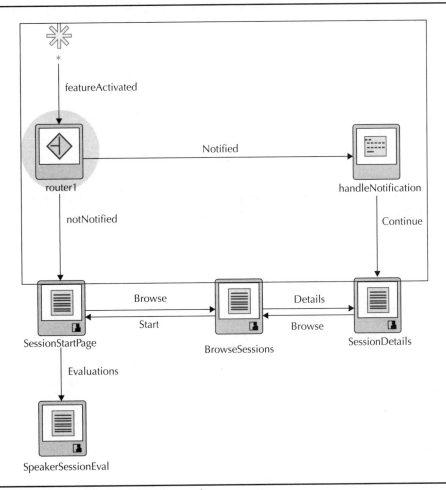

FIGURE 17-21.   *Modified taskflow for conference sessions*

Working with the Push Notifications Payload

In the section where the provider application was explained, you learned how to send notifications with a specific payload. Once the notification arrives at the device, it would be nice if the TAMCAPP app were able to work with the payload that is associated with the notification. That specific payload contains information about a given feature and a given session. Let's see how TAMCAPP can work with this.

First let's have a look at the specific part of the notification that is sent from the provider application. First for Android:

```
Message message = new Message.Builder()
                         ....
                    .addData("FeatureName", "Sessions")
                    .addData("SessionId", "12")
                    .build();
```

And then for iOS:

```
payload.addCustomDictionary("FeatureName", "Sessions");
payload.addCustomDictionary("SessionId", "12");
```

Both send a message with the same payload. To work with this payload, a custom class is created that represents the structure of the notification payload:

```
public class PayloadServiceResponse {
    private double from;
    private String collapse_key;
    private String customMessage;
    private String sound;
    private String alert;
    private String FeatureName;
    private String SessionId;

    public PayloadServiceResponse() {
        super();
    }
    // all getters and setters
}
```

In the onMessage() method of the PushNotificationListener, the payload can now be deserialized into our own custom object, and the specific values can be retrieved and worked with.

```
public void onMessage(Event event) {
    AdfELContext adfELContext = AdfmfJavaUtilities.getAdfELContext();
    JSONBeanSerializationHelper jsonHelper = new JSONBeanSerializationHelper();
    PayloadServiceResponse serviceResponse =
            (PayloadServiceResponse)jsonHelper.fromJSON(
                    PayloadServiceResponse.class, event.getPayload());
    serviceResponse.getSessionId();
    serviceResponse.getFeatureName();

    // more..
}
```

Summary

Push notifications are a great mechanism to push information to the users of an Oracle MAF application. Although the setup requires some work and understanding of Apple Push Notification Service and Google Cloud Messaging Service, the result is great. The provider application can send notifications to specific devices or to a whole batch of devices. The TAMCAPP application can respond to a notification and invoke functionality required for the user to take action based on the payload of the notification.

In this chapter you learned how to

- Set up Apple Push Notification Service
- Set up Google Cloud Messaging Service
- Create a simple provider application
- Configure an Oracle MAF application for push notifications
- Work with push notifications and payload

CHAPTER
18

Enhancing TAMCAPP

I s "good," good enough? Will the TAMCAPP application exceed our users' needs? Arguably, the functionality as we developed it in the second part of this book works great, but there is still some room for improvement. One of the things that we did not look at so far is the support for tablet layouts. You will learn how to implement this in the next section. After that, you will learn two different ways of adding a barcode scanner to TAMCAPP. First, you will see how to do this using URL Scheme, and after that you will learn how to add barcode scanning functionality to the TAMCAPP application using a Cordova plugin. This barcode scanner can be used to check whether or not an attendee actually registered for a conference session by simply scanning the barcode on his conference pass. This will speed up the process of entering a conference room.

Another enhancement that will be added to the TAMCAPP application is a custom component to support type-ahead search functionality for conference sessions. Finally, you will implement a background process that can be used to check the availability of network connectivity.

Implementing Tablet Layout

The TAMCAPP application was primarily designed and developed for smartphones with relatively small screen real estate. The application will run without a problem on tablets; however, the layout is not optimized for tablets with larger screens. In this section you will learn how the framework can help you to implement a layout that is optimized for tablets. Before we explain how to implement this, you need to know some of the considerations involved when creating specific layouts for tablets.

Design Considerations and How the Framework Can Help You

There are many devices on the market, and there are about as many different screen sizes. You as a developer have to decide how to respond to this. You can use built-in framework properties that inform you about the device's measurements such as availableWidth, availableHeight, and diagonalSize.

As stated earlier, an Oracle MAF application runs on a tablet without any changes. If you decide to use the same application, you are good to go. However, if you want to change the application to utilize the extra screen real estate of tablet devices, you have several options. The first thing you can do is dynamically show or hide content on individual pages based on the form factor. You would use an expression like this one:

```
rendered="#{hardware.screen.diagonalSize > 6}"
```

The second option you have is to create a specific route in your task flow, one with activities that caters for tablets, and the other for smartphones. Based on the form factor, the application would automatically navigate to different AMX pages in your task flow.

```
<router id="formFactorRouter">
    <case>
        <expression>#{hardware.screen.diagonalSize > 6}</expression>
        <outcome>toTabletPage</outcome>
    </case>
    <case>
        <expression>#{hardware.screen.diagonalSize < 6}</expression>
        <outcome>toPhonePage</outcome>
```

```
  </case>
  <default-outcome> toPhonePage </default-outcome>
</router>
```

Although these two options work fine, the recommended approach for creating one app that is optimized for both phone and tablet is to create separate MAF features for phones and tablets, respectively. This is somewhat more laborious but very flexible. This approach will be explained in the next section.

Tablet Layout Patterns

There are several common and popular layout patterns for tablets that can be created with the framework. The following patterns will be explained in this section:

- Flow layouts
- Stretch layouts
- Swim lanes
- Tiled layouts

To create a flowing layout, simply use a table component and add more rows to it than the page can show. If you add more and more rows, the application will automatically flow down.

If you need a layout that adjusts to the size of the available space rather than flows, you can create a stretch layout.

For instance, if you want to divide an area into four squares, you could use the following approach: use a table component that has a width property of 100 percent and two rows and inside the rows, each two cell components take 50 percent of the available width. The height of the cell components can be derived from the available height of the device (Figure 18-1).

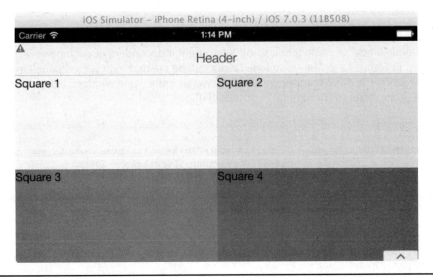

FIGURE 18-1. *Stretching layout that takes all available space*

TIP
To get a more accurate setting for the height of a cell component to fit the entire screen, you can use the following expression:
`height="#{deviceScope.hardware.screen`
`.availableHeight-<height of header>}"`
Height of the header is whatever height is defined for the header. The default for the framework is 44.

You would end up with code that looks like the following code sample:

```
<amx:tableLayout id="t1" width="100%" shortDesc="Container">
    <amx:rowLayout id="r1">
        <amx:cellFormat id="c1"
            height="#{(deviceScope.hardware.screen.availableHeight-44)/2}"
            inlineStyle="background-color:yellow" valign="top" width="50%">
            <amx:outputText value="Square 1" id="ot1"/>
        </amx:cellFormat>
        <amx:cellFormat id="c2" inlineStyle="background-color:Aqua;"
                    valign="top" width="50%">
            <amx:outputText value="Square 2" id="ot2"/>
        </amx:cellFormat>
    </amx:rowLayout>
    <amx:rowLayout id="r2">
        <amx:cellFormat id="cf3"
            height="#{(deviceScope.hardware.screen.availableHeight-44)/2}"
            inlineStyle="background-color:red" valign="top" width="50%">
            <amx:outputText value="Square 3" id="ot3"/>
        </amx:cellFormat>
    <amx:cellFormat id="c4" inlineStyle="background-color:green;"
                valign="top" width="50%">
        <amx:outputText value="Square 4" id="ot4"/>
        </amx:cellFormat>
    </amx:rowLayout>
</amx:tableLayout>
```

Finally, you can create a swim lane layout. This is a layout where you have one or multiple horizontal "lanes" of content that scroll left to right independent of each other. An example can be seen in Figure 18-2. The swim lane layout can be created with nested panelGroup layout components. The outer component should have an inline style width of 100 percent and the layout property set to "horizontal" and scrollPolicy="scroll".

```
<amx:panelGroupLayout id="pgl1out" inlineStyle="width:100%" layout="horizontal"
                    scrollPolicy="scroll">
    <amx:panelGroupLayout id="pgl2a" styleClass="adfmf-panelGroupLayout-groupBox"
                    inlineStyle="width:100px;height:100px">
        <amx:outputText value="First Box" id="ot1a"/>
    </amx:panelGroupLayout>
    <amx:panelGroupLayout id="pgl3a" styleClass="adfmf-panelGroupLayout-groupBox"
                    inlineStyle="width:100px;height:100px">
        <amx:outputText value="Second Box" id="ot2a"/>
    </amx:panelGroupLayout>
...... more boxes…
</amx:panelGroupLayout>
```

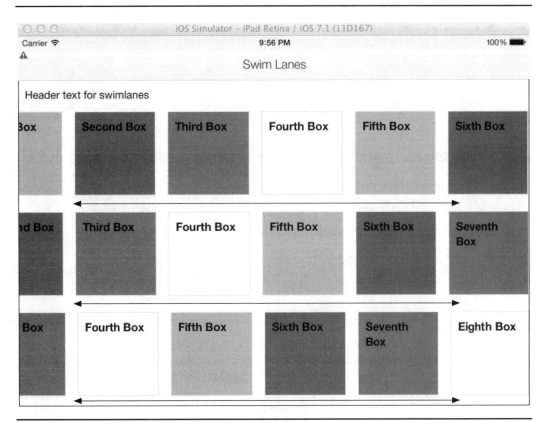

FIGURE 18-2. *Independently scrolling swim lanes*

When you have multiple constructs like this on one AMX page, they will scroll independently.

Tablet Layout for TAMCAPP

As mentioned before, the TAMCAPP application runs on tablets just as well as on smartphones. There is no direct need to create a specific tablet version for TAMCAPP. For the purpose of this book, one feature of the TAMCAPP application will be optimized for tablet layout. This feature is the Conference Session feature.

The first optimization step is to make the TAMCAPP application respond to different screen sizes. In other words, whenever the screen size exceeds a certain maximum measurement, we assume that it is a tablet and we will use different feature content and layout. To tell the framework that the tablet content should be used in specific situations, feature constraints can be used (Figure 18-3). You can simply use the built-in property "hardware.screen.diagonalSize." All of this can be configured in the feature definition file. Note that the constraint is exactly the same as the one that was used in the previous section for the router and the rendered property.

The constraint configures the TAMCAPP application to only use the tablet feature when the size of the screen exceeds 6. In all other cases, the "phone" feature is used.

The layout we want to achieve for the tablet feature is displayed in Figure 18-3. It contains a left sidebar where the user can search for specific sessions. After searching, the results are displayed

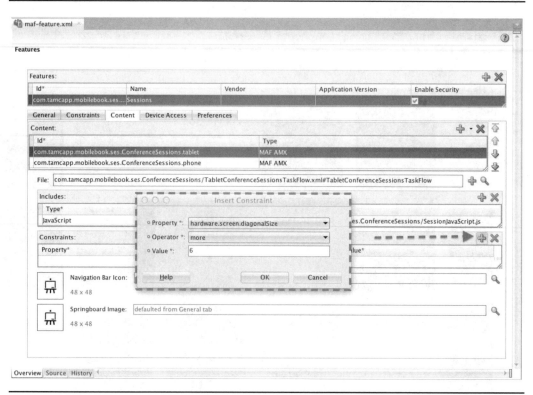

FIGURE 18-3. *Add a constraint for the tablet feature content.*

in a list on the sidebar. If the user selects one of the search results, a detailed view is opened on the right-hand side of the screen. To achieve this layout, a panel splitter component is used. It contains a navigation facet that can be used to render a list that controls the content of the panel item components of the panel splitter.

In Portrait mode, the navigation facet is automatically collapsed into a popup to provide more space for the panel items. When in Landscape mode, the navigator will appear normally. Both landscape and portrait orientations are shown in Figure 18-4. The "position" attribute is used to define the size of the navigator facet.

For all the functionality of the TAMCAPP tablet feature, the previously developed code can be reused. The main thing in the tablet layout is to reorganize the content on the AMX page. For the Conference Session feature, a flowing layout with a swim lane will be implemented. All main content goes into the flowing layout. The evaluations are in separate areas; the overall evaluation is in the flowing layout and so is the container for individual evaluations. The individual evaluations themselves will be displayed in a swim lane.

Let's take a closer look at how this can be achieved. The content area as a whole is a flowing area. Inside this flowing area there are rows and columns. All of these can be achieved by using a table component. This table component has as many rows as you need. By just adding rows to it, it will render as a vertically flowing content area.

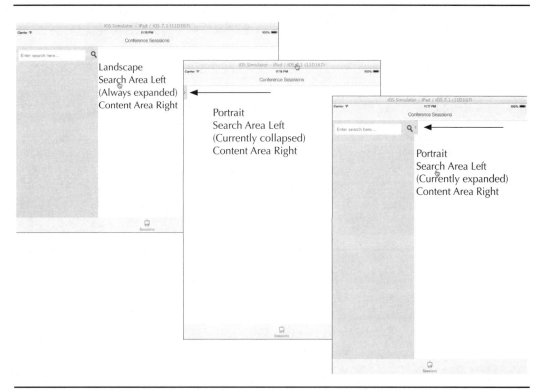

FIGURE 18-4. *Possible orientations of a panel splitter component*

Note that the general layout of the content area consists of four individual rows. Inside these rows, there are one or more columns. These columns are defined by cell components.

The first row is more or less a header row for the content area. It uses columnSpan = 2 to stretch over the two columns that are in the next row.

```
<amx:tableLayout id="tab1" width="100%" shortDesc="Content Area">
    <amx:rowLayout id="rw2">
        <amx:cellFormat id="c11" columnSpan="2" width="100%"
                    shortDesc="Detail Cell">
```

The next area contains two columns. These columns are implemented by using two cell components instead of the one that was used in the first row. Both cells use width = 50 percent, so combined they will use all available space.

```
<amx:rowLayout id="rw2">
    <amx:cellFormat id="c21" width="50%" shortDesc="Left Header" height="30">
        <amx:outputText value="Details" id="ot21"/>
    </amx:cellFormat>
    <amx:cellFormat id="c22" width="50%" shortDesc="Right Header" height="30">
        <amx:outputText value="#{bindings.title.inputValue} abstract"
                    id="ot22"/>
    </amx:cellFormat>
</amx:rowLayout>
```

The third row is somewhat special. It also contains two columns, but the column on the right stretches over several rows. For that, you can use the rowspan property.

```
<amx:rowLayout id="rw3">
    <amx:cellFormat id="c31" height="50%" shortDesc="Cell" valign="top">
    ….. content for first cell
    </amx:cellFormat>
    <amx:cellFormat id="c32" height="50%" shortDesc="Cell" valign="top"
                    rowSpan="7">
      ….. content for second cell
    </amx:cellFormat>
</amx:rowLayout>
```

This results in the flowing layout that we want. It is displayed in Figure 18-5.

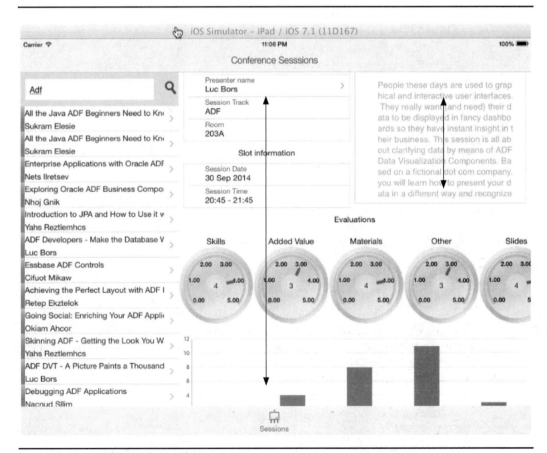

FIGURE 18-5. *Flowing layout for content area*

The next row contains the swim lane that contains the evaluations. This swim lane is implemented by using the nested panelGroup layout components as described in the previous section.

```
<amx:rowLayout id="rw3">
    <amx:cellFormat width="100%" halign="center" columnSpan="2">
        <amx:panelGroupLayout id="pgOUT" inlineStyle="width:100%"
                              layout="horizontal" scrollPolicy="scroll">
            <amx:panelGroupLayout id="pgIN1" inlineStyle="width:150px;height:150px">
                <dvtm:dialGauge minValue="0" maxValue="5" indicator="needleDark"
                                background="rectangleDarkCustom"
                                value="#{bindings.skills.inputValue}"
                                id="dg1" animationDuration="2500">
                </dvtm:dialGauge>
            </amx:panelGroupLayout>
            add more panelgroup layout components here….
        </amx:panelGroupLayout>
    </amx:cellFormat>
</amx:rowLayout>
```

The swim lanes are visible in Figure 18-6.

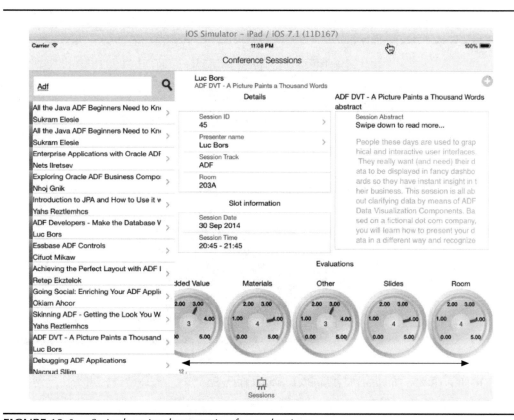

FIGURE 18-6. *Swim lane implementation for evaluations*

Using a Barcode Scanner to Register Conference Session Attendances

In Chapter 11 the headcount functionality was described. Headcount in a session is implemented as a kind of "digital clicker" (Figure 18-7). This is simple functionality. Each and every attendee in a conference session is added to a grand total by simply tapping a button. After all have entered the room and have been counted, the total is submitted.

Now what if the conference requires some kind of preregistration for sessions? Only if you really registered, are you allowed to get in. Or what if the organizing committee wants to keep record of exactly who attended a session? They'd really need to have more information. Usually, a conference issues conference passes or badges (Figure 18-8) that contain an attendee's name, company, and other information.

One could ask to fill out some kind of form before entering the room, but it would be more convenient for all people involved if TAMCAPP was able to record all this information. What if a barcode scanner could be used to scan a barcode on the conference pass and return the scanned value to the TAMCAPP application? That would be really nice, and guess what: it is possible, as you can see in Figure 18-9.

FIGURE 18-7. *The initially designed "digital clicker"*

FIGURE 18-8. *A typical conference badge*

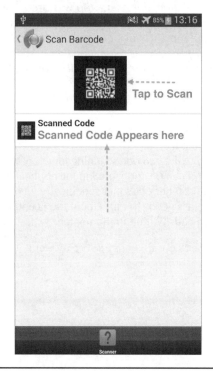

FIGURE 18-9. *"Barcode scanner application"*

Explaining the Use of URL Scheme in Oracle Mobile Application Framework

In Chapter 14 you learned how to invoke the phone function and Skype by using URL Schemes for both telephone and Skype. Oracle MAF also supports the concept of URL Scheme. By specifying a custom URL, you can allow an application to be called when this specific URL is invoked on a device. This means that you can actually define a custom URL Scheme for an MAF application. Once an MAF application has its own URL scheme, it can be called from other applications running on the device.

Such a URL Scheme for an Oracle MAF application must be defined at the application level in the maf-application.xml. The URL Scheme must be unique. If there are two apps using the same URL Scheme, the supported operating systems have no mechanism to determine which app to call. This means that there is no guarantee that the right app is called.

Using a Barcode Scanner

Barcode scanning is a very common requirement for mobile apps. There are several barcode scan apps available from the various app stores. For the purpose of this book, the ZXing app is used. ZXing (pronounced "zebra crossing") is an open-source barcode image processing library implemented in Java. The focus of ZXing is on using the built-in camera on mobile phones to scan and decode barcodes on the device. ZXing supports all kinds of barcodes.

NOTE
For the purpose of this section, the ZXing app was used. You can also use other barcode scanning apps, as long as you know the URL Scheme of the barcode app and how it can return the scanned code to the calling mobile application. The functionality described in this section was also tested with the pic2shop application that can also do barcode scanning:
`"pic2shop://scan?callback=p2sclient%3A//EAN"`

The idea for TAMCAPP is to scan the barcode, call a web service with the scanned barcode, and show the results on the page.

Step one in implementing the barcode scanning functionality is the creation of a URL Scheme for TAMCAPP. This is simple and can be configured in the application configuration file (Figure 18-10).

Step two is to create a Listener class that specifically will listen to the opening of TAMCAPP via its URL Scheme. This class needs to implement the EventListener class. In this class, the functionality to respond to calls will be implemented.

```
public class UrlSchemeCalledListener implements EventListener {
    public UrlSchemeCalledListener() {
        super();
    }
    public void onMessage(Event event){
    }
    public void onError(AdfException adfException){
    }
    public void onOpen(String string){
    }
}
```

maf-application.xml ×	

Application		
Device Access	Name:*	TAMCAPP
Feature References	Id:*	com.blogspot.lucbors.mobilebook.TAMCAPPfull
Preferences		
Security	Description:	
Cordova Plugins		
	Application Version:	1.0
	Vendor:	
	Lifecycle Event Listener:	mobilebook.full.application.LifeCycleListenerImpl
	URL Scheme:	tamcapp
	⊟ **Navigation**	

FIGURE 18-10. *Defining the URL Scheme for TAMCAPP*

Step 3 is to add a Listener in the start() method of the application's life cycle listener.

```
public void start(){
    EventSource openUrl = EventSourceFactory.getEventSource(
                        EventSourceFactory.OPEN_URL_EVENT_SOURCE_NAME);
    openUrl.addListener(new UrlSchemeCalledListener());
    // other code down here….
```

NOTE
Do not use an underscore in the URL scheme for the app. If you use, for instance, TAMCAPP_SCHEME, the app cannot create an EventSource properly. The app starts, but because the EventSource is not created properly, any reference to the URL Scheme from outside the app is not intercepted by the Listener.

Now the TAMCAPP application is configured so that it can be called using its URL Scheme. Now we can build an AMX page to call out to the barcode scanner and show the scanned code.

URL Scheme calls can be done by using an <amx:goLink/> component. This component has a URL attribute that can be used for this.

In the ZXing barcode scanner documentation, the following information can be found. The URL Scheme for ZXing is zxing, and within the call you can use scan to invoke the barcode scanner. This adds up to : zxing://scan. The scanned barcode is available in the URL's "{CODE}" placeholder. The callback URL, that is, the URL where ZXing sends the scanned barcode, should be put in the "ret" parameter.

So when TAMCAPP calls ZXing, ZXing should return the barcode to TAMCAPP. This is where TAMCAPP's URL Scheme comes into the picture. The URL Scheme for TAMCAPP is tamcapp. We also want to make sure that TAMCAPP knows that this is a callback from a scanning event.

```
<amx:goLink url="zxing://scan/?ret=tamcapp://scan?scannedCode={CODE}" id="gl2">
    <amx:image inlineStyle="height:102px;width:102px;margin-top:4px"
               source="/images/Barcode.png"/>
</amx:goLink>
```

NOTE
An application can only define one URL Scheme. If you want to invoke the application in multiple different ways, such as from a scanner, a second Oracle MAF app, and more, you should use the part between the URL Scheme and the returned parameter to distinguish between the different scenarios.

Once the ZXing application (Figure 18-11) has scanned the barcode, it immediately returns control to the calling application, in this case, TAMCAPP. This will lead to the invocation of the

FIGURE 18-11. *The barcode scanner application in action*

onMessage() method in the UrlSchemeCalledListener class. In this method, we have to find all the information about the scanned barcode and make sure that the ConferenceSession feature is called.

The first step in this process is to find out what caused the event and what barcode was scanned. In order to find this information, the payload of the event needs to be processed. This payload contains the callback URL tamcapp://scan?scannedCode={CODE}. In this URL we need to locate the string "scan." This is how the scan event can be distinguished from other URL Scheme calls.

Next, we need to get the value of the scanned barcode. We know exactly where the barcode is located and we need to take it out of the string. The exact location is right after the "?scannedCode=" string in the payload of this event.

It can now be extracted from the payload by using the substring and assigning it to an applicationScope variable. Finally, a resetFeature is issued on the ConferenceSession feature.

```
public void onMessage(Event event){
    AdfELContext elctx = AdfmfJavaUtilities.getAdfELContext();
    String url = event.getPayload();
    // Isolate the action. We do this because if there are more URL-Scheme
    // callbacks, we are able to respond to this in this one single method
    String action = url.substring(url.indexOf("//") + 2, url.indexOf("?"));
    if (action.equalsIgnoreCase("scan")) {
        String codeScanned =
                url.substring(url.indexOf("?scannedCode=")+ 13, url.length());
        ValueExpression val2 = AdfmfJavaUtilities.getValueExpression(
                            "#{applicationScope.scannedCode}", Object.class);
        try{
            val2.setValue(elctx, codeScanned);
        }
        catch (PropertyNotFoundException ex){
                ex.printStackTrace();
        }
        catch (Exception exw){
            exw.printStackTrace();
        }
        AdfmfContainerUtilities.resetFeature("com.blogspot.lucbors.scan.Scanner");
        AdfmfContainerUtilities.gotoFeature("com.blogspot.lucbors.scan.Scanner");
    }
}
```

The scanned code (Figure 18-12) is now available in applicationScope and can be used in a web service call to get the information about the scanned "Attendee." This mechanism has been described previously. You can simply call out to the getAttendees operation on the TamcappWsAttDc data control.

FIGURE 18-12. *The Tamcapp barcode scan app with the scan result*

Using Cordova Plugins

The previous section explained how to use URL Schemes. The example was to implement interaction with a barcode scanner. The barcode scanner functionality could also have been implemented using a Cordova plugin. A Cordova plugin bridges functionality between the WebView powering an application and the native platform the application is running on. Plugins are composed of a single JavaScript interface used across all platforms, and native implementations, following platform-specific plugin interfaces that the JavaScript will call into MAF, do not ship with third-party Cordova plugins. If you want to use a Cordova plugin, it must be developed using the SDKs for the platform to which they will be deployed. In other words, you create a plugin for an iOS application using Xcode and use the Android SDK to create plugins for applications targeted to Android devices. The plugin must be delivered with accompanying instructions in a readme or Manifest file that describes how to add the plugin's resources to the application.

NOTE
Whenever you want to use a third-party or custom-built Cordova plugin, you must make sure that the plugin is compatible with the Cordova version supported by MAF. Check the latest MAF documentation for the supported Cordova version.

This section does not go into details of creating custom Cordova plugins, but you will learn how to use an existing Cordova plugin for barcode scanning in Oracle MAF applications.

Preparing the TAMCAPP Application

When you want to use a Cordova plugin in a MAF application, you must add and configure the plugins on the Cordova plugin page of the application configuration file.

In order to properly configure the plugins in the MAF application, you must make sure that you have the appropriate plugin information available. This information consists of the plugin integration instruction and the plugin itself (source code and JavaScript file).

Next you must add the plugin library and the plugin JavaScript file to the MAF application that will use the plugin. The plugin library must reside in the ApplicationController project:

`ApplicationController\src\plugins\BarcodeScanner\Android\bin`

or

`ApplicationController\src\plugins\BarcodeScanner\iOS\bin`

The accompanying JavaScript files must go in the viewController project:

`ViewController\public_ html\plugins\BarcodeScanner\Android\js`

or

`ViewController\public_ html\plugins\BarcodeScanner\iOS\js`

Once the application is prepared and the plugins' artefacts are added, the workspace should look like the one you see in Figure 18-13.

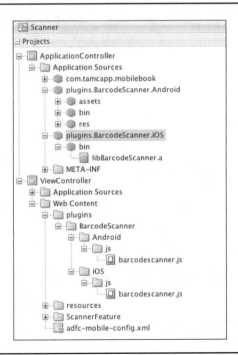

FIGURE 18-13. *Cordova plugin-specific files in the MAF application workspace*

Adding the Android Barcode Plugin

To add the Android plugin to your application, you must carefully follow the steps described in the readme file that ships with the plugin. You will learn from the readme file what the fully qualified name and the implementation class of the plugin are. Typically, the readme file will tell you to create an entry of the following form into the config.xml file of the Android application:

```
<plugin name="BarcodeScanner"
        value="com.phonegap.plugins.barcodescanner.BarcodeScanner"/>
```

In an MAF application, you enter this information when you add the plugin to the MAF application as shown in Figure 18-14. The name goes into the Fully Qualified Name field and the value goes into the Implementation Class field.

The readme file will tell you to add activities to your AndroidManifest.xml file. This step is supported by MAF in the application configuration file. Simply copy the text from the readme file and paste the content into the Android Manifest Activities box as shown in Figure 18-15.

NOTE
This is the standard way to configure Cordova plugins for Android. At deployment time, MAF uses this information to configure the Xcode project exactly as described in the readme file.

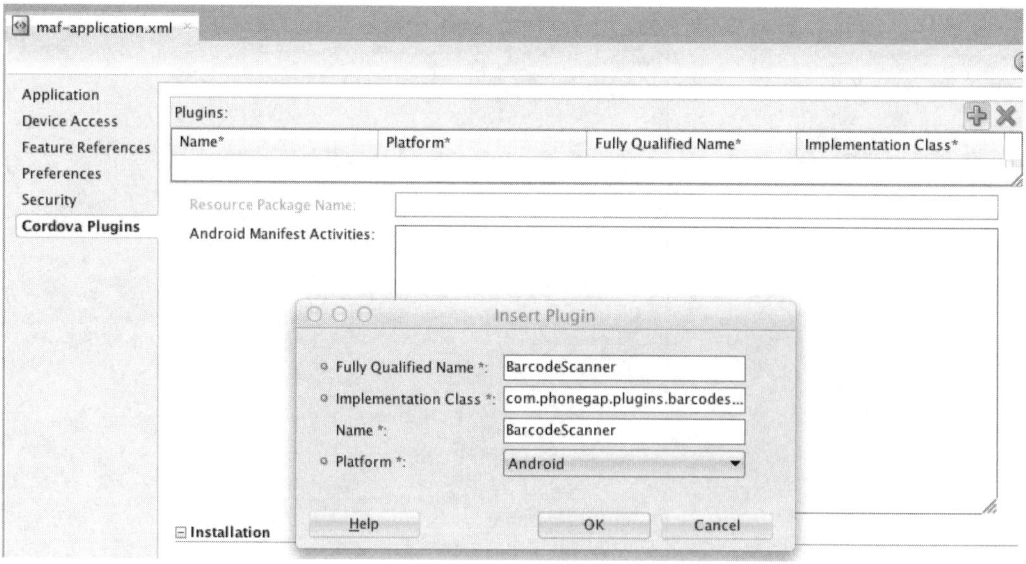

FIGURE 18-14. *Adding the Android Barcode Scanner plugin*

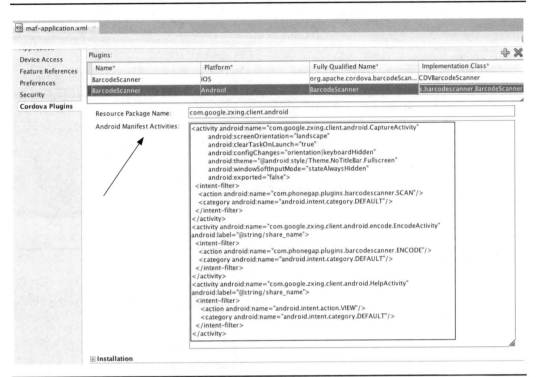

FIGURE 18-15. *Configuring Android manifest activities*

Adding the iOS Barcode Plugin

When you add the iOS Barcode scanner plugin to your project, as with Android, you must make sure to follow all steps in the readme file. An example of such a readme file can be seen here:

```
Copy the .h, .cpp and .mm files to the Plugins directory in your project.
Copy the .js file to your www directory and reference it from your html file(s).
In the Supporting Files directory of your project, add a new plugin by editing the
file Cordova.plist and in the Plugins dictionary adding the following key/value pair:

    key: org.apache.cordova.barcodeScanner
    value: CDVBarcodeScanner

Add the following libraries to your Xcode project, if not already there:

    AVFoundation.framework
    AssetsLibrary.framework
    CoreVideo.framework
    libiconv.dylib
```

All this information can be added in the application configuration file when you add a new plugin. The fully qualified name and the Implementation class (Figure 18-16) refer to the key/value pair that goes into the Cordova.plist's plugins dictionary.

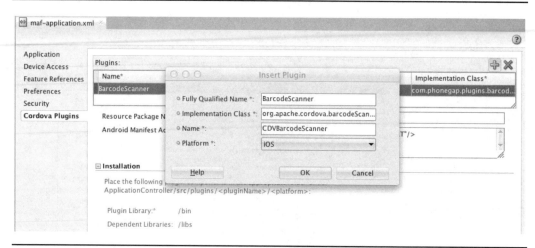

FIGURE 18-16. *Adding an iOS Cordova plugin to the MAF application*

Finally, the libraries that must be added to the Xcode project can be entered in the Linker Flags section as shown in Figure 18-17.

NOTE
This is the standard way to configure Cordova plugins for iOS. At deployment time, MAF uses this information to configure the Xcode project exactly as described in the readme file.

The plugin is now added to the MAF application. The final thing is to create a feature and the MAF content to actually use the plugin.

FIGURE 18-17. *Adding the Linker Flags for the Xcode libraries*

Using the Plugin in the Oracle Mobile Application Framework Application

With the plugin added to the MAF application, it is now time to create MAF content to use the plugin. This content can either be AMX content or Local HTML content. This section describes how to use AMX content. It is obvious that when you create a plugin for both iOS and Android, you must also create different content for both operating systems. For both operating systems, a different JavaScript file is used. The feature must be configured to use the right JavaScript file. This can be easily achieved by adding constraints to the content, based on the operating system, as you can see in Figure 18-18.

For Android, this constraint is defined as follows:

```
<adfmf:constraint property="device.os" operator="equal" value="Android" id="c2"/>
```

And for iOS, it looks the same:

```
<adfmf:constraint property="device.os" operator="equal" value="iOS" id="c1"/>
```

This will make sure that the appropriate plugin is loaded for the operating system.

Now the AMX content to use the plugin must be created. This will be a simple AMX view with a button to invoke the scanner and a text component to show the scanned code. The logic to invoke the barcode scanner from the button is placed in a Java method.

```
<amx:commandButton text="Scan"
                   id="cb1"
                   actionListener="#{viewScope.BarcodeBean.scanBarcode}"/>
```

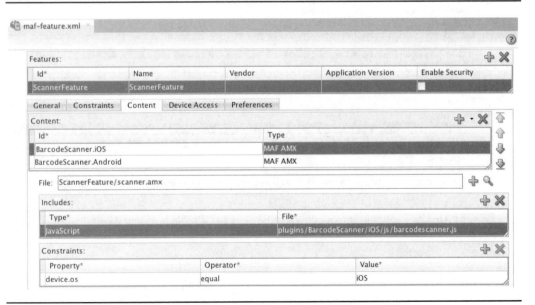

FIGURE 18-18. *Add constraints based on the device's operating system.*

The corresponding method, scanBarcode, actually calls a JavaScript function that resides in a custom JavaScript file to invoke the Cordova API and call the barcode plugin:

```
public void scanBarcode (ActionEvent event)
{
   // The feature includes a small JavaScript function which wraps the Cordova
   // barcode scanning function in a manner that makes it more suitable for
   // invocation from Java bean code. This function is invoked below:
   AdfmfContainerUtilities.invokeContainerJavaScriptFunction (
            AdfmfJavaUtilities.getFeatureName (),
            "scanBarcodeFromJavaBean",
            new Object[]{ });
}
```

This JavaScript file (BarcodeScannerFromJava.js) must be created and also be added to the feature as a specific JavaScript include (Figure 18-19).

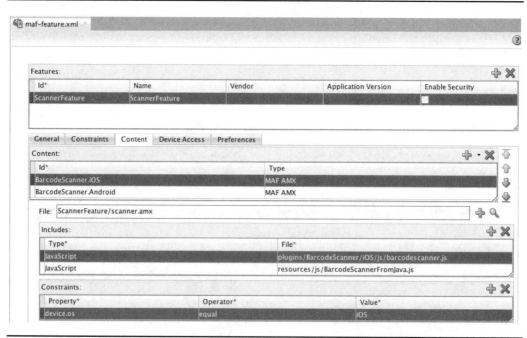

FIGURE 18-19. *The BarcodeScannerFromJava JavaScript file is added as an include.*

The corresponding JavaScript function wraps the Cordova barcode scanner so it can be invoked from Java code:

```
(function () {
      scanBarcodeFromJavaBean= function (options)
      {
        window.plugins.barcodeScanner.scan(
          function(result)
          {
            adf.mf.api.setValue( {
                "name":"#{viewScope.BarcodeBean.barcodeResult}",
                "value": "barcode = " + result.text + ",
                          Cancelled = " + result.cancelled},
                function() {},
                function() {});
            },
            function(error)
            {
                adf.mf.api.setValue( {
                  "name": "#{viewScope.BarcodeBean.barcodeResult}",
                  "value": "error = " + error.text },
                  function() {},
                  function() {});
            }
        );
      }
})();
```

This JavaScript function is also responsible for returning the scanned barcode to the MAF AMX view.

This section showed you how to implement a Cordova plugin in an MAF application and how to use this plugin in an AMX page by combining Java methods and JavaScript.

Add a Custom Search Component to TAMCAPP

Sometimes, when you develop MAF applications, you can encounter a situation where the functionality you need is not part of the MAF Component library. In those situations you would really want to create your own component to implement this functionality, and luckily, Oracle MAF supports the creation of custom components. This enables you to create your own components whenever you need one. The creation of such components is pretty straightforward. Using a combination of JavaScript and APIs provided by MAF, you can create new, fully functional interactive UI components and add them to a tag library to be used in your MAF AMX application feature.

Let's take a look at how you can create a custom search component and implement this component in the TAMCAPP app to search conference sessions. This search component supports autosuggest and a clear button, as displayed in Figure 18-20.

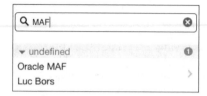

FIGURE 18-20. *The custom search in action*

Steps to Create the Custom Search Component

Typically, there are four steps involved in creating a custom component. First, you need to create a JavaScript file (Figure 18-21) that will be used to register a tag namespace and a series of one or more type handlers using the adf.mf.api.amx.TypeHandler.register API. The namespace will be used to avoid conflicts between element names when two (or more) different specifications are in use.

The namespace and component registration are handled by a TypeHandler:

```
// TypeHandler for custom "tamcappsearch" tags:
  var tamcappsearch = adf.mf.api.amx.TypeHandler.register("http://xmlns.lucbors.
blogspot.com/tamcappcustom",
"tamcappsearch");
```

This is the namespace that must be used later on when the custom component is used in an actual MAF AMX page. The component's name is tamcappsearch, and it will be registered in the *lucbors.blogspot.com/tamcappcustom* namespace.

After declaring the component name and the namespace, a rendering function for the custom component must be implemented:

```
tamcappsearch.prototype.render = function(amxNode, id)
    { ....
.....}
```

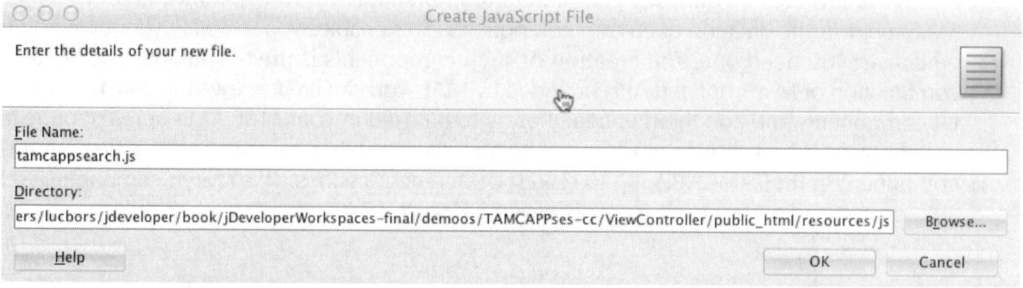

Create JavaScript File

Enter the details of your new file.

File Name:
tamcappsearch.js

Directory:
ers/lucbors/jdeveloper/book/jDeveloperWorkspaces-final/demoos/TAMCAPPses-cc/ViewController/public_html/resources/js   Browse...

Help   OK   Cancel

FIGURE 18-21. *Add a new JavaScript file.*

In this function, write the code to render the custom component and also add an eventListener that is used by the component to respond to user input, for example. In the case of this custom search component, two listeners are added: one on the input component for a keyup event so the component responds to user input, and a second one to the element that holds the clear button so that each time the user taps the clear button, the search field is actually cleared. Note that these eventListeners call a separate function in the JavaScript file that implements the actual logic for handling the text change or to clear the search field.

```
adf.mf.api.amx.addBubbleEventListener(
        inputElement,
        "keyup",
        this._handleTextChange,
        eventData);


adf.mf.api.amx.addBubbleEventListener(
        anchorElement,
        "tap",
        this._clearText,
        eventData);
    }
```

The function to clear the search area (_clearText) is a function that not only clears the text field, but also sets a className on the element. This className refers to an entry in a CSS file that accompanies this custom search component. The className clear_button is a styleClass that renders the clear button invisible.

```
tamcappsearch.prototype._clearText = function(event)
{
  var inputElementId = event.data["inputElement.id"];
  var inputElement = document.getElementById(inputElementId);
  inputElement.value = "";
  var anchorElementId = event.data["anchorElement.id"];
  var anchorElement = document.getElementById(anchorElementId);
  anchorElement.className = "clear_button";
  var context = event.data["context"];
  context._handleTextChange(event, true);
};
```

As already mentioned, this component "ships" with a CSS file that holds style classes for the custom component. This stylesheet needs to be created first (Figure 18-22).

The stylesheet that is part of the custom component holds the style classes that are used to display a clear icon or to hide it. These are two simple style classes that use the display property and a background image as can be seen in the code sample.

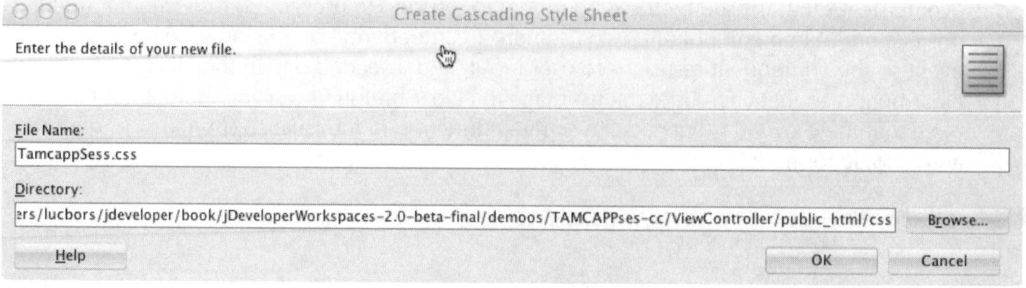

FIGURE 18-22. *A new CSS for the component's style classes*

```
.clear_button {

  display: none;

  background-image: url("x_icon.svg");

}

.clear_button_visible {

  display: inline-block;

  background-image: url("x_icon.svg");

}
```

Preparing the Feature to Use the Component

Once the JavaScript file for the custom component and the CSS file that accompanies it are finished, both need to be attached to all features that will be using your newly created custom component. This is configured in the feature configuration file, as you can see in Figure 18-23.

Now you can start using the custom component in the MAF pages. First, you must add the namespace of the component to the MAF AMX page that uses your custom component. Simply add an xmlns entry in the view element:

```
<?xml version="1.0" encoding="UTF-8" ?>
  <amx:view xmlns:xsi=http://www.w3.org/2001/XMLSchema-instance
    xmlns:amx=http://xmlns.oracle.com/adf/mf/amx
    xmlns:dvtm=http://xmlns.oracle.com/adf/mf/amx/dvt
    xmlns:tamcappcustom="http://xmlns.lucbors.blogspot.com/tamcappcustom">
    <amx:panelPage id="pp1" styleClass="tampcapp-background">
```

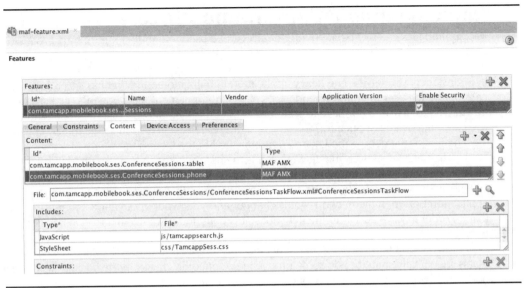

FIGURE 18-23. *Adding CSS and JavaScript files to a feature*

With the namespace declaration in place, the custom component can be added to the AMX page:

```
<tamcappcustom:tamcappsearch id="custom1"
        value="#{bindings.searchString.inputValue}"
        hintText="type search value here"
        valueChangeListener="#{bindings.searchConferenceSessions.execute}"
        inlineStyle=""
        rendered="true"/>
```

When you use the component at run time, you will see that initially the hintText is visible. Once you start typing in the search area, the hintText disappears and the Clear icon becomes visible as displayed in Figure 18-24.

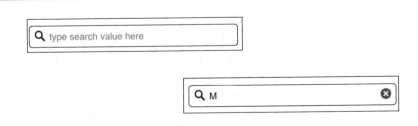

FIGURE 18-24. *The search box with hintText and Clear icon*

Implementing a Background Process

Background processes or background threads can be used to handle long-running processes or to continuously check application status both on the device and remotely in the background. The thread will run without the user noticing it until the thread specifically notifies the user interface. If, for instance, you have some heavy application initialization code that has several web service calls before the user interface is rendered, you could implement this code in a background thread. The user would not have to wait for the thread to complete before the application can be used, and the overall application would feel more responsive. As soon as the thread completes, any changes to the data in the UI are communicated to the UI and the user will see it.

In Chapter 13 you used the network status to check whether or not data had to be saved on-device in the SQLite database or at the enterprise server database. The network status can change at any given time; however, the framework currently only checks the network status at application startup. If the network status changes after this, your application cannot respond to that. In order to have access to the network status continuously, we can create a background thread that checks the network status.

A background thread can be implemented very simply. You can look at it as a worker thread that is specifically started to do some processing or ongoing checks in the background without bothering the user with long wait time or a stalled application.

To create a background thread, you simply create a new class that implements Runnable (Figure 18-25).

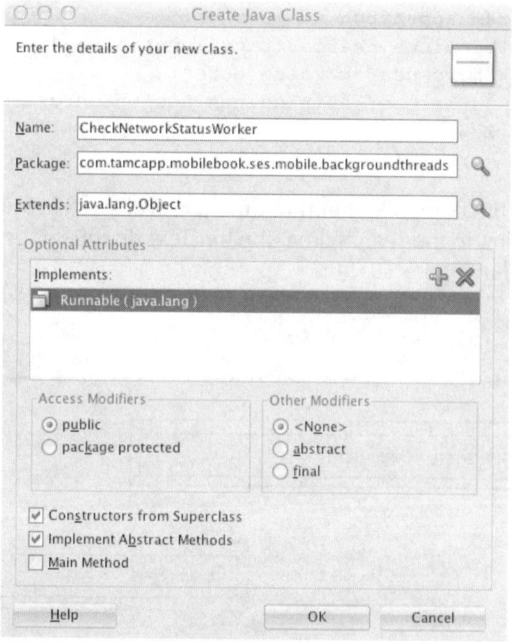

FIGURE 18-25. *Create a Java class that implements Runnable.*

You can now create a new instance of this class and start it in a separate thread. As soon as you invoke the start method on this new thread, the run method in the Class is executed in a separate thread.

The background thread we use for the network status check is started in the life cycle listener of the Conference Session feature. It is started in the activate() method. And when the feature is deactivated, the thread is interrupted in the deactivate method.

```java
public class SessionFeatureLifeCycleListener implements LifeCycleListener {
    private CheckNetworkStatusWorker cnsw = new CheckNetworkStatusWorker();
    private Thread cnswt = new Thread(cnsw);

    public SessionFeatureLifeCycleListener() {
        super();
    }
    public void activate() {
        cnswt.start();
        ..... other code here
    }
    public void deactivate() {
        cnswt.interrupt();
    }
}
```

You could use a background thread to call a web service without the user having to wait for the result. In the case of TAMCAPP, we use a background thread that continuously checks the network status. It will do this every 60 seconds. The call to AdfmfJavaUtilities.flushDataChangeEvent() is needed in order to inform the user interface of any changes to the data in the model that were caused by this background thread.

In the CheckNetworkStatusWorker class, which holds the logic that is executed in the thread, we just loop forever and check the network status every 60 seconds. If the thread is interrupted, an exception is thrown. This is caught, and the loop is exited.

```java
public class CheckNetworkStatusWorker implements Runnable {
    public CheckNetworkStatusWorker() {
        super();
    }
    public void run() {
        for (int i = 0; i <= i; ++i) {
        try {
            AdfmfContainerUtilities.invokeContainerJavaScriptFunction(
                    "com.tamcapp.mobilebook.Sessions",
                    "application.checkConnection",
                    new Object[] { });
            AdfmfJavaUtilities.flushDataChangeEvent();
        } catch (Throwable t) {
            System.err.println("Error in the background thread: " + t);
        }
        try {
            Thread.sleep(60000); /* sleep for 60 seconds */
        } catch (InterruptedException ex) {
```

```
            break;
        }
    }
}
```

If you use background threads, you should be aware of the fact that iOS and Android behave differently when the application goes to the background, for instance, by switching to another application. On iOS, the application is suspended; on Android, the application will continue running in the background. You need to take care of these differences. For this, you can use the lifeCycleListener. Whenever the feature (or application) is activated, you start the thread, and if it is deactivated, the thread should be stopped. In this way, the difference between both OSs is no longer an issue, as you always stop the thread. If you need to save the state of the thread, you can use application scope to do this and retrieve information from the application scope once the feature and thread are restarted.

Summary

This is the final chapter of this book. You already knew all about the Oracle Mobile Application Framework, and in this chapter, you learned some extra information. The importance of applications that can interact with each other and how this can be achieved using URL Schemes was explained. The fact that devices come in virtually any size makes it important for your application to respond to the size of the device. Oracle MAF enables you to do so and also provides you with several layout components specifically targeting tablet layouts. The implementation of threads that run the background also adds extra power to your application. You now know how to use these.

In this chapter you learned how to

- Implement tablet layout
- Work with URL Schemes
- Implement barcode scanning
- Work with background threads

Index

Beta Test Oracle Software

Get a first look at our newest products—and help perfect them. You must meet the following criteria:

- ✔ **Licensed Oracle customer or Oracle PartnerNetwork member**

- ✔ **Oracle software expert**

- ✔ **Early adopter of Oracle products**

Please apply at: pdpm.oracle.com/BPO/userprofile

Reach More than 700,000 Oracle Customers with Oracle Publishing Group

Connect with the Audience that Matters Most to Your Business

Oracle Magazine
The Largest IT Publication in the World
Circulation: 550,000
Audience: IT Managers, DBAs, Programmers, and Developers

Profit
Business Insight for Enterprise-Class Business Leaders to Help Them Build a Better Business Using Oracle Technology
Circulation: 100,000
Audience: Top Executives and Line of Business Managers

Java Magazine
The Essential Source on Java Technology, the Java Programming Language, and Java-Based Applications
Circulation: 125,000 and Growing Steady
Audience: Corporate and Independent Java Developers, Programmers, and Architects

For more information or to sign up for a FREE subscription:
Scan the QR code to visit Oracle Publishing online.

Join the Largest Tech Community in the World

 Download the latest software, tools, and developer templates

 Get exclusive access to hands-on trainings and workshops

 Grow your professional network through the Oracle ACE Program

 Publish your technical articles – and get paid to share your expertise

Join the Oracle Technology Network
Membership is free. Visit oracle.com/technetwork

@OracleOTN   facebook.com/OracleTechnologyNetwork